America the Prisoner

America the Prisoner

The Implications of Foreign Oil Addiction and a Realistic Plan to End It

Lewis Reynolds

Relevance Media, Inc.
Charlotte, North Carolina 28210
© 2010 by Lewis Reynolds
All Rights Reserved, Published in 2010

Printed in the United States of America

ISBN-13: 978-0-9842478-0-6
Library of Congress Catalog Number: 2010900819

Publisher's Cataloging-in-Publication Data

Reynolds, Lewis.
　　America the prisoner : the implications of foreign oil addiction and a realistic plan to end it / Lewis Reynolds.
　　　　　p. cm.
　　Includes bibliographical references and index.
　　ISBN: 978-0-9842478-0-6
　　1. Petroleum industry and trade—Political aspects. 2. Energy policy—United States. 3. Biomass energy.　I. Title.
HD9560.6 R39 2010
333.79`0973—dc22

2010900819

Cover Art by Neil White

10 9 8 7 6 5 4 3 2 1

Printed on Acid-free Paper.

For all of those who have lost their
lives in the unwitting pursuit of oil

Contents

Illustrations

Preface

It may no longer be fashionable, but, as those who know me are well aware, I love the United States of America. I have seen what oil dependence has done and continues to do to our country, and I know that it need not be so. Armed with this knowledge, I could not simply sit by, say nothing, and do nothing. I had to write this book so that more people could know what I know.

I hope that this book will help many Americans wake up to the realities of the modern world and take action. Whether that means investing in alternative energy, choosing it as a career, becoming involved politically, or some other path, the important thing to remember is that strength comes in numbers. If this book's message has an impact on you, help make others aware. Ignorance is bliss, but only for a while. Eventually, what you do not know can and will hurt you, and such is certainly true when it comes to the USA and oil addiction. It isn't too late to reverse course, but we must all recognize the challenge we face and work together.

Fortunately, I am hardly a lone warrior out to save the USA from its oil addition. There are already many who I consider kindred spirits working for the same ends. Even if their means may be different, I appreciate all of their efforts. There are many people that I would like to thank for their gracious contributions and assistance in the preparation of this work. I am particularly grateful for the patience and support of my beloved Melissa with whom I share my life and my heart.

I would also like to thank the most loving and nurturing parents anyone could ever hope to have. As I was growing up, they always told me that I could be anything I wanted to be. Thank you for the many years of encouragement and belief in me. You made me the man I am today.

My oldest friend in the world who I have known since kindergarten, Frank McHone, provided inspiration and a sounding board for ideas, and was, along with Melissa, the first to read this book. Frank, your feedback shaped this work and you deserve credit for helping craft the message as well as for being a great friend through thick and thin, my brother from another mother.

I am also grateful for the extraordinary efforts of my editor, Dr. Ray Craig, who is a gentleman of the first order and really helped to clean up this book. Ray, you have gone above and beyond the call of duty to sharpen my words and weed out the errors. I owe you one.

I would also like to say thank you to the many people that played a role in furthering my knowledge on the subject matter herein, particularly those who helped me discover or discovered with me the wonders of modern technology available to eliminate foreign oil dependence. Among those men are Col. Frank Wilbourne, USMC, Ret., Lt. Col. Jay H. Van Dyne, USMC, Ret., Phillip Danforth, Harry H. Graves, Richard A. Bailey, Dwight N. Lockwood, Kenneth M. Salzman, and Frank W. Scroggins.

This work would not have been possible without the dedicated public service of the men and women of the US Department of Energy and the national laboratories funded by it. The American people appreciate your work, even if most of them aren't intimately aware of your day to day efforts. I would also like to think the people of the US Department of Defense for taking the problem of oil dependence seriously and endeavoring to actually do something about it.

For all of those who have been willing to devote your own resources, whether time or money, to help ensure America's future, I say thank you. In particular I would like to mention T. Boone Pickens, who has spent many millions of dollars and appeared personally in television advertising to inform Americans of the perils of foreign oil dependency. His willingness to use his wealth to try to make America stronger sets an example for all of us. Although the path to energy independence presented in this book is different from the "Pickens Plan," there are many roads to energy independence that need not be mutually exclusive.

Finally, I would like to thank the many authors, historians, economists, and scientists that came before me. A particular debt is owed to Daniel Yergin for his Pulitzer Prize-winning and intimately revealing history of the oil industry, *The Prize*. I would also like to pay homage to Thomas Friedman, Charles Krauthammer, James Woolsey, Colin Campbell, and Fareed Zakaria. Although these men have different perspectives and sometimes divergent opinions, all of their contributions to the public debate about oil are important.

Abbreviations

AD	Anno Domini (Latin for "in the year of our Lord")
°API	a scale used to measure the density of oil developed by and named for the American Petroleum Institute
ANWR	Alaskan National Wildlife Refuge
BEA	Bureau of Economic Analysis
BP	BP plc (formerly British Petroleum)
BTC Pipeline	Baku Tbilisi Ceyhan Pipeline
Btu	British thermal unit
CAFE	Corporate Average Fuel Economy
CCE	Chicago Climate Exchange
CENTCOM	US Central Command
CENTO	Central Treaty Organization
CEO	chief executive officer
CFC	Chlorofluorocarbons
CIA	Central Intelligence Agency
CO	carbon monoxide
CO_2	carbon dioxide
CPI	consumer price index
DNA	deoxyribonucleic acid, the molecule responsible for genetic instruction in most life forms
DOE	US Department of Energy
E-85	blend of 85% ethanol and 15% gasoline
ECB	European Central Bank
ECN	Energy Research Centre of the Netherlands
EIA	Energy Information Administration
EPA	US Environmental Protection Agency

EU	European Union
euro	currency issued by the European Central Bank, official currency in a majority of the member nations of the European Union
FFV	flexible fuel vehicle
FT	Fischer-Tropsch
FT-IPK	Fischer-Tropsch ISO-Paraffinic Kerosene
GDP	gross domestic product
GM	General Motors Corporation
GVWR	gross vehicle weight rating
H_2	hydrogen gas
H_2O	water
HCl	hydrochloric acid
HF	hydrofluoric acid
IEA	International Energy Agency
IGCC	integrated gasification combined cycle
IMF	International Monetary Fund
IPCC	International Panel on Climate Change
MIT	Massachusetts Institute of Technology
mpg	miles per gallon
MSW	municipal solid waste
MTBE	methyl tertiary butyl ether
NASA	National Aeronautics and Space Administration
NATO	North Atlantic Treaty Organization
NO_2	nitrogen dioxide
NYMEX	New York Mercantile Exchange
O_2	Oxygen
OCS	outer continental shelf
OPEC	Organization of Petroleum Exporting Countries
ORNL	Oak Ridge National Laboratory
P/E ratio	price-to-earnings ratio

PDVSA	Petróleos de Venezuela, S.A.
PEM	polymer electric membrane
pH	the common measure of acidity of a solution (abbreviates power of hydrogen)
POX	partial oxidation
ppm	parts per million
PROALCOOL	Brazilian Alcohol Program
psi	pounds per square inch
RFI	request for information
SAVAK	Sazeman-e Ettela'at va Amniyat-e Keshvar (Iran's Secret Police)
SEC	US Securities and Exchange Commission
SFC	US Synthetic Fuels Corporation
SO_2	sulfur dioxide
SPR	Strategic Petroleum Reserve
SUV	sport utility vehicle
TARP	Troubled Asset Relief Program
TPC	Turkish Petroleum Company
UAE	United Arab Emirates
UAR	United Arab Republic
UAW	United Auto Workers
UN	United Nations
US, USA	United States of America
USDA	US Department of Agriculture
USGS	US Geological Survey
USSR	Union of Soviet Socialist Republics

Telling All My Secrets

We live in an era of short memories and even shorter attention spans. The world has some serious problems, but far too often they are simply ignored or Band-Aids are embraced over long term solutions. Nowhere has that truth been made clearer than with one of the most critical issues facing the United States, a debilitating weakness that is usually treated as an afterthought, only really noticed in periods when the consequences are particularly obvious and egregious. More often this problem's far reaching tentacles are disguised by the complexities of the global economy and by the obtuse nature of global geopolitics. But make no mistake; whether it is the focus or forgotten, it is perhaps the most serious issue facing the US and the world over the coming decades.

Like most problems, this one has a solution. The answer is not easy or quick, and most Americans remain oblivious to it. In large part, it remains in obscurity because at its heart lies a secret, well kept by the few who are aware of its power to change the world's economic dynamics and shift countless fortunes forever. But to truly appreciate its importance, some context is necessary.

Americans are regularly polled to determine what issues facing the country are the most important. The percentages move around, but among the categories always at the top of the list are the economy, wars, and terrorism. Perhaps the most important issue, one that affects virtually every other issue on the list, is always absent. The issue I refer to is the overwhelming US dependence on foreign oil.

Perhaps nearly everyone reading this book is already well aware that oil dependence has become a major issue for the US, but the perceived importance ebbs and flows with its price. Prices go up and down with astounding volatility, but the effect on the consumer is broad and inescapable regardless of the price level. Although most Americans are conscious of prices, too many are dreadfully oblivious to the wide-ranging effects of imported petroleum on the US economy or to the foreign policy implications of dependence on foreign nations for economic survival. The costs go well beyond the actual price at the pump. While oil has found its current place at the center of the world economic system, the need for it has created trade deficits and wealth transfers unrivaled in US history.

The US economy is suffering right now, and a major reason for that pain is the exportation of American wealth. When the US sends hundreds of billions of dollars overseas in exchange for oil, it is swapping wealth for short term consumption. The fuel received in the trade quickly and quite literally goes up in smoke. That momentary convenience was pleasant to be sure, but when the dust settles, the oil exporters, many of whom are sworn enemies of the West, are left in ownership positions of US assets. Because the US is producing fewer exportable products and has a trade deficit exclusive of oil, foreign financing is required to pay for Americans' consumptive habits. As a result, net foreign ownership of assets in the US has grown to nearly $3.5 trillion as of the end of 2008 (until 1986, the US owned more assets abroad than foreigners owned in the US).[1] Consumption is ever-expanding, and the outward flow of capital across US borders is ever-quickening. When a people's ownership stake in their own country is diminishing in favor of ownership by foreigners, their society is in decline.

Even with the serious economic issues associated with oil, there remains a whole other class of issues in the related but distinct political world. US oil dependence has unquestionably shaped world events and American foreign policy for the last century. Other nations and, yes, the US have made some shortsighted decisions to maintain the oil flow, some of them in the foreign policy realm, others involving convert actions, and a few ending in full scale war.

Any reasoned and thorough analysis would reach one inescapable conclusion: oil has been at the center of many, indeed most major military conflicts in the world, particularly those involving the West. From providing the impetus for Hitler's invasion of the Soviet Union and Japan's attack on Pearl Harbor in World War II to Saddam Hussein's invasion of Kuwait, the resulting Gulf War and the US return to Iraq in 2003, oil has bred a century of conflict. Whether or not you blame the Iraq War on the seemingly eternal quest for oil, it is certainly not the first battle to be fought over it.

It isn't just hot wars that have been driven by the oil question. The entire US-Middle East foreign policy has been structured around the obvious importance of the region for the world's oil supply. Policy makers don't like to discuss it openly, but oil is always the elephant in the room. To be sure, America has made some bad choices to guarantee the uninterrupted flow of oil, often acting in ways very much in conflict with our national identity. Although the costs of the wars we have fought, both in terms of blood and treasure, have been great, the compromise of American values is perhaps even more disturbing.

There is no better example than the US relationship with Iran. For most of the 20th century, the US and British governments supported dictators and manipulated the domestic political situation in Iran, often at the expense of the people. The rational was, of course, to ensure the continued flow of cheap oil. Those policies backfired when the harsh rule of the US-backed Shah was overthrown by a popular revolution. The Iranian population was left angry with the US, and the door was opened for the anti-American Islamic theocracy that followed. As we all know, addicts make poor choices and take extraordinary risks to make sure they can get their fix. It is really no different for a nation than it is for an individual.

What is most important now is not what has been done in the past, but what the US does in the future. By most estimates worldwide oil production is at or near capacity. Meanwhile, demand for oil is on the rise in the US and worldwide, especially in China. While economic crises have the ability to cause an occasional yet brief retrenchment, the long term trend is indisputable. The result will be an unfortunate future with constrained resources unable to meet growing demand. The situation leaves the US with essentially two choices. The first choice is to continue on the present path. The long term consequences will be upward trending global prices and supply constraints. The domestic economy will further deteriorate, depressing the value of the dollar and making oil imports more expensive still. America's wealth will continue to be exported and foreign ownership in the US will continue to grow. Because of competing global interest in the oil supply, there will be more conflicts, more forced foreign policy decisions, and, perhaps, more wars.

There is another choice. The US economy does not have to continue its downward spiral. The US does not have to be beholden to foreign resources. Despite what you may hear from some misguided leaders in government and industry, energy independence is possible. As much as the US may be a country without a sound energy policy that is being crushed by its own thirst for oil, it is still is the greatest industrial power in history.

Although industry has played a decreasing role in the US economy in recent years, energy independence can be the first step in reversing that trend. Aside from creating millions of jobs, a move toward energy independence can begin the process of rebuilding the US industrial base. It will provide one of the most stable and secure energy supplies in the world. Best of all, the new domestic energy can be both renewable and sustainable. Never again should America depend on overseas sources for its vital national interests.

The need for energy independence is hardly a secret, but the specific means to achieve it has proven much more difficult to pin down. The secret I mentioned in the opening paragraphs, the secret that will be revealed in this book is, at its essence, really quite simple. Many are already aware of the core principles but have not yet realized the implications or studied the technological means to capitalize on them. The secret begins with the well established scientific knowledge regarding the origins of petroleum.

The oil used today began millions of years ago as living organisms. The energy stored in oil, like virtually every other energy source on Earth, originated with the sun. That energy was collected through a process called photosynthesis, where energy from light converts carbon dioxide to an organic molecule. Oil is really only a collection of organic molecules that have been subjected to geological forces over millions of years.

As it turns out, the geological forces and the millions of years are not necessary to the process. The energy was not produced deep in the earth over those millennia; it was there from the beginning. All of that time can simply be skipped and the organic molecules produced by photosynthesis in plants living now can be refined directly into fuel using technologies very similar to those used in petroleum refining. This is the secret to which I have been referring.

Later in this book, I will describe the technological processes required to accomplish this "miracle" and the economics of the production process. The conclusions are inescapable. Not only is the technology real and, at least in its component parts, mature, it is also economically feasible and very much competitive with the petroleum market. The solutions offered in this book are not dreams; they are reality.

We all know that alternative fuels have been tried in the US before. Unfortunately, many of those efforts have taken a direction that could never result in energy independence. Ethanol from corn, for example, simply cannot make the US energy independent because the entire process (growing corn, producing fuel, etc.) is far too inefficient.

What I am describing is something different that has gotten precious little mention and only fleeting attention, perhaps because few understand its full potential. There is, however, a small but growing chorus of national leaders who are embracing these technologies publicly and a collection of prominent investors, particularly from Silicon Valley, who are showing their support quietly, not with words but with dollars. For America to turn back the disturbing forces it faces, however, it will take more than just a few politicians, academics, investors, and entrepreneurs.

The first step to realizing the dream of energy independence is that the US must overcome its one greatest weakness – the American attention span. In the era of the twenty-four-hour news cycle, little seems to matter that happened before last week, and there is precious little thought about the future. The American public has a history of short memories and a short term view when it comes to fuel prices and energy policy. This view is exacerbated by media coverage that focuses almost exclusively on short term price fluctuations.[2]

As evidence to the forgetfulness of Americans, one should take a good hard look at the parallels between the early 1970s and the late 2000s. In October, 1973, the seemingly perpetual conflict between the Arabs and Israelis came to yet another tipping point, a conflict that would become known as the Yom Kippur War. To make a political statement, the Arab nations imposed an oil embargo against the United States and its European allies for supporting Israel. Oil supplies were constrained and the price was thrust up fourfold in a very short period of time. When the dust had settled, the international economy was driven into a period of high inflation and recession from which it would not fully recover until 1982.

The events of 1973 and the years that followed are seldom recalled, but they are eerily similar to those of the present day. Skyrocketing oil prices followed by economic crisis and global recession could describe the headlines in the mid-1970s or of the late 2000s. In case I have not been clear enough, yes, I am absolutely saying that the spike in oil prices between 2003 and 2008 is indeed to blame, at least in part, for the global financial crisis.

What will it take for the US to finally learn its lesson? After the events of 1973, the US began efforts to curb its foreign oil addiction. There were initiatives for improved fuel efficiency and for the production of alternative fuels, but those efforts were quickly jettisoned when oil temporarily became a little cheaper. Today, the US is much more dependent on foreign oil than it was in 1973, yet American political leaders have done nothing to stop foreign oil from continuing to gain market share. Few national leaders seem to recognize the ongoing damage to the US economy from foreign oil addiction, and fewer still understand how the capital flows created by overwhelming overseas oil dependence can and have helped create asset bubbles and recessions, including the current one, a phenomenon that will be explained in detail in this book. Rather than blaming the system that actually created the mess, it is more politically expedient to blame greedy individuals. Mere theft and greed, even on a grand scale, is still far too miniscule to create such a crisis on its own.

When energy issues are discussed in the US, the debate has far too frequently centered on trivial proposals such as drilling for oil in the Arctic National Wildlife Refuge (ANWR) and off-shore exploration on the outer continental shelf (OCS). Whether you support or oppose such initiatives, the fact is that neither would have any material impact on the US energy landscape. Even if every square inch of US territory (including offshore waters) was opened to oil exploration, the resulting production would be sufficient to offset only a tiny fraction of US imports. The fact is that the US simply does not have enough oil to meet domestic resource needs regardless of the amount of drilling.

Today, it is time for America to recognize not only its strategic vulnerability resulting from overwhelming overseas petroleum dependence, but also the precarious economic situation that results from it. Just as importantly, Americans must remember what made it great and make sure that those qualities are not lost. America does indeed face a threat, but it also, as it turns out, faces an opportunity. The opportunity is not just for America as a nation; there is also boundless opportunity for individual Americans. Domestic energy production offers the potential to realize millions of American Dreams and create unimaginable wealth for those willing to take the lead and the risk. In a country that has seen its share of struggles in the labor market, the promise of more than 14 million new jobs from domestic energy production and the construction effort to make it possible could be an answer to many prayers.[3]

One of the keys to the unprecedented success of the US has been capitalism. Politicians from both sides of the aisle practice demagoguery at its finest as they engage in the newly fashionable demonization of the pursuit of profit. Many of the corporate executives who have been particularly targeted have more than earned the criticism that they have received, and a few undoubtedly belong in prison, but the politicians' tactics set a dangerous precedent. As they paint the desire to gain wealth as an evil endeavor, they chop at the underpinnings of the system that has allowed America to rise to gloried heights.

This book is not a defense of corporate executives. Many of them accomplish little and create even less while sleepily guiding their companies like a driver on a deserted highway at four o'clock in the morning. There are, however, some true innovators who deserve even more than they receive. The real leaders for the future are entrepreneurs that make a business of tackling serious challenges and the investors that support and believe in them.

Too often, the approach of energy futurists and environmentalists is to advocate overreaching government intervention. The solutions to our energy problem involve government, but cannot best be accomplished by government. Energy independence, like the computer revolution that came before it, will succeed only if the innovators and the investors that make their plans possible stand to profit.

Particularly frustrating is the unfortunately widespread belief that alternatives to oil can never be profitable or competitive. So many people, whether pundits in the popular media or experts writing about energy, economics, politics, or some combination thereof, have repeated that fallacy so frequently that I have almost come to believe it myself. They are, however, misguided.

The fact is that there are profitable alternatives to petroleum. Unlike those with the opposing viewpoint who have decided that non-oil solutions are uneconomic, I am not going to ask you to simply take my word for it. This book will describe in detail how alternative fuel can be produced at a break even cost equivelant to $45 per barrel of oil. Each and every fact-based assumption about the technological capabilities that are available comes from documented research, all of which is available directly from the US Department of Energy, the national laboratories they fund, another government agency, or widely recognized and respected pcer-reviewed scientific journals. The facts show that energy independence can be achieved not only in theory, but in practice using the technology and policies described in this book.

Although clearly possible, energy independence will not be easy, nor will it come without substantial domestic investment. Underestimating the commitment and financial resources that will be necessary to achieve it is at least as dangerous to the quest for energy independence as are those who contend it isn't possible. Politicians tend to be the culprits in the all-too-familiar refrain of over-promise and under-delivery. They are frequently well-intentioned but tragically uninformed about what an endeavor like energy independence would really require.

Think about it; if the US spends over one half trillion dollars a year on foreign oil, does it really makes sense to invest only a few billion, or even a hundred billion, to get an infrastructure capable of replacing all of it? If it were that easy, the solution probably would have been implemented years ago, and this book would not be necessary.

The calculations in later chapters will show that energy independence can be accomplished for an investment of roughly $900 billion. Even with all those zeros, the new industry can and will be profitable. The only missing ingredient, the only thing holding us back is awareness. Because energy independence will require the involvement of many Americans, the first step must be education. These words are the beginning, but the knowledge they share are only tools. The goals can't be accomplished unless people believe it is possible, for the true answer for America's problems lies not the pages of a book but in the hearts of its people.

Part One – The Economy and the Environment

1
Going Up in Smoke

The US has the largest economy in the world by a substantial margin, but it is an economy with cancer. That cancer, oil dependence, is slowly eating away at the true source of American power as each year the US exports more and more of its wealth in exchange for oil. The implications are far-reaching and almost universally negative. Energy independence is a way to reverse the shameful damage the US inflicts on itself every day. It is not just about protection from the whims of hostile regimes; it is also about reversing disastrous economic policies that have made America into its own worst enemy.

Even those who don't see a problem with overwhelming US dependence on foreign oil will concede that there are costs associated with oil use that aren't reflected in the price at the pump. The price of gasoline paid directly by consumers is but a fraction of the true cost of bringing fuel to market. It does not reflect the enormous burden of external costs associated with the securing the supply chain, environmental costs associated with oil usage, and economic costs stemming from volatile price fluctuations, just to name a few.[1]

The most easily quantified consequence of foreign oil dependence is the transfer of wealth and the related issue of the trade deficit. When a country imports more than it exports, it is said to have a trade deficit. The US was once a mighty industrial power supplying a considerable percentage of the world's manufactured goods and raw materials. Those days have long since passed and now the US has what economists have termed a "service economy." More importantly, the American economy is based less on producing either goods or services and more on consumption. The United States has maintained a trade deficit every year since 1976.[2]

To any remotely observant consumer, the shelves at Wal-Mart make it more than obvious that many products consumed by Americans are produced overseas. Consumer goods can be produced more inexpensively in developing and underdeveloped countries because of dramatically lower labor costs. Despite all of the imported consumer products, the US trade deficit's largest contributor has nothing to do with the disparity in labor costs; it is imported petroleum.

Importing petroleum or, for that matter, importing any foreign goods will not in-and-of-itself create a trade deficit. After World War II, Japan was able to grow its economy into one of the largest in the world despite having to import virtually all of its natural resources, including petroleum. What keeps the Japanese economy from imploding by virtue of all of those imports is the fact that Japan also produces lots of export goods as an offset. Japan has consistently maintained a trade surplus every year since 1981.[3] That is not to say that Japan's economy hasn't seen its share of other challenges.

A national economy is really not all that different from the economy of a family. While national economics is full of all kinds of fancy terminology generally unfamiliar to the average American, the concepts are quite basic. Unfortunately, simple ideas like "don't spend more than you earn" seem to be passé, not sophisticated enough for the preponderance of the economics establishment.

A trade deficit quite simply means that a nation is buying more than it is selling in international markets. When a country has a trade deficit, it must find a way to finance its purchases. In macroeconomics, this is called the "capital account." Generally, for the US to have a trade deficit, it must have a capital account surplus; the two accounts offset each other. There are other factors, but they are usually too small to make much of a difference.

For an individual, a trade deficit is simply analogous to spending more than you earn; imports constitute spending, while exports represent income. There are basically two ways for either an individual or an economy to spend more than it earns: borrow or sell assets. The US has done a lot of both. Examples of borrowing include the issuance of treasury securities, bonds, and bank deposits, while assets such as stocks and real estate can be sold to overseas investors.

In 2008, the total US trade deficit was $696 billion. Of that, over $453 billion came from the importation of petroleum and petroleum products, which means that a startling 65.1% of the total trade deficit came from imported petroleum in 2008.[4] If that fact alone is not disturbing enough, consider that the volume of consumption of imported petroleum has steady increased, but the effect has been even more striking in dollar terms, a result of the degradation of US currency value. Because payment must somehow be made for imported petroleum, the petroleum trade deficit and the wealth transfer from petroleum imports are really the same thing.[5] For that reason, it is also true to say that the importation of

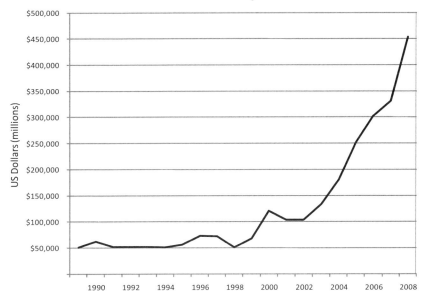

US Petroleum Imports

Based on complied data from the US Department of Commerce, Bureau of Economic Analysis and the US Department of Energy, Energy Information Administration.

petroleum resulted in the transfer of $453 billion of wealth from the US to foreign suppliers in 2008.

After a while, all of those deficits start to add up. A persistent national trade deficit means that net foreign ownership of US assets will continually grow. The US net foreign investment position was once positive, meaning the US owned more assets abroad than foreigners owned in the US. The position turned negative in 1986, and net foreign ownership of US assets has grown larger and larger ever since. At the end of 2008, the running total of net foreign investment in the US (which represents foreign ownership) had grown to almost $3.5 trillion, a value of 24.2% of US gross domestic product (GDP).[6]

To avoid increasing net foreign ownership of domestic assets, the trade deficit, as a percentage of GDP, generally should not exceed the economic growth rate. Most economists believe that trade deficits that exceed 3% of GDP are unsustainable.[7] In 2008, the trade deficit was 4.8% of US GDP.[8] With such large trade deficits, the net foreign investment position will continue to worsen.[9] As long as the US continues to be so heavily reliant on imported petroleum, it will be nearly impossible to eliminate the trade deficit.

Historically, the trade deficit has been financed mostly with foreign private investment. In recent years, however, the private investment has

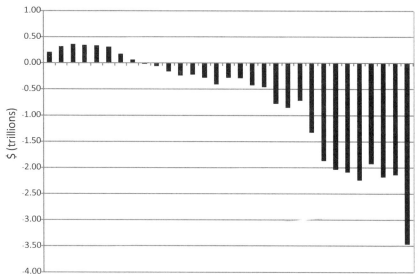

Net International Investment Position of the US

Data from the US Department of Commerce, Bureau of Economic Analysis.

been replaced by expanding sovereign (foreign government) investment associated with massive reserve accumulation in oil exporting countries and China.[10] China's motivation for holding dollar assets is pretty obvious: depreciation of the dollar relative to the yuan would make Chinese exports more expensive in the US market, likely resulting in sharp reductions in trade. With the Chinese economy dependent on exports (especially to the US), significant depreciation of the dollar relative to the yuan would be harmful for economic growth in China.[11]

Although similar forces are at work with the oil exporters, they also face another problem. Many of them simply can't spend all of the cash coming into their economies. Although some countries make an effort toward doing so by escalating defense spending or with extravagant domestic projects, a significant amount of the income from the petroleum trade becomes capital that has nowhere to go other than into the international financial system. Much of it inevitably lands right back in the US. The effect for the oil exporters is to swap oil for American financial assets. For Americans, the effect is to swap short term consumption for long term liabilities.

The whole system has created a dangerous co-dependency. The oil exporting governments are dependent on a high oil price for the stability of their own economies and, in most cases, their regimes. Meanwhile the

US, in addition to its oil dependency, has also become reliant on foreign capital. A slowing of foreign capital inflows and the resultant reduction in the availability of capital in the US could lead to a collapse of the dollar, sharply higher interest rates, and an economic crisis even worse than one the US has already experienced.[12]

The US economy has been driven for many years by consumption. Americans are among the world's most reckless consumers, but it isn't entirely their fault. For years, the US government has promoted wonton spending, believing it was the best means to promote economic growth. Those policies did create growth in the short term, but also planted the seeds for a major crisis, the effect of which are being seen today. Among the solutions is to begin adopting policies that promote domestic savings and curb expenditures.[13] An excellent place to start is with petroleum.

The Petrodollar System

US trade deficits have created a situation that forces reliance on overseas capital to support the economy. Much of that capital comes from the petroleum exporting countries that, in turn, get it from oil consumption by American businesses and consumers. The cycle of flowing money is not merely a manifestation of the market; it is the product of careful planning.

Toward the end of World War II, it became apparent that the allies would prevail, that Europe would need to be rebuilt, and that stability would be needed in the international economy. With this in mind, a series of international conferences were held. The Bretton Woods Monetary Conferences, as they became known, that took place in 1944 and 1945 established a new international monetary system. The product of the conferences was the formation of the World Bank and the International Monetary Fund (IMF), the establishment of a gold standard at $35 per ounce, and selection of the US dollar as the backbone of international exchange.[14] The "gold standard" allowed holders of US currency to exchange dollars for actual gold.

Under Bretton Woods, the Federal Reserve's ability to inject liquidity (money) into the financial system was constrained by the volume of physical assets (gold) possessed by the Treasury. By 1967, redemptions of dollars for gold had seriously depleted the US government's reserves of gold bullion. Soaring US budget and trade deficits placed enormous pressure on the value of the dollar. Increasingly, foreign central banks were demanding gold redemptions. On August 15, 1971, President Nixon announced that the US was abandoning the redemption policy all-together, ending the gold standard and international monetary system established by Bretton Woods. Thereafter, a system developed whereby most major world currencies were allowed to float in value against one another. With the collapse of Bretton Woods, all restrains on the Federal Reserve's printing presses were lifted, allowing for unlimited expansion of the money supply in the US.[15]

Because the US was once the world's largest oil exporter and because the Bretton Woods system established the dollar as the primary currency of international exchange, oil has traditionally been priced in dollars regardless of where in the world it is bought or sold. The dollar's status gives the United States a tremendous economic advantage over other nations. Because of the importance of oil to every nation and the fact that it can only be purchased with the US dollar, the dollar effectively becomes a natural resource itself, a resource essential to every nation.[16] When the gold standard was abandoned, the dollar was no longer backed by gold. Because of its status as the medium of exchange on the world petroleum markets, the dollar instead became effectively backed by "black gold."[17]

The petrodollar system, which is the product of the dollar's international status and central role in the petroleum market, is a complex system of currency flows. It begins with the purchase of oil by the US consumer, which sends massive dollar-denominated cash flows to oil exporting countries. In addition, US consumers buy imported goods, such as products from Japan and China, resulting in flows of dollars to those countries. In turn, the manufacturing nations must purchase oil, which they accomplish with the dollars they obtained from selling products in the US market. At this point, the oil exporters are awash in dollars, which they must either spend or invest.

One way or another, a large percentage of that money tends to end up back in the US. It is used to purchase US Treasury securities, is deposited in banks, or is used to buy dollar-denominated assets like US stocks, bonds, and real estate. From a macroeconomic perspective, the American economy does not have to actually produce anything to exchange for the oil unless and until members of the Organization of Petroleum Exporting Countries (OPEC) or some other exporter use the dollars they receive to purchase goods or services.[18] When the merry-go-round stops, the US government has gained access to cheap capital, allowing for lavish government spending while consumers have plenty of cheap consumables, an abundant supply of petroleum, and easy credit.

The supremacy of the dollar and the petrodollar system affords the US the unique ability to perpetuate annual trade deficits, allows the government to spend outrageously without necessitating offsetting revenue (taxes), and yet the dollar is still accepted as the primary medium of international exchange for goods and services.[19] As described earlier, a nation cannot run such deficits unless they are financed with foreign capital. Studies have shown that the availability of financing, in fact, determines whether countries run fiscal deficits rather than the presence of deficits predicting which countries seek foreign capital.[20] In other words, if capital is available, governments will spend it.

After the Arab oil exporters placed an oil embargo on the US at the onset of the Yom Kippur War of 1973, oil prices rapidly increased more than four-fold. The expansion of revenues was so swift for the Arab countries that they immediately went from embargo-imposer to investment partner needing some way to dispose of all of their newfound cash. Although the embargo ended without meeting the Arabs' stated goals, it had the effect of meeting an unstated one – increase the price of oil dramatically and, thereby, empower the Arab countries with massive and unrivaled wealth. While some would argue that the consequences also included making the Arab nations even more dependent on the West,[21] it was really more a tale of co-dependence with the fortunes of the Arabs and the West becoming more and more inextricably linked.

Between 1973 and 1982, OPEC ran a surplus of $400 billion, half of which went to Saudi Arabia. The United Arab Emirates (UAE) and Kuwait accounted for another $100 billion. Saudi Arabia placed approximately 45% of its surplus in banks, and used another 30% to purchase obligations of the US government. For all of OPEC, 22% of the surplus went to purchase US government obligations.[22] All of that capital provided a means to finance the ballooning trade and fiscal deficits of the US.[23]

The same trend held true during the price escalation from 2003 to 2008. During that period, OPEC once again ran a surplus; this time it was $1.65 trillion.[24] Saudi Arabian net foreign assets balloon by over 800% to more than $449 billion.[25] Meanwhile, the trade and fiscal deficits in the US also exploded, enabled by the influx of foreign capital and, consequently, the growth of net foreign asset ownership.[26]

The Petrodollar System

When net foreign portfolio holdings of US securities are combined with net foreign banking assets in the US, it becomes clear that OPEC members acquired US assets worth about $418 billion between June 2003 and June 2008, 25.3% of the OPEC surplus. When other major oil exporters Russia and Norway are included, the total rises to $747 billion.[27] Although large, those figures still underestimate the petrodollar flows because they do not account for investments made through intermediary countries. Financial centers such as Switzerland, Luxembourg, Bermuda, and the Cayman Islands together held more than 26.5% of net foreign portfolio holdings of US securities and net foreign banking assets in the US, which were nearly $1.8 trillion as of June 2008.[28]

While the petrodollar system funneled hundreds of billions, perhaps over a trillion dollars into the US, financing the trade deficit and, to a large extent the US government, it also finances many other governments, particularly those of developing countries. Much of the capital that flows from the oil exporters back into banks is re-loaned to developing nations. Those loans are (not surprisingly) denominated in dollars because the banks have dollars to lend. Furthermore, loans from the International Monetary Fund (IMF) and World Bank are generally denominated in dollars. The result is that much of the world's sovereign debt is dollar-denominated.

In an attempt to combat out of control inflation in the late 1970s, the Federal Reserve increased interest rates to levels previously unseen in the US. Developing countries that had been on the receiving end of floating rate US dollar-denominated loans faced massive increases in their interest accruals.[29] A series of countries were pushed to the brink of bankruptcy.

Demand for the dollar created by the petrodollar system ensures that the dollar is the world's most liquid currency, which helps explain why seventy percent of all international trade takes place in the dollar. The dollar is the currency that central banks accumulate as reserves, but they don't simply stack the currency in their vaults. Instead, they use them to buy the most liquid, interest bearing dollar-denominated assets, usually debt instruments of the US government.

Some economists would argue that with freely exchangeable currencies, it doesn't really matter what currency is used because it can be freely converted to another currency. Those economists would be wrong. Liquidity is often an illusion; it exists in practice when relatively small quantities are traded. Large trades tend to change market values for the commodity in question. Dumping a large quantity of any commodity on the market will likely cause a freefall in its price. So, when holders dispose of large quantities of assets they are forced to do so either through a privately negotiated sale to another block purchaser or by selling small quantities over a period of time.

This same concept helps explain why trade in the US dollar becomes so important for oil importers, particularly those with small economies or weak currencies. With a truly liquid international currency system, a country could simply exchange its own currency for dollars so that it could buy oil for importation. Because oil is such a large part of most economies, however, such transactions would represent significant sales of the home currency, placing downward pressure on the home country's currency value. Exporting goods in exchange for dollars circumvents the need to engage in currency swapping.

The dollar's unique role in the international financial system has allowed the Federal Reserve to print tremendous volumes of dollars. With such an expansion of the money supply, why has there not been a problem with inflation? According to Federal Reserve Chairman Ben Bernanke, "U.S. dollars have value only to the extent that they are strictly limited in supply."[30] When the money supply is expanded, the value of each unit of currency normally decreases. If a dollar is worth less, more of them are needed to buy a given product.

To help answer the question, it is important to understand that there are numerous measures of inflation. The most commonly used is the consumer price index (CPI), which measures prices paid by consumers for a basket of consumer goods and services. The CPI has been remarkably stable since the early 1980s. Consumer price inflation has been the primary focus of the Federal Reserve in its attempts to control inflation, which it has come to view as its primary mission. Although the CPI includes a wide range of goods and services consumers might purchase, it does not include the price of assets.

In sharp contrast to consumer goods, increases in asset prices have generally been thought of as highly desirable. You want your stocks to go up, not down. The same is true for the value of your home. The petrodollar system accomplishes just that. As capital flows back from the oil exporters, it goes not into consumer goods but rather into capital assets. The purchase of stocks and real estate directly inflates those assets values, while the purchase of Treasury securities, corporate debt, and time deposits depresses interest rates and makes financing for asset purchases more readily available, which indirectly inflates asset values.

Although it sounds like a utopia on the surface, it is far from it. The upward pressure on asset prices is not supported by underlying fundamentals. The consequences have been a series of asset bubbles. Although the unprecedented run up in real estate prices is the most recent example, there have been others such as the internet bubble of the 1990s. The asset bubble phenomenon is a serious risk to the economy.

The housing bubble, which spectacularly burst in 2008, has been the most damaging event for the US economy in recent memory, but few realize the central role oil played in creating it.

Oil's Role in the Economic Crisis of 2008

As those who have closely followed the financial crisis are aware, the trouble first became evident in the real estate sector. Throughout most of the country, housing prices had been rising steadily. For years, consumers in the US enjoyed what can only be described as "easy credit." Few asked why the real estate market kept inexplicably climbing or why the river of money invested in it and in mortgages backed by it kept flowing with unbounded vigor. There is, of course, a reason for it just as there is a reason for everything that happens, and it was no accident that the cycle continued.

At the core of the issue is credit. The entire nation, from the functioning of the government to the humble affairs of the average working American, is based on credit. The US is, as has been popularly stated, a "debtor nation." Before addressing how and why so much credit is created, it is first helpful to understand how the real estate bubble actually worked.

As with all free markets, the price of any commodity is based not on its true value but on the perception of its value. This fact is obvious in the stock market where the prices of companies' stock go up and down, sometimes in wild swings, on a daily basis. The true value of the company, its outlook and prospects, usually hasn't changed that quickly, but the perception of its value changes minute by minute. Most markets are not as volatile or as liquid as the stock market, but all of them work on the same principles. Asset bubbles occur when the perception of value substantially diverges from the true value. The bubble bursts when the market quickly and broadly realizes that discrepancy.

Until recent years, the real estate market was financed primarily by banks, whose funds came from customer deposits. Today, long-term mortgage financing is almost exclusively provided by a relatively new invention, the mortgage-backed security. Mortgage-backed securities are basically bonds that are supported by the value of and cash flow generated by mortgages. Creating them involves assembling large numbers of mortgages into pools. The pools are then carved up so that it is possible to issue a wide range of different securities, each with different maturities, credit ratings, and payment terms. The pools are sliced and diced in every conceivable way with the range of potential structures limited only by the imaginations of the pool aggregators, some of whom have pretty wild imaginations.

When the dust settles, some piece of the average home mortgage might be owned by hundreds, perhaps even thousands, of different investors. The disconnection between borrower and the ultimate investors, coupled with the efficiency of mortgage securitization, enabled mortgage issuers to offer consumers loan structures that would have previously been thought ridiculous. With features like "interest-only" and "flexible payments", these mortgages were ultimately predicated on the largely universal assumption that real estate values would be ever-increasing.

The shocking profitability of the whole system, in part driven by accounting rules that heavily favor securitization over traditional lending, created an environment where mortgage issuers were increasingly hungry for product. Even banks, previously competitors to the mortgage-backed security system, jumped in full-throttle. The effect of the abundance of easy credit is now obvious in retrospect. Many people bought homes that were far more expensive than their incomes could justify. Others purchased homes for purely speculative purposes much like trading stocks. There was wild overbuilding. In some of the nation's hottest real estate markets, particularly south Florida and Las Vegas, housing projects were completed and sold entirely to speculators. With no end users, some condominium projects remained virtually unoccupied, yet prices still kept climbing.

Housing was booming and the hysteria of buyers was surpassed only by the orgy of credit. Then, one day people started to look around, and they noticed that all of these new housing units were empty. The sea of investors realized that they had no cash flow to support their mortgage payments. The pressure to sell began to mount as those monthly payments grew painful. More and more units hit the market, and suddenly reality dawned. Panic spread throughout the country, impacting the values of everyone's homes even in small towns far removed from the excesses.

When real estate values plummeted, the ripple effect was felt swiftly in the financial sector. Not only did the profits associated with new issuances evaporate, the value of all of the securities that had been issued in the past became suspect. Many of the holders were banks and Wall Street brokerage houses, who themselves operate on massive levels of financial leverage (in other words, debt). Many of the country's largest financial institutions saw their institutional equity quickly erased.

As the banks and Wall Street firms sank, so did consumer confidence. Fear is the most powerful weapon of all in markets. When consumers are afraid for their jobs or their savings, they cease to be consumers. The sales at retailers plummeted; the sales and profits of manufacturers evaporated; travel decreased, companies cut costs and workforces; and so on.

With the financial sector crippled, credit became essentially unavailable. Most industries are dependent on the flow of credit. When that flow is cut off, companies can no longer purchase inventory or finance their operations. In an economy based primarily on credit and consumption, a freeze in credit markets coupled with an abrupt loss in consumer confidence is basically a doomsday scenario.

This brief description of the series of events that led to the most recent recession may leave out some of the details, but it outlines all of the major issues except, perhaps, the most important unanswered question. Whose money was being used to buy those mountains of mortgage-backed securities? The run up in real estate values and the subsequent calamity would never have been possible without liquidity to buy all of that paper.

The intrinsic qualities of mortgage-backed securities (MBS) in and of themselves dramatically expanded the pool of capital available for mortgage lending, making it just as easy to invest in them as buying stock or treasury bonds. Most of the excess liquidity that made the asset bubble possible, however, came from two sources.

The first culprit was the petrodollar system. American consumers paid for billions of barrels of oil. That money landed with the oil exporters. The exporters could not absorb such large financial inflows, so they invested it back into the US market where it went to a wide range of places: bank deposits, the stock market, corporate debt. The largest single bucket, however, was Treasury securities. From 2003 to 2008, the US spent $1.65 trillion on overseas petroleum, but at least $747 billion (45.3%) was sent directly back to the United States to purchase securities or be deposited in banks. Of that sum, $369 billion was invested in US government and agency securities.[31] When the dust settled, 22.4% of all dollars used to purchase foreign oil can be directly traced to the purchase of obligations of the US government. To put all of this in perspective, the inflow of petrodollars amounted to at least 20% of the total increase in mortgage balances from 2003 to 2008, a period of unprecedented borrowing.[32] Large additional sums were undoubtedly also repatriated to the US via financial conduits in major offshore financial centers.

With nearly three quarters of a trillion dollars flowing into financial assets in the US, it should come as no surprise that the plethora of excess funds in the market kept downward pressure on interest rates. The low interest rate environment made the issuance of mortgage-backed securities much easier and more cost effective. Lower interest rates increased borrowing power and placed upward pressure on consumer demand. Credit became more widely available, a phenomenon especially evident in the mortgage market.[33]

Mortgage backed securities also compete with US Treasury securities for investment dollars. As the yields on Treasuries were depressed, the yields on MBS investments seemed relatively attractive, particularly since the prevailing wisdom at the time deemed many MBS bonds to be virtually equivalent in risk to US government obligations, a view reinforced by major credit rating agencies who gave the top tier MBS bonds the highest possible credit rating.

Perhaps the best way to truly illustrate the effects of the petrodollar system is to describe the alternative. Imagine for a moment that the US is energy independent. Americans would still purchase fuel for their vehicles, but that fuel would come from domestic energy sources, perhaps some combination of domestic oil, natural gas, and biofuels. The funds from those purchases, instead of going to oil sheiks and petro-state autocrats who then buy financial assets, would go to domestic companies that would use those funds to employ more Americans and invest in domestic capital assets. Instead of being concentrated in financial assets, the money going to buy fuel could be an engine for employment and economic growth.

The second part of the liquidity game was the Federal Reserve. The Fed is responsible for regulating the money supply, which is another way of saying they decide how much of it to print. In the often quoted words of Federal Reserve Chairman Ben Bernanke, "the U.S. government has a technology, called a printing press (or, today, its electronic equivalent), that allows it to produce as many U.S. dollars as it wishes at essentially no cost."[34] In recent years, the Fed has printed more and more and made it available to banks, which then made loans in the market. Of course, the Fed also controls bank reserve requirements and short term interest rates, which they can manipulate to create still more liquidity. They are constantly pumping out dollars, but they do so with particular aggressiveness when there are serious market challenges like September 11, the onset of the Iraq War, oil price spikes and the economic crisis. Many, indeed most, of the events that have prompted the Fed to "loosen" over the last decade are themselves the product of oil dependency.

Increasing liquidity in the market does indeed have a stimulating economic effect, but there are consequences to all of that liquidity. It must go somewhere. Among other places, it ended up in questionable mortgage investments simply compounding the effects of petrodollar recycling. With interest rates already artificially depressed by virtue of the flow of capital from oil exporters back into Treasury securities and other bonds, homeowners found a favorable environment and plenty of capital to encourage over-borrowing. Many homeowners took out progressively larger home equity loans, the proceeds of which were used for more spending. The lunacy of the whole system seems obvious now, but not long ago it was accepted practice, encouraged by the US government through both policies and comments of officials.

With the path to economic crisis illuminated, there are some inescapable conclusions. Without foreign oil dependence, the system that made possible the excessive borrowing that led to the crisis would not have existed. The $747 billion that was concentrated in financial assets would have instead been in the hands of consumers, not as consumer debt or real estate loans, but as earnings. Circumstances would have been different for the Fed as well, and there would have been no need to furiously print dollars to prop up the economy. Massive excess liquidity was the problem, a problem largely created, in one way or another, because of foreign oil addiction.

The economic contraction has already had the effect of temporarily reducing global petroleum demand resulting in a drop in oil prices, but the world has been here before. In the mid-1980s, petroleum prices hit record lows, and the efforts aimed at replacing petroleum were abandoned. As we have been made painfully aware, prices didn't stay at all-time lows. Instead, they came back with a vengeance.

If the US were not dependent on foreign oil, is it possible to truthfully proclaim that the economic crisis could have been avoided? Although the business cycle would still exist and there would still be recessions and retrenchments, this particular crisis could indeed have been avoided. Without oil addiction and its long list of consequences, the US economy would be much more fundamentally sound, and without that addiction, the conditions and economic climate that allowed the crisis to fester would never have existed.

Decline of the Dollar?

The price of oil is a function of the confluence of several factors including global supply and demand, responses to geopolitical forces, actions of OPEC, and the dynamics of the financial markets. One of the most important (yet frequently overlooked) factors is the value of the US dollar.[35] As discussed earlier, oil trading throughout the world is conducted almost exclusively in the US dollar, and the dollar has been falling. From 2002 to 2008, the US dollar lost more than a third of its value against the euro.[36]

In theory, a weak dollar will improve the trade deficit, eventually eliminating it all together if the dollar's value declines enough because a free-falling dollar makes imported products more expensive in the US and makes American exports cheaper in world markets. Such an effect, however, can take a very long time, and very large movements in the dollar may be required, particularly considering the massive size of the trade deficit.[37] A slew of politicians and economists have long advocated a weak dollar to help US export industries, but the idea is more effective in theory than in practice because exports account for a relatively small percentage of the US economy.[38] Declines in the dollar have failed to produce corresponding declines in imports.

A variety of policies domestically have contributed to the devaluation of the dollar, and most of them have nothing to do with making US exports more attractive overseas. For starters, the value of the dollar depends on the widespread trust in the sanity of US fiscal policy. The falling dollar bears witness to a loss of trust by the international financial community.[39] The dollar is falling because, among other reasons, the ever-growing US fiscal deficit presents the prospect of too many US treasury bonds on the market. Financial markets and oil exporters are afraid that the future glut of bonds will drive up interest rates and drive down the value of those bonds.[40]

As guardian of the world's primary reserve currency, America has some unbecoming habits. Rampant borrowing, furious spending, and a trade deficit big enough to bankrupt any other country all make dollar devaluation inevitable if the trends continue.[41] The aforementioned factors also jeopardize the special benefits gleaned by the US by virtue of the petrodollar system.

Just as important is monetary policy, which directly controls the supply of dollars in the market. As it happens, the price of oil itself has had an effect on monetary policy affecting the value of US currency. In years past, an increase in oil prices was viewed in the context of overall domestic price increases. In other words, it was thought to be part and parcel to inflation, not only because energy prices are a factor in consumer purchases but also because energy is a component of many other consumer goods and services. Bernanke and the modern Fed, however, have viewed increasing oil prices as a lever more likely to cause a recession than inflation. Instead of fighting increasing oil prices with measures designed to control inflation, the Fed has responded by increasing the money supply in hopes of stimulating aggregate demand. So, as the falling dollar contributes to increasing oil prices, the Fed prints more money. Increasing the money supply makes a given dollar worth less, which means that more dollars are needed to buy a given quantity of oil. In effect, the falling dollar and the increasing price of oil elicit policies from the Fed that cause the dollar to fall still further and the price of oil to increase even more, accelerating and intensifying the effects.

But the Fed's policies are not entirely unreasonable. Instead, they are a choice between two evils. Tightening monetary policy in the face of rising oil prices would also have negative consequences since history has shown that rising oil prices coupled with constrained liquidity will almost certainly lead to a recession. The choices by the Fed have been essentially to attempt forestalling a recession with short term monetary stimulation at the expense of the long term value of the dollar. The opposite policy would probably cause recession and short term suffering, but avoid the challenges of a free falling currency.

Exchange rates play a key role in domestic oil pricing because two-thirds of the oil consumed in the U.S. is imported. Thus, even if other supply and demand factors remain constant, Americans will see the price of gasoline increase at the pump if the dollar weakens significantly. The price of oil has less to do with the exchange rate between the currencies of the oil exporters and the dollar (many of which are fixed) as it does the value of the dollar relative to the major international currencies.

Since oil is priced in dollars, conventional wisdom would have it that a change in the dollar's value would not influence the price of oil in dollars, but rather the price would change in other currencies. In practice, however, that is not necessarily true. When the dollar depreciates against other currencies, the euro for example, goods denominated in those currencies become more expensive relative to the dollar. Because the exporting countries also engage in trade with and buy large quantities of goods from Europe and Asia, their purchasing power is reduced in those markets when the dollar declines. The volatility of the dollar also makes the purchasing power of oil exporting countries more unpredictable.[42] The exporting countries, therefore, have an incentive to increase the price of oil in dollar terms. Just as one might expect, in the long term an increase in the price of oil results in significant depreciation of the dollar relative to the currencies of other nations with the exception of countries whose economies are also heavily dependent on imported petroleum like Japan.[43]

At the same time, a weak dollar tends to stimulate oil demand in the rest of the world, which acts to place upward pressure on prices.[44] Particularly, dollar depreciation has a positive impact on Chinese economic activity because its exchange rate is effectively fixed against the dollar. A declining dollar also means a decline in the Chinese yuan. Depreciating Chinese currency means Chinese exports are cheaper on world markets. The consequence is greater demand for Chinese goods, which entails increased demand for oil and, therefore, a rise in its price.[45]

Because of the multiple compounding effects, a decline in the dollar causes oil prices to increase in the US much more rapidly than in many other markets that have floating currencies against the dollar. At the end of 2002, the real cost of oil in Europe and in the US was about the same. From that point forward, however, there was a growing disparity between the price increases witnessed in the US and those in Europe. Between February 2002 and February 2004, the price of oil in dollars rose by 51%, but it rose by only 4% in euros. Over the same period, the dollar went from being worth 1.16 euros to only 0.80.[46] The conclusion is obvious. A declining dollar has intensified price shocks in the US.

As the virtually exclusive medium of exchange in the international oil market, the dollar clearly enjoys some special benefits, but that status is not perpetually assured. There has long been talk among some world leaders, particularly in Asia, of replacing the dollar with a basket of currencies or even with the euro (although recent economic developments in Europe have illuminated the inherent weaknesses of the euro, and talk of using it instead of the dollar has consequently evaporated). There has even been one direct challenge to the dollar's status by a major international oil exporting nation, although the effort was short-lived. As fate would have it, the leader of that nation, Saddam Hussein, was to be short-lived as well.

After the first Gulf War, Iraq was faced with UN-imposed economic sanctions. Out of humanitarian concerns for the Iraqi people, the UN Oil-for-Food Program was born. Under its auspices, Iraq began conducting oil transactions in the euro instead of the dollar in October 2000. The move, clearly political, was intended to serve notice that world oil transactions need not be conducted in dollars as they had been since the birth of the industry.[47]

Under the Oil-for-Food Program, the US purchased around 65% of Iraq's oil production.[48] A twisted world was spawned where US-based oil multinationals were actually forced to use the euro instead of the dollar to make purchases from Iraq. In 2002, a senior Iranian oil diplomat suggested that euros could have a wider role in pricing Middle Eastern oil. Russia, too, took up the issue.[49]

The invasion of Iraq and replacement of Saddam didn't take long after Iraq's shift to the euro. Some theorists have suggested that the timing was not a coincidence and that the decision to go into Iraq was influenced substantially by the need to defend the dollar's status. Not surprisingly, immediately after the fall of Saddam's regime, one of the first actions by the occupation force was to abandon Iraq's practice of pricing its oil in euros and reestablish the dollar as the currency used in the petroleum trade.[50]

The dollar is not without its own defense mechanism. Decades of petroleum trade has left the oil exporters holding dollar-denominated asset positions in the trillions. As a consequence, Saudi Arabia has long been an ardent defender of the dollar. The Saudis have much to lose if the value of the dollar diminishes, which means that they stand to lose if oil were no longer traded in dollars.[51]

Out of their own self-interest, the Saudis have resisted attempts to replace the dollar. As King Fahd, the previous Saudi monarch stated it, "...if we were to accept the basket of currencies, our dollar income and investments would be affected, and this is what we are trying to avoid as the biggest producer."[52] This entanglement illustrates yet another facet of the web of co-dependency that has developed between the US and the Saudis.

Dollar-denominated assets held by oil exporters (and China) do serve as a disincentive for them to embrace a switch that could diminish the dollar's value, but there are other factors to be considered. As long as oil continues to trade in dollars, the oil exporters will continue to accumulate more dollar-denominated assets. With the increasingly unstable fiscal situation in the US led by nightmare fiscal deficits and the downward trending dollar, countries may take the long term view and sacrifice some of the value of the assets they currently hold to avoid accumulation of still more dollars. The days of the petrodollar system may indeed be numbered, and it is vital to US economic security to ensure that such a transition, which may well be inevitable, does not precipitate an absolute economic collapse.

The Hidden Cost of Oil

By now, it should be clear that oil dependence takes a toll on the US economy. The petroleum trade deficit is growing, as is the wealth transfer and consequential growth in foreign ownership of US assets. These effects are clear and measurable, but the story does not end there. Even exclusive of the international trade and investment consequences, there is a striking impact from the dependence on imported petroleum. The cost of petroleum goes well beyond the cost at the pump.

Direct government subsidies to the petroleum industry are estimated to be $4.5 to $10.9 billion a year.[53] The largest such subsidy is the Strategic Petroleum Reserve (SPR). It may seem strange to consider the SPR a subsidy. If, however, the US were not dependent on foreign oil, it would not need a Strategic Petroleum Reserve, the primary purpose of which is to act as a buffer against overseas supply disruptions.

The costs do not end with subsidies. They are, in fact, relative child's play when compared with the drag on our economy associated with some of the more unsavory consequences of foreign oil dependence. While there are often disagreements about quantifying those costs, by any estimation, they are quite large.

One of the more obvious money pits as it relates to foreign oil dependence is the need to defend those overseas supplies using the US military. The US military spends considerable resources and much of its time maintaining military control over shipping routes vital to the movement of oil. The US has also spent exorbitantly on wars that are indisputably oil related. That spending is very much part of the cost of the national energy supply, yet is not readily visible to consumers at the pump. Instead, it is camouflaged as part of the federal budget and is, therefore, seldom considered when tabulating fuel costs. Instead of paying at the pump, Americans shoulder those costs by paying more in taxes or by running up the national debt. Well hidden though the costs may be, Americans still must inevitably pay.

When evaluating military costs, it is useful to remember that there are both ongoing costs (such as for operations, personnel, equipment, munitions, and other items that would be necessary even in the absence of conflict) as well as costs associated with specific military actions. Precisely calculating the cost of the military protection of oil interests is impossible because, among other reasons, military units serve multiple purposes. Determining the percentage of the total cost to allocate to securing the oil supply is, therefore, necessarily subjective.[54]

There are several methods that can and have been used to create estimates. One of the more useful techniques was developed by Milton Copulos of the National Defense Council Foundation. He suggests isolating the costs of the US Central Command (CENTCOM), the military command responsible for the Middle East and surrounding areas. More than half of all military actions undertaken by CENTCOM have been in the Persian Gulf region. Therefore, it is reasonable to allocate at least half of the costs of CENTCOM operations as related to securing oil supplies, an estimated $40.6 billion per year as of 2003.[55] The estimate represents the cost for personnel and equipment only and does not cover the cost of military conflicts including the first Gulf War or the more recent Operation Iraqi Freedom.

A strong case can be made that $40.6 billion per year for the military protection of oil is an extremely conservative estimate. First, it is certainly conceivable that well over fifty percent of CENTCOM's budget actually goes to protecting oil related assets. In fact, almost all of its activities are probably related to oil in one way or another. In addition, oil protection is not confined to the Middle East. There are other military commands that also protect oil exploration and shipping operations. The Pacific Command is responsible for protecting the vital oil shipment lane through the Strait of Malacca, which connects the Indian and Pacific Oceans and, consequently, the Middle East and the Pacific, as well as the entire Pacific region. The European Command is responsible for oil shipments through the Mediterranean. The Southern Command is responsible for South America, which is a vital oil supply region for North America. Clearly, a portion of the budgets of these military commands should also be considered when evaluating the cost of securing the US oil supply.

Absent any military conflicts, most of the oil supply line protection duty falls upon the US Navy. In 2007, the US Navy, in total, spent about $24.4 billion on personnel and another $35 billion on operations and maintenance.[56] It is reasonable to calculate that at least 20% of US Naval activity goes toward protecting global shipping and offshore oil exploration. That adds another $11.8 billion to the tab for making the world's shipping lanes safe to move oil.

As will be described in later chapters, the quest for oil played a major role in World War II. In fact, the war in the Pacific theater precipitated directly from conflict over oil resources. Wars can be some of the most costly undertakings in which a nation can participate. The Gulf War, the first of the major modern oil wars, was actually quite a bargain as far as military conflicts are concerned. The financial burden was low because the vast majority of the costs were reimbursed by other nations. Because the Gulf War was indisputably the product of Saddam Hussein's oil lust, the cost of the conflict should be included in any tabulation of the costs of securing the oil supply. After reimbursements, the tab was roughly $6 billion.[57] Because that conflict took place more than 15 years ago, however, it is not relevant to a present-day calculation of the financial burden.

Since September 11, 2001, the US military has undertaken several large operations. The most important and expensive of those operations are in Afghanistan and Iraq. The Afghan conflict began as a direct response to the attacks of September 11. Osama Bin Laden, who was ultimately responsible September 11, cited the 1990 Gulf War and subsequent occupation of Saudi Arabia as justification for the attacks. The attacks were, in part, retaliation against the US for its own military actions to secure oil resources, but there were also other factors motivating al-Qaeda. Therefore, including all of the expenses associated with the military conflict in Afghanistan as specifically related to defending the oil supply could be over-reaching. The conflict in Iraq, however, is a different matter.

While the first Gulf War was clearly and openly a conflict over oil resources, the later Operation Iraqi Freedom was veiled in concerns about Saddam Hussein's alleged weapons-of-mass-destruction programs.

Even if the justification used by the Bush Administration is taken at face value, the primary reasons the US considered Saddam a threat can still be traced directly to the original Iraqi invasion of Kuwait and subsequent events. Before Saddam got greedy for Kuwait's oil, he was not considered an enemy of or threat to the US. On the contrary, the US had maintained military ties with Iraq since at least the early 1980s.

The 2003 invasion of Iraq was not a military action conducted in isolation from previous world events. It was actually a continuation and escalation of an ongoing conflict that started with the oil-inspired invasion of Kuwait and the effort to reverse the invasion and protect Saudi Arabia's oil fields. If Operation Iraqi Freedom is really just an extension of the original oil conflict, then it is, consequently, also an oil conflict.

The Congressional Research Service estimates that the total appropriations for the operation in Iraq, through fiscal year 2009, are $641.5 billion. In addition, the Obama Administration has requested another $42.5 billion for fiscal year 2009, bringing the grand total cost for the seven year conflict to $684 billion.[58]

Spending in Iraq is now off of its highs due to success on the ground, but not before over half a trillion dollars has been sunk in the effort. That money is not coming back to the US Treasury. Although an end seems more imaginable after the success of the "surge" and the election of a president who has campaigned on a plan to withdraw American troops, the future remains murky with many unanswered questions about timing and cost. The operation is still ongoing and more expenses will be incurred annually for at least several years.

While historical costs are known, future costs will be dependent on the outcome of a series of political decisions. Because the most important factor determining future costs is the rate of withdrawal, the best estimates are probably those provided by the Obama Administration, which forecasts a total of $87 billion through 2014, with most of that amount being spent prior to 2012.[59] When those figures are combined with historical costs and valued as of 2009 using the US government cost of capital (inferred from the 10 Year US Treasury rate), the total net present cost is roughly $840.3 billion.

If the cost of Operation Iraqi Freedom (annualized over a 10-year amortization period as has been suggested by previous studies)[60] is combined with the general annual defense budget related to oil that was earlier calculated to be $52.5 billion, the result is an estimated $136.4 billion per year for oil-related military spending. In 2008, the US

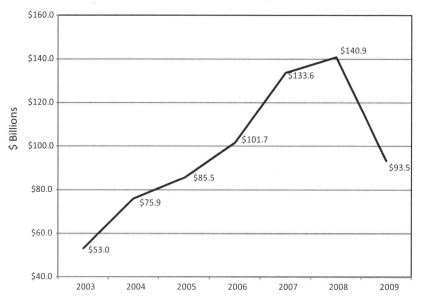

Annual Cost of the Iraq War

Data from Congressional Research Service, *The Cost of Iraq, Afghanistan, and Other Global War on Terror Operations Since 9/11*, p. 9.

imported about 4.7 billion barrels of crude oil and petroleum products of the roughly 7.1 billion barrels consumed.[61] Based on those volumes, military costs add another $29 per barrel of imported crude and over $19 for all barrels of crude consumed by the US on top of the price paid in the open market.

In addition to the cost associated with wars and defense, there is also the very real and significant impact on the economy from the effects of importing oil. Some of the most intensive research into the role oil plays in the economy has centered on the correlation of oil price spikes and economic recessions. The global financial crisis, which was preceded by a dramatic escalation in oil prices between 2003 and 2008, is only the most recent in a long line of oil-led recessions that have occurred since 1972. Some even take the analysis further to concluded that since price spikes have usually been associated with political events in the Middle East, political events in the Middle East can cause recessions in the US.[62]

The economy does not need to experience a recession to feel negative effects from oil dependence. A recession is generally defined, at least in the popular media, as two or more consecutive quarters of negative growth in real gross domestic product (GDP); however, growth need not be negative or even stagnant for oil dependence to levy economic costs.

As discussed earlier, foreign oil dependence causes a substantial wealth transfer and has important consequences for value of the dollar. The wealth transfer is quite simply movement of national wealth from the US to oil exporting nations. From 1989 to 2008, the cumulative US petroleum trade deficit was $2.6 trillion, which represents a substantial wealth transfer to overseas suppliers, but this cost is already reflected in the pump price. There are, however, other economic costs not as visible.

One impact not included in the pump price is the loss of potential economic output. As the price of oil increases, it becomes, from an economic standpoint, scarcer. When an economy has less available oil, its ability to produce goods and services is reduced from what it otherwise would have been. Since GDP is the sum of what an economy produces in a given year, the effect is a loss of potential GDP.[63]

One way to illustrate the phenomenon is to examine the travel industry. As the price of gasoline increases, people tend to travel less. Less travel impacts the hospitality industry, the airline industry, and a host of others. Increased fuel costs also have an effect on shipping. Workers who travel for business (like sales professionals for example) tend to be less productive as their ability to travel cost-effectively is reduced. There is a ripple effect throughout the economy that impacts industries far and wide.

Another hidden cost stems from the concept of macroeconomic adjustment. The fundamental concept behind these costs is that our economy has trouble immediately reacting to sudden, large price changes.[64] Because oil prices are always changing and those changes are unpredictable, our economy is always trying to adjust. The adjustments involve migration toward the optimum deployment of resources, capital and labor. Such migrations cannot happen as quickly as the price of oil changes; the redeployment of resources takes time and lags oil price changes. This phenomenon presents an economic cost. To exacerbate the problem of adjustments, it has also been demonstrated that rising oil prices retard aggregate U.S. economic activity by more than falling oil prices stimulate it.[65] Accordingly, oil price changes have asymmetrical affects on the economy.

In 2005, researchers at Oak Ridge National Laboratory completed a study that, among other things, calculated the cost of loss of potential GDP and macroeconomic adjustments resulting from oil dependence. The study found that economic costs were significant. Between 1973 and 2004 the total was over $5 trillion, which equates to about $160 billion per year over that period (although the impact in each given year may have deviated significantly from the average over the entire time period).[66] Using the same 2008 import volume figures from earlier military cost calculations, $160 billion equates to $34 per barrel of imported fuel and $23 for each barrel of crude consumed in the US overall (on top of the price paid for the crude itself).

When hidden economic costs and costs of military support are combined, at least $63 per barrel of imported fuel and $42 for each barrel consumed overall should be added to the price paid at the pump to reflect the true cost. Of course, as mentioned previously, this does not include the wealth transfer or the negative impact on the value of the dollar, yet they are truly significant hidden costs. As substantial as all of these financial costs are, they are only the beginning of the story.

2
It's Getting Hot in Here

Fossil fuels are dirty, nasty, icky substances. If you don't believe me, just ask the residents in the coastal areas of the Gulf states. As this book is readied for press, a deep water oil well drilled by BP plc in the Gulf of Mexico continues to spout oil into the open sea. That oil is killing wildlife, polluting beaches, and creating all kinds of havoc. Humans don't mix well with oil. The nature and scale of the international oil extraction effort guarantees that there will be accidents. Tankers leak, as was the case of the *Exxon Valdez*, and there are periodically explosions and other industrial accidents around the world. As serious as all of these accidents are, they could be minor compared to the potential impact from what is not an accident – the burning of fossil fuels.

Earth has witnessed almost unfathomable swings in its climate and environment. Lest we forget, at the time our planet was first formed there were rains of concentrated acid and virtually no oxygen in the atmosphere. The planet has evolved significantly over the last five billion years with no help from us. The changes we fear and debate today are relatively tiny shifts. Although our capacity to morph the environment exists only at the extreme margins, humans activities can and do influence climatic conditions. Subtle changes are sometimes all that is needed to produce pronounced impacts on the world in which we live.

Global warming is one of the key problems frequently discussed with respect to the environment, but even in the extreme, it is a matter of just a few degrees. Since the changes are subtle, there are deep divisions over whether humans are causing the planet to warm. The environmental community insists that the reality of anthropogenic (human-caused) global warming is indisputable, but there remain many skeptics who interject with equal vehemence, "not so fast." While the debate rages on, this book will present the facts and allow the reader to form his or her own conclusions.

Global warming is not the only potential threat to the environment. Before it dominated the news, there were other environmental crises. Over the past few decades, phrases like "the ozone layer" and "acid rain" became commonplace in our collective national lexicon. Fortunately, the environmental challenges associated with both of these have been largely addressed through new laws and concerted global action.

The ozone layer is a relatively thin layer of gas, specifically an unusual type of oxygen molecule found in the lower stratosphere that shields Earth from ultraviolet light. Ozone contains three oxygen atoms (O_3) instead of the two present in a normal oxygen molecule (O_2) that animals breathe. Ultraviolet light can degrade DNA, which causes a variety of problems with living organisms. In humans, the most common serious effect is skin cancer.

In 1985, a startled world learned that there was a growing hole in the ozone layer over Antarctica. At the time, most people probably had never even heard of the ozone layer. Subsequent ground-based research conducted in Antarctica during 1986-1987 and NASA stratospheric aircraft flights into the Antarctic region in 1987 showed conclusively that the ozone loss was a direct result of chlorine-catalyzed chemical destruction. The chlorine was coming from man-made chlorofluorocarbons (CFCs) that had migrated to the stratosphere. The gases were being broken down by ultraviolet light, freeing chlorine atoms. At the time, chlorofluorocarbon chemicals were commonly used as refrigerants, in aerosols, and in certain packaging materials.

The US Congress passed the Clean Air Act of 1990, which allowed the US Environmental Protection Agency (EPA) to phase out CFCs. For most applications, they were banned in the US after January, 1996. CFC concentration should reach maximum levels in the first few years of the 21st century, after which the recovery of the Antarctic ozone hole can begin. The reversal of ozone degradation, however, will be a long process and will likely not be complete until the year 2050 or later.[1]

Ozone depletion is not directly related to energy production or fossil fuels, but it does represent a successful intervention to stop environmental damage that was being caused by human industry. It is an example of using legislation to protect the environment without serious economic repercussions.

Another environmental challenge that has been on the radar for several decades is "acid rain". Acid rain, as it is called, is caused primarily by emissions of sulfur dioxide (SO_2) and nitrogen dioxide (NO_2). Unlike the ozone problem, acid rain is a direct result of energy production. Like many pollutants, SO_2 and NO_2 are emitted as gases when fossil fuels are burned. Once in the atmosphere, they react with other molecules to form sulfuric acid and nitric acid.

Acid rain, as the scary-sounding name implies, has serious environmental effects. It is not well tolerated by plant life. In forests that are susceptible, it can turn leaves and needles brown and cause them to fall off of trees. In many high elevation areas (which tend to be closer to high-concentration clouds), its effects are clearly visible. There are areas where acre after acre of dead trees, devoid of foliage, still stand as monuments to human carelessness.

To reduce acid rain, an overall cap on sulfur dioxide (SO_2) emissions was imposed on fossil fuel-based electric power plants by the Clean Air Act. The EPA developed a system of allowances to allocate the cap among utilities. The magic of the system was that power generators could trade allocations. Utilities that found it more expensive to cut sulfur emissions could buy allowances from others who were able to make large cuts in their sulfur emissions at a low cost. The first allocations were auctioned in 1993 by the EPA.

Under the SO_2 program, emissions were reduced faster than required under the law. Costs of reductions were below most forecasts, and there has been steady growth in the trading of allowances. The volume in 1995 was 700,000 tons, but by 2001, it increased to approximately 12 million tons with an annual value of $2 billion.[2] Many environmentalists hope that the SO_2 "cap and trade" program could serve as a model for solving other environmental concerns, particularly emissions of CO_2, which many believe to be a key contributor to global climate change. That idea, however, has become the subject of fierce political debate in the US.

Oil Spills

Oil spills are relatively common, but occasionally there is a major accidental release of petroleum into the environment. In recent memory, there have been two very large spills of crude oil in the territorial waters of the United States. The first such spill began on March 24, 1989 in Prince William Sound off the coast of Alaska when the *Exxon Valdez* (a large tanker) struck a reef, piercing several of its storage tanks.

Before the leaking ceased, 11 million barrels of heavy petroleum were released into the Alaskan coastal waters precipitating one of the worst environmental disasters in US history. The ecosystem was devastated. Cleanup operations took more than three years. Exxon eventually agreed to pay just over $1 billion in criminal fines and a civil settlement with the State of Alaska and the US government. In 2006, the government reopened the case to ask for more money claiming that there remain significant quantities of oil in the area that require further remediation – 17 years after the spill first occurred.[3]

The *Exxon Valdez* incident was a serious disaster, but it was nothing compared to a gushing well on the seafloor in the Gulf of Mexico off the Louisiana coast. On April 20, 2010, an explosion on BP's *Deepwater Horizon* drilling rig killed eleven workers and resulted in a release of petroleum unrivaled in US history. Several factors make the *Deepwater Horizon* different. First, as this book goes to press nearly three months later, the oil is still flowing from the well head – located nearly a mile below the surface. At such a depth, the task of plugging the leak has proven particularly challenging. The pressure down there is too great for humans, but perfectly suitable for modern underwater television cameras. Unenvisioned at the time of the *Exxon Valdez*, there are now a handful of twenty-four-hour cable news networks that regularly feature images of the gushing oil. There is also, of course, a live feed on the internet. It makes for a striking visual. Every day, Americans are reminded of the awful reality of the incident.

At the time of printing, BP and federal officials have been unable to accurately estimate the rate of flow. Estimates tend to place it somewhere in the 50,000 to 100,000 barrel per day range, an amount on the order of about one quarter to one half percent of average daily petroleum consumption in the US.[4] For comparison purposes, the flow is about 10-20% of the average volume going through the Trans-Alaskan Pipeline as of 2010 (about half of which is also, incidentally, produced by BP).[5]

Another important aspect of the Gulf spill is location. The *Exxon Valdez* spill was in a more remote location (Alaska), whereas the *Deepwater Horizon* is off the coast of Louisiana and has the potential to affect major population centers and tourist destinations along the Gulf coast and even the eastern seaboard. In short, the incident is much more visible to the average American.

Only three weeks before the spill began, President Obama held a major event at Andrews Air Force Base to announce his support for increasing offshore oil exploration. The leak in the Gulf has led to skepticism about the safety of offshore drilling. Many from Obama's own political base have begun to loudly and publicly question the wisdom of his decision to support offshore oil exploration. In a classic public about-face, Obama announced at a news conference on May 27, 2010 (less than two months after embracing increasing offshore drilling) that the government would stop issuing new permits for a six-month period.

The *Deepwater Horizon* incident will have long term implications. There are already environmental consequences, but as the oil migrates more areas will be affected. Birds and fish will die, and the tourist-based economy of the area will continue to be severely impacted. The long term environmental and economic consequences will be substantial. The $1 billion paid by Exxon for its Alaskan spill has already proven to be a drop in the bucket compared to BP's liability. BP has agreed to pay up to $20 billion for damages associated with the spill, but that amount is not a cap. Some prominent analysts have gone so far as to predict an eventual bankruptcy and breakup of BP.

The economic fallout goes well beyond the Gulf coast tourist industry. BP's financial commitment *already* represents a full one percent of the UK's 2009 gross domestic product.[6] BP is the UK's largest company, and the media in Britain has fueled the flames of anger of the British public against what has been perceived as a rhetorical flogging at the hands of politicians in the US. The incident is even straining relations between the Obama Administration and David Cameron's new government in London. Because of BP's significant role in the British economy, both the US and the UK may suffer long term economic ramifications.

Finally, the political impact in the US is still unfolding, but there may be important long term implications. Polls indicate that the public has largely disapproved of President Obama's handling of the affair. Analysts have compared the episode to perception of President Bush's handling of the aftermath of Hurricane Katrina, from which he never fully recovered politically. Most striking has been the criticism levied by members of Obama's own political party complaining that not enough has been done to stop the leak, control the spill, and support American suffering from the economic fallout. The potentially more impactful political fallout, however, is what all of this might mean for offshore oil exploration and public support for it. Most petroleum resources in the US that are not already fully exploited are offshore. Limits on offshore exploration will likely make the problem of foreign oil dependence just that much worse.

Global Warming and Atmospheric Carbon

Today, global warming is the predominant concern among environmentalists. Most scientists agree that the world is getting warmer. A study performed by the National Academy of Sciences at the request of Congress shows conclusive evidence that Earth's temperatures have indeed been increasing. The study found that the planet warmed by about 1° Fahrenheit (0.6° Celsius) during the 20th century. It further projected that Earth would warm between 3°-10° Fahrenheit (2°-6° Celsius) by 2100.[7]

Scientists believe that current global temperature levels are the highest the planet has seen in at least the last 1,000 years. Accurate temperature readings have only been kept for the last 150 years, so a bit of ingenuity is required to determine earlier temperature levels. Evidence from ice cores and boreholes, tree rings, records of glacier length, and historical documents have all been used to estimate historical temperatures. This evidence indicates that there was a warm period around AD 1000 and that there was a significant cooling from 1500 to 1850, a period referred to as the "Little Ace Age". The evidence is not conclusive, but it is believed that current temperatures are greater than those during the warm period a millennium ago.[8]

Consequences of increasing global temperatures are most evident at the far ends of the planet, the arctic and Antarctic, where is it possible to see ice melting right before your very eyes. Satellite images clearly show the reducing size of the polar ice caps. Even the most ardent opponents of global warming theories cannot deny that the ice is melting. The disagreement is over the cause.

There are lots of theories as to why the planet is getting warmer. Some believe it is part of a natural cycle of the planet. The most popular theory, however, is that it is the result of greenhouse gas discharge created by humans as we produce energy from fossil fuels. The basic principal in question is a well known phenomenon – the greenhouse effect. The greenhouse effect is unquestionably real and helps to regulate the temperature of our planet. All Americans have certainly experienced it by getting into a car on a sunny day only to find that it is warmer inside than outside. Without the greenhouse effect, Earth's average temperature would be about 0° Fahrenheit (-18° Celsius) instead of the present average of 57° F (14° C).[9] On the planetary scale, the effect occurs when heat is absorbed by certain gases in the earth's atmosphere and is then re-radiated downward toward the surface. Many different types of gases can produce it, the most common of which are water vapor and carbon dioxide. When greenhouse gas concentrations begin to increase, the greenhouse effect intensifies. The effect of this intensification is that more heat is re-radiated toward the planet's surface causing the average temperature to increase.

Carbon dioxide is of the most concern because its atmospheric levels have been steadily rising. Modern technology allows us to measure the concentration of carbon dioxide (CO_2) in the atmosphere going back thousands of years by taking ice core samples. A variety of samples have been taken in Antarctica where the ice is deep enough to contain a historical record going back at least 420,000 years.

To put the most recent findings in context, it is helpful to examine the data going back more than four ice ages. The planet's recent history, say the last one million years, has been characterized by a series of climatic cycles each lasting about 100,000 years.[10] For the last four cycles, the period covered by the empirical data from the ice core samples, our climate has been within a remarkably stable range. Although it has been constantly changing, the climate has stayed within very finite boundaries. Stability of the climate may have contributed significantly to the development of civilizations.[11]

What is of particular interest, however, is that the ice core data shows that atmospheric greenhouse gas levels have correlated very well with global temperatures. The correlation suggests that greenhouse gases may have significantly contributed to the climate cycles.[12]

With that data in mind, it is startling to look at information from the last two centuries. It is during this period that the world truly became industrialized. Subsurface oil and the refining process were discovered, and automobiles began to pepper the landscape. Large scale production of electricity from fossil fuels also became commonplace. Leading up to the industrial age, atmospheric concentrations of CO_2 were in line with the historical record over the last 420,000 years. If one examines the data between 1832 and 2007, however, there is a striking pattern of constantly-increasing CO_2 levels.

Levels of carbon dioxide in the period before the Industrial Revolution were around 280 parts per million (ppm).[13] Average global concentration in 2007, however, was 382.7 ppm.[14] The following

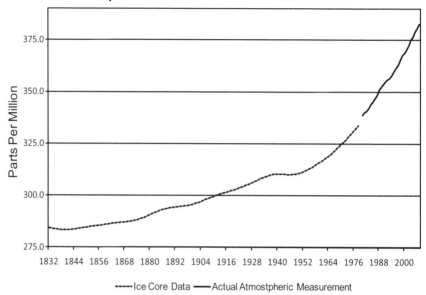

Atmospheric Carbon Dioxide Concentration

Ice core data data from Etheridge et al., "Historical CO$_2$ Records from the Law Dome DE08, DE08-2, and DSS Ice Cores." Atmospheric measurements from Dr. Pieter Tans, NOAA/ESRL, http://www.esrl.noaa.gov/gmd/ccgg/trends (accessed February 6, 2008).

chart depicts a dramatically increasing trend. Put further into context, current levels are the highest at any point during the last 650,000 years and probably during the last 20 million years,[15] perhaps as much as 27% higher than at any time during that period.

If the trend continues on its forecasted path, atmospheric CO$_2$ levels could increase even more. According to the Intergovernmental Panel on Climate Change (IPCC), the world could see carbon dioxide concentrations of anywhere from 490 to 1260 ppm (75-350% above the pre-industrial concentration) by the end of the year 2100.[16]

Even many oil company executives recognize that atmospheric CO$_2$ has greatly increased in the last century. This is particularly true of the retired ones who aren't risking their positions by saying so. Lord Ronald Oxburgh, the former Chairman of Royal Dutch Shell, is among those who are willing to admit the obvious:

> If you look at the historical records of the atmospheric CO$_2$, you can see us undulating along...and you reach the last century, and suddenly this spike goes through the roof. And it is probable that the earth has never

experienced a rate of increase of CO_2 in the atmosphere at anything like this rate in its history.[17]

Most scientists agree that there are two major factors increasing CO_2 levels in the atmosphere: emissions from fossil fuel combustion and industrial processes as well as increases resulting from land use change, mainly land clearing. In 2005, land use changes resulted in the emission of 1.5 billion tons of carbon, but fossil fuel combustion resulted in much greater emissions – 7.9 billion tons of carbon. Emissions from land use changes have remained relatively stable, but emissions from fossil fuel have been accelerating.[18] The total global emissions grew at 1.1% during the 1990s, but grew at the alarming rate of 3.3% between 2000 and 2004.[19] This rapid increase in growth can be attributed in large part to the accelerating industrialization and economic growth in the developing world, China and India particularly.

It is a simple fact that burning hydrocarbon fuels such as coal and oil produces carbon dioxide as a waste product. Actually, any form of combustion produces CO_2. Humans (as well as all other animals) even emit it when we breathe. Fortunately, nobody is suggesting that you should hold your breath to control CO_2 emissions.

Science does not suggest that the past climate cycles as a whole are a function solely of the atmospheric CO_2 concentration. Levels of atmospheric carbon dioxide are not the only determinant of global temperatures. Rather, much of the variability in past major climatic cycles can be explained by variations in Earth's orbital path.[20] Furthermore, a far greater determinant of global temperatures than CO_2 levels is the ability of the planet's surface to reflect or absorb sunlight. These absorptive properties could be responsible for accelerated temperature change in the future.

Even young children understand that darker surfaces get hotter, quicker in sunlight than do light colored surfaces even if they don't understand the science behind it. They quickly learn that while they may be able to walk bare-foot on light colored cement, black asphalt will burn their feet. This fact is a clear illustration of how darker-colored substances absorb more energy from light. This same phenomenon may accelerate warming of the planet.

Ice at the poles tends to be bright white and highly reflective, whereas the oceans have a deep blue color allowing for the absorption of

Annual CO$_2$ Emissions (1900-2004)

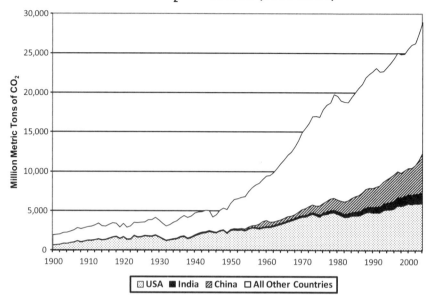

Data from Marland, Boden, and Andres, "Global, Regional, and National Fossil Fuel CO$_2$ Emissions."

more sunlight. As the reflective surface area of white ice melts and gives way to the absorptive deep blue of the sea, heat will be trapped. This effect can snowball. The trapped heat could create more polar melting, further deceasing the area of the ice caps, which, in turn, would create still more absorption and global warming.

It is also possible that the melting of the polar ice caps (which are composed of fresh rather than salt water) could change the salinity of the oceans at the poles. Theoretically, such a change could affect ocean currents, thereby having a dramatic impact on global climates. It was this phenomenon that formed the basis of the doomsday movie *The Day After Tomorrow*. While global climate shifts are possible and have occurred in the past, "abrupt" climate change generally means a change over the relatively short geological period of a decade or so, not a change over a few days. Most scientists agree that there would have to be significant melting well beyond current levels for a shift in ocean currents to occur.

So, that brings us back to greenhouse gases from fossil fuels. Most of the coal and oil that we are recovering today was actually formed millions of years ago – at the time of the dinosaurs. At that point in our planet's history, greenhouse gases had warmed the planet to levels so high that ice did not exist anywhere on the planet's surface. Waters at the poles were warm enough for humans to take a comfortable swim. Logic dictates that the burning of all of the fossil fuels stored in the earth would re-release back into the atmosphere that same carbon dioxide that was once sequestered. Why then shouldn't we expect the planet to trend toward the conditions that were present when atmospheric CO_2 was at similar levels?

Consequences of global warming could be severe. The matter is far too serious to simply ignore. Without question, the greatest impact would come from melting of the polar ice caps. Consequences of such a melting could be numerous and have a substantial effect on global climatic systems as well as sea levels.

Among the most immediate concerns related to melting of the polar ice caps is that it will add volume to the oceans causing sea levels to rise. Low-lying areas might find themselves under water. As Americans learned during Hurricane Katrina, the City of New Orleans is below sea level. Many other parts of the country that lie along the east and west coast are only slightly above sea level. Much of the State of Florida falls into this category, as does much of the City of New York. Rising oceans could submerge substantial tracts of land, resulting in the loss of trillions of dollars in property value.

Some would say we are already beginning to feel some of the consequences of increasing global temperatures, one being more severe weather events. A warmer planet will result in greater uptake of water through evaporation and, therefore, more precipitation. These precipitation events could be more severe, resulting in flooding and other undesirable events. Hurricanes could be more numerous and harsh. In other places, there could be changes in climate patterns that result in the area being much dryer and less able to support agriculture. In short, the potential effects are numerous and uncertain.

It is important to note, however, that not all of the potential consequences of global warming are bad. Some are actually positive, such as the possibility that a greater portion of the planet would be able to sustain agriculture.

Some say the global temperature increases are the result of natural phenomenon, not related to the widespread use of fossil fuels. This hypothesis, however, ignores the timing of the near simultaneous increase in temperature and atmospheric CO_2 concentrations, and it fails to offer evidence for a plausible alternative theory for the cause of temperature increases. For the CO_2 levels to have jumped so dramatically in the last century when compared with the last half-million years, it strains credibility to say it is merely a coincidence that the same period has also seen a temperature increase.

Indeed, there have been studies that estimate the relative contributions of natural temperature changes and changes caused by human activities concluding that most of the temperature increase seen in the 20th century is the result of human activity,[21] but the legitimacy of such studies has fallen under suspicion.

Whether humans are causing global warming will remain a subject of debate, and it is not all-together clear what will happen if humans continue to discharge uncontrolled levels of CO_2 into the atmosphere. As a general rule, however, it is unwise to continue any human activity that changes the relative concentrations of atmospheric gases or otherwise changes conditions on the planet. Anthropogenic global warming may or may not be real, but can we really afford to take the chance? There are other ways to produce energy that not only avoid the same environmental consequences but also enhance economic and national security.

Carbon Neutrality

Since fossil fuel consumption has been the primary contributor to carbon emissions, there has been burgeoning interest in energy sources that do not emit carbon. In that quest, the deceptively simple concept of carbon neutrality reigns supreme. Carbon neutrality means, quite simply, zero *net* emissions of carbon. In other words, it is acceptable to emit carbon into the atmosphere but only if somewhere else in the process you take an equal amount of it out. Since combustion produces carbon dioxide regardless of the fuel, for energy production to be accomplished on a carbon neutral basis, production must either not involve combustion or, if it does, production of fuel used in combustion must remove carbon from the atmosphere.

The simplest way to be carbon neutral is to avoid the carbon issue completely. Wind, solar, nuclear, and geothermal power generation do not involve carbon, but have limited applications for vehicular travel. Unfortunately, even the most promising new technologies for fueling vehicles involve carbon in the fuel cycle. Fuel cells technologies, for example, require hydrogen. While it is possible to obtain hydrogen gas (H_2) by separating the hydrogen and oxygen in a molecule of water

(H_2O) through a process called electrolysis, the process consumes a tremendous amount of energy. The energy invested to separate the water molecule must be produced from some other means. In producing this "seed energy," as in all methods of energy generation, there are implicit inefficiencies where energy is lost. The separation process itself does not conserve all of the molecule's energy. The result is a process that quickly becomes very expensive. When hydrogen is examined as a potential large scale source of fuel, assumptions usually include extracting it from hydrocarbon fuels (such as coal, oil, and natural gas) or from biomass, a process that must be considered in the context of carbon release.

By far the simplest technology that has potential for carbon neutrality is the use of biomass. Most of us have burned wood at some point in our lives. Burning wood can give us a lot of insight into what is actually happening when we convert biomass to energy. First, there is an open flame that reduces the wood to coals, giving off heat and light energy in the process. If the fire is extinguished at this point, the coals, as they cooled, would be a flaky black substance. That substance is carbon. If the fire is not extinguished, those coals would continue to burn slowly, giving off a great deal of heat as they seem to evaporate. In fact, carbon dioxide (as well as other greenhouse gases) is actually forming right before your eyes as the carbon in the coals is oxidized.

By burning wood, a carbon cycle is completed. The cycle begins with a growing tree. During photosynthesis, the tree takes in carbon and stores it as it grows by "breathing" CO_2 directly from the atmosphere. When wood from that tree is burned, the stored carbon is released back into the atmosphere. No more carbon can be released than was stored. Looking at the entire cycle, the net effect on the atmosphere is the same as if the tree had never existed in the first place. Accordingly, the cycle and energy harnessed from combustion of the tree are carbon neutral, and the process could go on forever without increasing the amount of carbon in the atmosphere.

Since fossil fuels were once living organisms, the carbon they contain also originated in the atmosphere. In their case it was absorbed millions of years ago when the atmosphere was much richer in carbon. Burning them now is the conclusion of a very long cycle that simply re-releases carbon back into the atmosphere from which it originally came. Because humans were not yet walking the earth, from our perspective the release of carbon from fossil fuels represents a net addition of carbon to the atmosphere and could theoretically set the environment on a course toward conditions similar to those prevalent when the carbon was originally absorbed.

Carbon Sequestration

One of the ways to combat increasing carbon emissions is a process called sequestration. Carbon sequestration is essentially extracting carbon dioxide directly from the atmosphere or at a plant site as it is about to be emitted and storing it. If mankind continues to use fossil fuels, sequestration of carbon is the only way to control or substantially reduce greenhouse gas levels in the atmosphere.

Sequestration occurs naturally through, for example, absorption of carbon dioxide by the oceans. The average person in the United States emits 120 pounds of CO_2 each day, about a third of which goes rather quickly into the oceans.[22] Oceans hold the vast majority of the earth's carbon, and they have the potential to contain significantly more. They have already absorbed more than 500 billion tons of CO_2 generated by the consumption of fossil fuels and are continuing to do so at the rate of about 1 million tons per hour.[23]

Of the total amount of carbon dioxide that has been emitted resulting from human activity, less than half remains in the atmosphere. The balance has already been absorbed by the oceans and other natural devices of sequestration.[24] One reason for growing scientific concern is that those natural carbon "sinks" are slowly losing their ability to remove CO_2 from the atmosphere. Estimates indicate that between 19% and 51% of the increase in atmospheric CO_2 growth rate since the 1970s has been due to a declining capacity for natural absorption.[25]

Despite the sheer volume of the oceans and their absorption capacity, the increasing rate of discharge and growth in atmospheric CO_2 levels renders natural oceanic absorption far too slow to significantly impact rising carbon dioxide levels in the atmosphere caused by the consumption of fossil fuels. For the oceans to continue to maintain control over global warming, the natural absorption process will have to be complemented by direct disposal of carbon dioxide.[26]

Carbon dioxide can be sequestered either actively or passively. Active sequestration requires us to extract CO_2 directly from exhaust streams, such as at the smokestack of a power plant. That CO_2 would then have to be transported to a disposal site. The cost of separating the CO_2 and transporting it would be a very important consideration in any active sequestration solution, but there may also be some positive economic benefits to the extent that CO_2 be used productively (such as through enhanced oil recovery).

Passive sequestration involves the absorption of CO_2 from the atmosphere. This would tend to be accomplished by absorption either in the oceans or through some terrestrial means. From an economic standpoint, costs of isolating CO_2 and transporting it are not relevant; methods can be judged solely upon the actual costs of disposing of the CO_2, and, of course, based upon its safety and environmental consequences.

There are several ways to sequester carbon in the oceans. Among the methods that have been studied by scientists are the formation of a plume of liquid CO_2 at depth, formation of a hydrate mass (which involves the reaction of CO_2 with water to form a solid), and formation of a lake of CO_2 on the sea floor.[27] All of these are active sequestration technologies. They rely on the fact that at great ocean depths CO_2 has greater density than seawater. Something with greater density than seawater will tend to sink rather than rise to the surface. All of these ideas are technically feasible, but they are in early stages of research. Deliberate injection of large quantities of CO_2 directly into the ocean is unlikely to be a practical solution, however. It faces quite a few daunting challenges.

For starters, it is quite possible that it could prove prohibitively expensive. Furthermore, the potential impact on ocean ecosystems would warrant serious consideration. Carbon dioxide tends to make the ocean more acidic, thereby harming a variety of ocean life forms. The CO_2 absorbed by the oceans since the onset of the industrial age has already resulted in lowering the surface ocean pH (a measure of acidity) by about 0.1.[28] Although this change is small, small changes on a large scale can have serious consequences.

Direct dumping of wastes into the ocean is also prohibited by international treaty. The London Convention, and its updated form, the London Protocol, are international treaties that restrict the dumping of wastes into the oceans. These treaties, at least in their current form, would prevent the direct disposal of CO_2 in the oceans, but would allow disposal in geological formations below the oceans.[29] It is possible that the treaties could be altered to allow deep ocean disposal of CO_2, but it's highly unlikely that such a consensus will be reached anytime soon. The phrase "dumping wastes in the oceans" tends to conjure some pretty strong public reaction, both in the US and abroad. Despite any potential technological promise, ocean dumping simply has too many political obstacles to overcome.

Another way to use the oceans to sequester CO_2 is by fertilizing phytoplankton to enhance the natural uptake from the atmosphere. Fertilization could be accomplished by adding chemicals to the oceans, such as nitrates, phosphates, and iron. The chemicals would be added to the upper ocean to increase photosynthetic activity and, thereby, result in the biological absorption of more carbon. As the phytoplankton die, they sink down into the deep ocean, taking carbon with them. The sinking phytoplankton would continually decrease concentration of CO_2 at the surface allowing for greater absorption from the atmosphere.

If this were the end of the cycle, the sequestration would be permanent – but it isn't. Once the phytoplankton and their carbon "cargo" reach the ocean depths, the carbon will eventually be re-oxidized when the phytoplankton decompose. This will result in a re-release of CO_2 back into the ocean and could lead to escape back into the atmosphere. All that would really be accomplished is temporary storage. At best, this would delay the atmospheric CO_2 problem for a few centuries.[30]

Ocean fertilization could also have severe consequences on ocean ecosystems. Part of the problem is that phytoplankton carry not only carbon but also other essential nutrients when they sink to the deep ocean. As a result, biological activity in other parts of the ocean would diminish.[31] Again, international treaties prohibiting the dumping of chemicals in oceans would be an obstacle to this approach, not to mention the possibility that it could be quite expensive. Given all of the challenges and obstacles, ocean fertilization is not likely to play a part in the ultimate carbon solution.

With the ocean options crossed off our list, there remain several alternatives. Among the most actively discussed is the capture of carbon dioxide at the site of emission, and subsequent sequestration in underground geological repositories. Geological repositories come in quite a few varieties. Hydrocarbon reservoirs are the easiest and at least appear to be the best option for underground sequestration. The reason is simple – they have a proven track record of long term hydrocarbon containment. If they have managed to contain oil and natural gas for millions of years, they should be able to contain CO_2 without leaks for a very long period of time.

Enhanced oil recovery is already a well established technology. Enhanced oil recovery involves the injection of CO_2 into deep geological formations, thereby creating pressure to assist in oil extraction. This process could be scaled-up to use a greater amount of CO_2, gas that would have otherwise been discharged directly into the atmosphere.

Much of the enhanced oil recovery in the US has been concentrated in west Texas. The CO_2 used has been mostly natural CO_2 rather than wastes created by burning fossil fuels. Scale has been small, with the total amount of CO_2 injected equivalent to only about one-half of one percent of the annual CO_2 emissions from fossil fuels combustion.[32]

Sequestration could also be accomplished in coal beds. It is well known that coal beds contain methane (natural gas), a reality made clear by explosions in mines that have trapped miners underground creating a series of high-profile national dramas. About five percent of the natural gas produced in the US comes from coal beds.[33] Clearly, those formations would also be capable of containing CO_2. The pressure of the CO_2 could also be used to enhance coal bed methane recovery since CO_2 and natural gas are slow to mix.

Both enhanced oil recovery and enhanced coal bed methane recovery have the added benefit of actually producing something useful. The carbon dioxide actually creates a revenue stream, obviously making the technologies more attractive. In the absence of governmental intervention (such as taxes, incentives, and the regulation of carbon emissions), profitability of geological sequestration will be a direct function of the cost of capturing and transporting CO_2, the cost of the injection and extracting the desired product, the quantity of oil or natural gas that can be extracted per unit of CO_2, and the price of oil or natural gas.

In addition to hydrocarbon reservoirs, there are other underground geological formations that are capable of containing CO_2. The most abundant of those formations are aquifers. Aquifers, like hydrocarbon reservoirs, are found in porous rock formations. They are far more abundant than oil and gas reservoirs. Many people actually obtain their water supplies from wells that reach these fresh water aquifers. Far below those, however, are brine (or salt water) aquifers. Brine aquifers are much larger and more extensive than fresh water aquifers. Incidentally, underground oil reserves were first discovered when drilling for brine to manufacture salt.

Brine aquifers are capable of holding vast quantities of CO_2. There are several challenges, however. The first and most important challenge is that, unlike hydrocarbon reservoirs, there is no guarantee that an aquifer will actually trap CO_2 underground. Hydrocarbon reservoirs have a proven seal, a formation of impermeable rocks that trap oil and natural gas. There may not be such a formation with brine aquifers. This problem is exacerbated by the chemical properties of CO_2. Carbon dioxide dissolves in both brine and fresh water, creating an acid that is capable of dissolving carbonate rocks.[34] A great deal of testing and research would have to be completed before aquifers could be considered viable for CO_2 disposal.

All methods of geological sequestration suffer from pronounced logistical challenges. Even with an acceptable repository, there are still significant technological issues associated with capturing CO_2. By some estimates, the cost of CO_2 capture may account for as much as 75% of total sequestration cost.[35]

In the last section, I described the cycle of growing, then burning, and then again growing wood, a process that is ultimately carbon neutral. My simplistic description of the cycle left out one key possibility that could play a huge role in offsetting discharges from fossil fuels combustion. Suppose the wood was not burned.

Without intervention, vegetation eventually dies and begins to decompose. Decomposition releases carbon dioxide just as burning does. Both are means of oxidation where the carbon atoms are combined with oxygen. Much of the plant, however, is below ground in the plant's root system. For some types of plants, this can be more than half of the total mass. Even after the plant dies, those roots are not exposed to air (and therefore oxygen) so they don't have the ability to release their stored carbon into the atmosphere as a greenhouse gas. The result is that we have sequestered carbon in the soil using a natural biological process – growing plants.

Clearly, if growing plants were enough, our dilemma would be over and there would be no need for future concern of atmospheric CO_2 concentrations. Although plants continue to grow, land use changes, such as deforestation, are actually taking away from the ability of terrestrial ecosystems to remove carbon from the atmosphere. If we want to use plant life to sequester carbon, intervention is necessary.

There are three ways to increase the ability of terrestrial ecosystems to absorb carbon. The first is to increase the productivity of the ecosystem, which can be accomplished by increasing the density of plant growth. Another way is to skew the type of plant growth to longer-lived species. That process might involve such actions as converting grasslands to forests. Finally, we can ensure longer retention of carbon in the soil. Practices such as no-till farming can be used to add longevity to carbon sequestration.

As a whole, the terrestrial biosphere (which encompasses all of the plants in the world) removes about 2 billion tons of carbon each year. Through a variety of manipulations such as reforestation, restoration of degraded lands, and improved agricultural practices, the global potential might be as high as 5 billion tons per year, which could be sustained for 10 to 50 years. The result would be the potential sequestration of 50 to 250 billion tons of carbon,[36] an amount far from trivial when compared with the 7.9 billion tons of annual carbon emission from the use of fossil fuels as of 2005.[37]

Even with all of the sequestration options, growth in the consumption of fossil fuels is too large for sequestration to offset all carbon emissions. If you subscribe to the theory that atmospheric CO_2 concentrations must be controlled, there is really only one solution. As is frequently the case, the best option is the simplest. The use of fossil fuels must be decreased.

Regulating Carbon Emissions

In America, regulation of carbon discharge is a hotly-debated issue. Those in favor of regulation argue for it based on concerns about global climate change and its consequences. Those opposed argue that it will cost too much, place a burden on industry and consumers, and stifle economic growth. There is certainly logic to be seen in both sides of the debate.

Aside from the fact that significant disagreements remain about to what extent release of carbon into the atmosphere affects the environment, another reason the prospect of carbon emission regulation remains hotly contested is that it is nearly impossible to assign an actual economic value to the environment. Flowers, trees, clean water, breathable air and polar ice caps are nice things to have, but the value of such "public goods" cannot be quantified. They have subjective, not objective value. In other words, value is going to be different based on how an individual assigns his or her priorities. Some environmental consequences do have objective costs. To the extent that global warming causes the polar ice caps to melt and raise ocean levels, there is the potential for waters to reclaim real estate. Submerging valuable beachfront property inflicts very real economic damage on the property owner. Similarly, if global warming causes the frequency and severity of storms to increase, also destroying property, the result is a very real economic cost to owners of that property, companies that insure it, everyone who pays insurance premiums, and, often, the taxpayer.

A clean environment or, for that matter, a stable climate is not a private good. One person cannot prevent another from having access to it. Furthermore, one person's enjoyment of a good environment does not take away from another's enjoyment of it.[38] Given these facts, the environment has no intrinsic economic value to any given individual in the "market." Put another way, why would you pay for something you can get for free? Perhaps the more relevant question, however, is: Why would you protect something unless you have an economic incentive to do so? These points show why market forces are not capable of keeping the environment clean.

To be sure, there are lots of noble people in the world who want to protect the environment just because they think it is the right thing to do. Markets on the macro scale, however, don't operate based on what is right and wrong. They operate on what is profitable or costly and on what is legal or illegal, or, more accurately, on what is punishable and how severely. As an illustration, in many industries it is commonplace for companies to violate laws they consider too cumbersome to follow; instead, they chose to pay fines and consider them a cost of doing business. Sometimes paying a fine is cheaper than following the law.

The problem with the environment, however, is that it has no price tag at all – at least as it relates to CO_2 emissions. You can emit as much as you like and face absolutely no cost for doing so. When any resource is free, it is going to be overused. Imagine how overweight the population would be if cheeseburgers were free.

This concept is what brought the petroleum business into vogue in the first place. You may be surprised to learn that whaling was the primary source of oil for illuminating lamps before kerosene from petroleum was available. There were lots of fish in the sea, and anyone was free to hunt them in any quantity they wished. As a result of intensive hunting of whales, many became endangered species. Whale oil became scarce. This all happened because there was no constraint on the hunting of whales.

When such problems present themselves, the solution that is often proposed is regulation. Regulation, although sometimes in the public interest, can be burdensome and costly. More often than not, regulation tends to benefit the largest firms in an industry. Firms with enough resources to navigate a complex matrix of arcane rules and standards and to employ lobbyists to get the rules tailored to their particular advantage tend to be the winners in heavily regulated industries. The effect over time is to concentrate power at the top among a few very large firms. Regulation is the antithesis of entrepreneurship.

As this book is readied for press, the prevailing political winds are in favor of more regulation. As a loose regulatory environment has made a popular target for politicians eager to cast blame of the economic crisis and recession, everyone should remember that just as a free-wheeling laissez-faire system has consequences, so does tight government control. Regulatory schemes often do much more harm than good. Far too often the winners are not the public but legions of lawyers and consultants that rack up billions of dollars in new fees.

The evidence is fairly convincing that carbon dioxide emissions from humans have had an impact on the environment, so despite the pitfalls of regulation, there is a problem that needs to be addressed, one that does not have a purely market-based solution. One suggestion, referred to in the media as "cap and trade," is to place a cap on total carbon dioxide emissions. Based on the cap, increments of allowable emissions would be carved up; shares would then be created; and they would be sold at public auction. The shares would be traded much the same way as stock. If you need to emit CO_2, you buy a share or a permit to do so either through the original auction process or through ongoing aftermarket trading.

Such a regulatory system would, like any system, require that emissions of CO_2 be monitored on an ongoing basis. Some authority would have to ensure that those emitting CO_2 had purchased enough shares to cover their emissions. Otherwise, they would be subject to a fine. To ensure compliance, the fine would be set well above the price of purchasing a permit on the open market.

The idea of this system is that those who can cut emissions more efficiently and cost-effectively will do so. Those who face higher costs will pay for the privilege of having someone else (with lower emission reduction costs) do it for them. Big business rarely can compete with small entrepreneurial business when it comes to innovation and problem solving. Accordingly, under such a system big utilities tend to be net purchasers while smaller, more entrepreneurial companies are better able to cut costs or efficiently mitigate emissions.

The problem with such a system lies in where to set the cap. In theory, the cap would be set based upon how much CO_2 the environment can tolerate. In practice, however, there is no consensus on just how much carbon that is. Any such decision would ultimately be political rather than scientific. The lower the cap is set, the greater the cost and impact on our economy.

The idea of regulating emissions this way is not new. Earlier, I described how a system based on trading SO_2 allowances was established to control sulfur dioxide in response to the Clean Air Act of 1990. The system was an astounding success. Aside from accomplishing the goal of cutting in half SO_2 emissions and greatly reducing acid rain, it worked with surprising efficiency.

Original estimates for the cost of reducing SO_2 emissions were in the range of $350 to $1,000 per ton. Over the first ten years of trading, however, the price of a credit has averaged $135 per ton. The result was that total annual cost of cutting SO_2 emissions in half was $1.2 billion, less than 1% of the production cost of electricity. Estimated benefits of the SO_2 reduction are on the order of $10 to $30 billion in avoided costs associated with SO_2 damage.[39] That's not a bad return on investment.

Starting in 2003, the Chicago Climate Exchange (CCE) began trading carbon credits in the US. Because there is not a legally mandated cap on CO_2 emissions as yet, the whole system is voluntary. Companies participating are doing so to gain first mover advantages, many anticipating that CO_2 soon will be regulated. Large utilities, assuming there will eventually be some regulatory system, clearly want the lowest cost system – one that will allow them to continue to operate and profit. A trading regime offers them an attractive option since it allows them to purchase the right to emit, almost certainly at a cost lower than what they would have to spend to reduce their CO_2 emissions.

At first blush, the cost of a CO_2 credit may seem like a useful quantity for measuring environmental impact, but it is not. It represents the market value of reducing carbon emissions, not the cost of actual damage to the environment. To illustrate this fact, one need only view the price history of a "Carbon Financial Instrument" traded on the CCE. The value has proven remarkably volatile, ranging from a low of less than $1 to a high of more than $7 over the past 5 years.[40] Quite obviously, the cost to our environment is not nearly so variable.

The first major attempt at an international regulatory scheme to control carbon emissions was the Kyoto Protocol. It was an international treaty negotiated in December 1997 by more than 160 nations with the aim of reducing net emissions of CO_2. The Protocol is fairly lengthy and complex, but it essentially requires that signatory countries maintain their net CO_2 emissions below a certain percentage of a "base year." The US signed the treaty during the waning years of the Clinton Administration, but it failed a ratification vote in the US Senate.

One of the primary objections to the Kyoto Protocol is that not all nations are expected to have the same level of reductions. Although Article 3 of the Protocol states that each country should have "a view to reducing their overall emissions...by at least 5 per cent below 1990 level in the commitment period 2008 to 2012," the actual binding requirement for reduction under the Protocol is an individually prescribed amount for each country. The US has one of the highest commitment levels, with the Protocol calling for a reduction to 93% of 1990 levels. Some other countries, notably Russia, were expected only to maintain levels at 100% of 1990 levels. Meanwhile, China and India, who are behind only the US in total CO_2 emissions, were not parties to the Protocol at all.[41]

Naturally, given the fact that the US could find itself at a competitive disadvantage in the world economy, many lawmakers were reluctant to embrace Kyoto. With a large reduction expected of the US, while modest or no reductions were expected in other large CO_2-emitting nations, impacts on the US economy was sure to be more pronounced. Between 1990 and 2004, CO_2 emissions in the US had already risen by more than 25%.[42] To comply with the Protocol, the US would have to cut emissions enough to erase that increase, plus cut another 7% over 1990 levels. The Clinton Administration's own report, prepared by the Energy Information Administration (EIA), estimated that the result could be an increase in energy prices to consumers of as much as 83%.[43]

Electricity production would feel the greatest impact from Kyoto. In 2008, 49.0% of electricity generated in the US was produced from coal,[44] and coal is the most carbon-intensive of the fossil fuels. The EIA estimated that Kyoto would force an increase in the delivered price of coal of between 153% and 800%. The coal price increase was expected to result in increases in electricity prices by 20% to 86%.[45]

Even though coal would have seen a greater impact than liquid fuel because burning it emits more carbon dioxide than does combustion of oil, the petroleum market is far from unaffected. The EIA projected that the price of gasoline would increase by between 11% and 53%, resulting in a drop in travel. Even air travel was expected to decrease.[46] Damage to the economy would be swift and severe, with an estimated reduction in GDP of between 0.1% and 0.8%.[47]

Perhaps most alarming, however, is that the size of the federal government, as a percentage of GDP, would increase dramatically. If the government sold permits via an auction system, the net effect would be a tax – a very big tax. Projected revenue collection under Kyoto would have been $585 billion in 2010 if the US met its reduction targets.[48] To put this in perspective, income taxes on individuals accounted for just over $990 billion in 2005.[49] It is unclear where the new revenue would have been diverted – to other tax reductions, paying down government debt, to new government spending, or some combination of these. In any case, the carbon auctions would have represented one of the largest tax increases in US history.

Another facet of Kyoto that raised eyebrows was the ability of countries to trade credits. While a splendid idea in and of itself, the feature promoted inequity in each country's negotiated reduction requirements. As I mentioned earlier, Russia was not required to reduce CO_2 emissions below 1990 levels. The Energy Information Administration projected that as much 165 million metric tons of CO_2 emission reductions in the US could come from purchasing credits from the countries of the former Soviet Union, especially Russia. The Protocol's target emission levels were set in such a way as to require no net reduction from Russia, yet Russia could sell excess capacity abroad. The result of this anomaly was a built-in transfer payment from the US to Russia and its neighbors. For all of these reasons, Kyoto faced stiff opposition from a host of political and business interests.

Kyoto failed to gain support in the US not so much because of opposition to controlling carbon emissions, but rather due to perceived inequities in how it would be applied to nations around the world and because there was not a clear means by which it could work in the US without far reaching implications for the economy. If a case could be made that the Protocol did not hurt US consumers or put the US at an economic disadvantage relative to China, India, and Russia, it is likely that it could have gained more traction. As is too often the case with legislation, the devil was in the details.

Although there are continued efforts toward a broad new international climate change treaty and, as this book is readied for press, continued interest in the Obama Administration and among Congressional Democrats in passing cap and trade legislation, neither may be necessary before greenhouse gas emitters find themselves subject to regulation. In 2007, the US Supreme Court ruled in *Massachusetts vs. EPA* (in a 5-4 decision) that the Clean Air Act gives the EPA authority to regulate emission of greenhouse gases including carbon dioxide. The Court went on to say that if the EPA does not regulate greenhouse gases, it must give a scientific basis for failing to do so. Under the Bush Administration, the EPA took no action toward enacting regulations, but the Obama EPA began the process of collecting public comment and drafting proposals almost as soon as President Obama took office. Although the Obama Administration seems to prefer new legislation, it seems that some form of greenhouse gas regulation may be inevitable.

Based on all of the evidence, it is clear that unchecked CO_2 emissions are an environmental and, consequently, an economic risk. Something must be done to slow the effect. The US needs prudent policies to combat increasing atmospheric CO_2 concentrations without the far-reaching economic fall-out. Whatever methods are chosen to curtail net emissions of carbon dioxide, the architecture must be better than the Kyoto regime to maintain American competitiveness and to gain the necessary political support.

The best options for decreasing CO_2 emissions without curbing industrial activity lie in the development of new technologies. Innovation can give the US a simultaneous economic and energy advantage in the global marketplace. Nuclear energy is one of the best options with respect to power generation, but there are also options for transportation fuels that can reduce pollution as well. As it happens, the solutions described later in this book will accomplish just that without the particular need for government regulation.

Part Two – Oil and Geopolitics

3
And on the 8ᵗʰ Day, Oil

The US oil addiction problem did not happen overnight. It took a long time for today's oil-based world to evolve. The story goes back over a century. Not every consequence of the rise of oil has been negative. Things were very different before oil came to prominence, and it has been central, perhaps indispensable, to transformation into the modern world we know today. In fact, the story of oil is *the* story of the last 150 years. Without oil, air travel may never have become widely accessible. In all likelihood, shipping would still be coal-based, requiring much larger, more inefficient ships. The automobile may not have become the fixture it is in modern society. The populace would be far less mobile, and the story of the twentieth century might have looked very different

Neither big business nor global politics can be fully understood without the oil centerpiece. The first modern global corporations were oil companies and many of the largest corporations today have their roots in oil. Oil has produced the greatest fortunes in history, fortunes that still remain unrivaled by those produced in the computer era. Oil markets have distributed power, prestige, and capital to those who have controlled access to oil, and the wealth generated by the industry is still creating dynasties and concentrating power.

The greatest impact of the oil age has not been financial but rather political. As I will discuss in this chapter, it was the strategic importance of oil at the end of World War I that was at the heart of decisions that drew the maps of the modern Middle East. These decisions were just another step along the way that brought us to the situation we have today, where America becomes ever more entangled in the world's oil-producing regions with each passing day. US fixation with the Middle East does not make sense without oil. Each and every move the US makes in the region can be traced directly to the need to quench the thirst for it.

To make sense of the present or to have any hope of foretelling the future, one must first understand the past. So, this chapter will go back to the beginning. It will describe how the modern oil industry unfolded from the first commercial wells through the era of Standard

Oil, probably the most powerful company in the history of the world. With the importance of oil comes the importance of the region that is responsible for producing, by far, more oil than any other. The Middle East is home to 60% of the world's oil reserves,[1] but has failed to offer much else other than bloodshed.

Throughout history, the Middle East has been an area of particular strategic importance. It was home to some of the earliest known civilizations, but today remains largely primitive. In some respects, it has changed little in the last thousand years. Although the region is united by Islam, there are deep divisions between sects that have not infrequently resulted in war.

Just as oil was becoming important, the Middle East was forced into a major political transformation. The Ottoman Empire, which had ruled the region for centuries, found itself on the losing side of World War I. Political upheaval combined with the discovery of oil created quite a setting for intrigue. The recipe breeds a fascinating story of how the beginnings of the modern Middle East were shaped.

Oil Becomes Big Business

Before commercial exploitation of petroleum, there was still a need for flammable liquids – mainly used as fuel in oil lamps. Oil lamps easily date back to the pinnacle of the Roman Empire, where vegetable oil and rendered animal fats were the main fuels. Eventually, whale oil became the primary source of fuel for lamps.

By all accounts, the whaling industry was a tremendous commercial success, but it became increasingly expensive as the world's whale population was decimated. Meanwhile, petroleum (literally Latin for "rock oil") was extremely cheap to produce and refine. The combination of these factors eventually rendered whaling uncompetitive, which is really the only thing that saved some whale species from the brink of extinction.

Up to the beginning of the 19th century, to the extent that petroleum was used, it was obtained from the surfaces of springs and streams. The realization that it could be found far below the surface of the earth is a more recent revelation, an accidental discovery during the process of drilling for brine to be used in manufacturing salt. Not infrequently, drillers found that their brine was mixed with a noxious substance, a contaminant eventually recognized to be petroleum. In some cases so much oil was obtained with the saltwater that wells had to be abandoned. Certain of these deserted salt wells were re-opened years later when it was discovered that the troublesome substance that rendered them useless was actually far more valuable than the brine the original drillers had sought.[2]

Origins of the American petroleum industry are usually traced to a 69-foot-deep oil well drilled in 1859 on Oil Creek near Titusville, Pennsylvania, this first of its kind in the US. The industry took off slowly at first. Despite great interest in oil's potential, the US was in the midst of the Civil War between 1861 and 1865. At least twice, the entire oil industry came to a stand-still when men abandoned oil rigs to fight. When the war ended, however, a million men were released back into the civilian workforce. Veterans were given priority when seeking employment, and they were welcomed with open arms by oil companies. There were men of all rank, from privates to generals, scattered all over the fields. As it would happen, the small oil region of Pennsylvania absorbed a larger portion of men probably than any other spot in the United States.[3]

With a flood of new prospectors descending on western Pennsylvania and the surrounding areas, the industry began to grow rapidly. As early as 1861 the United States was exporting oil overseas. In 1871, petroleum exports were over 152 million gallons (62.5% of the total domestic production of the 243 million gallons or nearly 5.8 million barrels). By the beginning of 1872, nearly 40 million barrels of oil had been produced in total, and oil had jumped to fourth place among the exports of the United States.[4] To put this volume in perspective, in 2008, the US produced 1,811 million barrels of oil, which includes Alaska and drilling offshore in US territorial waters.[5]

As the oil industry grew, perhaps nobody had more effect on its eventual form than John D. Rockefeller. Rockefeller was a Cleveland produce merchant who saw an opportunity to invest in a refinery being developed by Samuel Andrews, an Englishman who had sought his backing. Rockefeller and his partner gave Andrews $4,000 and promised to invest more if necessary. As it would happen, Andrews was a mechanical genius. He devised new processes, which made a progressively better quality of products and got progressively larger percentages of refined product from the crude.[6] His investment was doing so well that by 1865, Rockefeller had sold out of his merchant business to spend all of his time on oil.[7] He built more refineries and opened a trading house in New York. In June of 1870, he combined all of his operations under one company, the Standard Oil Company.[8]

Rockefeller, shrewd businessman that he was, constantly sought to cut costs and streamline his operations. One of the key costs affecting the oil industry during that period was associated with shipping via railroads, which were the predominant means of transportation. To try to gain an advantage, Rockefeller set up cartels to negotiate transportation rates. He also set out to either buy up or bankrupt his competition. His favored tactic was simply to open his books, whereupon the competition tended to quickly capitulate. He enjoyed such a cost advantage that it was clear to most that they could not compete.

By 1882, when the Standard Oil Trust was created, Rockefeller enjoyed almost total control over the oil industry. He retired in 1896, but his company continued to dominate the market until, after a decade of litigation, it was finally broken up by the federal government in 1911. It spawned such companies as ConocoPhillips, ExxonMobil, and Amoco.

Rockefeller and Standard Oil left a lasting legacy in the oil industry. All the way up through the present day, quest for monopolies and oligopolies has been a hallmark of the oil industry and has guided its behavior, especially during times of overproduction or when seeking to avoid it. The legacy is most pronounced in modernity's closest cousin to Standard Oil – OPEC.[9]

Rockefeller was, by far, the richest man in US history as a percentage of the total economy. At the time of his death in 1937, his net worth was estimated to be $1.4 billion, which was more than 1.5% of the US gross national product in that year.[10] Bill Gates, Microsoft founder and the richest living American, was estimated to be worth $40.0 billion in 2008,[11] a year in which the gross domestic product was $14.4 trillion.[12] That represents only 0.28% of the economy. If one buys into this method of comparison, they could say that Rockefeller's wealth at the time of his death was more than five times as great as Gates' wealth, roughly the modern equivalent of $215 billion.

The early 1900s saw a structural change in the oil industry. As the government tangled with Standard Oil, a new era began. In 1901, oil was first struck near Beaumont, Texas. The well was unlike anything seen before on the world stage. It erupted with such violence that a new word entered the national lexicon – gusher. The fountain of oil was capable of producing 75,000 barrels a day, more than 3,000 times the capacity of Drake's first well in Pennsylvania. Soon after, another huge find in Oklahoma made the American southwest the center of activity. This boom spawned new competitors for Standard, companies that would be known as Texaco, Gulf Oil, and Unocal.[13]

At the same time the oil industry was booming in the US, major fields were also being developed in Russia. While the Rockefellers grew wealthy in the US, the Nobel brothers and Rothschild family grew rich from their investments in Russian oil industry, providing a source of nagging competition for Standard in the international markets.[14] As the Russian oil market share grew in Europe, Standard set out on an aggressive campaign to cut prices. Undeterred, the Rothschilds went on the offensive, going after the lucrative Asian market. At the heart of the Rothschilds' campaign was Marcus Samuel, founder of the Shell Transport and Trading Company. Samuel made Shell into a powerhouse by devising a tanker vessel capable of sailing through the Suez Canal, a feat Standard's ships could not match. They had to go around the horn of Africa to reach Asia. The result was an obvious transportation advantage.[15]

In 1892, oil started pumping from a third region, East Sumatra, a Dutch colony in what is now Indonesia. The new discovery brought a third major international competitor, Royal Dutch Company, onto the world stage. Shell also began producing in the region when it gained a concession and struck oil in Borneo in 1887. Although Rockefeller made a concerted effort to consolidate both Shell and Royal Dutch into Standard, each sought to maintain their independence. Because of Shell's overinvestment in shipping, now less useful with the Asian oil discoveries, it was in a weaker position.[16] Eventually, this forced a merger with Royal Dutch in 1907, creating the European oil powerhouse we know today as Royal Dutch Shell.[17]

By the end of the 19th century, internal combustion engines were beginning to power ocean-going vessels. At that time, most ocean vessels were steam ships (powered by coal). Oil offers many distinct advantages over coal. It is more thermally efficient, meaning that a given volume of oil can offer more power than an equal volume of coal. Second, ships can be refueled with oil derivatives while in transit, whereas coal had to be loaded at ports. Finally, oil is much easier to move around on board a ship. The steam ships of the time devoted as much as three quarters of the crew to moving around the coal. The obvious advantages quickly resulted in widespread conversion of the world's naval fleets. Winston Churchill, who was among the first to see the strategic benefits and importance of oil, lobbied for and won approval to convert the Royal Navy to an oil-based fleet in 1913.[18]

From that point forward, as oil became a key strategic military consideration, it greatly influenced world relations, wars, and geopolitics. Oil was no longer just about money, it was now about power. Oil continues to be the centerpiece of international policy in the modern world.

The Middle East before World War II

To understand the Middle-East, one must look back to well before oil became its chief product. Although borders and conflicts have evolved substantially during the last century's "age of oil", the history of the region important to modern geopolitics begins in the year 632. It was that year that marked the death of Mohammed, founder of Islam.[19]

Upon his death, the future leadership of Islam fell into question. Mohammed had left no clear line of succession. Some followers of Islam believed that the successor leadership should be chosen by the faithful, while others believed that Mohammed's blood relatives were the rightful heirs.

After a series of murders and bribes resulted in several shifts in power, war erupted. In the Battle of Karbala in 680, Shi'a forces led by Hussein, a descendent of Mohammed, were defeated.[20] Because of the Sunni victory, 80-85% of modern Muslims are Sunni. The much smaller Shi'a sect includes the majority of Iranians, Azerbaijanis, and 60-65% of the ethnically Arab Iraqis.[21] Eventually the Sunni leadership, known as the Umayyad Caliphs, established an empire that stretched from what is now Iran to Spain. Were it not for their military defeat in France in 732, they may have well conquered all of Europe.[22] A succession of Caliphs ruled over all the Middle East for centuries, but by the thirteenth century, their power was in decline. Persia, what is now known as Iran, broke away from the Caliphate and its history evolved separately from the Arabs.

Ethnic Persians share a religion with Arabs but very little else except, of course, vast oil reserves. Persians are entirely different culturally, politically, historically, and linguistically. The link between Arabs and

Persians comes through Islam, which was introduced to Persia when it was conquered by the first Caliph shortly after Mohammed's death. The conquest was complete by 650, but it would take several centuries before a majority of Persians joined the Islamic faith.

By the early 20th century, weak rulers opened the door in Persia to demands for civil rights for the people and a constitution, which was ratified on December 30, 1906. Only five days later, the death of the Persian monarch brought Mohammad Ali Shah to power, and he was determined to crush the constitution. In June 1908 he used his Russian-officered Persian Cossacks Brigade to bomb the Parliament building, arrest many of the deputies, and close down the assembly. In July 1909, constitutional forces managed to reestablish constitutional rule and depose the Shah, who was forced into exile in Russia.

While internal fighting for control within Iran was ongoing, the British and Russian governments decided to take advantage of the situation by dividing the country for purposes of trade. Under the Anglo-Russian Agreement of 1907, Britain and Russia agreed to divide Persia into spheres of influence. The Russians were to enjoy exclusive right to pursue their interests in northern Persia and British interests would enjoy the south and east. Areas not under exclusive control would be open to free competition for economic and political advantage.

In 1911, Winston Churchill became First Lord of the Admiralty in Britain. Churchill was one of the first political leaders to understand the strategic military importance of oil, especially for naval vessels that relied on coal in the early twentieth century. Churchill championed the cause of converting the British fleet to oil-power, and he succeeded in gaining approval in 1913.[23] The problem for the British, however, was that unlike coal, which is abundant in Britain, there was no domestic supply of oil. If the British fleet were to be converted to all-oil, the British would need a steady guaranteed supply. As luck would have it, oil had already been discovered in Persia.

In 1901, British entrepreneur William D'Arcy secured rights to prospect for oil in southwest Persia. After a long search, his team struck oil in May of 1908. Within a year, the Anglo-Persian Oil Company was born.[24] Anglo-Persian made significant capital investments, including the construction of a pipeline and a refinery. By 1914, however, the investments had exhausted Anglo-Persian's working capital and it teetered on the verge of insolvency. Anglo-Persian's misfortune was the British government's solution, and the British, at Churchill's behest, purchased at 51% stake in the company,[25] which made the Anglo-Persian Oil Company essentially an arm of the British state.

Meanwhile, the Ottoman Turks had emerged in the fifteenth century to rule over vast Arab lands in the Middle East. The Ottoman Empire continued to rule until the early twentieth century when they decided to back the wrong horse in World War I, siding with Germany and Austria-Hungary. When the war ended with its defeat in 1918, the Ottoman Empire's territorial fate was left to the whims of the victors, the British, French, and Americans.

The political climate among the allies was curious. President Woodrow Wilson was decidedly opposed to colonial rule and believed that all peoples were entitled to self-determination. Meanwhile, the prime ministers of Great Britain and France, David Lloyd George and Georges Clemenceau, respectively, had vast colonial empires to protect and, if possible, expand. Accordingly, in advance of Wilson's arrival in Europe, the British and French leaders met in December 1918 to carve up as much of the Ottoman Empire as possible.[26] Spheres of influence had already been established two years earlier via the Sykes-Picot Agreement. Clemenceau's attention was largely focused on punishing the Germans, and he had little interest in the Middle East aside from Syria.[27] So, the consequences of the meeting were that the British would determine the fate of most of the Middle East including what now encompasses Israel, Jordan, Iraq, and Iran, as well as much of Arabia. This was all later formalized with mandates from the League of Nations.

The British, for their own reasons, tended to prefer that leadership be vested in the backward Bedouin tent-dwellers rather than educated urban intellectuals. They believed that the less-educated desert people would tend to make better allies, less likely to oppose the British monarchy and colonial rule. This particularly applied to the Hashemites, descendants of Mohammed's own clan.[28] Heading the Hashemites was Hussein, Sharif of Mecca, and his particularly power-hungry sons, Faisal and Abdullah.[29] Sharif was traditionally a term for proven descendants of Mohammed and comes from a similar origin as the English word sheriff.[30] By the time of Hussein, however, the post of Sharif was an appointed one, granted by the Sultan of the Ottoman Empire.[31]

In 1914, before the beginning of World War I, Hussein's younger son, Abdullah, presented himself to the British ambassador in Cairo and inquired about the possibility of purchasing weapons to stage a revolt against the Ottoman government. To honor such a request could prove problematic for the British. At the time, the British Empire was one of the largest Muslim states in the world with millions of Muslims, mostly Sunni, living under their rule in India, which included not only modern India but also Pakistan and Bangladesh as well. Muslim inhabitants owed loyalty to the Ottoman Sultan as spiritual leader of the Sunni sect. To sell weapons to insurgents staging a revolt against the "rightful" ruler would be risky and could result in rebellion against the British.[32]

When the Sultan declared war against Britain and joined in World War I on the opposing side, the risk for the British suddenly became an opportunity. The British needed Islamic allies. If the ruler of Mecca, holiest place in Islam, were to back the British, it would give them some cover from the *jihad* declared by the Sultan.

So, in June of 1916, Hussein raised the Hashemite standard and joined the British in an assault on the Ottomans.[33] At this point, a legendary figure entered the fold. Immortalized through the movie *Lawrence of Arabia*, British officer T. E. Lawrence befriended Hussein's son Faisal and became a centerpiece of the Arab revolt,[34] as well as a very influential figure when the lines of the Middle East were later re-drawn. He was less influential, however, in the outcome of the war. By most accounts, contributions of Lawrence and Hussein to the ultimate allied victory were negligible.

At the end of the war, although the British had received its mandate for much of the Middle East, they still had to satisfy President Wilson. With his opposition to colonial rule, some satisfactory solution had to be crafted. To compound the problem, colonialism was very expensive. The British were faced with skyrocketing costs maintaining their territories in the Middle East. The financial burden was untenable and a way of cutting costs had to be quickly found.

The ultimate solution, one that has been repeated in the twentieth century with questionable efficacy, was the notion of client states. A similar arrangement was already in effect in Persia, which, although officially neutral in World War I, had become a battleground for Russian, Turkish, and British troops. When the War was over, Russia was preoccupied with its own Bolshevik Revolution leaving Britain as the dominant influence in Tehran. The Anglo-Persian Agreement of 1919 established what amounted to a British protectorate over Iran.

The British, bearing in mind their recognition of the military vitality of oil, were not satisfied with their recent acquisition in Persia and were most certainly on the look-out for new supplies. The British, as it turned out, believed that there were no other major oil fields to be had other than those in Persia and Mesopotamia.[35] The rest of the world's known reserves were already under the watchful control of other powers. Given the fact that Churchill was a driving force behind conversion of the British fleet to oil, it was fortuitous that he was now in a position to draw the borders of the Middle East.

By virtue of the victory in World War I and the subsequent League of Nations mandate, the British had inherited the Turkish Petroleum Company (TPC) from its Ottoman owners. The TPC controlled the concession in Mesopotamia (the region that is now Iraq). The British also owed the Hashemites for their support during the war and, at the strong urging of Lawrence, decided the best course of action was to reward them with kingdoms. The confluence of these factors presented an interesting solution to Britain's problems. The British saw the opportunity to solve several problems simultaneously: they could reward their friends the Hashemites by crowning them monarchs; reduce the burgeoning costs of maintaining control in the region; and secure another strategically important source of oil.

In March of 1921, a collection of politicians and "experts" on the Middle East gathered in Cairo to determine the fate of the territories for which the British had received a mandate, a meeting now referred to as the Cairo Conference. The conference did nothing less than determine the destiny of the entire Middle East for the next century – perhaps much longer.

The conference was personally headed by Churchill, who was serving as Secretary of State for the Colonies. The conference ultimately decided to create and draw the borders for modern Iraq, Jordan, Palestine, and Israel. Without question, the creation of Israel was the most controversial decision of the conference, but it wasn't the only one. The British also installed monarchs, Abdullah and Feisal, sons of the Hejaz's Hashemite ruler Hussein, on the thrones of Jordan and Iraq, respectively.

Although he was a foreigner, Feisal was accepted in Iraq and was able to maintain power, largely due to bribes paid by the British to Iraqi tribal chieftains.[36] Feisal's Iraqi throne came with conditions, chief among them that the oil concession for Iraq would be controlled by Britain. Formally, the concession would be held by the Turkish Petroleum Company, which would have a monopoly over all oil in lands formerly part of the Ottoman Empire. All of the shareholders of the TPC (British allies) agreed not to make any attempt to compete with the TPC or each other in those lands, a measure that effectively ensured the oil would remain under British control. With the combination of Turkish Petroleum Company and Anglo-Persian Oil Company, essentially all known Middle Eastern oil reserves fell under British dominion. Feisal and his heirs reigned in Iraq until 1958 when Feisal's grandson, Feisal II was overthrown and executed in a military *coup d'état* led by the Ba'ath Party, of which Saddam Hussein was a member and eventual leader.[37]

Meanwhile Feisal's brother, Abdullah, was also accepted in Jordan, where his rule lasted until his assassination in 1951. After a brief rein by his son, his grandson Hussein took the throne in 1953. King Hussein became one of the most recognizable figures in the West, in no small part because he took prominent American Lisa Halaby (more commonly known as Queen Noor), as his wife. Her father, Najeeb Halaby, was son of a Syrian immigrant and a former head of the Federal Aviation Administration as well as former Deputy Assistant Secretary of Defense. King Hussein's son, King Abdullah II, continues to rule Jordan and is the only Hashemite ruler who remains on a throne.

Despite receiving their kingdoms at the Cairo Conference, the Hashemites still had a problem with which to contend. The Saudis, who ruled over a region in central Arabia, were engaging in conquest. King Ibn Saud, their ruler, was a particularly dangerous adversary. As a boy, he had been driven into exile when his kingdom was invaded by another Arabian tribe. He was forced to live in relative poverty, which is ironic considering the Saudi royal family's presently unparalleled wealth.

As Ibn Saud grew into adulthood, he, along with some of his brothers and cousins, began to engage in raids – stealing camels and anything else of value. Eventually, he decided to attempt to re-take his kingdom. He began by seizing the city of Riyadh in 1902 with an armed force of only 20 men.

The Ottoman-backed rulers who he overthrew appealed to the Ottoman Turks for assistance. Although they mounted forces to defeat Ibn Saud, they were never able to complete their objective. Eventually, the larger Ottoman problems in World War I rendered them unable to continue the fight, and the Turks never regained control over central Arabia.

Ibn Saud, being a conqueror by trade, was not willing to stop with central Arabia. He had great interest in the western portion of the peninsula, the region called the Hejaz. It just so happens that the Hejaz region along the Red Sea includes the Islamic holy cities of Mecca and Medina, turf of Hussein, Sharif of Mecca. As ruler over the holy regions, Ibn Saud's prestige would be greatly enhanced. In 1925, Ibn Saud conquered the city of Mecca, unseating Hussein and ending Hashemite rule over the region.

He continued his conquests through 1932, at which point he controlled most of the Arabian Peninsula. He consolidated and renamed his lands Saudi Arabia, in honor of himself, and proclaimed himself king. Ibn Saud ruled the region until his death in 1953, after which the kingdom has been ruled by a succession of five of his sons, including the current ruler, King Abdullah.

Ibn Saud was one of the few national rulers of the twentieth century to actually personally lead his armies on the battlefield, a tradition not seen the West for centuries. Not many modern leaders have the stomach for personally spilling blood or for risking their own skin, preferring to leave it to their military. They lead push-button wars from offices or bunkers far from the action. Ibn Saud took his entire kingdom by force, mostly by his own hand and those of his family. The sons who have ruled thus far since his death are old enough to remember the building of the nation, albeit in some cases as small children. Not all of the sons have ruled with equal strength and wisdom, but most of them have been anything but soft, vastly different from the spoiled, lazy, and decadent image often portrayed in the West.

4
Foundations of Oil Geopolitics

Now that the lines of the Middle East had been drawn and oil concessions sliced up, the British had established a monopoly over oil in the Middle East. Their presence in Persia and Mesopotamia (Iran and Iraq) created a rub with the Wilson Administration, which was opposed on principal to colonialism and believed that all countries should be able to bid openly on oil concessions. Of course, friction was magnified by the fact that the US was among those frozen out despite its own efforts to find new sources of oil. The US would not get into the Middle East game until it was finally made a partner in the Turkish Petroleum Company in 1928.

The 1920's was a tumultuous period for the American oil industry. Public perception of the oil industry was already tarnished from the Standard Oil era. Gasoline prices were on the rise, leading to Congressional hearings, but that was only the beginning. In the mid-1920s, details of one of the most famous corruption scandals in US government history began to unfold. The affair would become known as "Teapot Dome". Eventually, Albert B. Fall, who had served as Secretary of Interior in the Harding Administration, would be convicted of taking kick-backs in exchange for granting sweetheart oil contracts to his cronies. He would be the first Cabinet Secretary to go to prison for actions undertaken while in office.

As more details came to light, it became apparent that the money trail didn't just lead to Secretary Fall. It led virtually everywhere, including to a wide range of oilmen who had been previously thought respectable and to, most shockingly, the Republican National Committee.[1] With public sentiment already soured against the oil industry in the wake of Standard Oil's abuses, the Teapot Dome scandal only made matters worse.

Sympathy was scarce for oilmen when the Great Depression struck in 1929. Not only was there a severe impact on demand, but supply was at an all time high. New discoveries, including a massive new field in east Texas in the early 1930s, threatened to dump still more product into world markets. The only hope for survival for many of the oil companies became collusion.

In moves foreshadowing the formation of OPEC decades later, heads of the major oil companies structured a series of "As-Is" agreements in an effort to avoid overproduction. They effectively created a cartel consisting of the largest international oil producers. The As-Is agreements allocated sales quotas in various markets. As demand increased, so would the quotas, but each company would continue to have the same market share. The As-Is never really functioned as intended, however, and there was constant cannibalism of the majors' market share from outside their circle, especially from the Soviets who were now engaged in a no-holds-barred effort to gather hard currency reserves. The issue was finally put to rest in 1939 with the beginning of World War II, after which a glut of oil on the market was no longer a problem.[2]

The Role of Oil in World War II

By the eve of World War II, oil had become extremely important in world economics and military strategy. The US was still, by far, the largest crude oil producer, accounting for more than 60% of the world's output.[3]

When Americans look back on World War II, it is often viewed as one big war. In practice, however, it was really two wars, one in North Africa and Europe against the Nazis and one in the Pacific against Japan. The goals of the Nazis and Japanese really had little to do with one another. Their alliance was one of convenience, not ideology. Their relationship could be likened to, for example, the alliance between the Western powers and Soviets. What Japan and Germany did share was a need for oil resources.

Even before Hitler came to power in Germany, he was thinking about the ramifications of Germany's oil dependence. Because Germany had no domestic oil resources, Hitler kept a lustful eye on the Caspian oil fields in the regions around Baku. To achieve his ultimate plans, Germany would need to have enough resources within its own borders to make its economy self-sufficient and self-contained, not vulnerable from the outside. With the inclusion of the fertile farmland of Ukraine and oil of the Caspian region, Germany would have all the resources it would need for its "thousand year Reich."[4]

In August 1939, the Nazi Reich and the Soviet Union signed a non-aggression treaty. The treaty addressed, in addition to a pledge of non-aggression, respective German and Soviet spheres of influence. Only a few days later, Germany invaded Poland and World War II began in earnest.

Besides Soviet oil resources, the only other major source of oil in the European mainland was in Romania. In June 1940, the Soviets used the terms of the Nazi-Soviet Pact to seize part of Romania, bringing Russian troops dangerously close to the Romanian oil fields. Hitler perceived the Romanian fields as essential to the survival of the Reich.[5]

The combination of a potential Soviet threat to the Romanian fields and lust for the Soviet Caspian oil fields was too much temptation. In June 1941, the Nazis broke the Nazi-Soviet Pact and invaded the Soviet Union, with oil being a primary motivation.[6]

Unfortunately for the Germans, they were already short on fuel. Although their initial military effort met with success, they were unable to make use of captured Soviet fuel supplies. Soviet tanks ran on diesel, whereas German tanks ran on gasoline. Unable to gain new sources of fuel, the Germans outran their supply lines and lost their ability to press forward through the Caucasus, home to the highest mountains in Europe. The mountain range, already difficult to pass, could be defended given time, which lack of fuel provided.[7] In their quest to seize oil from the Soviets, the Germans failed and were forced to retreat. The principal reason for their failure was lack of the very resource, oil, for which they had initiated the campaign in the first place.

The Germans also had a plan in Africa. Their ultimate goal was yet another drive eastward into Arabia, then Mesopotamia and Persia where they could also access oil supplies. Again, oil shortages contributed to their defeat. German supply lines were left exposed and were decimated. Petroleum re-supply was not able to reach ground forces, and by May 1943, the Germans and Italians in Africa were forced to surrender.[8]

Allies fighting against Germany were not without their own fuel difficulties. The US endeavored to supply the British with petroleum. Supply lines, however, were littered with German U-boats wreaking havoc on tankers. Supply getting through to Britain was woefully inadequate.

As part of efforts to supply Britain, Harold L. Ickes[9], Secretary of Interior and Petroleum Coordinator for National Defense, set up a program to encourage conservation in the US domestic oil market. There was a substantial public uproar against the conservation policy. As he quickly discovered, prevention is bad politics. The experience prompted Ickes to remark, "It is impossible to carry the American people along with you on a program of caution to forestall a threatening position."[10] Those are prophetic words, indeed. Much remains unchanged in the US since the early 1940s.

Eventually, the tide turned as the Allies broke Nazi codes and were able to ascertain positions of the U-boats. The Allies ravaged the German fleet, and the US was able to ship fuel to Europe at will. During the War, almost all of the allies' fuel came from the US, which supplied six out of seven barrels of oil consumed for both military and civilian purposes.[11] Even the Soviet Union was receiving American oil supplies, despite the fact that they had substantial production capacity of their own in the Caspian region. In the darkest days at a banquet honoring Churchill, Stalin offered a toast. He said, "This is a war of engines and octanes. I drink to the American auto industry and the American oil industry."[12]

Acquisition of oil fields was not the only scheme the Germans had in mind to supply their military machine. They were also renowned for their abilities in chemistry and had developed a process for producing synthetic fuel from coal. Actually, they developed two processes. The first was called hydrogenation, favored in Germany for political reasons. It combined coal with hydrogen under extreme heat and pressure to make a high grade liquid fuel.[13] The other process, known as Fischer-Tropsch, used steam to break down organic molecules into hydrogen and carbon monoxide. The molecules were then allowed to react in the presence of a catalyst to produce liquid fuels.

When the Nazis came to power in Germany, the purveyor of hydrogenation technology, I. G. Farben, was turned into essentially an arm of the state. A crash plan was implemented to ramp up synthetic fuel production as quickly as possible. By September 1939, when Germany invaded Poland initiating World War II in Europe, there were fourteen synthetic fuel plants in operation and another six under construction. Synthetic fuel production was almost one billion gallons per year in 1940, which accounted for nearly half of the German fuel supply.[14]

When hopes for procuring new oil supplies from the Caspian region and from the Middle East were quelled, the Germans had little choice but to focus all of their efforts internally. I. G. Farben even began to use Jews and other prisoners held by Hitler's S. S. as slave labor in their production facilities. One of Germany's largest synthetic fuel plants was actually located at Auschwitz, home to the most infamous concentration camp.[15]

Eventually, the Allies caught on to German weaknesses and began bombing the synthetic fuel plants. The Allies also bombed Romania's Plotesti refinery complex, halting its supply to the Nazis.[16] These actions slashed German fuel supplies to the point where it could scarcely put planes in the air. Lack of fuel was the undoing of Germany. By May 1945, the war in Europe was over.

Like Germany, Japan was dependent on imported oil, much of which came from the US. Although it was becoming a formidable industrial power in the early twentieth century, Japan was a relatively small island nation with limited natural resources. Then, as it is today, Japan was forced to import almost all of its raw materials. Being a small island hasn't stopped other nations from attaining great military power. The case of the vast British Empire proves that point. Like the British, the Japanese needed the blood that must flow through the veins of a modern empire, oil.

By the 1930s, Japanese nationalistic sentiment was growing. The pervasive political doctrine was expansionist in nature with many believing that Asia should be ruled from Japan. Although domestic society was not dependent on oil, the Japanese military was. Modern ships and airplanes needed fuel.

In July of 1937, war broke out between Japan and China. The US, experiencing a period of isolationism, was neutral in the conflict. As news of atrocities committed by the Japanese, particularly brutal and ruthless warriors, gained media attention in the US, the tide of public opinion quickly shifted in favor of the Chinese. Support mounted for economic sanctions.[17] An embargo of military supplies would have meant cutting off almost all oil flowing to Japan, considering that the US provided about 80% of Japanese supply.[18] Such an embargo would risk expanding the war to other parts of Southeast Asia, forcing Japan to invade other countries where it could find new supplies of oil.

After much diplomacy, debate, and escalating tensions, the US finally decided against a full oil embargo. Instead, Japanese financial assets in the US (the primary purpose of which was to purchase oil) were frozen. The freeze took effect on July 25, 1941. The intent of the policy was not to cut off oil to Japan, but rather to regulate it. Assets would be "un-frozen" to allow Japan to purchase oil on a controlled basis. Their purchases would be closely monitored with the intent of preventing further military expansion in Southeast Asia.[19]

The job of enforcing the new policy fell to Dean Acheson, Assistant Secretary of State for Economic Affairs. It would be his job to release funds for oil purchases on a controlled basis. Acheson, however, was in the camp that supported an all-out blockade of oil shipments to Japan. Because of his policy proclivities, he neglected to release any Japanese funds and, therefore, they were unable to purchase any oil. The net effect of the policy was a total oil embargo on Japan.[20]

Reaction in Japan was mixed. Many senior statesmen sought to reach a truce with the US and avoid war. Others, led by Hideki Tojo, thought diplomacy a waste of time and pressed for war. When efforts at reaching a diplomatic settlement failed, Tojo was made Prime Minister. In November 1941, an Imperial Conference decided that the risk of having no petroleum supply was too great for the Japanese military. Final demands would be presented to the US, and, if they were not quickly met, Japan would go to war.[21] When it became clear that there was no hope for a solution, the Japanese attacked Pearl Harbor on December 7, 1941.

The closest major oil supplies to Japan were in the East Indies. The Japanese naval fleet immediately moved to capture those petroleum assets. Western oil workers were forced to flee as the Japanese advanced. They adopted a "scorched earth" policy, destroying oil wells, storage tanks, and refineries as they quickly scrambled to escape arriving warships.

Although escaping workers did a fine job in their destruction, the Japanese were able to revitalize the oil industry. Production was slowed considerably during 1942, but by the following year production was back up to 80% of pre-war levels.[22] The Japanese also took advantage of a promising field in Sumatra that was previously untapped. They drilled their only exploratory well of the war and opened what would become the largest oil field between California and the Middle East. With the re-emergent East Indies oil production and the new field discovery in Sumatra, the Japanese believed that they had solved their oil problem.[23]

What the Japanese failed to take into consideration, however, was that the oil supply was far from the home islands of Japan. It had to be transported from the East Indies through perilous Pacific waters. Beginning in 1943, that transport began presenting a considerable difficultly. US naval forces began sinking Japanese tankers in large numbers just as the U-boats had done to tankers carrying fuel from the US to Britain. It became increasingly difficult to import oil into Japan. By the first quarter of 1945, oil imports ended completely.[24]

Even though the Japanese were, for all practical purposes, completely out of fuel, they were not prepared to surrender. Only after atomic bombs were dropped on Hiroshima and Nagasaki did the war in the Pacific finally come to a close in August 1945.

In light of the evidence, only one conclusion can be drawn with respect to oil's role in World War II. It was, in fact, a primary cause of war in both theaters. In both theaters, it determined the outcome. Oil was at the very heart of the conflict, central to it in every way. Nothing had a greater hand in creating it, in guiding its course, and in deciding its victors. The war also had important consequences. During and after, US oil consumption was increasing rapidly. In 1948, the US became a net importer of oil, no longer able to meet its own domestic needs, much less the needs of the world.[25] Winning World War II had exacted a price, US energy independence. As long as energy was synonymous with oil, however, dependence on external energy sources was inevitable. The economy was simply growing too quickly to be sustained on the relatively modest reserves in the US. Political forces at the time believed, as many believe today, that US energy independence was and is gone forever.

Beginnings of the US-Saudi Relationship

World War II also marked another pivotal moment in world history; it was the beginning of US entanglement in the Middle East. Well before World War II, Persia (Iran) and Mesopotamia (Iraq) had become important oil producers. Of today's major Middle Eastern oil players, only renegade Saudi Arabia had been left out of the game. In the early 1930s, Chevron and Texaco had agreed to purchase an oil concession from the Saudi government. At that time, the Saudis were in dire financial straits. The government had essentially no source of revenue. Most of their land was barren desert with few, if any, natural resources. Its population was mostly nomadic Bedouin. In fact, the only source of funds that Ibn Saud had at that time came from tourism – pilgrims on their way to Mecca for the Hajj.

In 1938, however, commercially viable quantities of oil began flowing in the eastern part of Arabia.[26] Shortly after its discovery, war broke out in North Africa, severely curtailing Arabian tourist traffic. With optimism high on the potential for oil production in Arabia, the US government sent Everett DeGolyer, the most preeminent oilman of the day, on an expedition to gauge the oil potential for the US government in 1943. When he returned, he reported officially that Saudi Arabia's proven and probable reserves were about five billion barrels, but he privately believed reserves could exceed 100 billion barrels – an unprecedented oil find.[27]

With Hajj traffic at a standstill, Ibn Saud was eager to find alternative financing. The US Lend-Lease Act (which was being used to funnel American resources to Britain and other allies) was a mechanism that could allow the Saudis to gain some much-needed resources. Roosevelt was, however, opposed to lending money to Saudi Arabia. He considered the country "a little far afield" for the United States. Considering practices of the time in Saudi Arabia – slavery, whipping, cutting off of hands, and decapitation (most of which are still practiced today) – the US position seemed quite reasonable.

US Lend-Lease funds were actually being funneled to Ibn Saud via the British as early as 1941, a fact that American oilmen impressed upon him as they worked to gain favor. They pointed out that the British were receiving American aide and were simply passing it on to him.[28] Ibn Saud was already suspicious of the British because of their support for some of his enemies, especially the Hashemites, so he was eager to make an alliance with the Americans. By 1943, Roosevelt was convinced of the importance of Saudi oil and agreed to directly offer the kingdom financial support under the Lend-Lease Act.[29]

Concern was mounting that accelerated wartime production could be rapidly exhausting US domestic reserves. To guarantee the US a steady supply, some advisors even argued that the US should establish a military protectorate over Saudi Arabia with permanent military bases and troops.[30]

In the closing stages of World War II, as Roosevelt was returning from the Yalta Conference meetings with Churchill and Stalin, he made a stop in the Suez Canal for a series of meetings with Middle Eastern leaders. The most important meeting of the trip, perhaps one of the most important meetings of the century, was with Ibn Saud.

Roosevelt and Ibn Saud got along quite well. On a personal level, the two men had much in common. Roosevelt was in a wheel chair from his childhood bout with polio, while Ibn Saud had trouble walking resulting from a series of war wounds to his legs. After a jovial debate about who was the greater cripple, Roosevelt gave Ibn Saud his extra wheel chair. It became one of Ibn Saud's most prized possessions.[31]

On a professional level, they discussed oil extensively. Records of the meeting are notably missing, but many believe Roosevelt guaranteed Saudi Arabia's security, agreeing to use US military power to defend the nation in exchange for access to Saudi oil. What really happened is only known at the highest levels of government, but a series of actions by the US since 1945 lend credence to the speculation of a secret agreement.

Oil in the Post-Colonial Era

After World War II tensions quickly grew between the US and the Soviet Union. In March of 1946, Winston Churchill gave a speech where he warned of an "iron curtain" descending to divide Europe, with the eastern countries, at best, under the influence of the Soviets or, at worst, under direct Soviet control. Within a year of Germany's surrender, many on both sides of the iron curtain believed war was inevitable.

In the West, attention quickly turned to ensuring that the Soviet sphere of influence didn't expand. In April 1949, the US and many of its allies, particularly in Western Europe, had signed the North Atlantic Treaty.[32] The Treaty formed the North Atlantic Treaty Organization (NATO), essentially a military alliance against the Soviet Union and its realm of communist influence.

Given the importance of the Middle East for oil production, interest grew in forming an alliance in that region similar to NATO designed to counter the potential for communist encroachment. But political dynamics were complicated by the many rivalries among the Arab counties and the recent independence of Israel. Ultimately, the US decided to set up a treaty organization in the region, but not to actually join it. Formal membership could have proven problematic for the US, trying to be everyone's friend in a region where everyone had plenty of enemies.

In February 1955, Iraq and Turkey signed a treaty for mutual resistance of outside aggression. In April, Britain announced its intention join with Iraq and Turkey in the pact. Pakistan and Iran followed shortly thereafter. The alliance became known as the Baghdad Pact. The United States signed individual agreements with each of the nations but didn't join in the alliance, although it has representatives present at committee meetings.[33] The Baghdad Pact would not enjoy the longevity or the success of NATO.

Arab Nationalism

In the aftermath of World War II, colonial empires were crumbling and former colonies seeking independence. The US was concerned that breakup of the colonial empires would weaken its European allies. But the greatest fear was that, with the eroding empires, the US could find itself deprived of access to vital bases and raw material (particularly oil) located in the formerly-dependent states.[34]

Although Egypt is not a major oil exporting country, it is certainly an important country in the Arab world. This importance is derived from its place in Arab history and from its strategically important location. Egypt is home to the Suez Canal, a man-made channel connecting the Red Sea with the Mediterranean Sea that was completed in 1869. Without the Suez Canal, ships would be forced to circumnavigate Africa, adding thousands of miles to the trip between Europe and Asia (including the Persian Gulf region).

Like most countries in the region, Egypt had been part of the Ottoman Empire and thereafter subject to colonial rule by a Western power, in their case Britain. As in other countries, the British installed a monarch of their choosing. In 1952, that monarchy was overthrown by members of the Egyptian military. In 1954, a new leader emerged, one who would have a profound impact on the Middle East well beyond his lifespan. That leader was Gamal Abdel Nasser.[35]

Nasser was a nationalist, but he had greater plans. His ultimate goal was to unite the entire Arab world under one flag with no internal borders,[36] a sort of United States of the Middle East. Perhaps Nasser's most significant long term contribution to global geopolitics was that he was among the first to call for the use of oil as a weapon to give Arabs more power.

Nasser was a man of vision. Among his ambitious projects was construction of a massive dam on the Nile, known as the Aswan Dam. He sought financing from the West, but was rebuffed. In response, he nationalized the Suez Canal in 1956, removing it from Western control so that its revenues could be used to finance the dam. The action solidified his image among Arabs as a strong leader willing to stand against Western powers. As a result, his influence throughout the Arab world grew, particularly in Saudi Arabia where the eldest of Ibn Saud's surviving sons, Saud, had ascended to the throne in 1952. Nasser's popularity easily exceeded that of the new king, who was a considerably weaker and less popular ruler than his father.

Britain and France, previously in control of the Suez, were quite displeased to see a canal of such importance wrested from their hands. At the time, the Suez Canal handled almost all of the traffic of ships carrying petroleum from the Persian Gulf to Europe.[37] The British, French, and Israelis (whose oil supply was also severely affected), immediately began to formulate a plan to retake the Canal through military force. The plan ultimately failed dramatically, not because of the might of the Egyptian military, which was hopelessly outmatched against the triumvirate, but rather because of an unlikely international intervention.

As it would happen, the US was strongly opposed to the plan to retake the Suez. At that point in American history, anti-Colonialist sentiment was particularly strong. In one of the few times that the US has sided with Arab countries against Western powers, the US stood up to the British, French and Israelis and called for a UN resolution condemning the action and demanding immediate withdrawal of military forces. The Soviets also sided with Egypt and even hinted that they might intervene with military force. The triumvirate was isolated and forced to withdraw. America played the role of beloved hero to the Arab world, and the victory propelled Nasser to legendary status among Arab peoples.

In February 1958, Egypt and Syria agreed to merge to form the United Arab Republic (UAR). Effectively, it was more of a takeover than a merger, with the reins of power ceded to Nasser. It was the first step in the realization of Nasser's vision – a Pan-Arab state. Syria was home to two of the Middle East's largest oil pipelines, one originating in Iraq and the other in Saudi Arabia. Now firmly in control of the Suez Canal and Syria's pipeline network, Nasser controlled virtually all routes that oil could take between the Middle East and Europe.[38]

Not everyone in the Middle East was thrilled about the UAR and the emergence of Nasser. There were quite a few Arab monarchs who were not inclined to surrender their kingdoms and unite under what amounted to Egyptian rule. Although King Saud tried to play nice with Nasser, the Hashemites were anxious to unite against him. At that time, Hashemite kings still ruled over both Jordan and Iraq. Shortly after the formation of the UAR, the Hashemite rulers created an alliance of their own designed to counteract the threat to their sovereignty, but it was short-lived. Only months later, the Iraqi king was overthrown and executed, bringing a bloody end to the British-created Hashemite kingdom in Iraq. The *coup d'état* was led by General Abdul Karim Qassim. Whether Nasser was involved is unclear, but it certainly did work in his favor.

The new regime quickly discovered that oil companies had left most of Iraq's oil fields undeveloped in an effort to control supply. The companies had been pumping freely for the more powerful governments in Iran and Saudi Arabia, but Iraq and its puppet government were largely ignored. In response, Iraq seized all oil fields that remained undeveloped. Although not technically a nationalization, the effect was essentially the same. Considering that almost all of Iraq's oil resources remained undeveloped, more than 99% of the nation's oil fields were taken back by the government.[39]

Qassim withdrew Iraq from the Baghdad Pact and opened diplomatic relations with the Soviet Union, providing another foothold for Soviet influence in the Middle East. With Iraq's withdrawal, the Baghdad Pact was renamed the Central Treaty Organization (CENTO).[40] Ultimately CENTO would prove to be a failure, one that is all-but-forgotten except for an occasional footnote in history books.

King Hussein, the Hashemite ruler of Jordan, was left without a lot of friends in the Middle East in the wake of the Iraqi "regime change". Nasser spewed anti-Hashemite propaganda into Jordan calling on the people to rise up and overthrow the monarchial rule. Only the help of the US, Britain, and even Israel kept Hussein in power. Jordan remains one of the few reliable Arab allies of the West, in no small part thanks to Western support against Nasser's assault.

Nasser may have been a visionary and populist, but he was a lackluster administrator for the Syrians. To make matters worse, Egypt's domination of Syria bred considerable resentment. Egyptians were sent to Syria to fill most prominent government positions while Syrian businesses were kept out of Egyptian markets. The reality of the UAR was not exactly what Syrian leaders had envisioned when they had initially embraced the idea.

In 1961, a military *coup d'état* in Syria put an end to its membership in the UAR, but it by no means meant an end to Nasser's ambitions. The question of a Pan-Arab state was not settled, and, despite the failure of the UAR, Nasser still enjoyed broad appeal and popularity in the Arab world, including in Syria.

Shortly after the coup, there was a regime change in Saudi Arabia as well. King Saud had been in a constant power struggle with his brother Faisal since Ibn Saud's death. In 1962, Faisal was able to depose Saud and take power, in large part due to the Saudi royal family's fear of Nasser's threat to their sovereignty. Faisal was, by all accounts, a much stronger leader.

In Nasser's desire to oust the Saudi monarchy, his reach exceeded his grasp, but he still longed to extend his influence in the Arabian Peninsula. So, when the opportunity emerged, he couldn't resist involving himself in a civil war in the southern Arabian state of Yemen. Yemen, which sits on the southwestern corner of the Arabian Peninsula, shares a border with Saudi Arabia. Yemen, although not usually thought of as strategically important for oil, was actually home to one of the largest oil refineries in the Middle East, a facility built by the British in 1954.[41] Ironically, it was the labor union formed at the plant that served as a base for the only Communist movement ever to take hold in the Middle East. Because of the union's resistance to British control, they were finding their position in Yemen increasingly costly. Eventually, they decided to pull out.

At the time, Yemeni rule was held by a succession of Imams, who could best be described as Shi'a theocratic monarchs. After formation of the UAR, the Imam Ahmad decided to ally with Nasser. Much of Yemen's military was trained in Egypt and, therefore, became sympathetic to Nasser and his cause. After Ahmad's death in 1962, military leaders sympathetic to Egypt attempted a coup in an effort to depose the new ruler, Muhammad Al-Badr, but they failed to kill or capture him. Instead, he escaped and fled to the north for shelter among the tribes, whereupon he threw himself on the mercy of the Saudis.[42]

For King Faisal, an Arab nationalist intrusion into the Arabian Peninsula was just a little too close for comfort. If Nasser could unseat a traditional Arab monarchy in Yemen, it took little imagination to guess where he might strike next.

The Saudis began providing aid to the royalists in Yemen, while Nasser funded the military. The Yemeni military was no match for the tribesmen in their own mountain terrain, and Egypt found itself sending more and more of its own troops to Yemen, taking over the fighting directly.[43] Meanwhile, Nasser was also broadcasting anti-Saudi propaganda via radio from Egypt onto Arabian airwaves. Among the chief complains was an assertion that the Saudi regime was a puppet for the West, particularly the US.

In addition to providing assistance to oppose Nasser, the Saudi response was essentially to play the Islam card. They portrayed themselves as protectors of true Islam and portrayed the secular movement of Nasser as un-Islamic. The Saudis, now well-funded by virtue of their oil exports, threw money at the problem. They paid for construction of mosques and madrasahs (Islamic schools) and set about exporting their fundamentalist brand of Islam. These actions would have profound implications in later decades.

Among those that originally supported the UAR was a political party that had significant appeal to certain communities in both Syria and Iraq – the Ba'ath Party. In February 1963, the Ba'ath Party took power in Iraq after a violent overthrow of military dictator Abdul Karim Qassim, who had staged his own violent coup against the monarchy in 1958.

The following month, the Syrian Ba'ath Party, working together with Nasser's supporters, staged their own coup and took power in Syria. The Ba'ath, having initially supported unification of Syria and Egypt, were now willing to revisit the issue – this time with the potential inclusion of Iraq.

On April 17, 1963, Nasser and the leaders of Syria and Iraq began a second try at a Pan-Arab state and signed a declaration providing for a federal union of their respective countries. The following day, President Kennedy wrote to Nasser with respect to the agreement:

> I should not let the occasion pass, Mr. President, without extending to you and to your Iraqi and Syrian collaborators, a word of congratulation on the agreement in principle announced in Cairo on the formation of a new and enlarged United Arab Republic. It seems that through a process of firm negotiation a sound constitutional structure is being created with a view to meeting the aspirations and views of the Arab peoples concerned.[44]

From the US perspective, Western interests were compromised in Iraq as Soviet influence had grown under Qassim. The hope was that Nasser's control over Iraq would eliminate a source of Communist influence in the Middle East.[45] As an Arab nationalist, Nasser was opposed not only to the outside influence of colonial powers but also the Communists. Communism was not compatible with his vision for a unified Arab world, but that fact would not stop him from turning to Soviet military and economic support when he could not get it from the West.

As Kennedy was congratulating Nasser, perhaps he had not yet considered the reactions of Jordan, Israel, and the Saudis. Each felt threatened as Nasser's power continued to grow. The US was walking a tight-rope, trying to keep everyone happy in the Middle East. This, of course, was a daunting task considering the hostilities between Nasser and Jordan, Nasser and the Saudis, and Israel with all of the Arab countries. The US found itself in an almost untenable position, where any expression in favor with one party was likely to cause resentment with another.

The US was also trying to find a way to end the civil war in Yemen, which threatened to bring Nasser and the Saudis into direct conflict. Although the US was attempting to retain its position as an ally of Egypt, sympathies clearly were with the Saudis who were far more strategically important to the US. Although US support for Egypt against colonial powers and Israel during the Suez Crisis of 1956 had endeared America to the Arab world, support for the Saudi regime over the more popular Nasser was fertilizing the dynamic pervasive today, one where many Arabs perceive the US as an enemy.

The merger of Egypt with Ba'athist Syria and Iraq never quite came to fruition. There were serious disagreements, chief among them being that the Ba'ath could not accept Nasser's desire for a tight federation under his personal rule. The second attempt at Pan-Arab state ended in mutual recriminations and open hostility.[46] The whole prospect of a three-nation merger ended for good when there was yet another coup in Iraq only nine months after the Ba'ath came to power.

Turmoil in Iraq began with an intra-Ba'ath struggle between extremist elements and moderates who differed over the speed of implementing full socialization and amount of power to be shared with non-Ba'ath groups.[47] Abdul Salam Arif, who was a lukewarm Ba'athist, took advantage of the dispute and ousted the civilian Ba'ath leadership, seizing power on November 18, 1963. The tone of the new regime was pan-Arab rather than Ba'athist.[48] Arif was succeeded by his brother in 1966 after his death in a helicopter crash. The regime of the Arif brothers was to be short lived, however. In 1968, the Ba'athists returned to power under Ahmad Hasan al-Bakr, Prime Minister in the earlier 1963 Ba'ath government. His ascension would set the stage for his protégé, Saddam Hussein, and usher in an era of Ba'ath rule that would continue until the US invasion of Iraq in 2003.

As for Nasser, his adventures in Yemen ended in failure. Although the royalists were never to return to power in Yemen, Egyptian forces were engaged in a prolonged conflict that tied down many thousands of troops, by some accounts as many as 85,000.[49] Historians compare the Egyptian experience in Yemen with the American experience in Vietnam. It took a toll on Nasser and would have strategic implications for his next major conflict, the Six-Day War of 1967.

The Curious Case of Iran

Iran is the most populous country in the Middle East and the second largest country by land area. Since ancient times, Persian states have held or sought a dominant role in the region and the world. Most recently, this has manifested as the Iranian quest for an internally-sustained nuclear program and, many believe, nuclear weapons. While Iran's nuclear program has become a prominent current political issue, most Americans remain unaware of the history of the Iranian relationship with the West.

In February 1921, Persian Cossacks Brigade officer Reza Khan marched into Tehran and seized power. After a series of shrewd political moves, Reza Kahn was able to move from military dictator to crowned Shah in 1925, and so the Pahlavi Dynasty was born.[50] From the beginning, he was somewhat of a nuisance for the British government. Persia had laid claim to the British protectorate of Bahrain, creating friction over the tiny island in the Persian Gulf. In November of 1932, the Shah announced he was cancelling the oil concession granted to the Anglo-Persian Oil Company. Although the rift came to a negotiated conclusion, it proved very costly for the British, who were forced to capitulate to many of the Shah's financial demands.[51]

At the onset of World War II, Reza Khan was sympathetic to the Nazi government in Germany. With its importance to the British, Persia could not be allowed to side with the Axis Powers. In 1941, the British ousted him in favor of his much more agreeable son, Mohammed Reza Pahlavi. The new Shah was only twenty one and was quite weak, essentially a puppet of the British, which is, of course, why he was chosen.[52]

After World War II, the Venezuelan government was able to shrewdly negotiate their oil contract under terms much more advantageous than anything seen previously. Iranians, particularly the nationalists, wanted similar treatment. The British government, however, was determined not to have Iran join the ranks of those with shiny new oil concession deals, but forces in Iran were rapidly aligning against the British. Many in the Iranian parliament were already resentful of British treatment of workers in Iran, which only added to their desire for a new oil deal.

In 1949, a group of Iranian parliament members led by Mohammed Mossadegh proposed the nationalization of British oil assets in Iran. The CEO of the Anglo-Iranian Oil Company (which had changed its name from the Anglo-Persian Oil Company when Persia was renamed Iran in 1935)[53] quickly flew to Iran to head-off the crisis. He presented a supplemental agreement, which the Shah was pressured to sign, but the new terms fell far short of anything approaching Venezuela's deal.[54]

In November 1950, parliament rejected the supplemental agreement, failing to ratify the deal that the Shah had signed. News of a newly-negotiated and highly-advantageous oil concession for Saudi Arabia shortly thereafter only fueled the flames of Iranian nationalism. In March of 1951, the parliament again voted, this time to nationalize BP's assets. The Prime Minister, who had been appointed by the Shah, tried to block parliamentary action. Before he could do so, however, he was assassinated. Under Iranian law, his successor would be chosen by parliament, and their choice was none other than Mossadegh, the same leader who had originally proposed nationalization. Backed into a corner, the Shah was forced to sign a nationalization order.[55]

Nationalization sent the British into a panic. The response was a suite of economic sanctions aimed at cutting off Iranian oil revenues. In November of 1951, however, the early architect of Britain's Iran policy reemerged – Winston Churchill. Given his role in shaping the post-World War I Middle East, his strategy probably shouldn't have surprised anyone – a secret plan to stage another *coup d'état* and overthrow the Iranian government.[56]

At first, the US had little interest in helping the British with their plans, but interest grew along with fears of Soviet expansionism in the region. Iran, which shared a border with the Soviet Union, was of strategic traditional importance to the Russians, who saw it as a potential route to gain access to the Persian Gulf. More recently, it had become important to the US as a supplier of oil for the Korean War effort.[57] The British were quick to take advantage of the new attitude of the incoming Eisenhower Administration by proposing that the Central Intelligence Agency (CIA) join efforts to stage a *coup d'état*.[58]

The CIA and British Secret Service concocted a plan that involved stirring up anti-Mossadegh sentiment; attacking religious leaders and blaming it on the government; bribing military and legislative officials; and paying demonstrators to stage a massive anti-government rally. The plan went into action in August of 1953, but failed initially. The Shah, who had secretly supported the plan, was forced to flee to Iraq.

The Western intelligence agencies didn't give up. They tried again and this time they were successful. Mossadegh was arrested.[59] The Shah quickly returned from Iraq, but to make sure that he stayed in power, he needed to consolidate control. A ruthless secret intelligence service was just the answer, and, with the help of CIA, SAVAK was born. SAVAK was one of the most infamous and ruthless intelligence agencies in history. Using it as his chief instrument, the Shah began a two-decade-long reign of terror in which political enemies were routinely tortured and murdered. US involvement in SAVAK's creation is an unfortunate stain on its national history.

Prior to the removal of Mossadegh, the British had controlled all of Iran's oil resources. Considering that CIA had led the coup effort, the US was not going to walk away empty handed. After the dust had settled, the British percentage of the Iranian oil concession had been reduced down to 40%, while the US divided another 40% equally between its oil majors: Exxon, Mobil, Gulf Oil, Texaco, and Chevron. The remaining shares landed with Royal Dutch Shell and Total S.A. (the French oil conglomerate).[60] In 1954, production resumed in Iran and the Anglo-Iranian Oil Company changed its name to British Petroleum.[61]

5
Losing Control

At this point, oil was firmly entrenched in the politics of the Middle East and the world. Global power had shifted away from colonial empires. Most of the world had aligned itself with either the US or the Soviet Union, and the two great powers were at the peak of the Cold War. The military machines of both sides were fueled by oil. The world economy was becoming more oil dependent each day, and Western countries began importing increasingly larger percentages of their oil supplies. Never had control of the vital oil resources of the Middle East been more important.

Since the emergence of a global petroleum industry, power had rested in the hands of Western nations and their multinational oil conglomerates, but the industry was changing. The West was growing more dependent on resources from oil-rich countries while the global political climate was making it more difficult to control many of the regimes in vital regions. Forces of nationalism, particularly in the Middle East, produced governments that the West found increasingly difficult to dominate. Governments wanted more money and more power for themselves. Nasser was the first Arab nationalist leader, but he was certainly not the only one. The rise of such leaders was part of a trend of shifting control over the world's largest petroleum reserves.

Despite the growing importance of oil, the West was moving away from seeking direct control of overseas oil reserves. In a world with growing demand and limited supply, and with decreasing direct government involvement in protecting their businesses, oil companies found themselves in an unfavorable bargaining position. Control was gradually shifting from buyers (oil companies and consumers) to sellers (oil exporting nations). This would mark the beginning of evolution toward the world we know today, a world where those with oil have the upper hand.

Historically, the greatest danger to the oil industry has been overproduction. Too much oil on the market drives down prices and, therefore, profits for oil companies and oil producing countries. It is in the interests of both to keep supply constrained enough to maintain relatively high price levels, thereby maximizing revenue. Several attempts were made to control production both domestically in the US and in the Middle East in the first half of the twentieth century.

In the early 1930s, the Texas Railroad Commission imposed a regulatory system in the US that was designed to control overproduction of oil. Although the system was declared unconstitutional by the US Supreme Court in 1935, it would have far-reaching implications, the most important one of which was that it would eventually be the model for OPEC, an international cartel effectively controlling the flow of oil throughout the world.[1]

After the end of World War II, oil was abundant and cheap, and almost all of the oil outside of the US, Canada and the Soviet Bloc was controlled by the "Seven Sisters", the largest multinational oil conglomerates. The Seven Sisters, through a series of mergers and reorganizations, exist today as ExxonMobil, BP, Royal Dutch Shell, and Chevron, comprising much of what we now know as Big-Oil. Despite overseas dominance, the Seven Sisters did not enjoy the same level of market share in US domestic markets. In the US, independents controlled most oil production. The fact that Middle Eastern oil was much cheaper to produce than oil in the US created significant friction between oil multinationals and the US independents. The independents wanted to keep prices high, while the Seven Sisters were quite content to keep them lower where they enjoyed an advantage on costs.

At that time, the independents enjoyed much more political influence in the US than Big-Oil. The independents employed many Americans and were politically active. Big-Oil's operations were mostly outside the US, and they did not have domestic workforces full of voters to put pressure on politicians. In 1959, independents successfully lobbied the Eisenhower Administration to cap imported oil at 13% of domestic consumption.[2]

As a result of the import quota, there was less market for Middle Eastern oil. The US was by far the largest market, and with a large chunk of it now closed to the oil exporters, the price of their oil came under pressure. Eventually, large multi-nationals were forced to cut prices, the effect of which was to slash royalties going to oil-rich governments.

Meanwhile, Juan Pablo Perez Alfonzo was reemerging as a major political figure in Venezuela. It was Alfonzo who had been among the first to challenge the financial terms of the prevalent oil concession arrangements in 1948, resulting in much more favorable terms for Venezuela. Contract renegotiations in the Middle East had followed, as did the turmoil in Iran. Although Alfonzo had fled Venezuela after a military takeover, a return to democracy paved the way for his appointment as Minister of Energy.

With his country's treasury being decimated by the price reductions, Alfonzo realized that oil exporting countries needed greater revenue stability. It is difficult to have effective, disciplined fiscal policy when a country cannot accurately predict its revenue. He found allies among the Middle Eastern countries who sought to move the balance of power more toward themselves and away from the oil companies.

Alfonzo was a man who had studied the oil industry in great detail. He came to believe that selling oil too cheaply was bad not only for the oil producing countries but also for consumers. Cheap oil would result in the premature exhaustion of a nonrenewable resource and would discourage new development. He was among the first to recognize that oil could play a negative role in the economy of a producing nation. He believed that oil and profits from selling it should be conserved, not treated like an income stream that would continue in perpetuity. Profit belonged to the people and should be used for infrastructure and development.[3]

Alfonzo also recognized that Venezuela was a high cost producer. The competition in the Middle East enjoyed very large oil fields and high internal pressure, which led to very low production costs. In a truly global free market, Venezuela would be at a competitive disadvantage. He was familiar with the Texas Railroad Commission quota system from his days studying in the US. If such a system could be introduced on the international level, it would offer Venezuela the ability to protect its market share from low cost competitors while also benefiting the low-cost producers by increasing prices and, therefore, profits. It was a win-win situation.

As one of the first American-educated Saudi leaders, Abdullah Tariki had been appointed to head the Saudi Directorate of Oil and Mining Affairs in 1955. In time, Tariki gained substantial autonomy as the Saudi royal family was distracted by the power struggle between Saud and Faisal.[4] Alfonzo and Tariki learned that they shared common visions with respect to a re-allocation of power in the oil industry – that the oil producing governments should have more of it and the oil companies less. In 1959, at the Arab Oil Congress in Cairo, Egypt, a clandestine meeting was arranged that included Alfonzo, Tariki, and representatives from

Kuwait, Iraq, and Iran. Although the representatives had no power to act formally, they did agree to recommend Alfonzo's ideas to their respective governments.[5]

In August of 1960, the inevitable happened. In the face of pressure from the Eisenhower oil import quota, Exxon slashed the posted price for Middle Eastern crude. Oil exporters, who had no warning of the cut and who were dependent on oil revenues for the health of their national economies, were outraged.[6] The Iraqi regime, then headed by Qassim, saw a great political opportunity in the making. The Iraqis quickly invited the oil producers for a meeting.[7]

In September of 1960, Venezuela, Saudi Arabia, Iran, Iraq and Kuwait met in Baghdad and officially formed the Organization of Petroleum Exporting Countries, well-known today by its initials OPEC.[8] The purpose of OPEC was clear – to defend the price of oil.[9] OPEC was born as a direct answer to the US-imposed import quota.

By no means was OPEC an early success. In the beginning, OPEC's members spent more time trying to compete with each other than working together for mutual benefit. Many of the members, particularly in the Middle East, had long-standing political rivalries that increased the challenge of cooperation.[10]

By 1963, both of the original founders, Alfonzo and Tariki, were gone from the scene. Tariki was a victim of the power struggle between Saud and Faisal and was ousted in 1962. Alfonzo became disillusioned and resigned in 1963. Both left with disappointment about the ineffectuality of OPEC. Alfonzo, in particular, heaped criticism on his organization and took to calling oil "the excrement of the devil."[11]

OPEC's legacy would be left to another generation. Given time, however, dynamics changed as Middle Eastern oil continued to gain an ever-increasing share of the world market. With a greater market share, OPEC's power would grow. With a common cause, its members might be able to finally work together. In the festering wound of the Arab-Israeli conflict, winds of a perfect storm were gathering.

The Six-Day War and Nasser's Legacy

Although weakened by his failures in creating a pan-Arab state and his military quagmire in Yemen, Gamal Abdel Nasser was still the most powerful Arab leader. Even more so than it is today, the Middle East was a tense place in the late 1960s. All of the countries in the region had plenty of enemies, but Israel was particularly isolated. Virtually every other country in the region was professing deep hatred for Israel and calling for its destruction.

Israel was being shelled from across the Syrian border in the Golan Heights area. There were numerous acts of sabotage and terrorism. The Israelis blamed the Syrian government for the aggressive acts.[12] Although evidence suggests that there was no troop buildup on the Israeli side of the border, the Egyptians claimed otherwise and that Israel was preparing for military action against Syria. The Israelis denied the accusations. United Nations observers in the area confirmed that they had seen no evidence of troop buildup.

Nasser believed that leadership in the real and symbolic war against Israel was a pre-requisite for maintaining leadership in the Arab world.[13] He seized the opportunity to again take the lead against Israel. Egypt began to mass troops on its border, remilitarizing the Sinai. They then closed the Gulf of Aqaba to Israeli shipping, instituting what amounted to an oil blockade of Israel.

The political situation in Jordan was fragile. King Hussein, the Hashemite ruler of Jordan, did not want a war with Israel. In fact, he would do all possible to avoid a confrontation. He pledged to the US, who was leading efforts to avert a confrontation, that he would not attack Israel if they responded to the attacks from Syria. On the other hand, if Israel attacked Egypt or attacked inside Jordan, internal pressure would force his hand. He would have no other choice but to counterattack.[14] As the situation escalated, King Hussein eventually put his forces under Egyptian command.[15]

By 1967, Nasser was openly hostile to the West, particularly the US, while heaping praise on the Soviet Union, on which he was growing more and more dependent for military and economic aid. The US came to believe that the Soviets had a "substantial degree of influence" in Egypt.[16] The Israelis actually believed that Soviets were in the background urging the aggressive Syrian and Egyptian action that led to the Six-Day War.[17] It may well have been the case considering that the Soviets were claiming that Syrian acts of terrorism were actually CIA activity.[18]

Rhetoric was flying full force from Nasser, whose public statements make clear that he had every intention of starting a war.

...Our basic objective will be to destroy Israel. I probably
could not have said such things five or even three years
ago. If I had said such things and had been unable to
carry them out my words would have been empty and
worthless. Today, some eleven years after 1956, I say such
things because I am confident...[19]

With international efforts to avert a crisis going nowhere and with
Egyptian troops massing on its borders, the Israelis decided to act. On
June 5, 1967, the Israelis made a preemptive move and destroyed most of
the Egyptian Air Force on the ground in the first hours of the conflict.
They then faced off with Egyptian ground forces in the Sinai. By the June
8 cease-fire, victory over Egypt was complete. Israeli forces occupied the
Sinai Peninsula and the Gaza Strip, reopening the shipping lanes.

Meanwhile on the Jordanian border, fighting began in response
to the preemptive Israeli action. After the Jordanian army opened fire, the
Israeli army quickly took the West Bank and the parts of Jerusalem that
they didn't already control. A cease-fire with Jordan became effective on
June 7. On June 9, Israel attacked Syria and took the Golan Heights. June
10 brought a cease fire to the Syrian front and the Six-Day War came to a
close.

Although defeated militarily, Arabs still had their oil, which they
had realized could be used as a weapon. The concept had been discussed
even before the formation of OPEC. Now the Arabs had a chance to test
it. The idea was not new, of course. In July 1941, the US placed what
amounted to an oil embargo on Japan.[20] The first Arab oil embargo was
put into effect on June 6, 1967, the day after the start of the Six-Day War.
As punishment for supporting Israel, shipments of oil to the US and
Britain were banned by Saudi Arabia, Kuwait, Iraq, Libya, and Algeria.[21]

Although some Arab countries (particularly Saudi Arabia and
Kuwait) were friendly toward the West, they found themselves backed into
a political corner by the conflict. If they were shown to support the West,
they risked a backlash by their own populations. At the time, however,
the US still had substantial unused production capacity, which it quickly
activated.

It is important to note that this was an embargo by Arab oil
exporting countries, not by OPEC. An embargo by OPEC would have
included Venezuela and Iran and perhaps would have had a greater

impact. Those countries were not involved, however, and instead actually guaranteed additional quantities of crude to offset Arab reductions.[22]

Within a month of initiating the embargo, it was clear that it was a failure. Supply was redistributed as needed. Leaders in the Middle East began to openly question the wisdom of giving up substantial oil revenues when the embargo was having essentially no effect on the intended parties. By September, the embargo was lifted.[23]

The Six-Day War was really the final blow to Nasser. Less than two months after the end of the war, Nasser was reported to be in ill health. A July 31, 1967 Central Intelligence Agency report indicated that Nasser was "pale, nervous, and has lost about 15 pounds." The report went on to suggest that his declining health might be the result of "tensions and strain that have beset Nasser in the last two months."[24] The Egyptian government was essentially bankrupt and now wholly dependent on its Arab neighbors and the Soviets for financial aid. Most senior military leaders in Egypt had been arrested to prevent any coup attempts.[25] Within three years, Nasser would be dead. The reins would be passed to his second in command, Anwar Sadat.

The Shifting Balance of Power

In 1969, monarchial rule ended in Libya when the king was overthrown by a group of young officials led by Muammar Abu Minyar al-Qadhafi.[26] After Nasser's death, Qadhafi was the heir-apparent to lead the quest for Arab oil-power. He considered Israel, and the US for supporting it, the greatest danger to Arabism.[27]

Qadhafi planned to use his newfound power in Libya to upset the fifty-fifty contract formula created by Alfonzo that had dominated the Middle East since the early 1950s. One particular oil company was especially vulnerable. Occidental Petroleum's sole source of supply was the Libyan oil fields. Consequently, Qadhafi had the company backed into a corner. Qadhafi's demands for a new contract were initially met with resistance from Occidental's infamous owner Armand Hammer. In response, Qadhafi cut production and squeezed Hammer until he was forced to agree to his terms.[28]

Given Qadhafi's victory, leaders of other oil producing countries started to scramble to get better deals. In Iran, the Shah was growing considerably less friendly toward oil companies, making threats and demanding a greater share for himself. Iran and Libya began competing to see who could strike the best deal. Once one country had struck a deal, the other would immediately go about trying to best them. The process continued, much to the dismay of the oil companies who had no choice but to comply in the tightening market.[29]

In OPEC, there was talk of an all-encompassing embargo to strengthen the hand of the producing nations against the oil companies. The embargo concept was supported by the closest of US allies, the Shah and King Faisal of Saudi Arabia. The oil companies, facing an embargo and lacking US government support, were forced to capitulate. The victory marked a turning point for OPEC, which proved that it could now act as a unit.[30]

By 1970, the world was much more dependent on the Middle East for its oil.[31] US oil production had peaked that year at 10 million barrels per day,[32] and energy demand was growing rapidly. In 1971, the Texas Railroad Commission approved putting all domestically available supply online. It was a decision that resulted in the elimination of the only spare production capacity in the Western world, making the US much more susceptible to supply shocks from overseas exporters.[33]

In September 1972, Ahmed Yamani, Saudi oil minister, publicly proposed a startling, unprecedented bilateral deal with the US that had the potential to solve US oil problems for the foreseeable future. Under his plan, Saudi oil would be supplied to the US at stable prices in return for technology and development assistance. Yamani even stipulated that surplus revenues received by the Saudis could be reinvested back in US oil refining and marketing operations.

Despite the fact that such a deal would have guaranteed the US a long-term energy supply, months passed with no reply from the US government. There are indications that senior policy officials were worried about the reaction to such a deal from US allies in Europe.[34] Concerns about the allies, however, were perhaps misplaced, since they were not at all shy about the prospect of making similar deals. No less than three governments made overtures to the Saudis with offers of attractive long-term contracts.[35]

By the time the State Department finally responded, the Saudis were no longer interested.[36] Although there remained a bilateral security arrangement with the Saudis, the US had missed its one chance for stable prices. Now, the global political dynamics were changing. In April of

1973, President Nixon announced that the oil import quota system that had been in place since the Eisenhower years would be abolished.[37] The US needed more oil.

The Arab Oil Embargo

Sadat, now in power in Egypt, had a very different agenda from Nasser. He had no ambitions to create a pan-Arab state. In fact, he was interested mostly in restoring Egypt's economy, which was left in shambles by Nasser's military adventurism. Sadat, unlike Nasser, had also managed to become friendly with the Saudis. While King Faisal engaged in a rivalry with Nasser and, eventually, a proxy war in Yemen, he was fond of Sadat.

Sadat recognized that in order to restore Egypt, he needed to negotiate a lasting settlement with Israel. Israel, having recently ravaged Egypt's military in the Six-Day War, was in no mood to negotiate. Sadat needed to extricate the Israelis from the Sinai to have any hope of gaining a favorable agreement; otherwise, he would be negotiating from a position of weakness. He saw no other choice; he began planning for another war.[38]

King Faisal was watching with concern as a Marxist regime was taking over in South Yemen. The Saudis wanted to get the troublesome Soviets out of the Middle East. Sadat was of the same mind. He resented the Soviet military presence in his country, which was home to more than 20,000 Soviet "advisors". Without Saudi support, however, Sadat would be forced to turn to the Soviets for aid with his fiscal shortfalls.

The Saudis were rolling in cash from their oil exports and agreed to provide Sadat the aid he needed. In turn, Sadat began to put pressure on King Faisal to deploy the oil weapon once again. This time, however, circumstances would be different. The US was now producing at full capacity and, unlike the previous attempt in 1967, this time they would not be able to increase production to make up for oil lost in an embargo. Faisal began to make his feelings known to the US. Unless the West adopted more even-handed policies in favor of its Arab friends, the Saudis might be forced to succumb to anti-American pressures.[39]

Although some viewed the Arabs as unsophisticated and ignorant, they were not. They, like Western powers, had economists performing calculations and analyzing supply and demand. They were becoming well aware of their position relative to the importing countries.[40] The Arabs, it would seem, had learned from their previous experiences using the oil weapon. This time, their embargo would be targeted at only a few counties. With a targeted embargo, producing countries would not see their petro-income as seriously impacted.[41]

In October 1973, conflict broke out yet again in what would become known as the Yom Kippur War. Sadat's strategy was to catch Israel by surprise at a time when it was least prepared. Both the US and Israel had disregarded the warning signs. When hostilities commenced, the Israelis were forced to fall back as the Egyptians and Syrians scored victories.[42]

Israel was desperately short of weapons and requested help from the US. The US government arranged a "secret" airlift that was supposed to take place during the cover of night, but high winds forced the flights to land during daylight hours, exposing the plan.[43] In the Arab world, the re-supply was taken as an overt and highly visible sign of support for Israel.[44]

On October 17, the Arab members of OPEC met to discuss the situation with respect to Israel. Their decision would have far-reaching implications for the US and world economies.[45] The policy would be an oil embargo against supporters of Israel. The Arab nations cited a host of reasons for the embargo: continued occupation of Arab territories by the state of Israel in defiance of UN resolutions; failure of Israel to restore the legitimate rights of Palestinians; failure of the oil importing countries to take positive action regarding the Arab-Israeli dilemma; support from the West to help Israel consolidate its occupation of Arab territories; and the US supply of Israel with sophisticated weapons systems before and during the Yom Kippur War.[46]

They announced that they would immediately cut production by 5%. For each successive month that Israel failed to withdraw from the territories it had seized in the Six-Day War, production would be cut another 5%. Finally, the policy would not apply to Arab-friendly states. Iran did not take part in the embargo and instead boosted production,[47] but the Shah did vote in favor of the price increases that accompanied the embargo – the best of both worlds for Iran (increased volume and higher prices).

It was clear that the embargo was intended to be most harshly targeted at the United States. Algerian minister of industry and energy, Belaid Abdesselam, summed up Arab objectives:

We are not, and we have not been, contrary to what has been often reported, asking for the United States to change its policy. We simply have asked the US to fit its action to its stated policy. One of the tenets of US policy has always been the refusal to recognize or accept the acquisition of territory by force. That is something that has not only been stated and repeated frequently by the United States, but also was voted by the United States as a member of the Security Council of the United Nations, which ordered the evacuation of the Arab lands seized by Israel in the 1967 war. All we are asking is that these UN resolutions be carried out.[48]

Such action on the part of the US, however, was easier said than done. The political landscape in the US made it almost impossible to criticize Israel, and support for it was basically a prerequisite for holding public office. Israel maintained that the Arab lands seized in 1967 were necessary for its security. In light of that, it was and is difficult for elected leaders to call for return of captured lands.

The design of the embargo was particularly clever. It countered the possibility of importing countries simply moving oil around to alleviate an embargo against a single nation with overall production cuts. For the US, however, there was a total embargo. Arab countries, including Saudi Arabia, stopped shipping oil to the US entirely.[49]

On the surface, it seemed like the US response was to simply take its lumps from the Arabs. After all, the US government did not respond militarily, nor did it cede to Arab demands. As it happened, there was actually a lot more complexity in the relationships and events of the early 1970s that are readily apparent. It seems that nothing is simple when oil politics and the Middle East are involved.

As was discussed in detail earlier, the world oil market operates in dollars, which is both a product of the international perception of its stability at the end of World War II and the fact that the US was once the largest exporter of oil. The end of the Bretton Woods financial system earlier in 1973 forced devaluation of the dollar, which prompted complaints among oil exporting nations about the decline of their purchasing power. They demanded compensation for the fall of the dollar relative to other currencies.[50]

Meanwhile, the US domestic oil industry was suffering. Oil production in the US costs considerably more than production in the Middle East, which creates a cost advantage for the Arab producers. With the price of oil low, Arab countries, even with the declining dollar, were profiting, but US producers were experiencing cash flow problems. The US independents wielded significant political influence in the US. The net result was that the interests of two powerful groups that were previously in conflict were now aligned, and they were both actively pressuring the Nixon Administration. The solution they sought was simple: higher oil prices.

Perhaps the second most powerful man in Saudi Arabia in 1973 was Ahmed Yamani. Yamani is an oil industry legend, a fascinating figure who served as Saudi Oil Minister from 1962 to 1986. During his tenure, he survived the assassin who killed King Faisal and a kidnapping at the hands of famed terrorist Carlos "the Jackal".

In a 2001 interview, Yamani offered some insight into the US political situation by making a striking claim. He professed that the US had actually, in fact, been behind the 1973 oil price spike. He claims he learned of the plot during a 1974 encounter with the Shah, when he was told directly that the US wanted prices to increase. "Ask Henry Kissinger," said the Shah. According to Yamani, US oil companies had, at that time, been saddled with too much debt. Some needed high oil prices to avoid bankruptcy; a price spike would afford them an escape. As proof, Yamani cited minutes of a meeting of the Bilderberg Group that indicate the US and UK planned the price spike.[51]

The Bilderberg Group is a favorite topic for conspiracy theorists. Some contend it is working to eventually subjugate the sovereignty of the US to a "New World Order" or a world government. The group is real, although those who attend the meetings tend to change from year to year rather than having a fixed cast of "conspirators". It was devised as a means to allow a cross-section of leaders from around the world to gather for discussion of important international issues.

While true motivations of the players remain in question, it is the actions of the Arab governments themselves that lend the most credence to the theory that the embargo was really all about increasing world oil prices. Once the economic objective of a higher price of oil was achieved, the political objectives of the embargo were quickly and quietly abandoned along with the embargo itself.[52] Years after the conclusion of the embargo, Yamani admitted that the Arabs knew they could not ultimately "...reduce imports of oil to the United States...The world is really just one market. So, the embargo was more symbolic than anything else."[53] The Arabs knew from the beginning that an embargo would not achieve their political objectives.

We will probably never know what really happened behind the scenes in 1973, but we do know that the US oil industry reaped significant benefits from higher oil prices, as did the US Treasury. While there is much evidence to support the conventional wisdom that the US was really a victim to OPEC's embargo, there is also evidence of collusion.

Regardless of what was happening behind-the-scenes, Nixon, despite the major distraction of Watergate, did what he could to try to satiate the masses as the crisis grew domestically. On November 7, 1973, he made a major presidential address and called on the country to develop "the potential to meet our own energy needs without depending on any foreign energy source."[54] His speech marked the first time a US president had publicly called for energy independence. Despite his calls, most in the Nixon Administration did not believe that energy independence was possible.

The net loss of oil from the market at the height of the embargo amounted to about 9% of world supply – 4.4 million barrels per day.[55] At the time, however, no one had accurate figures regarding the embargo's effect.[56] Fear of shortage had much more impact than any actual shortage. Fear is the most powerful market force, as financial markets continually demonstrate. As a result of the panic, the price of crude was driven up dramatically. Consumers and oil companies began to buy in even greater volumes than usual to stockpile oil resources. The result was artificially inflated demand.[57]

The most visible and memorable effect was gas lines. Just before the embargo began, an allocation system was instituted in the US because of growing tightness of the market that was intended to distribute supplies evenly throughout the country. The system prevented movement of supplies from well-stocked to under-stocked areas. The foolish result was that some areas had high levels of surplus supply while others faced scarcity.[58]

For people that found their way into lines at undersupplied gas stations that winter, the effect was inescapable. The realization quickly dawned that America's economic survival was now dependent on a collection of nations in a part of the world about which most Americans knew almost nothing.[59]

The final analysis of the effects of the embargo is still being written. It had many complex and unintended consequences. In December 1973, OPEC members gathered for a meeting in Tehran. At that meeting, the price of oil was reset to $11.65 per barrel, a level four times what it had been just two months earlier at the beginning of the Yom Kippur War.[60] The people of the US ultimately absorbed the shock and were forced to endure a deep, back-breaking, eight-year-long recession and unprecedented inflation.

The average American was definitely a loser, but there were winners. In the long term, the price spike served to dramatically increase the flow of investment (vis-à-vis the Arab oil exporters) into the US economy. It saved and returned to profitability a sagging US oil industry. It made Arab countries more politically dependent on the US because of broadening financial ties. I doubt, however, the suffering masses would have agreed that the ends justified the means.

As for Sadat, he had achieved his goals. He was able to secure his peace with Israel and restore the prestige of Egypt. It was Sadat, ironically, who urged the end of the oil embargo in meetings with his Arab counterparts. It no longer served Egypt's interests to have an embargo in place. Although there were some disputes among the Arabs, on March 18, 1974, oil ministers agreed to end the embargo.[61] The original demands were never met, but the embargo was over.[62]

Higher prices and production cuts were all very real. The gas lines and shortages that caused them, however, were largely the result of price controls and regional allocations in the US, not purely the actions of Arab countries.[63] Although the Arab countries had stopped the flow of Arab oil to the US, and even largely prevented redistribution of Arab oil through third party countries, they could do nothing to stop oil companies from increasing the percentage of Arab oil going to "friendly" countries so that supply from non-Arab sources could be freed up to be shipped to the US. The net result was that importing countries shared roughly equivalent supply cuts rather than the US bearing the full weight of the embargo.

Iran's Islamic Revolution

After the price of oil shot up in 1973, the Shah foresaw an endless sea of oil revenues for Iran. He envisioned using the plethora of petrodollars to modernize Iran and solve its domestic economic problems. The Shah was obsessed with modernity and wanted desperately to transform Iran into a modern world economic power. Under his plan, Iran would become a "serious" country.[64] Previously, he had been content to be a regional leader in the Middle East. But with so much newfound wealth and the prospect of even more in the future, he saw Iran as a potential world leader – a Germany, a Japan, perhaps even a USA.[65]

As the price of oil was increasing, the worldwide economy was experiencing inflation.[66] In the US, the inflation rate for the year following the embargo was 12.2%.[67] The US economy was suffering, and by 1975, unemployment was reaching the highest levels seen since the Great Depression.[68] The Shah did not believe that higher oil prices could cause inflation in the US and other Western counties; instead, the inflation only fueled his lust for even higher oil prices.[69] Like a dog that bites the hand that feeds it, the Shah was forgetting who his friends were.

The Shah was also coming into conflict with another adversary, one closer to home. The Saudis were very much opposed to the Shah's quest to drive oil prices ever higher. They believed, wisely, that continually pushing up prices to the point of creating recessions in importing countries was not in their best interests. They feared the logical eventual outcome of such policies – the move to other alternative fuel sources and greater efforts at conservation.[70] In other words, they were concerned that the upward pressure on prices would cause a long term structural weakening in demand for petroleum, thereby making their resources less valuable.

The Iranian economy was not immune to rampant inflation being experienced worldwide. Many of the products that Iran was buying abroad were increasing in price just as oil was increasing. The Shah's answer was domestic price controls.

The US had now embraced a strategy in the Middle East that came to be known as the Nixon Doctrine. The policy was for the US to avoid being brought directly into regional conflicts that were peripheral to the interests of the US. Instead, they would empower regional states that could take on this role as surrogate. In the Middle East, the US chose the Shah's Iran to fill the void. It was understood among US officials that an increase in oil price would be a way of indirectly financing the military buildup necessary to create Iran as the regional cop on the block in the Middle East.[71]

Meanwhile, the Shah's close associates, his family members and high ranking government officials, were awash in cash that they had gained as a result of the furious arms trade between the US and Iran. Bribes were just part of doing business in the Shah's government. Bribes were, in fact, so much a part of the economy that they led to a black market for goods that directly countered the Shah's price controls. The black market, in turn, fueled further inflation. Inflation took a particularly hard toll on the merchant class and civil servants. As merchants were being squeezed, they were squeezing the public, which led to popular discontent.[72] The seeds of revolution were being sown.

Corruption was so widespread that it was clearly apparent to the populace. The people could not help but be aware of massive arms purchases, which were being made for no obvious ends. The people, accurately or not, began to connect the dots – their economic problems were seen as linked to the Shah's military connections with the West.[73] At the time, there were as many as 60,000 US troops and contractors in Iran acting in various capacities.[74] Under the Shah's dictates, Americans were not subject to Iranian law. It was this issue that provided a catalyst for mullahs, particularly the firebrand Ayatollah Khomeini, to foment even more discontent.

The Shah's luck was running out. Unfortunately for him, Jimmy Carter, then President of the United States, began encouraging the Shah to open his society and embrace human rights just at the time when he was trying to repress rebellion. For him to maintain power, he needed to crack down. Without US support, the revolution grew and the Shah's grip on power was slipping away.[75] Strikes and demonstrations grew. In January 1979, the Shah was forced to flee the country. Khomeini returned from exile to massive crowds of supporters. By April, the Iranian people voted overwhelmingly to declare Iran an Islamic Republic in a popular referendum, and the Shah's reign was officially over.

The Ayatollah, now firmly in control, didn't forget about Iran's treatment at the hands of the Western powers. His government nationalized the Iranian oil industry, putting a final nail in the coffin of the long tenure of Western oil company control.

Khomeini's rise to power was a product, more than any other factor, of his ability to paint the West (especially the USA) as the enemy of the Iranian people. It was, in fact, Khomeini who famously bestowed the moniker "Great Satan" on the United States, and, according to the Ayatollah, the Shah was simply its puppet. Anti-Western sentiment was the cornerstone of Khomeini's power and pervaded Iran during the Islamic Revolution, the climax of which was the seizure of the US Embassy in Tehran by a group of Iranian students.

The reason students gave for their actions tie directly back to the early efforts to maintain Western control of Iran's oil. Students justified storming the embassy by claiming that it was a staging ground for the 1953 coup that removed Mossadegh from power, which was, of course, true.

Although Khomeini didn't know about the plan in advance,[76] he seized the opportunity to score political victories domestically and embarrass the US internationally. Today, his likeness remains familiar to most Americans because it was his face that became a nightly fixture on US television news as the hostage crisis carried on for 444 long days for the 52 Americans held in Tehran.

While the crisis damaged Iran's status internationally, it was viewed as an act of heroism in Iran, and it was a major political victory for the Ayatollah. One of the five students that originally planned the attack even went on to oversee Iran's oil industry as Minister of Energy, a post he held from 1997 to 2005. Notwithstanding the legitimate grievances of the Iranian people, seizure of an embassy is a reprehensible breach of international convention, a fact now admitted by the operation's regretful mastermind.[77]

Since the Islamic Revolution, Iran has been the principal architect of its own isolation, but the West must also shoulder some of the blame for the sour state of relations. After all, it was ultimately greed over an oil contract that resulted in a US-planned and staged *coup d'état* to depose a democratic Iranian government. In its place came a murderous tyrannical regime that repressed and abused the Iranian people for decades. Imagine how Americans might feel if the roles were reversed and a foreign power overthrew our government and imposed on us a ruthless dictator.

While some grievances are clearly legitimate, Iranian theocrats have taken to blaming the US for just about everything. Beginning with Khomeini, the US has been used as a scapegoat for a myriad of domestic problems, and the theocrats have propagated anti-American sentiment for their own political advantage. Khomeini and his successors have certainly proven that they aren't above inventing a few sins for the West when its own actions haven't been sufficient. To understand Iran, however, we must remember that the history between Iran and the West did not begin when the American embassy was overrun by revolutionaries in 1979. Iran didn't become a member of the "Axis of Evil" overnight. There is a much deeper context, and it all began with oil.

Implications of the Islamic Revolution stretched well beyond bilateral relations between the Iranian and US governments. Perhaps the ultimate loser, as has been the case far too often with political conflicts, was oil consumers. In October 1978, Iranian oil workers went on strike, and the price of oil spiked once again. Despite the resulting supply constraint, the world actually produced more oil than it consumed in the fourth quarter of 1978. Lack of sufficient supply cannot explain the price changes of 1978-1979.[78] Once again, fear would drive the markets.

The fall of the Shah also meant the failure of the Nixon Doctrine. To exacerbate already piqued security concerns in the region, in December 1979, the Soviet Union invaded Afghanistan. A fresh review of the security situation in the region would necessitate a new policy for ensuring oil security. That policy would be announced on January 23, 1980 during President Carter's State of the Union address. Carter declared that to protect the interests of the United States, he was prepared to use "any means necessary, including military force."[79] Carter was declaring that the US would use its military to make sure that oil continued to flow to the US.

Implications of Carter's policy were enormous. For the first time, a US President declared his willingness for direct military intervention in the Persian Gulf to protect oil supplies, a previously unfathomed approach to foreign policy in the region. Although President Carter would undoubtedly be reluctant to admit it today, to the extent that either the liberation of Kuwait or the removal of Saddam Hussein was an "oil war", the Carter Doctrine set the stage for it.

6
Everything Changed in 1979

The Middle East and the oil world had a big year in 1979. There were not one but three earthshaking events. The Shah of Iran was overthrown and his pro-Western regime was replaced by an anti-Western Islamic theocracy. The West's closest ally in the region was gone. One could scarcely imagine a more rapid or more dramatic shift in the regional dynamics.

Meanwhile, Iran's next-door neighbor was experiencing its own dramatic political shift. Within months of fall of the Shah, a new nationalist dictator came to power in Iraq. He was virtually unknown at the time, but he would soon make his mark. Few foreign rulers would garner the infamy in the US as the man who became colloquially known simply as "Saddam".

Finally, the Soviet Union invaded and took control of Afghanistan. All of these events were to spawn a monumental shift in US foreign policy. The entire regional dynamic in the Middle East was changing; old alliances were dissolving and new rivalries emerging.

In Iran, the Shah's departure brought considerable domestic chaos. Iranian society was experiencing a cultural reversal where the Westernization policies of the Shah were taking a one hundred eighty degree turn. Iraqi dictator Saddam Hussein decided to capitalize on the turmoil by quickly seizing the valuable oil producing regions along the Shatt al-Arab River (the confluence of the Tigris and Euphrates Rivers). He launched his attack on September 22, 1980.[1]

The Iran-Iraq border along the Shatt al-Arab River had been loosely defined and disputed. Indeed, the controversy predated modern Iraq and served as a source of conflict between Persia and the Ottoman Empire going back more than a century.[2] After the outbreak of war, the US decided to remain officially neutral and not to supply arms to either side.[3]

In Iran, a vicious power struggle was ongoing. Iraqi aggression had the effect of galvanizing Iranian society and mobilizing them to repel the invaders. Although the Iranian military, the pride of the Shah, had been gutted by the revolutionaries as soon as he was driven from power, the Iranians were able to withstand the onslaught. They were eventually able to drive the Iraqis back across their own border. It looked as if the Iranians would defeat the Iraqis completely, but the war wasn't to end so quickly. The two countries eventually fought each other to a standstill.[4]

By 1982, it was clear that there would not be a clear victory by either side any time soon. The US saw its opportunity to intervene and began restoring diplomatic relations with Iraq (which had been broken in 1967). Officials agreed to supply intelligence information on the Iranian military, as well as attempt to broker an end to the war. In exchange, Iraq agreed to renounce terrorism and support any Palestinian peace efforts.[5]

The US did, in fact, keep its end of the bargain. Even better, the US agreed to support the sale to Iraq of French-made fighter jets equipped with the Exocet anti-ship missile. The Exocet's purpose, as it would later become clear, was to sink Iranian oil tankers.[6] The US was, of course, well aware of the possibility of a disruption in oil flow, but consented to the deal anyway.[7]

In a peculiar twist of fate, Israel, apparently subscribing to the "enemy of my enemy is my friend" philosophy, became one of Iran's greatest allies during the Iran-Iraq War. Israel sold to them from a vast stockpile of Soviet-made weapons captured during the Six-Day War of 1967 and US-made weapons acquired during the Yom Kippur War resupply operations in 1973. Israel's motivation may have been partly political, but profit was clearly a key factor, if not the top priority.[8]

It was through Israel that the US began a back-channel relationship with the Iranians. The US began providing intelligence not only to Iraq, but also to Iran. In 1986, news of the Iran-Contra Affair broke in the US, making clear to Iraq that the US was actually a double agent. To make matters worse for the Iraqis, the US was not only supplying intelligence to Iran but also arms, including anti-tank missiles.[9]

The US was deliberately playing the Iraqis and Iranians off against one another. Perhaps some had the attitude that war between the nations was a good thing. It was a "let them kill each other" policy. By 1987, however, this strategy was beginning to impact US interests directly. Both countries had been engaging in a "tanker war," with the Iranians using Chinese "Silkworm" missiles to match Iraq's Exocets. The conflict was finally beginning to seriously disrupt Persian Gulf oil traffic.

Kuwait, also a major oil exporter operating in the northern Persian Gulf waters, began having its tankers fall victim to Iranian attacks.

In desperation, they appealed to the superpowers for defense of their oil shipments. The US responded by agreeing to "reflag" the Kuwaiti tanker fleet under US registry and grant US military protection.[10]

Reflagging of Kuwaiti tankers was a major victory for Iraq, which had been seeking overt US involvement for years. The action led to several direct military engagements between the US and Iran. In retaliation for an Iranian attack on one of the reflagged Kuwaiti tankers, the US destroyed two Iranian oil platforms.[11]

After a series of major Iraqi victories in 1987 to repel the Iranians and an offensive in the summer of 1988, the Iranian army had been decimated. Iran was a poor match for the Iraqi military with US support. The Iranians were left with no choice but to sue for peace.[12] The balance of power in the region had shifted in favor of Saddam's Iraq.[13]

Most analysts believe that America's surreptitious involvement throughout the conflict benefited Iraq, with board opinion supporting the notion that Iran would have prevailed militarily if not for US intervention.[14] It is conceivable that Saddam's regime would not have survived the Iran-Iraq War without it, thereby precluding his invasion of Kuwait and a long dirty episode for the US that continues to this day. On the other hand, a victorious Iran would have carried with it a whole different set of issues.

The reflagging of the Kuwaiti tankers, although not seen as pivotal decision at the time, marked the first instance of direct US military involvement in the Persian Gulf. Now that the US had a toe in the water, so to speak, involvement in coming years would only grow.[15] The US intervention not only realized the Carter Doctrine, it also set an important precedent. In less than a generation, the US transitioned from mere puppeteer to lead actor in perhaps the most violent and tumultuous region of the world. Implications for all were enormous, especially for Saddam.

Iraqi Invasion of Kuwait and the Gulf War

The Iran-Iraq War produced no clear victor after eight years of conflict, but was extremely costly in financial terms for Iraq. Wars are quite expensive, and this one left Iraq owing about $50 billion to Western and Russian lenders. It had gotten, by some estimates, another $100 billion or more from other Arab countries,[16] most prominently Saudi Arabia and

Kuwait.[17] The Iran-Iraq War had badly degraded oil production capacity in both countries.[18] If Iraq was to climb out from under its massive debt load, it would need an increase in oil prices. The Kuwaitis, however, had other ideas.

Kuwait, along with the United Arab Emirates (UAE), began producing in excess of its OPEC quota, that is to say overproducing.[19] Saddam accused Kuwait and the UAE of conspiring with the United States to keep oil prices low, a practice that he claimed was condemning Iraq's people to starvation.[20]

Iraq also had long-standing grievances against Kuwait related to a major oil field that straddled the border of the two countries. The field, called South Rumaila, is one of Iraq's largest. Saddam charged that Kuwait was exploiting the field by stealing its oil and decreasing the internal pressure, making it harder for Iraq to recover its share of the resources.[21]

To make matters worse, Saddam had been under the impression that the wartime financial contributions of Kuwait had been grants, not loans. The Kuwaitis made an announcement dispelling that assumption, which had the effect of making it extremely difficult, perhaps impossible, for Saddam to renegotiate his debts with European lenders.[22]

Saddam appealed to President Bush to intervene and use his relationship with Kuwait and the UAE to slow production, but Bush refused. On July 25, 1990, Saddam summoned the US Ambassador, April Glaspie, to an unprecedented meeting. Saddam explained Iraq's financial predicament to Glaspie and how he needed help from the US government to pressure Kuwait and the UAE to stop cheating on their quotas. Saddam also wanted help in stopping the campaign against Iraq in the US media, which he claimed was turning public opinion against Iraq and making it more difficult to negotiate with Western lenders.[23]

Glaspie explained that there was nothing that could be done about the press, but she took a conciliatory tone with Saddam. She confided that, like him, there were also domestic producers in the US that wanted higher oil prices. Saddam was, of course, aware of President Bush's background in the oil business, that he was very much a member of the domestic oil producer community. Given Bush's history, Saddam interpreted Glaspie's comments to mean that the President was among those who would be pleased by higher prices.

Perhaps the most controversial aspect of the meeting was Glaspie's response to Saddam's complaints about Kuwait. She told Saddam,

...I admire your extraordinary efforts to rebuild your
country. I know you need funds. We understand that,
and our opinion is that you should have the opportunity
to rebuild your country. But we have no opinion on
Arab-Arab conflicts, like your border disagreement with
Kuwait.[24]

Later, her comments would be cited as tacit approval for Saddam
to commence an invasion of Kuwait.[25] From Saddam's perspective, in light
of the context, such an interpretation was not completely unreasonable.
Glaspie, however, was actually just repeating standard US sound-bite
policy that had been in place for years. Although she had been made well
aware of the fact that Saddam was massing troops on the southern border,
it appears clear now that Glaspie had received little or no instruction from
Washington.[26] Bush's attention seems to have been focused elsewhere.
Glaspie, although an experienced diplomat, was unfamiliar with Saddam.
She was left to regurgitate standard policy intended to apply to all Arab
conflicts. Saddam, who was really a street thug by profession, rarely
engaged in formal diplomacy and heard what he wanted to hear.
    On August 2, 1990 Iraqi troops poured across the border into
Kuwait. The insignificant Kuwaiti resistance lasted only a few hours
before Iraq controlled the entire country.[27] At this point, a situation
that had previously been ignored became a grave concern for the Bush
Administration. Saddam now had around 100,000 troops massing only
10 miles from the Saudi Arabian border while the Saudis had fewer than
1,000 men stationed between the Iraqis and their rich Arabian oil fields.
The Saudis were naturally very anxious.
    From the beginning, the US was providing the Saudi government
with intelligence, and senior officials, notably Secretary of Defense
Cheney, were engaged.[28] US reaction was, however, anything but a
rush to war. The inclination, as was characteristically Bush, was to let
diplomacy settle the crisis. When Bush met with Margaret Thatcher
in Aspen, Colorado immediately after the invasion of Kuwait, it was
Thatcher who persuaded him that decisive action was needed. Up to that
point, the Bush Administration was largely apathetic. Thatcher, however,
was immediately talking about the prospect of military action.[29] This is
hardly surprising considering the importance of Kuwait to British oil
interests, not to mention the fact that Saddam had been guilty of several

previous provocative acts directed at the British, including the execution of a British national.[30]

On August 8, Bush announced that the US would be sending military forces to Saudi Arabia. The next day, American military units began arriving in the desert. Operation Desert Shield, the code name of the military operation designed to prevent Saddam from extending his invasion into Saudi Arabia, was in full swing. A broad coalition of forces from many nations assembled in the sands of the Arabian Desert. By the time Desert Shield became Desert Storm on January 17, 1991, coalition forces numbered almost 600,000.[31]

In the West, many believed that Saddam's military machine was highly capable. Particularly in the media, his army was depicted as the fourth or fifth most powerful in the world. He was also said to possess chemical weapons, missiles capable of reaching Europe, and possibly nuclear weapons. In retrospect, overestimation of his military seems ridiculous in light of the fact that for eight years he failed to defeat the armies of an internationally-isolated Iranian regime.[32]

On February 22, realizing that the war would be lost, Saddam desperately resorted to setting fire to the Kuwaiti oil fields. Even this move didn't cause oil prices, which had dropped considerably on the day hostilities were commenced, to increase.[33] Once the ground war began, coalition forces made quick work of what little was left of the Iraqi military. It took coalition forces less than three days after ground operations began on February 24 to extricate the Iraqis from Kuwait and hand an astounding defeat to what was then the world's fourth largest military force.[34] The air war had all but destroyed Iraqi fighting capability. Many had been killed by the bombing campaign or had fled to safety; others surrendered hastily without a fight, many to Western journalists roaming the area.

The Gulf War era saw the assembly of one of the broadest military and political coalitions in history. With the Cold War coming to a close, it seemed the world was moving forward in a spirit of mutual cooperation. That international harmony would be short-lived. The US had lived up to its "secret" agreement with the Saud family by protecting them from Saddam's aggression. Without intervention, there is little doubt that Saddam would have eventually found a suitable reason to march into Arabia. In the words of the late former US Representative Tom Lantos,

If it were not for the United States intervention in 1991, the House of Saud would be nothing more than a villa on the Riviera by now, and because of its petroleum wealth it continues to enjoy unwarranted indulgences where US interests are concerned.[35]

While some would like to describe the virtual world unanimity in those early months of 1991 as the product of collective distain for Saddam's aggression against the tiny desert monarchy of Kuwait, it was plainly and simply about oil. There is a whole lot of oil underneath that desert sand. The prospect of someone like Saddam controlling all of it was pretty scary, not only to the US but to the rest of the world as well. Had Saddam been able to control all of Iraq, Kuwait, and Saudi Arabia, he would have gained control of 38.2% of the world's oil reserves.[36] More importantly, he would have been the world's "swing producer" with virtually absolute power to dictate world oil prices by expanding or curtailing oil production as he saw fit. Operation Desert Storm, or the Gulf War as it would eventually be termed in the US, was not the end of Saddam. Instead it was the beginning of a long chapter of history not only in Middle East but in the US as well.

Oil and International Terrorism

The roots of international terrorism go back well before September 11, and, for that matter, well before Israel became a primary target in the 1970s. Terrorism has evolved. The al-Qaeda version that we know all too well today in the US is a far cry from terrorism from decades past. The phenomenon's original version consisted of airplane hijackings, kidnappings, and minor bombings. People were definitely injured and killed, but the numbers were smaller. From a macro perspective, old-school terrorism was really more of a nuisance than a strategic threat, and some would argue that there is no reason to view it any differently just because of a series of larger, more successful attacks. The problem with such a viewpoint is that it fails to consider the economic impact of a major terrorist act (such as what the US experienced in the aftermath of the September 11 attacks) and the growing likelihood that terrorist might eventually be able to procure nuclear weapons.

Terrorism, at least the version I am attempting to address, is rooted in fundamentalist Islam. The original Islamic fundamentalist society, the Muslim Brotherhood, got its start in Egypt even before the ascendancy of Nasser. The Muslim Brotherhood would become the inspiration for al-Qaeda and would count among its members the eventual September 11th mastermind, Ayman al-Zawahiri.

Terrorist groups of the Middle East, whether the Muslim Brotherhood, al-Qaeda, Hezbollah, or one of the other incarnations, are usually not focused on oil issues, at least not directly. They tend to have other, more immediate grievances. Complaints about Israel or Western policies toward the region are never far from the top of the list. Far too often, however, grievances relate to the effects of oil policies. Since al-Qaeda has had the most significant impact of any terrorist organization, their actions in the context of oil are particularly meaningful.

At the end of the "magic year" of 1979, the Soviets invaded Afghanistan. Afghanistan is primarily Sunni but also has a considerable Shi'a population. The Saudis and Iranians have a historic religious rivalry. When the Soviets invaded, both countries scrambled to organize competing insurgencies to fend them off.[37] Osama bin Laden was among those who took up the fight. Bin Laden was an incredibly wealthy Saudi who would become one of the key figures directing the CIA-sponsored mujahedeen insurgency. The invasion proved unsuccessful, and eventually the Soviets were forced to withdraw. Bin Laden returned to Saudi Arabia with folk-hero status.

When Saudi Arabia came under threat, the royal family turned to the US for assistance, but Bin Laden had other ideas. He opposed the use of US troops to defend the kingdom. Instead, he offered to defend it himself using his mujahedeen fighters. The royal family turned down his offer in favor of the clearly superior American military. Bin Laden was outraged at both the personal rebuff and at the presence of US troops in the holiest part of the Islamic world.

After the end of the war, an ongoing cycle of provocation and apparent capitulation developed between Saddam and coalition forces. For that reason, the US maintained a significant troop presence in the region. As many as 20,000 troops were stationed in Saudi Arabia, Kuwait, and other nations surrounding Iraq. The presence of troops began to breed resentment, especially in Saudi Arabia, where Islamic extremists were particularly insulted by the American presence so close to Islam's holiest sites. It was the decision to keep US forces in Saudi Arabia that many believe was the critical catalyst that would lead to the September 11 attacks.[38]

In June 1996, the US got its first serious warning. Al-Qaeda terrorists targeted Khobar Towers, a residential complex housing US military personnel in Saudi Arabia. The CIA, which was severely weakened by budget cuts during the Clinton years, relied on information they received from Saudi intelligence. The Saudis blamed the Khobar Towers bombing on Hezbollah, the Iranian-backed terrorist group, not the real culprits, al-Qaeda and Osama Bin Laden.[39] Whether it was incompetence or politics that led to the erroneous conclusion is unknown. In either case, the Saudis shifted focus from Bin Laden to Iran. The truth about Khobar wouldn't come out until several years later.

Meanwhile, the troop presence in Saudi Arabia remained an open, festering wound that provided fertile ground for recruiting more and more new terrorists.[40] Al-Qaeda attacks continued. The USS Cole was bombed while docked at port in Yemen, and there were major assaults on US embassies in Kenya and Tanzania. Still, the US failed to take the al-Qaeda threat seriously. Then came September 11, and everything changed.

Removing Saddam and the War in Iraq

At the conclusion of hostilities in the Gulf, the decision to leave Saddam in power was shockingly uncontroversial. The most ardent defender of preserving Saddam's rule was none other than Dick Cheney, then Secretary of Defense. He defended the decision by illuminating the political complexities, particularly as it related to how Iraq would be governed in Saddam's absence and the potential for ethnic conflict. When appearing on the Sunday morning talk show circuit to discuss the feasibility of using US troops to govern Iraq, Cheney remarked, "I think it makes no sense at all." Part of the problem for Cheney and others in the first Bush Administration was that victory came so swiftly that they were left without a post-war plan.[41] Strangely, Cheney would change his attitude for the second invasion, but post-war planning would again be missing.

After the Gulf War, almost everyone thought the successful military campaign would make Bush a shoe-in for a second term.

Unfortunately for him, the US economy hit a recession just before the 1992 election. Economic problems set the stage for the rise of the previously unknown Governor of Arkansas, Bill Clinton. Clinton was by no means a foreign policy enthusiast. His interests lay squarely in the domestic policy realm.

Circumstances had other ideas for Clinton, as is often the case for presidents. He quickly found himself engaged in a variety of foreign policy entanglements, a major one of which was Iraq. After the conclusion of the Gulf War and Saddam's removal from Kuwait, US policy toward the Persian Gulf region became known as Dual Containment. The policy was designed to keep pressure on both Iran and Iraq. The Clinton Administration devoted significant energy to the endeavor. In 1996, State Department memos make clear that, "Our policy of containment is time-consuming, fraught with repeated crises, and costly to maintain..."[42]

Although there were several small US military actions against Iraq during the Clinton Presidency, notably Operation Desert Fox, there was never any serious consideration of another ground war to remove Saddam from power. That all changed on September 11, 2001. By then, Clinton had been replaced by George W. Bush, who filled his administration with members of the neoconservative movement. Neoconservatives can generally be characterized as advocates for using US power to spread democracy and American influence abroad, by force if necessary.

After the September 11 terrorist attacks, US vulnerability, whether real or psychological, opened the door for revisiting the Iraqi situation. Almost immediately, members of the Administration were analyzing ways to go back into Iraq. Adding to fears were the anthrax attacks that occurred in the immediate aftermath of the destruction of the World Trade Center buildings.

One of the few things that both Democrats and Republicans have almost unanimously agreed upon since the fall of Communism was that Iraq possessed weapons of mass destruction. The virtually unanimous agreement that Iraq possessed, at a minimum, chemical weapons that could be used against the West; the psychology of the nation in light of the anthrax attacks and September 11; and Iraq's continually belligerent attitude all combined to create an atmosphere that made selling an invasion surprisingly easy. That nexus would allow a relatively small contingent of policy makers within the Bush Administration to conceive and promote an invasion that conjured very little opposition domestically yet received little international support. On March 20, 2003, US troops invaded Iraq. In only a few days, the country was completely under US control and, shortly thereafter, Saddam was in military custody.[43] In one of the great ironies of history, however, the one assumption that went virtually undisputed leading up to the invasion – that Iraq possessed weapons of mass destruction – would be discredited when weapons were never found.

Those at the center of the debate never hid their ambition to convert Iraq into a friendly country, a "client state" as some might describe it. The one thing that nobody talked about was all of that oil under the sands of Iraq. To the extent the US controlled Iraq, it would also control all of that oil – some 115 million barrels, about 9.1% of the world's reserves, nearly four times the amount underneath the entire US (including Alaska and in off-shore territorial waters).[44] Millions of barrels of oil could be added to world markets as embargos from the Saddam era were lifted. Many of the original war proponents envisioned privatization of the Iraqi oil industry and a subsequent free-flowing expansion.

In the immediate aftermath of the invasion, however, oil facilities were looted and sabotaged. Mismanagement, incompetence, and rampant corruption also plagued the industry. As a result, Iraq lost 75% of its oil export capacity.[45] Although eventually the industry began to recover, the dream of a free-flowing Iraqi oil industry was not to be. Under the direction of oil company executives working with the US State Department, the Iraqis disregarded the vision of an Iraqi oil industry operating on free market principals in favor of a state controlled industry operating subject to OPEC quotas.[46]

In a strange twist of fate, the US, by virtue of its occupation and administration in Iraq, found itself a *de facto* member of OPEC.[47] The harshest critic of the privatization of the Iraqi oil industry was the US oil industry itself.[48] No one benefits more from OPEC quotas and resulting higher prices than the domestic US oil industry. Free-flowing oil would simply bring down prices, something that oil companies clearly do not want to see. Losers in this scenario were, of course, American consumers, but the people of Iraq were negatively impacted as well. Although Iraq's long term interest may be aligned with other members of OPEC, in the short term it needs income to promote economic growth and reconstruction. Even with the impact on worldwide prices of a free-flowing Iraq, the country would still certainly receive more income under such a policy than by adhering to OPEC export quotas.

The man in charge of remaking the Iraqi oil industry, Rob McKee, was also, even during his tenure in Baghdad, chairman of a Halliburton subsidiary. McKee made no secret of the fact that he was against privatization of the Iraqi oil fields or that he was in favor of policies to keep the price of oil high, ostensibly to help the Iraqi economy.[49] Of course, the Iraqi economy is certainly not the only beneficiary of high oil prices. The US oil industry, including McKee's primary employer, Halliburton, also had much to gain.

US leverage over the oil industry structure did have one clear and tangible outcome: the proposed new Iraqi petroleum law would represent a return to the type of contract used in the earlier days of Middle Eastern oil exploration – a contract much more advantageous to oil companies than that of any other state in the Persian Gulf region.[50] The oil companies would have the best of both worlds: preventing the privatization of Iraqi oil fields and the resulting ramped up of production that would ensue, while still managing to get an "old-school" contract reminiscent of the pre-Arab nationalism days, one that decisively favors them.

After the invasion of Iraq, oil prices skyrocketed and so did oil company profits. In the five years after the onset of the conflict, profits of the five largest Western oil companies more than tripled. Moreover, oil revenues filled the coffers of some of America's fiercest adversaries in Iran and Venezuela, not to mention Russia and a handful of Middle Eastern despots, complicating US diplomacy.[51] Iraq became a case where oil interests got to have their cake and eat it too, but from the US public's perspective, the invasion of Iraq didn't quite meet the truth in advertising test.

Non-Middle Eastern Oil

Although the Middle East is home to what is by far the largest concentration of oil, accounting for 60% of the world's reserves, there remain other significant oil exporters outside the region.[52] The 2001 National Energy Policy suggested eight alternatives from which the US could source oil from outside the Middle East: Mexico, Columbia, Venezuela, Russia, Azerbaijan, Kazakhstan, Nigeria, and Angola.[53] Of those countries, only two have truly significant oil resources that would rival even one of the smaller Middle Eastern oil exporters, Russia and Venezuela, who have 6.3% and 7.9% of the world's oil reserves, respectively.[54]

Venezuela has long been a major player in the US market. Although most oil exporters have been content simply to sell their oil, the government of Venezuela has taken it much further. They are one of the few truly vertically integrated oil companies that operate in the US market. In September, 1986, the Venezuelan national oil company, Petróleos de Venezuela, S.A. (PDVSA), bought a 50% stake in CITGO Petroleum Corporation. PDVSA acquired the remaining half of CITGO in January, 1990. CITGO sells more than seven billion gallons of gasoline in the US market every year and owns three major refineries in the US that have capacity of almost 750,000 barrels per day.[55] Venezuela is no small player.

The complication associated with Venezuelan oil is that the country is under the near total control of Hugo Chavez, their renegade president. Chavez is a close friend and protégé of long-standing US adversary Fidel Castro. Like Castro, his political ideals are Marxist, and he is virulently anti-American. He is, perhaps, the most dangerous adversary the US faces in the world today.

Since coming to power in 1999, Chavez has endured considerable domestic resistance, eventually evolving into the primary antagonist to US interests in the Western hemisphere. Latin America, a region that has historically been vulnerable to Communist incursion, has proven a fertile ground for the Chavez brand of demagoguery.

Venezuela, although hardly a traditional world power, is gaining wealth due to its vast oil reserves, the largest outside the Middle East. That wealth is being deployed to purchase arms and build military capabilities to counter US "imperialist aggression." Chavez has even called for the creation of a NATO-like military alliance, the purpose of which would be to fight the United States.[56] Perhaps there is no more clear-cut case of cash flowing directly from the pockets of American consumers to procure weapons bought for the stated purpose of killing American soldiers. Chavez makes no secret of it; he openly brags of the irony.

Despite his ambitions, Chavez has been a terrible steward of Venezuela's oil industry. In the late 1990s, Venezuela embarked on a plan to expand capacity to 7 million barrels per day with an eye toward taking some of the Saudis' market share in the US. When Hugo Chavez came to power, he rescinded those plans and, instead, opted to expand capacity more slowly. Chavez's ascension to power has brought long-term political strife, a major oil worker strike in 2003, and significantly higher taxes, none of which has been beneficial to Venezuela's oil industry. As of 2003, lack of foreign investment, damage from an oil workers strike, and the constant threat of civil war have brought production capacity down to 2.2 million barrels per day from 3.7 million barrels per day in 1998.[57]

The political future of Venezuela is uncertain, but Chavez has only tightened his hold on control. As his power has grown, he has become increasingly radical. Given the deteriorating infrastructure within Venezuela's industrial complex and the political climate spawned by Chavez, Venezuela represents an unfavorable source of petroleum of the US markets.

The other major non-Middle Eastern oil player is Russia. For most of the latter half of the 20th century, the USSR was America's primary adversary, and the world was essentially divided between US and Soviet spheres of influence. The Soviet Union was a significant oil producer, the world's largest in the 1980s. It accounted for about 20% of world oil production at its peak.[58]

The Soviet Union collapsed in 1991. There were many contributors to its downfall, some of which were related to internal politics, others to nationalistic forces in the constituent states, but the failure of the Soviet economy was probably the most important factor. Even Soviet leaders complained through the years about waste and colossal inefficiency. Brezhnev, Soviet leader between 1964 and 1982, famously lamented the massive over-production of shoes in 1976, to the tune of 700 million – nearly three pair for every man, woman, and child – yet the Soviet people still had a shortage because the shoes never got to them. The Soviet Union led the world in steel production, but it was of poor quality and frequently went unused. It also led the world in cement production, but there were still perpetual shortages of that commodity as well.[59]

Although there were many problems with the Soviet system, it is hard to avoid the obvious reality that its downward spiral coincided with the significant drop in oil prices that began in 1985. Oil and gas accounted for almost half of Soviet exports and accounted for about 60% of convertible currency trade with the West.[60] The USSR was accustomed to maintaining a hard currency trade surplus; during the early 1980s it was about $4 billion annually. When oil collapsed, however, the 1985 surplus dropped to $534 million.[61]

Despite its robust industrial capacity, the Soviet economy produced very few quality consumer goods. Imported consumer goods from the West were highly prized in the Soviet Union, but they were also very expensive. With little for workers to buy under a deteriorating Communist system, money had essentially no value. In a world where money is worthless, why bother to work to earn it? As a result, the workforce under the Soviet system was largely unproductive, lazy, and, in many cases, intoxicated.

More consumer goods from the West could have bolstered activity in the workforce, but imports require hard currency. The problem for the USSR was that other than energy, it had little in the form of marketable goods. With energy prices dropping, the only other export that could save the Soviets was weapons.[62] The primary market for weapons is among other oil producers, especially in the Middle East. Reduced cash flow for oil producers meant weapons purchases were increasingly unaffordable. Key buyers such as Saddam Hussein in Iraq were forced to resort to credit with the USSR to keep the weapons resupplies flowing for his ongoing war with Iran.[63] Weapons were not going to provide the hard currency the Soviets needed.

In 1986, Soviet central planners were able to get their trade surplus back up, but not by increasing exports. Instead, the Communists slashed imports, which resulted in even fewer goods available for Soviet consumers.[64] To make matters worse for the Soviets, the oil industry began suffering from increasing production costs, falling productivity and efficiency, and, in some cases, deteriorating product quality.[65] The "easy" reserves close to industrial areas were being depleted, forcing more production to come from desolate areas of Siberia where extraction and transportation of oil were more expensive. This would have been fine in an increasing price environment, but the price of oil was falling.[66]

All things considered, lack of hard currency, shortage of consumer goods, and sinking profitability of the oil industry were major factors precipitating Soviet decline. Put bluntly, the fall of oil prices in the mid-1980s was an immediate cause of the collapse. The Soviet Union was doomed because Communism is an inherently flawed economic system, but the timing of its funeral was as much a function of oil prices as anything else.

After the fall of the Soviet Union, Russia's oil exports fell dramatically.[67] Russia lost much of its clout and influence. There was a rush during the Clinton Administration to admit former Soviet-bloc states to NATO. Poland, Hungary, and the Czech Republic, all former Communist states, joined. The idea was that membership in NATO would connect those that had lived behind the Iron Curtain to the rest of Europe and, by extension, to the US. The expansion of NATO also had the effect of further marginalizing Russia. It essentially moved the old Cold War sphere of influence boundaries eastward toward an increasingly isolated Russia. Early opponents of NATO's expansion felt that the creep toward Russia could leave them feeling cornered, set back Russian democratic reforms, and revive the Cold War.[68] A weakened and cornered Russia could prove dangerous; as most are aware, an animal is most dangerous when wounded and cornered.

Perhaps the most vivid illustration of the decline in Russian power was its inability to protect its longstanding ally Serbia from the US military after the Clinton Administration decided to intervene in the Balkans. Aside from direct US military encroachment into former Soviet client states, the Russians were also concerned about the precedent being set – that foreign powers could confront a regime over the treatment of its own population. They feared the example could too easily be applied to other places in the future, including Russia.

Russian complaints, however, were essentially ignored, which was a testament to just how weak Russian power in Europe had become. The whole affair in the Balkans set the stage for resurgent nationalism, and with promises of reasserting Russian power, it would pave the path to power for the new regime of Vladimir Putin.[69]

Putin proved quite an enigma for the West. After his first meeting with Putin, President George W. Bush famously responded to a question about whether or not Russia could be trusted by professing that he been "able to get a sense of his soul."[70] Putin was, however, much different from the portrait Bush painted early in his Presidency. He, even more so than his Soviet predecessors, used Russia's status as a major exporter of oil and natural gas to increase Russian political influence, often at the expense of his neighbors and in conflict with Western interests. Although now ostensibly out of power, it is widely believed that Putin maintains a firm grip on the reins of Russia from behind the scenes. In any case, his policies set a precedent for just how far Russia is willing to go to use its natural resources to increase its global influence.

One example of Russia's aggressiveness has been its decision to, on multiple occasions, cease or reduce the flow of natural gas to the former Soviet republic of Ukraine, which is dependent on Russian supply. Russia has, in effect, used natural gas as a weapon just as the Arabs used oil in 1973, but with arguably greater effect.

Far more serious than the natural gas incidents was the 2008 full scale military invasion of Georgia, also a former Soviet Republic. Georgia, strategically located in the Caucasus Region at the dividing line between Europe and Asia, has been home to a long-standing ethnic conflict over an area Russians refer to as South Ossetia.

During the Soviet years, Georgia was known as the Georgian Soviet Socialist Republic. As was the practice in the Soviet Union, the central government created three autonomous regions within Georgia for minority groups. One of the three was the South Ossetian Autonomous Region. As Georgians pressed for independence in the last days of the Soviet Union, South Ossetians resisted because of their ethnic kinship with Russians. After the Soviet Union was dissolved, South Ossetia was home to a fierce separatist movement. Eventually, ethnic conflict led to civil war. A shaky peace was finally forged in the late 1990s, but South Ossetia remained effectively outside central Georgian control.[71]

Georgia is not a major oil producer, nor does it have notable oil reserves. The country does, however, lie to the west of one of the world's most productive oil regions near Baku on the western Caspian Sea. Because the Caspian Sea is a land-locked body of water, the oil from the western Caspian must be pumped via pipeline toward deep water ports on either the Black Sea or the Mediterranean Sea to be shipped throughout the world.

Although there is a pipeline route that goes north from Baku to the Russian port of Novorosslysk, it is relatively small compared to the two pipelines that cross Georgia going to either the Black Sea port of Sup'sa or on to the Turkish port city of Ceyhan on the eastern Mediterranean. The newer of those two pipelines, the Baku Tbilisi Ceyhan (BTC) Pipeline, which came online in 2006, is by-far the largest pipeline in the Caspian Region, with the ability to move more than one million barrels per day.[72]

Before construction of the BTC Pipeline, virtually all of the Caspian region's oil flowed across Russian territory. As global concerns about the strategic value of oil have mounted, Western interests have devoted considerable effort to making sure that Caspian oil can be accessed through countries outside Russian influence. Since the breakup of the Soviet Union, Georgia has been one of the more Western-oriented republics. Development of the BTC Pipeline through Georgia was a major victory for the West on the world oil landscape and represented a major strategic loss for Russian oil power.

When the Russians invaded in 2008, the pretext was protection of South Ossetia from Georgian aggression. The context of the last twenty years of history in Russia and the Caspian region points to a different conclusion. The conflict, like so many that preceded it, was really about oil power. Although South Ossetia lies slightly to the north of the major oil pipeline routes,[73] Russia demonstrated to the Georgian government that it was willing to send troops into Georgia and was capable of seizing the pipelines if its demands were not met. Even with a Russian military withdrawal, South Ossetia will still be there to provide the excuse for future incursions.

Just as the Soviet collapse mirrored a collapse in oil prices, so too did the resurgence of Russian power mirror the rise in oil prices after the invasion of Iraq. The Russian economy is remarkably similar to the economies of Middle Eastern petro-states, but there is one alarming distinction. Russia has a military, although perhaps less fearsome than at the pinnacle of its war-fighting ability in the twentieth century, that is extremely formidable and nuclear armed. The leadership has demonstrated its willingness to use its military to protect Russian oil power and to use Russia's status as a major energy exporter as yet another weapon in a quest to restore Russia to superpower status.

Part Three –
Today's Energy World

The Oil Bidniz

Petroleum is, above all else, a business. So far, this book has largely been devoted to really big picture issues: geopolitics, international economics, and the environment. To begin solving the problems that oil dependence has created in our world, one must gain a better understanding of the industry itself.

It is important to remember that the petroleum industry and the energy industry are not necessarily the same. Petroleum is only one form of energy Americans consume; electricity is another. From a practical standpoint, electricity and the liquid fuels that power our vehicles are quite different. We get them through different distribution channels, and, most importantly, they originate from different sources. In today's world, liquid fuels and electricity are anything but interchangeable, although the introduction of electric hybrid vehicles may begin to blur the lines just a little.

At one time, much of the electricity in the US was produced from petroleum, but today petroleum accounts for only a negligible amount of electricity generation. Coal-fired power plants produce by far the largest share of electricity in the US, accounting for 49.0% of generation as of 2008.[1] Coal owes its popularity to its abundance and affordability in the US. In fact, although the US has only 2.4% of the world's petroleum reserves, it has 28.9% of the world's coal reserves.[2]

Widely debated in the US is the prospect of increasing electricity generation from nuclear energy. This debate is multi-faceted. Nuclear energy is actually fairly common in the US and in some other countries. There are 439 nuclear plants in 31 nations around the world that produce 16% of the world's electricity (6% of its total energy).[3] As of 2008, Americans get 19.6% of our electricity from nuclear power,[4] which is generated at 104 operating commercial reactors in the US.[5] A few counties get an even higher percentage of their electricity from nuclear power than the US. France, for example, generated 76.8% of its electricity from nuclear power in 2007.[6] Nuclear energy has some clear advantages, no carbon dioxide emissions being chief among them, but expanded use of nuclear energy would have little or no impact on the use of petroleum.

Regardless of the type of energy source, a debate about electricity must be conducted separately from a debate about transportation fuel. To illustrate the point, consider that the US has essentially no foreign energy dependency as it relates to electricity generation. We have plenty of energy resources for power production, although there remains a vigorous environmental debate surrounding many of the methods we employ. There are also environmental issues with oil usage, but the most serious concerns with respect to oil relate to foreign dependence and the political and economic ramifications of it.

The Basics of Oil

Petroleum literally means "rock oil" in Greek. It has been used for a variety of purposes since ancient times, but it has really come to prominence in the last 150 years as subsurface exploration and extraction has made it inexpensively available in large quantities. Advances in petroleum refining technologies have also allowed useful products to be manufactured from its raw form – crude oil.

The products of petroleum that are most familiar, gasoline and diesel fuel, provide energy for transportation both for people and for all of the "stuff" we are constantly moving around the world. Also notable is kerosene, which was originally used for illumination and was the first commercial product derived from crude oil. Today, jet fuel, which is basically kerosene, allows people to travel virtually anywhere in the world in less than a day.

Petroleum comes to us courtesy of trillions of tiny sea creatures known as plankton. Millions of years ago, Earth and its oceans were very warm. Dinosaurs roamed. The atmosphere was concentrated with carbon dioxide - much higher concentrations than are found today. It was a plankton paradise. Ocean currents concentrated plankton in certain areas, where they multiplied and grew in large numbers. As they died, their tiny carcasses fell to the sea floor, piling up layer upon layer.[7]

Much of the dead plankton disappeared through decomposition, a process that requires oxygen, but some remains were preserved in areas where oxygen was relatively scarce. The plankton were either quickly buried under other organic matter on the seafloor or were concentrated in remote corners of the oceans where waters were relatively stagnant and, therefore, mostly free of oxygen.[8]

Once buried, the organic matter was subjected to a variety of forces on its way to becoming petroleum. Temperature was the most important factor in the transformation. The minimum temperature to create oil is about 150°F, which occurs naturally at depths of about 7,000 feet. Oil can be generated from that point down to about 18,000 feet where temperatures reach 300°F, above which organic matter tends to be converted to natural gas rather than petroleum.[9]

Oil and gas tend to rise due to buoyancy as both are less dense than water. This movement process is called migration. Movement is along the path of least resistance, which often results in fossil fuels moving considerable distances from where they were originally formed, both vertically and horizontally.

Although early prospectors believed that oil moved in underground rivers and pooled in underground lakes, that isn't exactly how it works. There are no underground lakes or rivers of oil. Instead, it moves through and is contained in porous sedimentary rock, generally sandstone or limestone. These porous rocks are referred to as reservoir rocks. Sandstone tends to be formed on sand dunes, along shorelines, in river beds and river deltas. Limestone is largely the product of coral reefs. Of course, over millions of years the location of these rocks in relation to the seas has changed substantially. That is why oil can be found in areas that aren't necessarily near a present-day ocean. It is the ancient shorelines and ancient paths of rivers that are most important in determining where such rocks (and oil) are found.

As long as there is porous rock, oil can continue to move, and it continually migrates toward the earth's surface unless that migration is stopped by a trap.[10] A trap is formed at a high point in the reservoir rock that is sealed by non-porous rock. Shale and salt commonly act as seals preventing oil from continuing to migrate upward. One type of trap is a natural arch called a dome or anticline. It is in these anticlines, and in other subsurface traps, that oil can often be found.

Some areas of the world have no sedimentary rock. These areas, called shields, tend to be abundant with ore minerals like iron, copper, lead, gold and silver...but not oil. Other areas, called basins, have very thick sedimentary rock. The Caspian basin has about 85,000 feet of sedimentary rock, but most basin areas are 20,000 to 40,000 feet deep. Examples include the Gulf of Mexico and the Anadarko basin of southwestern Oklahoma. It is in these areas that oil and gas are typically found.[11] In all, Earth has about 600 sedimentary rock basins. Of the basins that have been drilled and explored, about 40% are productive. About 90% of the earth's oil occurs in just 30 basins.[12] Approximately 30% of basins remain unexplored.[13]

Not all crude oil is created equal. Oil is actually a mixture of hydrocarbon molecules of different sizes and molecular structures. The mixture is different for just about every oil field in the world. They are compared based on, among other things, density. A scale developed by the American Petroleum Institute is the most common method of comparison. It is known as °API. The °API of crude oil ranges from 5 to 55. Light crude is 35 to 45, while heavy oils are below 25.[14] Lighter crudes contain a higher portion of smaller, more hydrogen-rich molecules that are well suited to producing gasoline and other high-value transportation fuels. Heavier crudes have a higher portion of larger, more carbon-rich molecules, for which there are limited, lower-value uses such as asphalt and heavy industrial fuel.[15]

Crude oils also vary by the amount of sulfur they contain. Sweet crude has less than 1% sulfur, while sour crude has more than 1%. Heavy oils tend to have higher sulfur content than light crude.[16] Sulfur is an undesirable contaminant, which leads to more rapid corrosion of equipment in refineries and to greater emissions of pollutants. The sulfur content of finished products is controlled and has been the primary focus of environmental regulations.[17]

Generally, when we think of oil, we think of the black liquid that is gleaned from below the surface via wells, but oil can come from other sources. Oil shale is sedimentary rock rich in organic matter called kerogen. When oil shale is heated to about 660° F, the kerogen is transformed into a version of crude oil. High grade shale can produce as much as 25 barrels per ton of rock.[18] With most shale, however, yields are closer to one barrel per ton. Herein lies one of the biggest problems with oil shale – what do you do with all of that left-over rock? An economic use has yet to be found for it.[19] Furthermore, alternative means of producing oil are not always economically competitive with the traditional pumped liquid variety. Production from oil shale involves high costs, which are a major factor preventing widespread commercial development.

Another source of oil is from tar sands (also called oil sands). Tar sands are sand mixed with very heavy oil. The oil can be separated using steam.[20] Commercial production is occurring now in several locations in Canada, including at the Athabasca Oil Sands areas of northern Alberta. Because it takes more than two tons of oil sand, on average, to yield a barrel of crude, the process is cumbersome. It can also be very expensive because of the massive energy needed to separate oil from the sand.

Despite the challenges, production from oil sands is rapidly growing. In 1999, oil sands accounted for about 15% of Canada's total petroleum production,[21] but by 2008 that percentage had grown to 50%.[22] Canada is particularly important to the US since it, not Saudi Arabia, is by far the largest exporter of petroleum to US.[23]

In addition to petroleum-based fuels, there are also alternative fuels. The most common alternative fuel in use today in the United States is ethanol. Biodiesel is another alternative fuel that is growing in popularity. These fuels still represent only a small fraction of the total market in the US and the world. It is also possible to manufacture gasoline, kerosene, diesel, jet fuel, and other similar products from sources other than petroleum, in which case they can also be alternative fuels. In other words, it isn't necessarily the type of fuel that makes it an alternative; it is the raw material from which it is produced. For example, common fuels most people recognize as petroleum-derived can also be manufactured from coal and from biomass.

The Oil Supply Chain

The oil supply chain can be easily divided into three distinct parts. The first of these is oil exploration and production. It is the part of the business where oil deposits are found, drilled, and extracted. In essence, it is the process of going from zero to a barrel of crude oil. In the oil industry, this part of the business is often referred to as *upstream*.

One you have a barrel of crude oil, it has to be made into useful products. This process is called refining, which uses chemical process to convert crude oil to gasoline, kerosene, fuel oil, lubricants, plastics, and other products. Refining is referred to as the *midstream* part of the industry.

Finally, the products produced by refining must find their way to consumers. The process of distribution and marketing is referred to as *downstream*. In the world of corporate oil and gas, a few very large global conglomerates are involved in all of the three stages of the industry, but there are many companies involved in just one or two parts.

Extraction

As is well known, most oil comes from drilling wells and pumping it up from beneath the surface of the earth. Well technology has come a very long way from Drake's landmark 1859 well in Pennsylvania. Drake's well was constructed at a point where oil was already flowing to the surface from underground. The purpose of the well was to speed the flow. Many early wells were drilled near such seeps. This method of locating wells actually proved remarkably successful in the early days of the industry. It wasn't until much later that geology was better understood. Today, seismic technology and satellites are used to find locations of potential oil reserves.

As the technology of finding oil progressed, so did methods of extracting it. With that complexity came greatly-increased capabilities. Initially, oil was simply pumped from the ground through wells drilled straight down into the earth. Now, however, wells can change course. Nowhere is this capability more important than in offshore exploration.

Offshore oil platforms and rigs are extremely expensive. Accordingly, it is important to glean maximum utility from these high-priced capital assets. To achieve this goal, wells are often drilled outward at angles. Viewed from above it would look something like spokes on a bicycle wheel. Using directional drilling, an offshore rig can retrieve much more oil than it could from a single well.

With most fields, oil recovery is initially very easy because internal pressure in the fields forces oil to the surface once a well is drilled. After that pressure is released, however, oil extraction quickly becomes more difficult. Sometimes wells must be stimulated to increase the flow of oil. In the early times of petroleum exploration, all the way up to the late 1940s, a process called explosive fracturing was common. As the name implies, explosives were lowered down wells and detonated at depth, thereby shattering the rock and creating an environment more conducive to the free flow of oil.

Since use of explosives is dangerous, this method has largely been replaced by hydraulic fracturing. In hydraulic fracturing, large volumes of fluid are injected under high pressure into wells to fracture the reservoir rocks.[24] Fracturing can increase the rate of production anywhere from 1.5 to 30 times the original production level. The ultimate oil recovery of the well can be increased by 5% to 15%. About 30% of oil wells in the US are fractured.[25]

Wells can also be stimulated using acid to dissolve some of the rock around a well. Hydrochloric acid (HCl) is typically used for carbonate reservoir rock, while hydrofluoric acid (HF) is typically used for sandstone.[26]

Enhanced oil recovery is something entirely different from fracturing. It involves the use of a separate injection well drilled near the production well. Liquids or gases are injected through the injection well to force more oil out through the primary well. When this process uses water, it is called a water flood. A water flood can recover 5% to 50% of the oil in place remaining after traditional recovery means are exhausted.[27] Water flood is generally effective until the water "breaks through" to the primary well. Since water will always follow the path of least resistance, once it reaches a production well it will tend to flow along that same path, rendering it inefficient.[28] Modern practice starts the water flood early, often simultaneously with the commencement of production.[29]

The same goals can also be accomplished using carbon dioxide gas (CO_2) for enhanced oil recovery. The principals are similar to those of a water flood except that CO_2 is used instead of water. The CO_2 is pressurized and forced into the injection well. CO_2 is highly soluble in oil. As a result, an oil-CO_2 solution is created that has properties similar to carbonated water, something very familiar to the average consumer because of the popularity of carbonated beverages and sparkling water. As a solution, movement through the porous rock becomes much easier.[30] The added benefit, however, is that this process results in the disposal and sequestration of carbon dioxide.

Even with enhanced oil recovery techniques, only about half of the total oil in a reservoir is economically recoverable. Significant research has gone into new recovery techniques in an attempt to glean that remaining 50%, but, as yet, there are no promising solutions.[31]

Extraction technologies will continue to advance, as all technologies do over time. They will allow greater exploitation of existing wells providing more resources. Advancement, however, will not change the fact that the quantity of petroleum on Earth is finite. More efficient extraction is a way to buy time to transition to alternatives, but can only slightly delay the inevitable. Eventually, oil will not be able to meet the world's fuel needs.

Refining

Processing crude oil, known as refining, produces a wide range of products including, most importantly, transportation fuels. Every refinery is unique and is configured based on the characteristics of the crude oil it is designed to process and the slate and quality of output products, as well as environmental constraints.[32]

Before the refining process begins, crude oil is first treated to remove impurities like water, salt, and sediment. After being treated, the crude oil undergoes the initial step of refining, which is separation. Separation is accomplished through a simple distillation process where crude oil is heated and sent to a distillation column. The column allows the lighter molecules with lower boiling points to condense at the top, while larger, heavier molecules with higher boiling points are collected toward the bottom.[33]

Regardless of the quality of crude oil, the products derived through separation techniques alone do not match up with market demand. The process yields more heavy-molecule hydro-carbons and not enough lighter molecules suitable for transportation fuels. In the early years of the oil industry, separation was the only step in the refining process. Consequently, much of a barrel of crude was not used.

Today, refining doesn't stop with separation. Modern refineries employ other processes that go beyond physical separation of the molecules to convert heavier molecules to profitable products. Heavier crude, which contains a greater percentage of carbon, requires greater refinery complexity to produce valuable light product.[34]

A chemical process called cracking puts heavier molecules under high temperature and pressures and uses chemicals to split longer carbon molecule chains to form lighter products, such as gasoline.[35] Fluid catalytic cracking is the most common form. It involves heating the feedstock to high temperatures and then mixing it with solid catalysts on which cracking reactions occur.

Another variation, called hydro-cracking, requires the injection of hydrogen gas at high pressure. Lighter molecules have a greater percentage of hydrogen, which is the purpose of the stream of hydrogen gas: to produce the ideal ratio of carbon and hydrogen molecules in a reaction chamber to yield the desired product, most often gasoline. Hydro-cracking can be used to upgrade distillate streams from other processes (such as catalytic cracking), but hydro-crackers are expensive to build and operate. They generally require a secondary plant to produce hydrogen gas, which adds considerable expense.[36]

Where there is a catalytic cracking unit, there is usually also an alkylation unit. Alkylation combines gaseous by-products of other refining processes to produce a high-grade gasoline blending component. There are several other processes that are also used in refining operations to produce fuel-grade products, but they represent relatively small contributions to overall fuel output.[37]

Also worth mentioning is a process called reformulation in which the chemical composition of hydro-carbon molecules are altered to increase octane and, thereby, performance characteristics of fuel. The process is used to produce reformulated gasoline. Because the main chemical reaction in catalytic reforming, dehydrogenation, produces hydrogen in large quantities, reforming can be integrated with hydro-cracking. Reforming is the only refinery process that is actually a net producer of hydrogen.[38]

As with extraction techniques, improved refining technologies can allow more efficient use of limited petroleum resources. There are limits to its capabilities, however. There are only so many carbon and hydrogen atoms in a given quantity of crude oil. Once all of those have been transformed into useable fuel, it is simply not possible to go any further.

Distribution and Marketing

The final stage of the petroleum production cycle is distribution and marketing of refined products. Frankly, one of the attributes that has made petroleum so successful is how well it lends itself to distribution. Part of the magic of oil is that it is a liquid, which is much easier to move than a solid. It is this simple fact that has made oil such a key source of fuel in the modern era.

Liquids (and gases) share one quality with which solids simply cannot complete – they can be pumped. Most fuel is distributed throughout the country by pipeline. Pipelines are much easier to use than railroads, trucks, or other similar methods. They are also pumped from your gas tank to your engine – which is why you don't have to stop the car to shovel coal into the engine every few miles.

Once gasoline has been refined from crude oil, there are basically two different routes it can take to market. It can be sold directly via company-owned stores or franchises of an integrated oil company, or it can be sold in bulk to a middleman. The middlemen, referred to as petroleum jobbers, redistribute fuel to neighborhood gas stations. The amount of petroleum moving through each channel is roughly the same.

There is a common misconception among consumers about jobbers and gas stations. It is often assumed that if there is a major oil company's name on the station, it means that the oil company owns that location. That is not necessarily true. Most gas station locations are actually franchises, much like locations of McDonalds or another fast food purveyor. McDonalds Corporation owns very few of its restaurants; instead, they are owned by independent business people.

In our modern world, petroleum distribution is everywhere. Nearly every major intersection in the United States is home to a gas station. Distribution, as luck would have it, is one of the key barriers to entry of any new competing technologies. You can't fill up on hydrogen or recharge your electric battery at the local filling station, which is a major impediment to widespread adoption of these technologies. Even ethanol, although becoming more common, can be found at only a tiny fraction of the number of outlets compared with gasoline.

A Culture of Mobility

The advent of the internal combustion engine has spawned quite an evolution in modern culture. Its widespread use in automobiles has opened up the world in ways its pioneers could scarcely have dreamed. Today, Americans think nothing of hopping in their cars and driving to work, on errands, and even over long distances. Such trips may have taken days or weeks using the means of transportation available 100 years ago.

The first design for an internal combustion engine is generally thought to have been created by Leonardo DiVinci; it was among the many innovations that seemed unimaginable in his time. The first person to actually experiment with an internal-combustion engine was Christian Huygens in the late seventeenth century, but no effective engine was developed until 1859, when J. J. Étienne Lenoir built an engine that could self-sustain operation. In 1885, Gottlieb Daimler constructed what is generally recognized as the prototype of the modern gas engine with its vertical cylinder and fuel injection through a carburetor. In 1889 Daimler introduced an engine with an improved design having a much higher power-to-weight ratio. It is from this engine that most modern gasoline engines are descended.[39] In 1893, the Daimler engine was on display at the Columbian Exposition in Chicago, where it was seen by a mechanically inclined employee of the Edison Company, a man named Henry Ford.[40]

Ford was one of the most universally loved figures of his era. While he was most responsible for popularizing the automobile in the US, he was also a hero around the world. In the Soviet Union, his likeness could be found hanging in factories next to portraits of Lenin. Hitler also revered him and implemented his practices at Volkswagen, where cars were fashioned after the Model T. Of course Rockefeller was quite the fan as well, proclaiming his manufacturing facilities "the industrial marvel of the age."[41] Rockefeller's attitude was perhaps understandable, since Ford, more than anyone, contributed to the growth of the market for oil and, thereby, Rockefeller's wealth.

Ford's encounter with the Daimler engine inspired him. His dreams were of a "horseless carriage" and he immediately began to work on an engine of his own. He was finally able to get it to run on Christmas Eve, 1893.[42] Three years later he had his "Quadricycle," as it was called, off on its maiden voyage.

As it would happen, the debate about electric cars versus gasoline cars is not a new debate. During early development of the automobile, there were electric cars manufactured alongside gasoline powered cars. Ford clearly favored the gasoline vehicle, but his invention was validated by an unlikely mentor. Shortly after his first vehicle's maiden voyage, Ford, as an Edison employee, had an opportunity to meet Thomas Edison, a man he revered. Edison, keenly interested in Ford's invention, asked numerous detailed questions about it and its design, after which he exclaimed,

> Young man, that's the thing; you have it. Keep at it! Electric cars must keep near to power stations. The storage battery is too heavy...Your car is self-contained

– it carries its own power-plant – no fire, no boiler, no smoke, no steam. You have the thing. Keep at it.

It seems that some old problems die hard. The same issues are still apparent today in the quest to develop a reliable electric car. Edison's commentary, however, strengthened Ford's resolve. Eventually, he was able to collect investors to provide financing and his company was up and running.[43]

Ford's first two companies failed. The second one was later reorganized as Cadillac Automobile Company, which eventually did produce cars and later became a familiar division of General Motors.[44] For Ford, however, the third time was the charm. His third company, Ford Motor Company, made him the business legend that he is, and, more importantly, led to the popularization of the motor vehicle in America.

In the autumn of 1908, a new product hit the market – a product that would eventually garner more than 50% market share for vehicles on the road in the United States. Its target market was middle and working class families. Ford would sell more than 15 million units by 1920. This new product, known as the Model T, marked the beginning of a car culture that would forever change America[45]

What made the Model T special, aside from intangible aspects, was its affordability. Henry Ford was not the first to mass-produce the motor vehicle; that honor belongs to Ransom E. Olds. Ford's contribution, most of all, was development of the assembly line. It was this manufacturing process that ultimately allowed large scale, economical mass production of the automobile. By 1923, Ford was producing more than 2 million cars a year using his assembly line technique. Only by turning out cars on this scale could they reach the masses.

Up to this point, the primary means for traveling was either by horse or by foot. Railroads had opened up the west, but they were far from being an everyday means of transportation for most people. Even in the era of railroads, most travel was by horse. But with the mass production of the Model T, as well as its successors and competitors, America was well on its way to being an automobile nation.

At the beginning of the 1920s, Ford produced half of the new cars in the world and 60% in the US. In the following years, however, Ford would see its preeminence diminish in favor of Alfred Sloan and his General Motors Corporation. Sloan, also recognized as one of the business titans of the twentieth century, shaped the automobile industry into what it is today. It was Sloan who gave birth to the concept of diversified products in the automobile industry. At GM, car models were restyled each year, creating the habit of differentiation between year models that we know today. GM's cars also came in a variety of colors and with a wide range of options and accessories.[46] By 1927, there was an automobile for every 5.3 people in the US, and US automakers (mostly GM and Ford) accounted for 80% of the world's cars.[47]

As World War II came, most of the nation's industrial capacity was refocused on the war effort. Automobile manufacturers ceased production of civilian cars and instead produced military vehicles. When the war ended, however, there was more demand than ever for big-ticket consumer goods. Servicemen returned home and the baby boom was off and running, creating millions of new families. What does every family need? A family car, of course! Later, the concept of the family car morphed into the personal car with each person instead of each family owning one. A major reason for this change was that women began to enter the workforce in large numbers. In 1969, on average, 2.20 persons shared an automobile. By 1995, however, only 1.59 people were sharing an automobile. That represents a 28% decrease in vehicle occupancy, which also caused a 38% increase in energy use.[48]

As everyone started to own cars, they became closely associated with individual identity. Today, there are so many different kinds of cars, it is staggering. Most of them reflect the personalities of their drivers. Imagine the muscle car, the performance sedan, the minivan, the SUV, or a huge full-sized truck. Each one of these types of vehicles is so unique that it is almost possible to imagine the face of the driver that goes with it. None of these drivers would enthusiastically part with their car. Cars are convenient, but they are also a reflection of who we are. People love their vehicles. Perhaps no other material possession, with the possible exception of clothing, is a more accurate reflection of a person's personality.

As solutions to US oil dependence are evaluated, leaders should be mindful of that special relationship. Those who propose massive shifts to public transportation or other strategies that minimize the use of personal vehicles fail to consider the resistance to such measures that will surely come from American society. Asking Americans to give up what they so dearly love is an energy strategy that is destined to fail.

8
A Few 800-Pound Gorillas

The petroleum market is a very complex world. There are many producers, many consumers. Everyone has a hand in the game. It has created the world's greatest fortunes and enslaved nations. For the US, it is like mother's milk, and the economy simply cannot run without it. A serious disruption in supply would have incalculable effects on the daily lives of nearly every American.

Oil is important because it allows us to be mobile. Transportation is a key facet of daily life, and transportation demand is growing. The worldwide level and rate of growth of real per capita income, the rate of population growth, and migration of populations to urban areas are the primary drivers of the growth of transport demand.[1] In 2000, personal transportation demand was 32.3 trillion passenger-kilometers (p-km), but by 2050 it is expected to be 74 trillion p-km, a global annual increase of 1.7%. Goods transportation demand is also expected to grow rapidly, from 14.4 trillion tonne-kilometers (t-km) in 2000 to 45.9 trillion t-km in 2050, a global annual increase of 2.3%.[2]

The largest single determinant of personal travel demand is income. The cost of fuel and of vehicles plays a relatively small role in determining transportation consumption. Demand for travel in a particular market can be characterized at three distinct levels: a relatively inelastic demand at levels where incomes are very low (consumers simply can't afford vehicles or fuel); a highly elastic demand in medium income countries (where consumers are near the threshold of affordable travel; and a lower elasticity for high income countries (where travel is generally affordable for everyone).[3] It is not only the level of income that is important, but also income distribution. The more widely wealth is disbursed, the greater demand for passenger travel.[4]

The size of cities has always been constrained by ability of transportation systems to provide raw materials and food, to transport their finished goods to distant markets, and to enable their residents to congregate in numbers for manufacturing, commerce, and other face-to-face interaction. The first two of these problems were largely solved by the advent of low-cost waterborne transportation systems (like ships), which is why most major cities lie on navigable waterways. The final problem, getting people from home to work and back on a daily basis, still provides a challenge.[5] Anyone who commutes to work in a major US city is well aware of this problem.

A wealthier population demands more non-commute travel activity. In wealthier countries, work-related daily travel is actually a relatively small percentage of miles traveled. In the US in 2001, for example, commuting to work represented only 26% of personal travel, whereas social and recreational travel represented 30%. Driving children to school and other errand running was another 20%.[6]

Worldwide wealth is on the rise. Wider distribution of wealth is generally a good thing. Not only will more people's basic needs be met, but, greater wealth decreases hostility and violence in populations. Rising wealth solves many problems, but it also creates new ones, including increasing demand for petroleum.

Some Key Players

There are really only a few countries that play a significant role in world petroleum markets. As it relates to supply, Saudi Arabia and Russia are, by far, the most important producers. Saudi Arabia produces more than two and a half times as much oil (as of 2008) as its nearest Middle Eastern competitor, Iran. Russia produces about the same amount as Saudi Arabia. The US is actually the world's third largest oil producer despite relatively paltry reserves, a status that is the product of intensive resource utilization.[7]

Intensive US reserve utilization can be explained by the demand side of the equation. Although there is a real competition between Saudi Arabia and Russia for the title of world's largest producer (each have about 12%-13% market share) and a wide range of countries produce more than two percent of the world's oil, consumption is not nearly so well distributed. When it comes to oil usage, the US has no competition. Americans consume almost 23% of the world's oil, which is almost as much as is consumed in Europe and Eurasia combined. China, the second largest consumer, accounts for about 10%,[8] but oil consumption is growing much more rapidly in China. Over the course of time, the consumption gap between China and the US has been narrowing. If development trends continue in China, eventually China will overtake the US as the largest consumer of transportation fuel.

The China Factor

There is no better illustration for the growth of transportation demand than the world's two most populous countries, China and India, respectively. Combined they have more than two and a half billion people – almost half of the world's population. Both of them are developing rapidly, and incomes are rising. China, in particular, is emerging as a global economic power. From 1949 to 1979, China's energy policy was developed through a central planning model. The governmental system was basically patterned after the Soviet Union, and there were heavy subsidies for development of energy resources. In 1979, however, China began a transition toward a market economy.[9]

One of the great questions in the context of the geopolitical struggle for oil is whether the great oil consuming nations, which will soon include the US, China, and Russia, will view one another as allies, competitors, or some combination of both. Will two of these nations gang up on the third, and, if so, will the US be part of such a pact or will it be left to face a Chinese-Russian alliance determined to undermine American interests in the Middle East? Could a conflict over oil involving the three powers lead to a dangerous military confrontation?[10]

The US has love-hate relationships with both countries. There is a historic rivalry between the US and Russia leading back generations. When the Cold War effectively ended in 1989, there were high hopes that Russia could become a strategic US ally. It seemed that improvement in US-Russian relations were on the fast track with the storied "love affair" between George W. Bush and Vladimir Putin. As it would happen, Mr. Bush's love may have been unrequited as relations once again chilled with Russia's renewed imperial ambitions.

The US relationship with China is less familiar to most Americans. Historically, the two nations have been allies. It was US support for China in World War II that set off a series of events that eventually led to the attack on Pearl Harbor and US entry into the war. World War II left the nationalist government of Chiang Kai-shek weak. By 1949, the Communist forces of Mao Zedong took control of the mainland after a long civil war. Chiang Kai-shek was forced to retreat to the island of Taiwan. The "two Chinas" have existed under separate political leadership ever since. For practical purposes, Taiwan is now a separate country even though the US and most other nations do not recognize it as such. One of the most important long term political goals of the Chinese government is reunification with Taiwan.

After Mao's ascension to power, the US continued to recognize the government of Chiang Kai-shek as the proper and legitimate government of China. It was not until President Nixon visited the mainland in 1972 that relations were normalized. Over time, the government of China has evolved toward a more pro-Western view, largely because of their economic interests. Many now characterize China as more ally to the US than adversary. Today, China has a burgeoning market economy and is a key trading partner of the US. The economies of both countries are linked by a web of interdependence, which makes the stability of each country very important to the success of the other.

China has one of the fastest growing economies in the world. When coupled with the unrivaled scale of its population, implications for world energy markets will be far reaching. Between 1990 and 1995, China went from being a net energy exporter to a net importer of energy.[11] It became a net oil importer in 1993.[12] Between 1992 and 2005, China's total national energy consumption more than doubled, while petroleum's share of their energy went from 17.5% to 21%.[13]

It would seem that China has a problem, one with which the US has become all too familiar – it is becoming increasingly dependent on energy from abroad. China has even fewer petroleum reserves than the US (about half as much), yet its petroleum consumption grew at an average annual rate of 6.0% between 1998 and 2008. In the mature US market, consumption grew by only 0.2% annually during the same period,[14] which was still enough to dramatically increase US foreign oil dependence due to rapidly declining domestic production. By 2030, Chinese oil consumption is expected to more than double again while its petroleum production is expected to decline.[15]

Although China's total population is not expected to grow much over the next few decades, more people will be moving into cities. The growth of cities will create significant growth in transportation demand.[16] It is a well-established fact that urbanization of a population is one of the key drivers of demand for transportation. China is currently on pace to have as many vehicles on the road in 2030 as the US has on the road today. By 2035, China could have the largest number of highway vehicles in the world.[17]

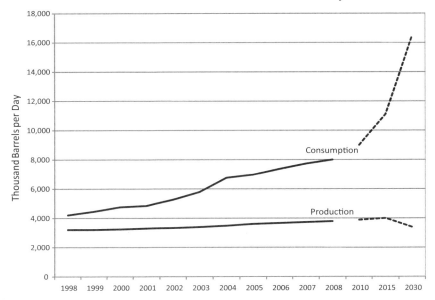

China's Petroleum Production & Consumption

Data from 1998 to 2008 from BP plc, *Statistical Review of World Energy June 2009*; projections from International Energy Agency, *World Energy Investment Outlook 2007*.

Increased demand can mean only one thing – higher prices. Chinese demand and demand from other developing countries are already major contributors to the upward pressure on worldwide petroleum prices. Consumers in the US will be among the victims of those requisite price increases.

For China to meet its transportation fuel needs, it is going to be forced to turn to the same unstable sources of petroleum as the United States. Europe and Japan have long relied on African and Middle Eastern oil for their domestic supplies, but now China and other rapidly industrializing counties will also compete for the same petroleum.[18]

As of 2000, more than half of Chinese oil imports came from Oman and Yemen. Production from those mature fields is expected to decline in coming years, which is forcing China to seek out new sources of supply, particularly in Africa.[19] The actions of China's government indicate an apparent distrust of the international market to deliver reliable supplies. China fears it may at some point be denied access to the oil it needs. To counter market risk, China has sought long-term contracts for access to supplies in nations with which China has a strong bilateral political relationship. The policy of establishing bilateral relations with oil producers has been a key factor in the development of relationships with states that have been known to be supporters of terrorism.[20] In particular, China's relationships with Iran, Burma, and Sudan have drawn criticism.[21] With their growing demand, however, it is unlikely that China will be able to fulfill all of its oil needs solely with bilateral deals; eventually, China too will be forced to rely on oil obtained in the international market.[22]

Just as the US has demonstrated a willingness to use its military to protect its oil supplies, China has likewise began designating military resources to ensure oil it has purchased or produced in other countries is protected and safely reaches the homeland.[23] China is almost exclusively dependent on the Strait of Malacca for oil shipments, which is currently patrolled and protected by the US Navy. China does not presently have the naval capability of ensuring safe passage for its petroleum trade, or, if it chose to do so, to challenge the U.S. naval presence in that area. This relative weakness is the key motivation for steps being taken to increase Chinese naval power.[24]

Modernization of China's naval fleet is only a first step. You can expect that China will continue to modernize and improve its military. In the back of the minds of some Chinese leaders is undoubtedly the potential for conflict with the US. If such a conflict ever did occur, the source of the dispute would most likely be competition over energy supplies. Even though the topic has garnered substantial attention from the political establishment in the US, a conflict resulting from Chinese military aggression to force reunification with Taiwan is a significantly more remote possibility. A military conflict over Taiwan is not in the strategic interest of either the US or China.

Unfortunately, events are already in motion that could set the stage for a US-Chinese confrontation. With the economies of both China and the US growing as worldwide petroleum production fails to keep pace, competition is inevitable. Responsibility lies with the governments of both countries to take actions to avoid the long progression toward a conflict. A Sino-American Energy War is far too likely if both countries continue on their present courses without development of substantial alternative sources of energy.

The Saudis

At the end of 2008, Saudi Arabia was the world's largest petroleum producer and exporter. Even with Russia's resurgent oil industry, which produces almost as much as Saudi Arabia, Saudi Arabia will probably remain the largest exporter for some time to come due to its own limited oil usage.[25] The US has had a long-standing "special" relationship with Saudi Arabia going back all the way to the first meeting between Roosevelt and Ibn Saud in 1945.

Saudi Arabia is the world's most advanced welfare state. Saudis get free healthcare and interest-free loans. College education is free within the kingdom and highly subsidized abroad. Electricity, domestic air travel, gasoline and telephone services are available at well below cost due to government subsidies. All taxes in Saudi Arabia were lifted in 1973. As a result, there is no revenue connection between the Saudi regime and society. Virtually all state revenue comes from either oil or foreign investment income, and petroleum makes up almost all of Saudi exports.[26]

Many analysts in the intelligence community are concerned about the stability of the regime in Saudi Arabia. Among the most vocal critics is former CIA officer Robert Baer, who spent a considerable portion of his career in the Middle East. Baer claims that the Saudi population largely believes the endless wealth has corrupted the royal family and that they have stood by while the population has grown poorer. They are seen as having failed to protect Islam as well as fellow Muslims in Palestine and elsewhere. He also asserts that the Saudi police force is corrupt and that the rule of law is a sham.[27] In short, political conditions are not all that different from those in Iran prior to the fall of the Shah.

Another harsh and surprising critic of the Saudi regime is the daughter of Sheik Yamani, the famous former oil minister. Speaking about the corruption and hypocrisy of the royal family, she remarked,

> ...It makes me very sad because you're watching this behavior, and you're watching the decay, and these people are putting their head in the sand and waiting until the place burns. The royal family has alienated vast majorities of the Saudi people to whom they give their names. They know they are losing power.[28]

Baer, whose book inspired the movie *Syriana*, made perhaps his most shocking assertion in a 2003 article. He claimed that if free and fair elections were held in Saudi Arabia, Osama Bin Laden would be elected the president in a landslide. Baer claims that his popularity stems not from Arab hatred for the West but from the fact that, "Bin Laden has dared to do what even the mighty United States of America won't do: stand up to the thieves who rule the country."[29]

Both a blessing and a curse for the Saudi regime is the size of the royal family. By most accounts, there are at least 5,000 princes in the royal family of Saudi Arabia. From a positive standpoint, such a large family gives the Saudis a broader base from which to rule. There are a lot of people with a vested interest in keeping the regime in power. On the other hand, royals, particularly Saudi royals, are very expensive. Few can hardly imagine spending as lavishly as a Saudi prince.

As if 5,000 were not enough, the Saudi royal family keeps growing and growing. A healthy prince might sire 40 to 70 children during his lifetime. With exploding populations, some believe the size of the family could reach 60,000 or more within a generation.[30] Royals receive special privileges and often stipends. As the size of the family continues to grow, the cost of royal perks will become increasingly burdensome to the Saudi economy, and greater strain between the royals and the population is likely.

To complicate matters for the royal family, the current ruler, King Abdullah, is not particularly popular within his own family. His mother was not from among the Saud, but instead from the Rashid tribe, who were among Ibn Saud's rivals as he sought to expand his control of the Arabian Peninsula in the early twentieth century. The marriage was political, intended to cement a truce with the Rashid.[31]

The political future for Saudi Arabia is uncertain. Next in line for succession to the Saudi throne is Crown Prince Sultan, who has been Saudi Defense Minister for over four decades. He is among those in the royal family with the closest ties to the West, but he is also widely perceived as corrupt. His succession is likely only to intensify criticism of the royal family's rule.

Meanwhile, the birth rate in Saudi Arabia has soared to one of the highest in the world. Half of the population is under the age of 18. The mere presence of so many young people entering the workforce places enormous pressure on an economy, particularly in an economy without an abundance of employment opportunities.[32] Demographics paint a bleak picture for the long-term viability of the Saudi regime.

Given the close relationship between the US and the Saudi government, it should probably come as no surprise that there are many current and former high-ranking US government officials with close ties to the Saudis and to the Saudi oil industry. Among those tied directly to Saudi cash through private sector dealings and investment partnerships are former Secretary of State James Baker, National Security Advisor Frank Carlucci, British Prime Minister John Major, Vice President Dick Cheney, and President George H. W. Bush. In addition, Secretary of State Condoleezza Rice, former US Senator Sam Nunn, former Treasury Secretary Nicholas Brady, former Senator and Democratic vice presidential candidate Lloyd Bentsen, and former CIA director John Deutch are among those who have served on the boards of directors of one or more companies partnering with the Saudis in various business ventures.[33]

Of course, there is nothing inherently wrong with doing business with the Saudis, which is often unavoidable given their wealth and pervasiveness throughout the business world. Merely doing business with someone does not mean you are corrupt or that you are willing to subordinate the interest of your country to the pursuit of profit. The close association of many top government officials with the Saudis does, however, have the potential to instill among policy makers a greater comfort level with the Saudis than their actions should warrant. Put another way, close association often leads to giving your associates the benefit of the doubt.

Although a continued friendly relationship with Saudi Arabia is beneficial for both countries, the US should be careful. Given the unstable conditions, the regime could fall. Such events usually occur without much prior warning, and the US intelligence community has a dismal track record predicting revolutions. If a change does occur, it is vital to US interests in the region to avoid the perception of trying to repress the Arab people in hopes of furthering economic interests.

The Economics of Oil

Oil is a commodity and it behaves as such in markets. The same forces of supply and demand that govern everything else govern oil. The difference between oil and other commodities, and the argument for why it is "special," relates to oil's strategic importance. Oil is important to almost every other economic activity, and there are currently no practical substitutes for it.

The primary concern of consumers is availability and price of transportation fuel, for which the most important determinant is the price of crude. Crude prices are, to a large extent, a function of the policies of the Organization of Petroleum Exporting Countries (OPEC). Therefore, OPEC, more than any other participant in the market, determines the price at the pump. Refining and marketing also play a role in setting price, as does the level of local competition. It is these midstream and downstream forces, along with variability in state and local gasoline tax rates, which account for differences in gasoline prices from one area to another.

World oil markets can be characterized as volatile and upward trending. Economic growth and highly expansionary monetary policies have been among the key drivers for crude oil demand expansion. Given inelastic oil demand and supply, any small excess demand would require a large price increase to clear oil markets. Conditions, therefore, are ideal to see oil price increases.[34]

A major shift in market power has been occurring in the oil industry over the last few decades. Although the oil multinationals still enjoy record profits, their dominance of the market has been ceded to national oil companies – the state-controlled ventures that monopolize the supply of their home countries. Most oil reserves are owned by national governments. Less than 3% of the world's proven reserves of conventional oil are owned by ExxonMobil, BP, Total, Chevron and Royal Dutch Shell combined.[35] Oil companies are really production, transportation, refining, and marketing companies, but the assets belong to players such as Saudi Arabia, Kuwait, Iran, Iraq, Libya, and even the US government.

The rise of the national oil companies introduces a new, disturbing dynamic to the market. Instead of purely commercial arrangements, oil transactions take on political character. Instead of seeking to purely maximize profits, national oil companies take on the goal of furthering the political ambitions of the leaders of their countries.

The consequence of this new trend is a rapid growth in so-called state-to-state arrangements, oil deals that come with military assistance, economic assistance, and trade concessions. Such extra concessions are a tool intended to establish preferential access to supplies. Preferential oil deals have the potential to be especially alarming when one considers that they represent a movement toward secret deals and away from transparent markets where allocations are made based on prices determined through forces of supply and demand. China and India are especially aggressive in promoting such arrangements. Chinese agreements for oil access with Sudan and Angola are good examples.[36]

Modern OPEC

There are significant disagreements about the true nature of the Organization of Petroleum Exporting Countries (OPEC). Some argue it is a cartel that acts as a monopoly, an oligopoly, or a dominant firm; others argue it is not a cartel at all and that its members compete. There are also more complex arguments that classify Saudi Arabia as a dominant firm within OPEC, while OPEC as a whole fits various other economic classifications.[37]

If one cannot look back into the past, analyze OPEC's behavior, and state with certainty whether OPEC is a syndicate, a cartel, or a trade organization populated with competing members, then how could it be possible to look into the future and predict OPEC's likely reaction to any series of events? OPEC's nature is constantly evolving. It is what it is at a given moment in time, and as surely as you classify it, it will change because the members all have different and evolving agendas.

There are two fundamentally different types of countries that comprise the members of OPEC, and, because of their divergent natures, they are often at odds. Where they differ is in their need for cash. Countries with large populations relative to their production levels need to maximize profits because they need large amounts of income to support their economy over a broad population. Iran, Nigeria, and Venezuela are examples of such countries. Kuwait and Saudi Arabia are examples of countries that have much higher production relative to their populations. They don't need (and indeed can't spend) the massive inflows of cash. They prefer to keep prices lower to defend their market share by depressing the popularity of conservation measures and alternative fuels. Ahmed Yamani, retired long-time Saudi oil minister, is well known for his arguments that higher oil prices are not in the interests of oil producers. Escalating costs, he warns, will force importers to seek alternative sources for their fuel. Of particular concern to Yamani is Hugo Chavez, a key figure within OPEC championing higher prices, a position Yamani attributes to \Venezuela's failure to invest in new production capabilities.[38]

OPEC is not all-powerful in the sense that they can determine the state of the overall global economy. Evidence actually supports the notion that OPEC responds to macroeconomic conditions, not the other way around.[39] Studies also show that OPEC quotas do affect production both in the short and long term. This means that OPEC does exercise market power over both production and prices.[40]

An analysis of OPEC's historical actions in response to changes in the market price for oil yield one inescapable conclusion: OPEC members are chronic cheaters on their production quotas, constantly producing more oil than the quotas allow. From 1986 through 2003, Saudi Arabia and Iran have most closely adhered to their quotas, while Algeria and the United Arab Emirates have been the more flagrant overproducers.[41]

OPEC has no monitoring system, no punishment for members who cheat on their quotas, and no overriding authority.[42] Higher oil prices invariably cause greater production by some individual OPEC members, which is competitive behavior that would not be expected in a classic cartel.[43] Evidence also indicates, however, that OPEC members share excesses and shortages, which undermines the theory that OPEC members are competing with each other for market share.[44]

The 1980s brought major changes to the world oil industry. In 1981, President Reagan removed all price and allocation controls on crude oil and refined products. Market forces alone were allowed to regulate the flows and price of oil. Shortly thereafter, an even more fundamental change was occurring in the oil industry. Before the 1980s, the price for most oil traded in world markets was determined by long-term contracts. By 1982, however, more than half of all oil traded internationally was priced based on the spot market.[45] In 1983, the New York Mercantile Exchange (NYMEX) introduced the trading of crude oil futures, which was the final blow to OPEC's ability to defend a specific price for oil.[46] OPEC saw that conditions were changing, and in 1982 it shifted to the system still in use today – setting production quotas for its members.[47]

Although the price now fluctuates, OPEC still largely controls the market. The wealth of real time market information, abundance of traders, and liquidity of the market give rise to the illusion of a market-derived pricing scheme. In the words of noted energy economist Morris

Adelman, "...the market sets the price...but who controls the market? Under competition, nobody does, because nobody controls supply. Since the OPEC nations change supply up or down to set the price, they control the market."[48] The shift in OPEC was therefore a distinction without a difference; monopoly power still rested in the same place.

OPEC's most significant recent challenge came from the liberation of Iraq. Under Saddam Hussein, Iraq kept production in line with the quotas, which are normally set at the same level as Iran's. Advocates of invading Iraq, however, envisioned a takeover of its oil industry by free enterprise. Under the "neocon" vision, Iraq's oil reserves would be auctioned off to competing operators. Those operators, without any government-imposed constraints, would quickly ramp up production to the highest level possible (estimated at 6 million barrels per day), thereby maximizing profits.[49] Of course, that didn't happen. Iraqi oil is now firmly under government control, with the idea that Iraq will continue to adhere to its OPEC production quota. The most significant threat to OPEC power in years was quelled not by forces within it, but rather by advocates for the US domestic oil industry.

Saudi Arabia holds a unique position in world petroleum markets. It maintains, by far, the largest idle production capacity. It is so large, in fact, that they can single-handedly replace, within a short period of time, a total loss of exports from any other oil exporting nation.[50] This makes Saudi Arabia the world's swing producer. Their swing production is not symmetrical, however. Falling prices reduce Saudi production faster than rising prices increase it; they cut production rapidly to prevent sharp price declines.[51] Their bias is toward defending prices more than staving-off price escalations, but that probably should not come as a surprise to anyone.

Because of its production scale, Saudi Arabia behaves differently in setting its oil policies than do other members of OPEC. Other members tend to take the lead of Saudi Arabia and set their policies accordingly, while Saudi Arabia tends to set its own policies without being considerably influenced by the other members. The role of Saudi Arabia seems to be a manifestation of the fact that other members are too small to impact Saudi price leadership.[52]

In response to the 1973 oil crisis, the International Energy Agency (IEA) was established in 1974. Its 26 member countries are obligated to hold stocks equivalent to 90 days worth of oil imports. The agency's real purpose, however, is an oil sharing mechanism. Under the IEA system, if one or more member countries experience a significant supply disruption, it can request the oil sharing mechanism be triggered. Depending on the severity, conservation measures may be instituted in other member countries or actual oil supplies may be shared. The system, as yet, has never been triggered.[53]

Although the OPEC cartel's monopoly power is widely discussed and frequently used to its members' advantage, the US is actually not without power of its own. The US market is a very large percentage of the world oil market. Accordingly, the US has monopsony power. If the US, or a group of countries including the US, takes actions to control purchases, it can influence the price of oil in much the same way as does the OPEC cartel.[54] Just as there are export quotas, importing countries could set import quotas. In fact, the US has done this in the past. To do it again, however, would require substantially greater political will than is pervasive with today's leaders.

Around the same time that the IEA was created, the US established the Strategic Petroleum Reserve (SPR), in part to meet US obligations under the agreement. The SPR is a system of huge salt caverns along the Gulf of Mexico designed to hold large quantities of crude oil. It contains, as of November 16, 2009, 725.0 million barrels of crude oil.[55] To put the volume in perspective, it is slightly less that the total petroleum reserves of Trinidad & Tobago.[56] Total capacity of the SPR was 727 million barrels as of 2008, but the Energy Policy Act of 2005 authorized its increase to 1 billion barrels.[57] At 2008 import levels, SPR inventory provides about 56 days of protection.[58] Private storage adds enough capacity to meet the IEA 90-day requirement.

Even with all of these countermeasures and US monopsony power, OPEC remains the dominant force in world petroleum markets. The SPR and IEA framework provide nominal protection against another supply shock, but the US remains vulnerable and exposed by virtue of its overwhelming oil dependence. An opportunity was missed in Iraq, but the real opportunity lies in curbing dependence on OPEC (and on foreign oil in general) with alternative fuels.

Oil-Based Economies (Petro-States)

Imagine, for a moment, that you are a citizen of an impoverished Third-World country. Suddenly, oil is discovered near your home. Have your fortunes just improved, or have you been cursed? It would seem that discovery of oil in a poor country would be a good thing for its people, that the new-found wealth would save its population from the scourge of poverty. Unfortunately, however, history has shown this logical premise to be absolutely untrue in most cases. In fact, the discovery of oil has tended to precede even greater poverty for a country's population, and standards of living have tended to drop dramatically below levels before the discovery.[59]

Such countries are often referred to as "petro-states." Perhaps the best way to illustrate the concept of a petro-state is to reminisce about the 1960s television program *The Beverly Hillbillies*. In the show, a backwoods family with no education and no exposure to the modern world suddenly strikes oil. With their newfound riches, they leave the backwoods and move to a mansion in Beverly Hills. It is there that their ignorance of the world contrasted against the lavish and cosmopolitan setting provides irresistible comedy. Petro-states are surprisingly similar. Cash-rich rogue states on the loose in the world, however, are hardly a laughing matter, and petro-states are seldom as endearing as was TV's Clampett family.

Oil-led development often initially seems to work. Per capita income rises and there are more employment opportunities. Countries have better nutrition, health, and infrastructure. These improvements, history has shown, have rapidly been undermined. The booms quickly turn to busts.[60]

The problem begins with governments, which, in most cases, are holders of the state's mineral rights. They negotiate with oil companies for capital investment and revenue sharing, a process that can be complicated by the fact that enormous oil multinationals often dwarf, in terms of sheer economic might, the countries in which they operate.[61] Powerful oil companies, both foreign and domestic, tend to have inordinate power in petro-states and play large roles in the decision making, often morphing laws and legal structure in their favor.[62]

Once deals are made and oil is flowing, governments must decide what to do with the profits from their oil exports. They determine national priorities, allocation of resources, and who should reap the rewards (generally some individuals, regions, or groups more than others). The government may not necessarily act in the public interest; it may be more interested in its own fortunes than its people's.[63]

In petro-states, ruling elites end up with the preponderance of oil revenues while the rest of the population suffers in poverty.[64] The reason for this phenomenon relates to a confluence of economic and political power. Even in the West, where governments are relatively transparent, there is a clear link between the rich and the powerful. The rich make campaign contributions; in return, the powerful provide them with high-level access and favors.

In the less-developed world, links are much more concrete. Because petroleum production is highly capital intensive, only the largest and wealthiest companies or states can participate. Petroleum production is also highly profitable, however, often dwarfing all other sources of revenue for a small, undeveloped nation. The combination of these factors tends to concentrate revenue where economic and political power is already highly concentrated. In effect, only the powerful can grant the opportunity to make money from oil, and only those who are granted the opportunity can provide resources needed to keep regimes in power. The result is a symbiotic relationship where both the rich and the powerful need each other to exist.[65]

To defend the elite, governments form large, well-equipped security forces that gain privileged status to ensure their continued allegiance.[66] Militarization goes hand–in-hand with oil wealth. From 1984 to 1994, OPEC countries spent three times as much as developed countries and ten times as much as non-oil exporting developing countries on defense.[67] In 2005, of the ten countries with the highest defense spending as a percentage of GDP, eight were in the Middle East (the other two were the US and Singapore, which is a major Asian oil refining center). Saudi Arabia trails only the US and Russia in terms of total defense spending and is, by far, the largest importer of foreign made arms.[68]

When oil is first discovered in a country, it often creates expectations that things will improve for a population. When it becomes clear that expectations and reality are very different, it can be a recipe for disorder and war. To quell the masses, governments often resort to using force against its own population. History has shown that oil exporters are among the most troubled, authoritarian, and conflict-ridden states in the world.[69]

In 2001, Michael Ross, then a visiting scholar at the World Bank, performed a detailed mathematical analysis of the relationship between oil production and political governance. His conclusions confirmed what many had already surmised from their own observations. Oil does hinder democracy – and not just in the Middle East. Furthermore, the poorer the state, the greater the effect will be.[70]

Volatility of oil prices also plays a major role in the weakness of petro-governments. Because of volatile price fluctuation, it is almost impossible to accurately estimate future oil revenues, which tends to result in unrealistic revenue projections. The projections further raise expectations and result in increased appetites for spending (and decrease its quality). More government spending often results in domestic inflation and the rapid growth of foreign debt.

The discovery of petroleum can even disrupt and replace pre-existing industries that were once healthy. Agriculture, for example, can often be sacrificed. It is easier to import food and manufactured goods than produce them domestically if the government is awash in foreign currency. As such, exportation of oil can serve to handicap development of other productive activities.[71] To amplify the effect, exportation of oil often causes a phenomenon known as "Dutch Disease," which occurs because windfalls from oil push up the real exchange rate for a country's currency, making other export products uncompetitive in the international marketplace.[72]

Although Spain is not a major oil producer, it has some experience with the same circumstances now being experienced by oil exporters. With the discovery and conquest of the Americas, Spain became one of the richest countries in the world by virtue of its discovery and plunder of gold. Spain would take gold from the New World and use it to buy things: food, manufactured goods, art, whatever it wanted or needed. By the time the flow of gold ceased, Spain had lost its ability to produce domestically and forever lost its status as a world power.[73]

Perhaps the best example of a quintessential petro-state is Saudi Arabia. The fortunes of Saudi Arabia are irreversibly tied to oil. Nowhere is a ruling elite more clearly defined. At least 5,000 Saudi princes receive stipends from the government, some in the multi-million dollar per year range, yet per capita income has seen great long term volatility. In 1981, it was $28,600, but by 2001 it had fallen to just $6,800.[74] By 2007, however, it had rebounded with the high price of oil to $20,700.[75] Even with prices increasing, it will probably never again reach its peak 1981 levels due to staggering population growth. Despite that fact, Saudi Arabia retains its title as having the largest per capita defense spending.[76]

The Oil Industry Cash Trap

Private industry is the engine and foundation of the US economy. It provides jobs to millions of Americans, feeds their families, and pays for the education of their children. It improves the standard of living for all Americans, and remains the primary source of US power in the world.

Profit has become a dirty word among some in the political intelligencia, but it is truly the primary motivation for productivity and innovation. The defects inherent in a system without a profit incentive, such as Communism, are apparent to all who have even a modest knowledge of the now-defunct Soviet Union. Even Maoist China is hurriedly transforming to a market economy. The only remaining traces of that flawed ideology are in Cuba and North Korea, neither of which have a problem with immigration. Profit is essential to spur innovation, motivate the workforce, and properly deploy capital.

The problem with the oil industry, however, is that it is largely excluded from the free market system. For starters, there are extremely high barriers to entry. For example, most of the world's oil is under the control of various governments. To be in the oil business one must convince these governments to grant an oil concession. That is no easy task considering all of the best resources (such as in the Middle East) are already taken. Entering the refining business is equally daunting, requiring years of permitting and overcoming aggressive environmental opposition in most developed countries. Of course, even if all of those issues are overcome, there is still the need for huge amounts of capital.

The oil industry has found itself the popular villain for many years going all the way back to Rockefeller. Over that time, the image of the industry has become monopolistic, over-powerful, speculative and risky, conspiratorial, wasteful, disorderly, out to gouge consumers, out to corrupt government, and a threat to public welfare.[77] Some of that criticism is well deserved, but much of it has been overblown.

The business of oil lends itself to centralized control. It is for this reason that there are very few major oil companies in the world. In fact, as discussed in an earlier chapter, it took John D. Rockefeller only 23 years to gain almost total control over the oil industry from the time the first commercial oil well was drilled in the US. Today the industry remains under the near complete control of just a few major players, almost all of which are either currently or formerly state-owned or are companies formed during the breakup of Rockefeller's Standard Oil. OPEC has effectively gained control over the actual oil resources themselves.

The fact that so much power is concentrated in the hands of so few sets the oil industry apart from many other industries. In a highly concentrated market forces of supply and demand are not allowed to operate freely, and the consumer usually becomes a victim. In the oil industry, there is not sufficient supply-side competition. Meanwhile, demand is highly inelastic. The confluence of these factors results in enormous market power for the few suppliers, which tends to result in very high prices.[78]

The era of the Bush Administration was one of the most profitable periods in the history of the industry, a fact that probably won't come as a surprise to many people. Some of that profit relates to upstream crude oil reserves. As the price of crude oil has risen in the world market, oil companies have benefited to the extent that they drill and extract crude oil. The increase in crude oil prices, however, does not completely explain the record profits. In fact, since the US invasion of Iraq in 2003, profit from the refining and marketing sector has, on average, doubled.[79]

The rise in oil company profits is not nearly as alarming as what those companies are doing with the cash flow. One might expect they would be using the funds for more drilling, or, as several oil companies' public relations campaigns would have you believe, alternative energy. Reality, however, is much, much different.

After the first oil shock in 1973, oil companies attempted a variety of diversification strategies with their improved cash flow. While most invested in related industries like mining and chemicals, a few ventured into such disparate ventures as retailing and meat production. By 1990, however, almost all of oil companies had counted their diversified investments as failures and returned to their core business. Reasons for their failures were numerous. One of the biggest problems was cultural. Managers in oil companies were accustomed to projects that require very long lead times – typically seven years. They were unable to adapt to other industries that require much quicker decisions and reactions to market conditions. Exxon's foray into information processing was particularly egregious.[80]

Considering Exxon's previous adventures and the fact that it is, by far, the most profitable corporation in the world, it is fitting to begin with it. In 2007, ExxonMobil Corporation earned $40.6 billion in net income, but it took in over $52 billion in cash from operations. While some of it was reinvested, mostly in overseas oil and gas exploration and production projects, nearly $40 billion was either paid out as dividends or used to repurchase stock. If Exxon spent anything at all on alternatives to petroleum, the amount was so small it didn't appear in their financial statements. In fact, the only mention of alternative energy in the company's annual report filing with the US Securities and Exchange Commission (SEC) was as a risk factor that may adversely affect their operating results in the future.[81]

A more interesting case might be BP plc. In 2000, the old name, British Petroleum, was jettisoned in favor of just "BP." The company created a new logo and rebranded itself with the slogan "Beyond Petroleum."[82] BP's marketing now portrays it as a next-generation company focusing on alternatives to oil. As with Exxon, the truth is revealed when we follow the money. BP generated just over $24.7 billion in cash from operations resulting in profits just short of $21.2 billion in 2007; $7.1 billion went to stock repurchases and $8.3 billion to dividends, a total of $15.4 billion. Unlike Exxon, BP claims to invest $1.5 billion per year in their alternative energy business. Upon further investigation, however, their alternative energy business is almost entirely comprised of manufacturing solar panels and generating electricity from wind and natural gas. While these businesses are certainly meritorious, they have very little to do with alternatives to petroleum.[83]

Even with so many billions in record profits, profits some considered outrageous, virtually nothing has been invested in alternatives to oil. Instead, oil companies used most of that money to buy back stock and pay dividends. Ultimately, it is not so much the public that should be upset about these practices, but rather the companies' shareholders. Managements are squandering a historic opportunity not only to profit in the short term, but to position their companies for the future. Unfortunately, they seem to be far too much like the petro-states with whom they so closely associate, living in the moment and relishing cash with little preparation for the days when the world will leave them behind.

9
I Think I Lost My Appetite

Oil addiction is indeed a multi-faceted problem. In a broad sense, there are two ways to tackle it: curb demand or expand supply. Without Americans' love for their cars and the personal freedom that they bring, reducing petroleum demand would not be so difficult. Mobility is a defining characteristic of America, both in the figurative sense (as in upward career and socio-economic mobility) and in a literal sense. It is a psychological underpinning of American identity. The philosophy of mobility, which has been bred into Americans for generations and has been a beacon to draw immigrants from around the world, will not easily be quelled, nor should it be.

Conservation is certainly an important concept, but meaningful reductions in fuel demand will require more. Wasteful, superfluous personal travel can be reduced, but the real impact will have to come from technological advances that improve the fuel efficiency of traditional vehicles and make possible the development of advanced vehicles that go farther on less fuel.

Environmentalists make fuel economy the centerpiece of their energy policies, but auto manufacturers claim that its costs will destroy their businesses. Commonly referred to as vehicle miles per gallon, fuel economy has sparked some of the most spirited and hostile debates in our quest for sound energy policy. The concept is simple – the farther a vehicle can go on a given gallon of fuel, the less fuel that vehicle will use. If spread over a large number of vehicles, improved fuel economy can have a considerable impact on the amount of fuel that a nation consumes.

There are a variety of ways that fuel economy can be improved. Estimates by the National Academy of Sciences show the potential for a safe and affordable 25% cut in average new vehicle fuel use within a dozen years.[1] Automakers acknowledge that they have many engineering options at their disposal, especially for improving the least efficient vehicles – SUVs and light trucks. In the future, advancements such as variable valve timing and lift control, displacement on demand, reduced aerodynamic drag, continuously variable transmissions, and engine friction reduction have the potential to improve fuel economy without sacrificing safety.[2]

GM is already developing displacement-on-demand technology that shuts down some cylinders when excess power isn't needed to save fuel. Ford has researched electric throttle control, continuously variable transmissions, adding valves, and taking excess weight out of engine and chassis components. Chrysler has touted a series of engineering tweaks that could improve efficiency in some vehicles by 25%.[3]

Many conventional technologies intended to improve fuel efficiency have already been researched extensively and implemented in at least some commercial vehicles. Using only technologies that (a) were sold in the US in 2005 in at least one mass-market vehicle and (b) can pay for themselves in fuel savings over 50,000 vehicles miles assuming fuel cost of $1.50 per gallon, average fuel economy of the car and light truck fleet could be improved by 24%-26%. Implementation of these technologies would add about $800-$1000 to the retail price of a vehicle.[4]

Additionally, technologies such as advanced lean exhaust gas after-treatment systems for high-speed diesels and direct-injection gasoline engines, which are currently under development, could offer further improvements on fuel efficiencies.[5] The cost of direct injection gasoline and diesel engines is not economical to deploy based on the 50,000 mile fuel savings standard at $1.50 per gallon, but with higher fuel prices the technology looks more promising.[6] Prior to widespread acceptance, however, significant improvements will have to be made in vehicle emission technology for direct-injection to comply with environmental regulations.[7]

Aside from technological advances to the power train, engine, and aerodynamic profile of a vehicle, the largest gains in fuel efficiency could come from decreasing a vehicle's weight. This approach draws criticism because studies have shown that occupant safety is a function of, more than any other individual factor, vehicle weight.[8]

Vehicles weights have actually increased over time. The increases are the result of two trends: the growth of the average weight of vehicles within individual vehicle classes and skewing sales toward larger vehicles classes (such as SUVs).[9] As vehicles have evolved, more and more features have been added that increase safety, reduce noise, reduce emissions, and improve the overall driving experience. Each of these additions has required the installation of new components. Increasingly, these components have been structural. The more components added to a vehicle, the more its weight increases. Although design improvements and materials substitution have curtailed weight of individual components, the sheer number of new features has led to a substantial growth.[10]

One way to reduce weight is to gravitate away from the use of heavy metals in favor of carbon composites. Carbon composites are widely used in aerospace because they can be stronger and tougher than steel but yet weigh considerably less (25%-35% as much). Because they are very strong, they can actually absorb more crash energy than steel.[11] Even with a stronger construction, a lighter vehicle remains at a safety disadvantage because, regardless of the strength of the materials, heavier vehicles provide a greater resistance to a change in velocity.

Although the technology is available, the market has been unable to produce significant advances in vehicle fuel economy. Where the market has failed, the government has shown a track record of success. Experience shows that government intervention will be necessary for any major improvements of fuel economy.

Regulating Fuel Efficiency

In the US, fuel economy standards are regulated for cars and light trucks, but not for other types of vehicles. In the wake of the Arab oil embargo, there was great interest in promoting fuel economy. Sadly, that goal seems less imperative today. In 1975, the Energy Policy Conservation Act was passed into law, which established standards for passenger cars and light trucks. The means for regulating fuel economy is a standard commonly known as CAFE.

According to the National Highway Traffic Safety Administration, the federal agency responsible for implementing the fuel economy regulations:

> Corporate Average Fuel Economy (CAFE) is the sales weighted average fuel economy, expressed in miles per gallon (mpg), of a manufacturer's fleet of passenger cars or light trucks with a gross vehicle weight rating (GVWR) of 8,500 lbs. or less, manufactured for sale in the United States, for any given model year. Fuel economy is defined

as the average mileage traveled by an automobile per gallon of gasoline (or equivalent amount of other fuel) consumed as measured in accordance with the testing and evaluation protocol set forth by the Environmental Protection Agency (EPA).[12]

Basically, CAFE requires car manufacturers to take an average of the miles per gallon efficiency of all the cars produced for the US market. That average must not exceed the CAFE standard, which has been unchanged at 27.5 miles per gallon since 1990.[13] Almost unfathomably, the government has not required any improvement in car fuel economy for a generation. Put another way, a baby born when the current standards were established was eligible to vote in the 2008 Presidential election.

Light trucks, which include sport utility vehicles (SUVs), are regulated differently. Under the law that established CAFE, authority to set the specific fuel economy standards for light trucks was delegated to the National Highway Transportation Safety Administration. Light truck standards rose from 17.5 miles per gallon in 1982 to 20.7 miles per gallon in 1996. They did not change again until 2005, when they began to rise gradually to 22.2 miles per gallon in 2007.[14]

CAFE has proven remarkably effective. From 1978 to 1985, a period of continuous increases in fuel economy standards, US oil usage steadily decreased. Reduced consumption from 1978 to 1985 was achieved despite a 15% percent increase in vehicle miles traveled during that same period.[15]

Fuel economy averaged just 13.6 miles per gallon in 1978. If it had remained at that level in 1992, the nearly 2.1 trillion miles traveled by passenger cars and light trucks over that period would have required an additional 46 billion gallons of petroleum,[16] an amount equivalent to more than all the proved reserves in the US and Mexico combined.[17]

Beginning in 1986, the US experienced a period of low oil prices. When oil prices collapsed, interest in increasing fuel economy waned.[18] It was no longer a pressing political issue. For this reason, along with resistance from the automotive industry, CAFE standards have been largely forgotten as a means of promoting increased fuel efficiency. While fuel economy standards have changed little, travel demand has grown due to increasing population, greater economic activity, higher incomes, and increasing geographical dispersion.[19] The result has been greater petroleum usage and greater dependence on foreign sources of oil.

Car manufacturers didn't stop innovating, however. Since 1975, car manufacturers have made considerable improvements in the basic efficiency of engines, drive trains, and vehicles aerodynamics, which could have been used either for improved fuel economy or improved vehicle performance. When emphasis was on improved fuel economy, innovations were targeted to achieve that goal, but thereafter, technology improvements have been concentrated principally on performance. Since 1990, fuel economy remained essentially unchanged while the average vehicle became 20% heavier and gained 25% on its 0-60 miles per hour acceleration time.[20]

Despite the auto industry's demonstrated ability to improve on vehicle technology, it aggressively opposes CAFE standards or at least an increase in the targets. The industry claims: higher efficiency targets could force it to market products that are inferior and out of step with consumer tastes and preferences; fuel economy gains will force increases in the retail price of the vehicles, adversely impacting sales; and increased standards could result in sacrificing safety in favor of fuel economy by decreasing vehicle size and weight. Finally, the industry argues that some manufacturers are disadvantaged relative to others because the structure of CAFE benefits companies that focus on a limited line of smaller vehicles at the expense of full-line manufacturers.[21]

Most of their justification for opposing fuel economy standards is pure rubbish. The same arguments that are directed at CAFE standards have been used by the automakers to decry catalytic converters and air bags. Once rules required those items, however, automakers quickly adapted.[22]

Efficiency standards imposed after the oil crisis of the mid-1970s forced automakers to improve efficiency in time for what would become the second oil shock in 1979 from the Iranian Revolution. The president of the United Auto Workers admitted in 1980 that the auto industry and its workers would have suffered much more if efficiency standards had not already been enacted.[23]

The final automaker argument, that some manufacturers are disadvantaged relative to others, is actually a legitimate concern. CAFE standards, which require all manufactures to meet the same targets regardless of product lines or mix, disadvantages domestic manufacturers.[24] Domestic manufacturers typically market a broad range of vehicle choices for consumers, from small lightweight compact cars to much larger high performance luxury cars and sport utility vehicles. The board product mix makes compliance with CAFE standards more difficult than for many foreign manufacturers who produce only smaller, more economical cars. US manufacturers have argued, therefore, that the structure of the standard is unfairly biased against them.

Clearly, CAFE has its structural inadequacies. Despite that fact, it is hard to argue against the overall goal of promoting fuel economy; the question is how, specifically, to do it. CAFE can be improved and there are certainly other options for fuel economy regulation. Almost every developed nation in the world has some type of fuel economy standard, but they vary widely from country to country. The US has CAFE, Japan and China have standards based on vehicle weight, and the European Union has comprehensive voluntary standards.[25]

One obvious problem with CAFE is that the penalty for violating it is absurdly low. Even with a recent increase in the fine, the amount a manufacturer must pay is only $55 per vehicle for each mile per gallon its fleet is below the standard.[26] Many manufacturers, particularly European luxury car makers, simply consider the fines a cost of doing business. They continue to make cars with lower fuel efficiency and simply pay the fines, passing the costs on to consumers. A fine does not dissuade an activity if is so low that paying it does not have a material impact on the company's profitability.

Another major criticism of CAFE standards is that once a manufacturer meets the goal, there is no incentive to continue to improve.[27] One proposed solution to this problem is a program called "fee-bates". Generally, a fee-bate imposes a government mandated system of charges and refunds on a revenue neutral basis to encourage a desired activity. Although there can be endless variations on the application of such a system, in the simplest form manufacturers (or buyers) of vehicles pay a charge when a vehicle has fuel efficiency below the average in their category. Proceeds from those fees would then be paid out as rebates for vehicles that have better than average fuel economy.

A key advantage of a fee-bate system is that it provides a continuous incentive to adopt new technologies and improve fuel economy with manufacturers always striving for improvement to avoid fees or gain rebates. This is particularly attractive considering the political difficulty associated with raising CAFE targets over the last 20 years.[28]

Some economists have long argued that higher fuel taxes in the US are a better way of promoting fuel economy than CAFE targets or other similar fuel efficiency standards. They believe an increase in fuel taxes will curb fuel demand by reducing vehicle miles traveled as transportation becomes more expensive. A related but distinct theory is that higher gasoline taxes would also create incentives for manufactures to build more efficient vehicles. Taxes tend to be favored because they theoretically give more flexibility to vehicle manufacturers and consumers.[29] Gasoline is, of course, already taxed at both federal and state levels in the US.

Gasoline taxes in the US have historically been low compared to taxes in Europe and Japan, where rates (and therefore fuel prices) have been much higher. Proponents of higher gasoline taxes cite studies showing that gasoline demand is highly elastic, so much so that a relatively small increase in fuel prices (about $0.50) would have the same effect in gasoline savings as a 25% increase in CAFE standards.[30] As evidence, they cite data indicating that, on average, a new vehicle travels 13,000 miles in the US, 8000 miles in Europe, and 6000 miles in Japan in its first five years.[31] Where the logic goes awry, however, is that this argument fails to consider that other factors (such as land use patterns and culture) can explain differences in vehicle use.

In practice, travel demand elasticity has been very difficult to measure. Travel volumes, fuel economy, and fuel consumption are dependent on fuel price but also on many other unrelated variables. In addition, fuel prices have tended to be highly volatile, complicating efforts to discern elasticity. Thus, there is considerable disagreement on the magnitude of the effect of fuel taxes on fleet fuel economy, travel volumes and fuel consumption.[32]

Several more recent studies have concluded that pump price is not a good means of regulating fuel economy. One study published in 2008 in *Energy Economics* contrasted the effects of various fuel economy standards and fuel taxes throughout the world. It concluded that fuel efficiency standards have induced considerable fuel savings but that achieving the same results via fuel taxes would require very high tax rates designed to keep prices at high levels for more than a decade.[33] Another 2007 study calculated short term and long term price elasticity as -0.36

and -0.81, respectively. These finding indicate that consumers are not very price sensitive, the implication of which is that higher fuel taxes would not be a very effective means of reducing consumption.[34] Empirical information from Canada, where they have experienced high fuel prices for the last 20 years, confirms the same conclusions.[35]

Price increases in the US between 2003 and 2008 offer the most direct insight. Those years brought substantially higher fuel prices without the levy of new gasoline taxes. Despite this fact, overall gasoline demand in the US was largely unaffected. Between 2002 and 2007, fuel prices more than doubled from a national average of $1.15 to $3.07[36] while total gasoline consumption increased by over 4.7% during the same period.[37] Based on these facts, it is clear that changes in fuel prices, whether market driven or artificially inflated with taxes, have very little effect on total fuel consumption or fuel economy. Travel demand in the US, as it turns out, is quite inelastic. Therefore, gasoline taxes are not an effective means of promoting fuel economy or of reducing petroleum consumption.

The other argument in favor of higher gas taxes is based on the belief that they will promote the sale of more fuel efficient vehicles. The theory is, once again, based on a false premise. Studies have, in fact, confirmed that consumers rarely consider fuel economy in their purchase decisions.[38] Higher fuel costs have impacted SUV sales on the margins, but the impact is small compared to the increase in fuel prices.

Among the drawbacks of higher gasoline taxes is the fact that they are highly regressive and tend to have the most impact on those with the least ability to pay them. Furthermore, taxes have the added complication of being highly unpopular, which has served as a political roadblock to legislation aimed at increasing them.

Without question, failure to improve vehicle efficiency, coupled with declining ability to produce oil domestically, has contributed substantially to increasing US dependence on foreign oil.[39] US production has declined from 8.0 million barrels per day in 1998 to just 6.7 million barrels per day in 2008.[40]

As much as any one group can be blamed for the failures, the American automobile industry makes a convenient villain. The industry's own twisted logic used to explain increasing US foreign oil dependence, while simultaneously justifying industry opposition to raising fuel economy targets doesn't help their case. As a follow up to his testimony before the US House of Representatives Committee on Science, Michael J. Stanton, representing the Alliance of Automobile Manufacturers, commented:

> ...Programs that succeed in reducing oil demand have always increased, in percentage terms, the world's dependence on the most insecure sources of supply. As demand falls, the market share of high-cost non-OPEC producers falls, and the market share of low-cost Middle Eastern OPEC producers rises.[41]

Mr. Stanton is, in effect, saying that reducing US oil demand must consequently increase dependence on foreign oil. Using his logic, increasing demand for petroleum (burning more oil) would have the effect of making foreign oil a smaller percentage of the US market.

If the price of crude were below extraction costs in the US, or if the US had endless quantities of domestic supply, his arguments might stand up to scrutiny. The US, however, is already producing at maximum capacity. Oil wells are not sitting idle waiting for the price of gasoline to increase to make pumping it profitable. During the 1980s, prices did fall to such a point, but that is not the case now. The US is not exchanging its domestic production for foreign production. Contrary to the assertions of Mr. Stanton, improving automotive fuel economy will reduce US dependence on foreign oil.

Advanced Vehicles

From the birth of the automobile industry until 1905, internal combustion engine powered vehicles, electric vehicles, and steam cars were all competitively marketed and sold in the US.[42] For a variety of reasons, the gasoline powered car won the battle for supremacy. New concerns for the environment, changes in cost relationships and economic forces, advances in technology, and geopolitical issues are prompting a revisit to the question long thought settled – how best to power vehicles.

Advances in technology often result in changes to consumer buying patterns. When the automobile was first introduced, horses were the primary means of transportation. It took only two decades for the economy to go from horse-dominant to automobile-dominant. Technology transitions tend to happen fairly rapidly, generally taking about two times the useful life of the capital stock.[43]

There are many proposed revolutionary innovations in vehicle design that could significantly impact fuel demand. Hybrid and plug-in electric hybrid vehicles are some of the most promising options. They offer the potential to increase fuel economy by making much greater use of the power produced in the internal combustion engine, storing that extra energy in batteries rather than wasting it. Plug-ins even allow the energy for the first few miles (the number of which varies by technology) to be supplied from the electrical grid rather than from liquid fuels.

Another novel idea is to move away from today's concept of general purpose vehicles. Most drivers use the same vehicle for in-city driving, commuting, and longer highway trips, but the idea of more highly specialized vehicles might be able to reduce total fuel demand. Vehicles designed specifically for urban driving, for example, could be much smaller and lighter (fuel economy tends to be at its worst in urban settings). Volkswagen has developed a lightweight urban car capable of getting up to 240 miles per gallon.[44]

The easiest and best step to immediately widen fuel options is to make all vehicles flexible fuel compatible. Flexible fuel vehicles, as the name implies, can run on a variety of different fuels including gasoline, ethanol, and methanol. Such a vehicle allows fuels to compete freely in the marketplace. There is no reasonable argument against flexible fuel vehicles; they are what some might call a "no-brainer." For the automakers, fuel flexibility is a feature that adds less than $100 to the manufacturing cost of vehicle.[45]

In 1990, Congress adopted regulations that would increase the manufacturing and use of flexible fuel vehicles. Car manufacturers have already begun to increase production of them, which helps them to comply with government pollution standards and breeds goodwill with environmentalist critics, all at negligible cost. There are already five million flexible fuel vehicles on the road in the US, most driven by people who aren't even aware their vehicles have the capability of using alternative fuels.

Hybrids & Electric Cars

Electric cars have been around as long as gasoline powered cars, but they have not been manufactured commercially for many years. The reason is simple – electric cars run on batteries that have to be recharged. In the early days of the automotive industry, electric cars enjoyed a more even playing field. They were well suited to the small cities of the time. Longer trips were rare since roads between towns were generally of such poor quality that they were not suitable for vehicular travel. Even then, however, the inadequacy of electric vehicles was evident.[46]

Employing the most modern technology available now, an electric car can go only a fraction of the distance of a gasoline vehicle without refueling. While the range of gasoline cars are limited by size of the gas tank, that tank can be quickly refilled at any one of thousands of service stations located across the country. Recharging a battery, however, is a much more time-consuming process. If an electric battery could be recharged in a matter of minutes and give similar range to a gas powered car, electric vehicles would surely capture substantial market share. At present, however, nobody is really contemplating a technology that would allow rapid battery recharging.

Electric vehicles could, however, have a limited market. Consumers planning to drive their car for only short distances each day (back and forth to work, for instance) might find an electric car appealing, particularly if that consumer had a second vehicle with an internal combustion engine available for longer trips.

A much more attractive product lies where the electric vehicle and internal combustion engine meet. The so-called electric hybrid vehicle is a product that has features of both. It has an internal combustion engine that allows it to burn fuel, but it also has a battery system that stores energy. The next generation of hybrids, the so-called plug-in hybrid, can be recharged by plugging in to the electric power grid.

There are already hybrid vehicles on the market. The Toyota *Prius* is one of the more well known versions. Of the cars and trucks sold in the US in 2008, 2.5% were hybrids (up from essentially none in 2003).[47] Although they still represent a very small segment of the market, it is growing quickly. Today's hybrids extend fuel efficiency, but most are not yet capable of taking a charge from an external power source.

There are several ways the hybrid systems lower fuel consumption: First, the internal combustion engine can be shut down completely when the vehicle stops. A battery both restarts the engine and propels the vehicle when the driver wishes to resume moving. Second, the vehicle can operate off of battery power at low speeds where the efficiency of gasoline engines is at its worst. Third, engine design can be optimized for hybrid operation since the battery is available to offer extra power when needed, such as for acceleration when the vehicle is already traveling at high speeds. Fourth, a continuously variable transmission can be used to optimize vehicle performance. Finally, the electric motor also functions as a generator, storing energy.[48]

Hybrids have their greatest impact when driving in the city (stop and go conditions). They tend to have much less, if any, impact under high speed highway conditions. The amount of benefit received during city driving is a function of trip length and ambient conditions.[49]

Although not yet on the market, the Chevrolet *Volt* has been aggressively marketed by General Motors. After several delays, the *Volt* currently planned for launch of its inaugural 2011 year model in November 2010. GM promises that its battery system will allow drivers to travel up to 40 miles on a single charge. Once the initial electric charge is depleted, the gasoline-powered generator will produce enough energy to continue to power the car for a range similar to most standard gasoline-powered production vehicles.[50]

By all accounts, there is significant demand for the *Volt*. Ability to recharge each night from the grid and maintain the flexibility of a fuel-powered vehicle has its obvious advantages. Fifty percent of cars on the road in the US are driven 20 miles a day or less. A plug-in vehicle with at least a 20-mile range battery would reduce fuel consumption by, on average, 85%.[51]

Another mystery that remains is the cost of the car. If the price significantly exceeds the savings from reduced fuel consumption, demand will be confined to buyers purchasing for reasons related to their social consciousness or product novelty, leaving out most of the market. If, however, costs are reasonable, the plug-in hybrid can be a significant contributor to getting energy problems under control and reducing US dependence on foreign sources of oil.

Hydrogen & the Fuel Cell

Hydrogen is the most abundant element in the universe, accounting for approximately 90% of all molecules.[52] It was first used commercially for cutting steel.[53] Later, it was used to fill lighter-than-air airships, the most famous being the Hindenburg. The Hindenburg caught fire in 1937, resulting in dozens of fatalities and an international media frenzy.[54] The incident scarred the public's perception of hydrogen's safety, but hydrogen is actually much less explosive than gasoline.

Interest in hydrogen as a fuel blossomed in the wake of World War I.[55] It wasn't until recent years, however, that the media and some prominent political figures took up the cause. The reason for all the renewed interest is because hydrogen can be used much more efficiently in a device called a fuel cell when compared with the use of fossil fuels or other liquid fuels in an internal combustion engine. Fuel cells are not subject to the same thermodynamic limits as internal combustion engines because they are electrochemical devices.[56] Far less energy is lost as waste heat, which results in conversion efficiency more than double that of combustion engines.[57] The power produced in fuel cells can be transferred to the drive mechanism of a vehicle by wire rather than by a mechanical transmission, which allows virtually unlimited design flexibility.[58]

A fuel cell is essentially a battery whose reactants are fed in from an external source rather than being packaged inside.[59] The fuel cell was invented in 1839 by Sir William Grove, but it was not produced for a practical application until the NASA space program in the 1950s. The best use of fuel cells might have nothing at all to do with vehicles and transportation. For example, fuel cells can be an excellent means of storing electrical energy, allowing more production to be generated with renewable technologies that are intermittently or unevenly available (such as wind and solar).[60]

Fuel cells are, by no means, ready for commercial use in the US vehicle fleet. A fuel cell vehicle is a very complex machine requiring numerous high technology components that must be integrated and manufactured at low cost and high reliability.[61] Producing fuel cells is extremely expensive. To compete with the internal combustion engine, the cost of hydrogen fuel cells has to be dramatically reduced.[62]

Now, more than 150 years after the invention of the device, low temperature fuel cells still use the same basic materials, particularly platinum.[63] As anyone who has purchased jewelry will attest, platinum is an extremely expensive metal. The cost of platinum is a major part of the cost of producing fuel cells. It is clear from current research that platinum loading must be greatly reduced to make the cost affordable.[64]

New materials are needed not only for the catalysts (platinum) but also for proton exchange membranes, gas diffusions layers, and bipolar plates, fuel cell parts, which together account for 70% of the cost of the system.[65] Materials must perform at much higher levels, lower costs, and for longer lifetimes than those currently available. In many cases, these developments will require revolutionary, not evolutionary, advances in technology.[66]

In 2003, the Bush Administration announced a Hydrogen Initiative intended to promote rapid movement toward a "hydrogen economy." The Initiative set a goal for commercial use of fuel cells by 2012 and competitive use of hydrogen in commercial transportation by the year 2020. Because technological developments are not progressing at the pace envisioned in the Initiative, the American Physical Society predicts that the 2020 timeline "may slip."[67]

Despite the reality that fuel cells are many years away from commercialization, nothing has been more aggressively promoted in recent years as an answer to the world's energy problems as much as hydrogen. Both oil companies and car companies have been the chief architects of the hype, along with a slew of unlikely allies in the environmental community.

What all the hype conveniently leaves out is that hydrogen is not an energy source like oil, coal, biomass, or solar power. It is, instead, an energy carrier, more analogous to gasoline which, like hydrogen, must be produced from a raw material.[68] Since hydrogen must be manufactured from another energy source, adoption of hydrogen will do absolutely nothing to provide more energy to the US or any other domestic market.

Once a full understanding of the realities of hydrogen and the fuel cell comes to light, it brings up questions about why the Hydrogen Initiative and the whole concept of a "hydrogen economy" has gotten so much attention. Perhaps since oil companies are currently the primary producers of hydrogen and that it is mainly manufactured from fossil fuels has something to do with their support, a strategy designed to protect their market share as alternative fuels are explored.

The Hydrogen Initiative involves such a small investment in research that it is unlikely to produce much, if any, technological progress.

Commitment of $1.2 billion isn't trivial, but like any sum it can become irrelevant if spread over a long period of time. For example, the actual budget appropriation for 2004 to the Hydrogen Initiative was $159 million. Of that amount, however, about $42 million disappeared into earmarks. That means only about $117 million went for the Initiative,[69] an amount that would not be sufficient to build one average power plant in the United States. Some have estimated that as much as $100 billion is actually needed over a ten year period to make significant progress.[70]

Although technology for the fuel cell remains a significant problem, it is by no means the only problem or really even the most serious one. Perhaps the greatest obstacle against widespread adoption of hydrogen as an energy carrier is the inability to store it in sufficient quantities onboard a vehicle.[71] Hydrogen is very light, but its energy content by volume is also very low. Hence, great volumes are required. For example, hydrogen contains only 30% of the energy of natural gas for an equal volume at the same pressure.[72] Even when hydrogen is highly compressed, it still only contains a fraction of the energy of an equivalent volume of gasoline. At 10,000 pounds per square inch pressure (psi), hydrogen contains only about 14% as much energy as the same volume of gasoline. Tanks capable of 10,000 psi represent the most advanced technology currently available. In fact, 10,000 psi tanks were only recently demonstrated and certified.[73]

There are other options for on-board hydrogen storage, but they are even less-practical than the compressed gas method. It could be stored as a cryogenic liquid, but liquid hydrogen achieves only a slight decrease in volume for the same energy content as a 10,000 psi tank. There is also the option of "solid-state" storage in which hydrogen molecules are embedded in a material, but it is difficult to find a material that binds hydrogen tightly enough to store it but readily releases it for use at reasonable temperatures and pressures.[74] Incremental improvements in current on-board storage technologies will not be sufficient for the commercialization of hydrogen in vehicles. Breakthroughs in fundamental research are needed to create new, high-efficiency, recyclable hydrogen storage materials.[75]

It is conceivable that hydrogen could be made on board the actual vehicle, with an on-board reformer converting gasoline, natural gas, methanol, or ethanol to hydrogen.[76] Such an approach would eliminate the need for storing large quantities of hydrogen on board the vehicle, but necessitate substantial additional equipment to produce and purify the hydrogen on-board, resulting in substantial vehicle cost increases. For this reason, commercial viability of such an approach is hard to envision.

Even if the on-board storage issues are overcome, hydrogen production and delivery remains another significant challenge. Hydrogen can be manufactured from oil, coal, natural gas, biomass, and the electrolysis of water. It is already used extensively in the petroleum refining industry for production of low-sulfur gasoline and diesel fuel. Almost 90% of high-purity hydrogen used commercially today is produced from the steam reforming of natural gas.[77]

Production of hydrogen from natural gas is in the range of 70%-85% energy efficient (or 30% to 15% of the energy from the source – natural gas – is lost in the process), but the conversion might still be justifiable if the efficiency of the fuel cell makes up for the loss of efficiency from the conversion. For example, gasoline well-to-wheels efficiency is estimated to be 14%, whereas using natural gas to produce hydrogen that powers a fuel cell is estimated to be around 42%.[78]

Simple steam reforming of natural gas does not yield hydrogen of sufficient purity to operate in the low-temperature fuel cells under development for transportation applications. The hydrogen must be extremely pure, as carbon monoxide left behind from the production process will contaminate the fuel cell. The added steps necessary to purify the hydrogen add significantly to the cost and complexity of the production process.[79]

Aside from steam reforming of natural gas, hydrogen can be produced in several other ways. One is the gasification of hydrocarbon molecules (typically either coal or biomass). Gasification produces primarily hydrogen and carbon monoxide, which must then be separated. This method probably has the most economic potential. As with steam reforming, the hydrogen must be further purified for use in fuel cells.[80]

The "cleanest" method of producing hydrogen is by separating the atoms in a water molecule. Water is two parts hydrogen and one part oxygen (H_2O). Electrolysis can break the molecular bonds yielding hydrogen (H_2) and oxygen (O_2). Electrolysis, although "clean" at the point of production, requires vast amounts of electricity and is generally considered the least competitive means of manufacturing hydrogen. It is, at best, only 75% efficient,[81] but that is without considering energy lost in the production of electricity, a process that is below 50% energy efficient for technologies currently in use. The last major improvements in process efficiency came about 50 years ago, and a major technological leap forward is therefore unlikely.[82]

The cost of transporting hydrogen is also a major factor that will inhibit its future use. Hydrogen is less dense and takes more energy to compress than natural gas, but in theory it could be transported through existing natural gas pipelines.[83] It is possible to produce hydrogen with distributed technologies (close to the point of purchase for the end user).[84] Local production, however, has its own set of challenges.

Aside from the specific technical hurdles standing in the way of conversion to hydrogen, there is one major overarching factor that must be overcome – the investment challenge. To deploy hydrogen, an entirely new infrastructure would have to be built for delivery. It presents a classic "chicken versus egg" problem. Which comes first, the hydrogen infrastructure or the hydrogen fuel cell powered vehicle? For manufacturers and consumers to accept hydrogen and convert to it, it must be readily available all across the country, just like gasoline is today. For the infrastructure to develop, a sufficient number of cars must be on the road so that hydrogen sales volumes make it profitable to invest in the capital equipment necessary to manufacture, distribute, and sell it.[85] For this reason, any conversion to hydrogen as a primary fuel choice will be necessarily gradual.

Since the environmental community has embraced it, a discussion would be incomplete without evaluating the environmental impact of transition to hydrogen. It poses several environmental challenges. First, its production, depending on the method, can result in significant releases of carbon dioxide (CO_2). Some environmentalists fail to recognize the environmental dangers of hydrogen because at the vehicle level, the greenhouse gas emissions are essentially zero. At the hydrogen manufacturing level, however, CO_2 is generally released as a by-product. This is particularly true when it is produced via steam reforming of natural gas, by far the most common method.

As explained earlier, hydrogen can be produced without any greenhouse gas emissions through the electrolysis of water, but that also requires electricity, which, to maintain carbon neutrality (zero net CO_2

emissions), must be produced by carbon neutral means, ruling out coal, natural gas, and petroleum.

Hydrogen is not carbon neutral unless produced from a carbon neutral energy source. Because fuel cells are more efficient than internal combustion engines, however, use of hydrogen, regardless of how it is produced, has the potential to emit less CO_2 than gasoline powered vehicles.[86] Concerns about carbon emissions should be viewed through that prism.

It is unclear how or if it will ever become a major factor in the US transportation market. Far too many leaps in technology are required not only to refine and improve existing technologies but also to invent new ones from scratch. What is clear is that hydrogen will not solve the imminent problem of oil dependence.

10
Drill, Baby, Drill!

Sharp debate generated by the proposition of curbing petroleum demand pales in comparison with the disagreements over expanding supply. Demand can at least be quantified; we know how much oil is consumed. The amount of oil in place underground, known as "reserves," is much more difficult to ascertain. An even greater challenge lies in predicting what reserves can ultimately be recovered at reasonable cost given currently available technology (referred to as "recoverable reserves").

As was revealed earlier in this book, the planet has about 600 sedimentary rock basins. About 90% of Earth's oil occurs in just 30 of them.[1] Once oil is found in a particular basin and there is some production from the area, it is possible to establish with a fairly high degree of certainty the amount of oil in the reservoir. The process is not guesswork, but rather well established science. When a well is drilled, sensors are inserted that give readings of porosity, thickness and oil percentage in the well. Readings from all of the wells in a field are then combined to measure total oil in place.[2] From there it is easy to make calculations of the amount of oil remaining by simply subtracting the oil already extracted. Estimation of total recoverable reserves can be accomplished by comparing the percentage of recovery for similar fields.

BP plc is widely thought to publish reasonable reserve estimates; it is their estimates that are used most frequently throughout this book. BP estimates total remaining reserves to be 1,258 billion barrels at the end of 2008.[3] Other published reserve estimates commonly cited in the petroleum industry include 1,342 billion barrels according to *Oil and Gas Journal* and 1,184 billion barrels according to *World Oil*.[4] Much more conservative estimates have been prepared by Colin Campbell, a famous petroleum geologist and key figure in the "peak oil" movement. Mr. Campbell calculates remaining reserves to be 791 billion barrels as of the end of 2005.[5]

The primary source of the gap between highest and lowest resource estimates stems from the belief that some official reserve estimates, particularly among OPEC members, are determined with political rather than scientific motivation. Former executives from both the Saudi national oil company and the Iranian national oil company have publicly stated that Middle Eastern reserve estimates are significantly over-inflated.

Unfortunately, politics do play a major role in establishing official reserves estimates. During the 1980s, OPEC considered tying production quotas to each member's proven reserves. If enacted, such a policy would strongly encourage countries to state the highest possible level of reserves to ensure that they gain the maximum share of the overall production quota. Anticipation of such a policy has been one factor that has encouraged countries to overstate their reserve levels. During the 1980s, several OPEC nations made sudden upward restatements of their official reserves estimates without any clear explanation. In 1988, Venezuela also restated its reserves to include heavy oil resources, which more than doubled its stated reserves from 25 billion barrels to 56 billion barrels.[6]

Similarly, Canada began including its oil sands in its reserve estimates. When the change was made in 2003, Canada's reported reserves went from 4.9 billion barrels to 180 billion barrels. As a result, Canada landed in the number two spot on the US Geological Survey (USGS) list of nations having the largest oil reserves (behind only Saudi Arabia).[7]

Many experts believe many (if not most) of the OPEC members are engaged in a systematic deception about the volume of their own oil reserves. Given that most of the countries in question are controlled by authoritarian regimes, transparency is lacking. It is therefore impossible to know for certain whether or not those governments are actively engaged in inflating their stated oil resources, but the evidence (particularly the sudden, unexplained restatement in the 1980s) certainly seems to support the notion.

The other source of controversy relates to estimates of future discoveries. Not all basins have been explored, and there remain other untapped potential sources of petroleum. Many believe that frontier regions, such as the Arctic, South America, the Indian Ocean and the southeast Pacific Ocean, are likely to produce significant new discoveries of oil.[8]

Among those that estimate future oil discoveries is the USGS. The USGS calculates that eventually another 732 billion barrels will be discovered worldwide in previously unknown fields.[9] The USGS includes in its forecasts basins that are not yet accessible but may be in the next 30 years. Basins in deep water and environmentally sensitive areas are considered and given a "probability factor" that they can achieve production.[10] Many experts believe USGS estimates are overly optimistic.[11] In contrast, estimates prepared by Colin Campbell reflect the expectation that only 142 billion barrels of oil remain undiscovered, although his estimates exclude deep water or polar oil.[12] It is in these areas that all agree most new discoveries are likely to occur.

    The truth is that nobody knows how much more oil will be found, which is probably why that oil is called "undiscovered". With modern equipment, exploration has become much easier and more accurate. Given the profitability of oil, essentially the entire world has been evaluated for petroleum potential. While history has shown that new sources of oil will continue to be found, the possibility of finding major new fields, such as those that exist in the Middle East where resources are abundant and extraction is easy and inexpensive, is extremely remote. World oil content is finite and eventually new discoveries will cease. The time will come when technological capabilities will exceed the earth's ability to hide oil, a moment that is rapidly approaching.

Expanding Drilling

    The US presidential campaign of 2008 gave birth to the slogan "Drill, baby, drill!" Drilling is a short-term tactic, not a long term strategy. The US has been drilled, drilled some more, and then re-drilled again. In fact, there are more than 300 times as many producing oil wells in the US as there are in Saudi Arabia.[13] Unfortunately, the average production of each well in the US is paltry by comparison.

    The US has only 2.4% of the world's oil reserves but accounts for 22.5% of world oil consumption. Year after year, US oil production goes down while oil consumption goes up. In 2008, production was just 84% of the level it was just 10 years ago.[14] With limited reserves, thousands of oil wells, and dwindling production, it defies all reason to claim that drilling more oil wells in the US can solve America's energy problems. Sadly, it seems there are people out there who still believe more drilling is the solution.

    Over the last decade, the most controversial area in which new drilling had been proposed was the Arctic National Wildlife Refuge (ANWR), a deserted area in northern Alaska. Despite the spirited

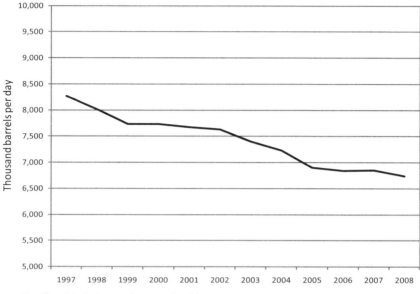

US Petroleum Production

Data from BP plc, *Statistical Review of World Energy June 2009.*

disagreements, ANWR and similar sites are simply not sufficient to make up for even a small percentage foreign petroleum imports.[15]

The US Department of Energy (DOE) projected that ANWR, if opened to oil exploration, would achieve its peak output of 1.0 to 1.3 million barrels per day twenty years from commencement of operations.[16] That volume of petroleum constitutes 5.2% to 6.7% of US consumption in 2008.[17] While ANWR provides a source of supply that s not insignificant, it is not large enough to make a serious dent in US oil imports. After all, US petroleum imports were 13 million barrels per day in 2008,[18] ten times the most optimistic ANWR production projections. No amount of drilling in ANWR can stave off the day when the US will have to shift to petroleum alternatives.

Even though exploration in ANWR is not the panacea that proponents would have the public believe, it may still be worthwhile. Every little bit of new domestic supply could help, and there are some other important benefits to be gleaned from drilling in ANWR. For example, the Trans-Alaskan Pipeline needs at least 325,000 barrels per day to operate. If production falls below that level, the remaining oil reserves would become stranded. ANWR could extend life of the pipeline and its usefulness by up to 20 years.[19]

ANWR is not the only controversial potential drilling location under consideration. Drilling on the outer continental shelf (OCS) has been a hotly-debated subject in the media and was also a key issue in the 2008 elections. Some claim that offshore drilling off the Atlantic and Pacific coasts could provide a substantial new petroleum source. ANWR and the OCS have one thing in common – they have, like so many energy issues, ended up pitting pro-drilling interests against environmentalists.

In 2010, a watershed event changed the perception of offshore drilling. In April, there was an explosion at BP's Deepwater Horizon drilling platform. The incident resulted in a major release of oil from the seafloor into the Gulf of Mexico, creating the largest oil spill in US history. Repeated efforts to curb the flow of oil, despite the combined resources of the US government and BP, failed, and the oil leak continued long after the onset of the disaster. As this book is readied for press, oil is still flowing. The episode has served as a painful reminder of the technical challenges of petroleum exploration at sea, the potentially devastating consequences of accidents, and just how much is still remains unknown. Support for offshore drilling, particularly in new areas, has quickly eroded.

Debate about expanding offshore drilling is actually just as pointless as the debate over ANWR. The government's own estimates, which tend to be on the optimistic side, project that almost 62.3% of US deepwater resources are in the Gulf of Mexico, mostly in areas already home to extensive petroleum exploration and production. After the Gulf, the Pacific and off-shore Alaska are the next richest areas, respectively (although they each have much smaller resource bases than the Gulf). The most hotly debated area, deepwater off the Atlantic coast, is home to only 3.3% of total national deepwater petroleum resources.[20]

In light of these facts, drilling in the Atlantic, with its relatively small resource base, would seem to be a waste of time. There are probably some areas, perhaps off the Gulf coast of Florida, that are currently off-limits to drilling but could add some domestic oil supply at the margins. It is not, by any means, going to be a major contributor to reducing foreign oil dependence. Drilling, we can conclude, is not the answer, certainly not if foreign oil dependence is the question.

Is the World Running Out of Oil?

Perhaps the simplest questions create the most debate. Is the world running out of oil? The answer is yes, and it has been since the day the very first barrel was pumped. Without a doubt, there is a finite amount of oil in the world. The earth is not producing any more of it, at least not quickly enough to be relevant. We know that it takes millions of years and extreme environmental forces for oil to be made in nature. The relevant question isn't whether the world will run out of oil, but when?

To put the issue in context, perhaps the most illustrative exercise is to compare world oil consumption to world oil reserves, which can be thought of as kind of sales to inventory analysis. Combined proven reserve and future discovery estimates range from the most conservative assessment of 844 billion barrels[21] to the liberal appraisal at 1,990 billion barrels.[22] World oil consumption was 84.5 million barrels per day in 2008.[23] Given that consumption rate and those inventory estimates, the world has, on the conservative side, 10.0 years, and on the optimistic side, 23.6 years of inventory remaining as of the end of 2008. Such figures are illustrative but also misleading because the world will not be able to produce at current levels all the way up until reserves are completely gone.

Most economists will actually tell you that we will *never* run out of oil. They are quite right. The reason, however, isn't that the world has plenty of it; rather, it is because that last barrel of oil would be so expensive that nobody would be willing to pay for it. Market forces will increase the price of oil as it becomes increasingly scarce. As Morris Adelman, a professor at the Massachusetts Institute of Technology (MIT), explains it,

> ...Optimal allocation over time between us and our posterity is a phantom problem. No mineral, including oil, will ever be exhausted. If and when the cost of finding and extraction goes above the price consumers are willing to pay, the industry will begin to disappear.[24]

It is a well established principal of economics that constrained supply equals higher prices. Scarcity is the reason gold, for example, costs more than steel or that diamonds cost more than granite.

The trouble with viewing oil as just another commodity subject to supply and demand is that it fails to take into account the fact that there is presently no other commodity that can be suitably substituted for oil. The function of society as a whole depends on its availability at affordable prices.

Technically, Adelman is, of course, right. When oil becomes too expensive, we simply won't buy as much of it, or any of it, as the case may be. But, what would be the effect on the economy if the price of gasoline went to, say, $30 per gallon without a suitable alternative? Supply and demand would technically be balanced, but much less oil would be bought and sold. As a consequence, most of us would not be able to afford transportation, even for work, and movement of goods vital to the economy would stop. The economy would be decimated, and the American way of life as we know it would come to an end.

A doctorate in economics is not necessary to realize that a dwindling oil supply will result in higher prices, nor is a PhD in petroleum geology required to figure out that if the amount of oil in the world is finite, eventually the ability to pump it will begin to decrease. Gasoline prices may not reach $30 per gallon, at least not in the next few years, but some argue that "peak oil" is only around the corner. "Peak oil" is the point where world oil production reaches its maximum point and then begins to decline.

Those who believe that the point of peak oil production is rapidly approaching generally follow the teachings of King Hubbert, a geophysicist who, in 1956, correctly predicted that US oil production would peak around 1970.[25] Most members of the modern peak oil movement believe only the most conservative estimates of world oil reserves, and they believe that most of the world's major oil reservoirs have already been discovered.[26] Some peak oil theorists have a very bleak vision of the future, with a few predicting an impending "Armageddon" resulting from scarcity of petroleum resources.

Not everyone agrees that peak oil is upon us. Some experts take the other side of the debate, embracing optimistic estimates of world oil reserves and the expectation that there will be plenty of oil for everyone for many years into the future. They tend to believe that Hubbert's equations predicting an oil production peak will be rendered obsolete by new access to closed areas, resurgence in Russia, and an abundance of new technologies.[27] Of course, the characterization of estimates as "optimistic" is a little deceiving. For example, estimates are usually deemed "optimistic" if they indicate that there is enough supply to meet demand through 2020,[28] which is not really a reasonable standard.

Dire oil predictions are nothing new. They have been historically undone by the opening or reopening of new territories to oil exploration and introduction of new technologies.[29] For example, better technology and management practices have increased Russian output by 45% since 1998, catapulting Russia to its current position as the world's second largest petroleum producer.[30]

There have been a variety of predictions about the timing of a world oil production peak performed by both optimists and pessimists. Results of those calculations depend mostly on whose assumptions you use for reserve estimates. Not surprisingly, the use of more conservative estimates tends to indicate that peaking is more imminent. Kenneth Deffeyes, a well-known petroleum geologist and peak oil pessimist, previously predicted that world oil production would peak in 2005.[31]

Growth in world crude oil production has been virtually flat since 2004, hovering between 80 and 82 million barrels per day.[32] It is too early to tell if the peak oil theorists are right, but data clearly shows that production has leveled off to a very narrow range. Whenever there is an ultimate peak in oil production, it will become clear only several years afterward.

For those who claim Deffeyes and his colleagues are simply alarmists, that they are using overly conservative reserve measurements to reach their conclusions, perhaps a more optimistic approach will shed some light on the situation. In 2006, several researchers at Oak Ridge National Laboratory, one the US Department of Energy's primary research facilities, prepared an optimistic estimate of world oil peaking. Their analysis used data from the US Geological Survey (USGS). As mentioned earlier, USGS estimates tend to be the most optimistic.

The Oak Ridge simulation predicted that it was highly likely that conventional oil production would peak between 2016 and 2028, with an average of 2023. Using the more conservative reserve data often used by some peak oil theorists, however, Oak Ridge predicted little chance world oil production would peak any later than 2010 and that it was likely to peak by 2006. The study concluded,

> Peaking of conventional oil production is almost certain to occur soon enough to deserve immediate and serious attention...Even from the optimist's perspective, oil peaking is a serious issue.[33]

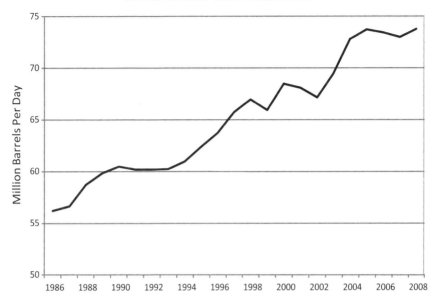

World Crude Oil Production

Data from Davis, Diegel, and Boundy, *Transportation Energy Data Book.*

Oil production peaking does not, in and of itself, spell disaster. The problem is that demand is growing. With a production peak, supply will begin to decrease. Those converging forces will result in price increases. The increases may not be along a straight line; occasionally prices will leap forward and then recede. Oil shocks, and perhaps even mild counter-shocks, have occurred and will continue to occur in the future. The underlying fundamentals, however, are undeniable: oil production will peak, but with growth of developing countries like China, the world will still want more and more oil.

Regardless of whether conventional oil production is already at or near maximum output or whether it will peak within two decades, the time to do something about it is now. Sure, there have been wolf-cries about running out of oil several times in years past. Things, however, are different this time. In the past the petroleum industry was not fully mature. The market did not have production coming from every corner of the globe (including deep ocean waters). More importantly, in the past, rapidly expanding world demand (driven by the seemingly overnight industrialization of the world's most populous nations) was not a factor. Now, Americans have front-row seats as rapidly expanding worldwide demand meets a fully mature petroleum industry already producing at full capacity.

The Refinery Challenge

As of 2007, there were 149 petroleum refineries in the US, 145 of which were operating. In 2007, those 145 operating refineries had an operating capacity of 17.4 million barrels per day, not including downtime for maintenance (which resulted in refineries operated at 88.5% capacity, below the 91.9% 10-year average). All together, an average of 15.4 million barrels of crude per day were processed. The problem was that the US consumed 20.7 million barrels per day.[34]

No new refineries have been built in the US since 1976.[35] Considering that demand is increasing while refinery capacity is not, the gap between American needs and production capability will continue to widen.

Even if the US produced enough crude oil to meet its needs domestically, that oil could not be refined into enough gasoline and other end products to meet domestic needs. The fact that the US has developed no new refining capacity is both a failure and a triumph, depending on your perspective. If you are a consumer or if you are looking at the industry from the perspective of national security, it is a terrible failure. If you are an oil company, however, it is a great triumph.

There is a large spread between the price of crude and the price of gasoline, which, except for gasoline taxes, goes to the refining and marketing industries. To illustrate the point, just look at industry profit margins.

The spread is determined not so much by the price of crude but by the number of refineries, capacity, competition, and, of course, demand.[36] Constrained capacity unquestionably benefits the refineries. Consumers, on the other hand, should be concerned that a not-so-insignificant portion of gasoline prices comes not from crude prices, but from refinery profits.

The refining industry is virtually unanimous in its belief that no new oil refineries will ever be built in the United States. A new refinery would face a range of political hurdles in federal, state, and local permitting process. Even existing refineries face regulatory problems as evidenced by the fact that most investment capital into the refining industry pay not for expansion to increase production volume but to instead to upgrade processes to keep in step with new regulatory mandates.[37]

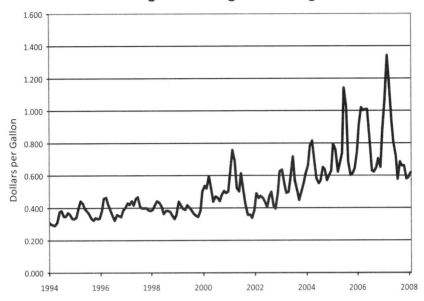

Refining / Marketing Profit Margin

Based on data compliled from the US Department of Energy, Energy Information Administration and the US Department of Transportation, Federal Highway Administration.

Alternative Fuels

Biofuels first became a part of the energy alternative fuels conversation in the wake of the Arab oil embargo. The Carter Administration devoted significant resources to studying the potential of biofuels, subsidizing the construction of a limited number of plants. The popularity waned when oil prices cratered in the mid-1980s. After the beginning of the war in Iraq, gasoline prices in the United States started to shoot upward. With the increases came both a consumer desire to find cheaper alternatives and an entrepreneurial quest to find ways to produce products rendered profitable by the upward trending fuel market.

Biofuels are just what the name implies, fuel that comes from living things. Oil, coal, and natural gas were all once living things as well, but because they were alive millions of years ago, they are categorized as fossil fuels rather than biofuels. Fossil fuels were created through a process of chemical reactions and geological forces over long periods of time. The realization that the oil used today was once living organisms begs an interesting question. Why shouldn't we be able to collect biological material today and replicate the processes of the earth in a modern industrial plant achieving the same ends but foregoing the millions of years required for the natural process? Such an approach is not only possible but has been successfully used commercially at locations around the world.

The use of plant and other biological materials as energy sources has been around ever since the discovery of fire. Biofuels are, in fact, among the oldest of human technologies. Ever hear of burning wood? Going from an organic solid, like wood, to a liquid with high energy density comparable to oil distillates, like gasoline, requires a little more ingenuity. Using modern technology mankind does indeed have the knowledge and skills to convert biological material into liquid fuel that can perform like gasoline.

The first step in producing any biofuel is procuring raw material, which, in most cases, is going to be plants or processed versions thereof (vegetable oil, etc.). The US has traditionally enjoyed a strong agricultural industry. Today, the agricultural industry in the US is unrivaled. Although much of the US manufacturing base may have moved overseas, it is still the world's dominant agricultural producer. The US is good at growing things, and it is just beginning to harness that dominant ability to produce liquid fuels.

At present, the most common non-petroleum fuel in the United States is ethanol. Ethanol has traditionally been manufactured through the fermentation of sugars (similar to the making beer). Fermentation takes place when yeasts, which are tiny living organisms, feed off of sugar and produce alcohol and carbon dioxide. By far the most common raw material for ethanol production in the US is corn.

Ethanol, an alcohol, is chemically much different from gasoline, which is a mixture of hydrocarbon compounds (benzene, octane, toluene, and up to 15 others). Historically, ethanol's primary purpose has been to serve as an octane extender or oxygenate additive for gasoline. Much of the gasoline sold today, particularly in the mid-west, contains a small portion of ethanol.

With the advent of the gasohol[38] programs during the Carter Administration, there was serious exploration of the potential of ethanol as an alternative to oil. Many years before that, however, when automobiles first began to pepper the landscape of America, industry pioneer Henry Ford thought that ethanol was the natural and most logical fuel for his fleet of automobiles. Those plans were put on hold, however, as the abundance of cheap petroleum made it more economically expedient to fuel cars and trucks with gasoline.

In recent years, the ethanol industry experienced a boom and a subsequent bust. The resurgence began when it was discovered that a gasoline additive called methyl tertiary butyl ether (MTBE) was seeping into groundwater. Concern about environmental damage and the potential health risks led to aggressive pursuit of alternatives. Although there is not a federal ban of MTBE, at least 25 states now have full or partial bans in place or about to take effect. One of the alternatives to MTBE is ethanol.

The second major catalyst for the expanded use of ethanol was the dramatic increase in oil prices that began in 2002. Prior to the spike in gasoline prices, ethanol production was not economically attractive, costing more per gallon to produce than the wholesale price of unleaded gasoline. Only through tax credits offered to those who blended ethanol with gasoline was the industry sustainable. With profitability came an explosion in the construction of ethanol plants and a rapid increase in ethanol production.

Despite the development of numerous new ethanol plants and a more than five-fold increase in production over the last ten years, the total ethanol output capacity in the US is still only a drop in the bucket compared to gasoline consumption. Total fuel ethanol production in the US in 2008 was just short of 8 billion gallons while total gasoline consumption was over 138 billion gallons.[39] In many areas of the country ethanol, commonly marketed as E-85 – a blend of 85% ethanol and 15% gasoline, is still unavailable for purchase at the pump.

The economics of fermented ethanol are basically a function of the price of gasoline and the net cost of the raw materials used in production, as well as other variable costs and tax incentives. For US-based ethanol plants, the raw material used in production is almost exclusively corn. Its net cost, the price of corn less the value of by-products (mostly distillers' grains, which are sold as animal feed), is by far the largest variable cost of production.

The major risk associated with the ongoing operation of a fermentation ethanol plant relates to the fact that corn does not have any price relationship to fuel ethanol. Falling gasoline prices coupled with a rise in corn cost can result in severe constraints on a plant's cash flow. Unfortunately for ethanol producers, that is exactly what happened in 2008. The explosion in the number of ethanol plants dramatically

US Fuel Ethanol Production

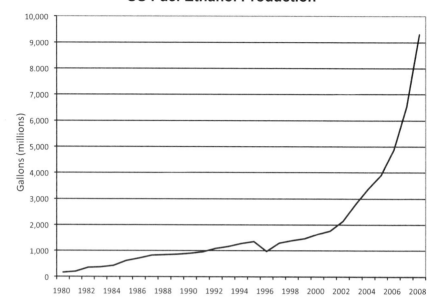

Based on data compliled from the US Department of Energy, Energy Information Administration and theRenewable Fuels Association,

expanded the demand for corn causing prices to increase. When the price of gasoline began to drop in 2008 in the face of the global recession, so did the price of ethanol. Margins evaporated, and the industry was left in financial turmoil.

The other major factor affecting the ethanol industry is tax incentives. The most important incentive is the federal excise tax credit. Ethanol blends have been either wholly or partially exempt from the federal excise tax on gasoline since 1978. This tax exemption generally serves as an incentive to gasoline blenders to include ethanol in its gasoline formulations.

The present incentive system is called the "Volumetric Ethanol Excise Tax Credit" (VEETC). It requires blenders to pay the full rate of tax (18.4 cents per gallon) on each gallon of a gasoline-ethanol mixture, but provides a $0.51 cents per gallon tax credit or refund for each gallon of ethanol blended.[40] The effect of the system is to eliminate the federal gasoline tax on any gasoline/ethanol blend that contains more than 36% ethanol. There are also incentives for the installation "clean fuel refueling facilities", in other words, an E-85 fuel pump.

One of the most important long-term challenges to ethanol is that, as it turns out, a gallon of ethanol has only 67% of the energy content of a gallon of gasoline.[41]   Because the energy content is less, a driver will not get the same miles per gallon using ethanol as with gasoline. Conventional wisdom is that fuel economy would be reduced in direct proportion to the reduction in energy content based on the blend of ethanol. In practice, however, the relationship is not linear. Different vehicles react differently to ethanol and differently to the level of ethanol in the blend (E-10, E-20, E-30, E-85, etc.). In some cases, adding ethanol to a fuel blend actually increases the fuel economy.[42] In light of the recent research, it is not possible to embrace a particular conclusion about the fuel economy of ethanol versus gasoline. More study in this area is needed, but it is still clear that the lower energy content is a disadvantage.

Ethanol has other challenges, including the fact that it is also more difficult to transport than gasoline. Because of its chemical composition and its affinity to attract water, it cannot currently be moved by pipeline, leaving truck and rail (for longer distances) as the primary distribution methods. These methods tend to be more expensive.

In the US, not all vehicles can use fuel that is primarily comprised of ethanol. Generally, only flexible fuel vehicles (FFV's) can use fuel blends that are predominately ethanol, such as E-85 (85% ethanol and 15% gasoline). Although there are already a large number of flexible fuel vehicles on the road and the car manufactures are producing more, a dramatic shift in the national automobile fleet will take time. That shift will be necessary for ethanol to play a larger role in the US energy landscape.

From an environmental perspective, ethanol is particularly attractive because it is, at least theoretically, "carbon neutral" because carbon dioxide discharged during its production and use is offset by the carbon dioxide absorbed by growth of corn. In practice, fermentation-based ethanol production is not truly carbon neutral. Fossil fuels tend to be used at several points in the production cycle. Petroleum based diesel and petroleum derived fertilizers are often used on the farm to produce corn. Furthermore, natural gas is typically used in ethanol plants to dry the distillers' grain so that it can be kept longer without spoiling and to make transportation easier.

The Brazilian Experience

As it has become increasingly obvious to Americans that dependence on foreign oil compromises national security, ethanol has gained more attention. Brazil, once a major energy importer like the US, has recently achieved energy independence thanks, in no small part, to producing large quantities of ethanol, proving that such a feat is possible even for countries without substantial oil reserves. Not all of Brazil's fuel comes from ethanol, however. Brazil still gets a little over half of their fuel supply (on an energy content basis) from domestic oil production.[43]

The Brazilian Alcohol Program (PROALCOOL) was established in the 1970s to reduce oil imports.[44] The Brazilian government recognized, particularly after the supply shock of 1973-1974, that dependence on unstable foreign sources of energy could be a long term challenge for their country. A long term, consistent effort has led Brazil to unprecedented results.

In Brazil, ethanol is manufactured from sugarcane using a traditional fermentation process. In 1970, Brazil produced 50 million tons of sugar cane, which yielded 5 million tons of sugar. By 2002, they were producing 200 million tons of sugar cane, which yielded 19 million tons of sugar and 12 billion liters of ethanol.[45]

Accordingly to the Ministry of Agriculture, Brazil has about 320 million hectares suitable for cultivation, only 53 million of which are under agricultural production. Sugarcane accounts for less than 10% of agriculture in Brazil, despite the booming ethanol industry.[46]

Brazil's ethanol production costs are the lowest in the world at around $0.80 per gallon. A favorable climate, low labor costs, and a well-developed infrastructure, along with several decades of experience, all help maintain the cost advantage.[47] Given the available land and low production costs, Brazil is now poised to become a net energy exporter, an almost unthinkable concept for a country with few fossil fuel reserves.

The dividends for the Brazilian economy have been substantial. For the period 1975-1989, $4.92 billion was invested in the alcohol program in Brazil. The result was savings on the purchase of foreign oil amounting to $43.5 billion.[48] In addition, the ethanol industry employs more than 700,000 people.[49]

Brazil has been able to preserve its hard currency reserves by not spending them on foreign oil. Reduced energy imports also has improved the balance of payments (trade deficit), reducing the need to attract foreign capital. For a country like Brazil, the effect is less dollar-denominated external debt.[50] The alcohols program in Brazil has been, by any financial or political measure, a resounding success.

As with any initiative, there is always an opposition. Critics of the program point to concerns about deforestation, but sugarcane for Brazil's ethanol industry is overwhelmingly grown in the southern regions, well away from the Amazon and Atlantic Rainforests.[51] Brazil is actually a very large country almost the size of the continental US, and it therefore, has a wide range of climates, a fact that is frequently overlooked.

The long term effort in Brazil is meaningful for other countries, especially the US. Although American challenges (as well as European and Chinese challenges) are different from those of the Brazilians, their success can be an example of what a sustained effort can accomplish. The US cannot become energy independent using the same strategy as Brazil; the climate is different and US energy needs are currently too great. The Brazilian experience does, however, serve as an example of what is possible even for a country with very few oil resources.

Next-Generation Biofuels

As the ethanol industry has grown, the increasing demand for corn and concerns about the potential for pressure on production margins has led companies to seek new technologies that use other raw materials or that offer much greater efficiency in corn ethanol production. There are two types of ethanol technologies that show promise for allowing wider-scale production of ethanol from a range of raw materials. These technologies are commonly referred to as "cellulosic" technologies.

The first process uses enzymes to break down cellulose into sugars that can then be fermented into ethanol. "Bio-processing" can use a wide variety of raw materials including agricultural plant wastes (corn stover, cereal straws, sugarcane bagasse), plant wastes from industrial processes (sawdust, paper pulp), and some energy crops grown specifically for fuel production, such as switchgrass. Enzymatic bio-processing has some distinct advantages over simple fermentation. In the end, the manufacturing process is the same – sugars are fermented using yeasts to produce ethanol. The initial steps in production, however, are where the process gains its advantage.

Corn or, for that matter, sugar cane, already have high sugar content; yeast feeds off of the sugar, which is what produces ethanol. With grasses and other high-cellulose plants, sugars are locked in complex carbohydrates called polysaccharides. As a result, traditional fermentation technologies can't convert them to ethanol.

A process called acid hydrolysis can break down the complex carbohydrates into simple sugars. An alternative method, enzymatic hydrolysis, utilizes pretreatment processes to first reduce the size of the material to make it more accessible to hydrolysis, after which enzymes are employed to convert the polysaccharides to fermentable sugars. The final step is fermentation of the simple sugars yielding ethanol and carbon dioxide.

Since these processes can use agricultural wastes as a feedstock, they have the ability to tap a largely underutilized resource. Currently, agricultural residues are plowed back into the soil, composted, burned or discarded at landfills. As an added benefit, collection and sale of crop residues can create a new source of income for farmers without requiring any additional acreage.

A key impediment to large scale development of these technologies is the high cost of cellulose enzymes, which have historically rendered enzymatic bio-processing uneconomic. Many companies are currently working on ways to reduce the cost of enzymes.

Pretreatment technologies are also a key focus of research and development efforts. Pretreatment is required to break apart the structure of biomass to allow for the efficient and effective hydrolysis of the polysaccharides. Up to 70% of the total mass of biological materials is composed of structural carbohydrates. Pretreatment's primary purpose is to achieve higher yields from these sugars without degrading the materials.

The second process that differs from traditional ethanol production is truly a total departure from the biological fermentation. It instead uses thermochemical processes that promote chemical reactions in the presence of heat and pressure to convert biomass to fuel. The thermochemical production of synthetic fuels was invented in petroleum-poor but coal-rich Germany in the 1920s. In Germany, the process used coal rather than biomass. One of the greatest advantages of thermochemical conversion is the wide range of raw materials that can be used to produce fuel including coal and biomass, as well as virtually any other organic material.

In 1939, at the beginning of World War II in Europe, Germany was operating fourteen synthetic fuel plants and had another six under construction. By 1940, synthetic fuel production was almost one billion gallons per year, which accounted for nearly half of the German fuel supply during the war.[52] At the end of World War II, captured German scientists were brought to the US where they continued to work on synthetic fuels. Since then, the technology has progressed substantially.

Using biomass to manufacture fuels using thermochemical processes is the most promising development in the biofuels industry. It is by far the most efficient means of production because it has the ability to use all of the hydrocarbon material in a feedstock rather than just sugars and carbohydrates that are or can be made suitable for fermentation. The potential products go way beyond ethanol since the synthesis process can produce a wide range of fuels including synthetic gasoline and diesel fuel.

Thermochemical fuel production from biomass could well be one of the most important technological revolutions of the 21st century. The remainder of this book is devoted to discussing the technology, its cost, and how it can be applied to combat US dependence on foreign oil. Given sufficient quantities of biomass, the process could indeed provide a means to replace imported petroleum and eliminate all of the negative effects of the result from foreign oil addiction.

Part Four –
A Path Forward

11

How to Squeeze Oil from a Twig

Petroleum is really nothing more or less than a black liquid that comes out of the ground. There is nothing wrong with it, just as there is nothing wrong with a shiny rock called gold. It is *pursuit* of petroleum – the wars, greed, and lust for power – that makes it so dangerous. The quest has caused untold suffering for so many around the globe. The problem is significantly worse for countries that don't have enough of it to meet their own needs and must seek it from outside their borders.

In the US, the problem has, until now, existed mostly on paper. Americans have yet to experience the great suffering that has plagued peoples in petroleum-producing regions. Petroleum conflicts aren't fought in the streets of the US where housewives roam freely in their SUVs. Petro-state dictators stay in their corners of the world, while most Americans remain oblivious to their existence. Meanwhile the US economy is like a functioning addict, only leaving its relatively country club-like Western world behind to sneak into skid row to get its oil fix. Petroleum is like a national heroine – the US simply can't live without it. Without a steady supply, the economy would convulse like a junkie in withdrawal.

Every day, more wealth from the US becomes the property of foreigners. Oil has dominated US foreign policy since World War I, and most of the conflicts involving the US military from World War II to actions in the Middle East have had, at their roots, oil. The expense of continued global policing, of wars, of wealth transfers, of the price shocks, and of the outsourcing of the energy industry far outstrips any other individual avoidable cost to society. Finally, our problem is emerging from the shadows.

Energy security, for which some have called, is not an adequate response to US foreign oil addiction. Importing oil from allies or any supposedly secure supply would solve a few problems. Perhaps it would lessen supply shocks and the need for periodic military action. It might even reduce US involvement in the Middle East and, consequently, Islamic terrorism. But importing energy from friendlier nations would not solve the fundamental economic problems associated with imported energy (including the ongoing wealth transfer, trade deficit, and long term stability of the dollar). What the US needs, what it must have to continue to be a great economic power for the next century and beyond, is energy independence.

Contrary to popular opinion, the US is not short on energy resources; most just don't take the form of petroleum. There are many energy options: wind, sun, tides and waves of the oceans. For transportation fuel, however, besides petroleum there are essentially three important resources: natural gas, coal, and biomass. While some advocates of natural gas claim it is the answer to America's petroleum challenges, the truth is that the US only has 237.7 trillion cubic feet of proven natural gas reserves, about 11.6 times the current annual production rate.[1]

Proponents of using natural gas to replace oil point to a study that concluded that the US has "a 100 year supply of natural gas."[2] What they fail to mention, however, is that such calculations are based on current usage levels. Displacing even a small percentage of foreign oil with domestic natural gas would mean much higher consumption rates and would, therefore, drive down that "100 year" number significantly. Furthermore, reserve estimates employed in the study go far beyond proven reserves to include probable and even possible reserves, the most optimistic measure of potential reserves. Although domestic natural gas could be *part* of an answer to foreign oil dependence, it is clearly not available in sufficient quantities to be a panacea.

In contrast with natural gas, the US has enormous coal reserves, 28.9% of the world's resources.[3] It is, quite simply, plentiful. Coal does, however, have another significant challenge. The carbon to hydrogen ratio of coal is much higher than for either oil or natural gas. The consequence of that fact is that, absent some means of carbon sequestration, the combustion of coal is a much more significant contributor to carbon dioxide emissions. Even those who remain unconvinced that carbon emissions are affecting global temperatures must recognize the reality of a substantial political movement in favor of limiting carbon emissions. Because efforts toward achieving energy independence stand a much better chance of success if there is relative political unanimity and because the production of fuel from coal is sure to draw fire from the environmental community, coal makes a less-than-ideal energy source.

Finally, there is biomass. The US has an abundance of fertile land and forests that already produce vast quantities of biomass and could produce much more with a dedicated production effort. Biomass is, by definition, a carbon neutral fuel so long as no fossil fuels are consumed in its production. But perhaps the best reason to favor biomass is that it is not a finite resource. Biomass can be regrown as fast or faster than it is consumed, which makes it a truly sustainable energy source.

The technology already exists to refine any of the aforementioned resources into clean, domestically produced transportation fuel. Using natural gas as a transportation fuel is more familiar, but producing fuels from coal and biomass is not a new idea. One of the first such efforts in the US was a Bureau of Mines Synthetic Fuel Project originally championed by President Truman. The project attempted to capitalize on fuel research inherited from Germany after World War II with the aim of utilizing the vast coal reserves in the US. The program was later terminated by the Eisenhower Administration because it "wasn't competitive" in light of the abundance of cheap foreign oil.[4]

Cheap oil is the reason that the US has not developed a significant alternative fuel industry. In truth, oil has never been cheap, but many of its costs have been external – they weren't included in the price visible to consumers when filling up at the local gas station. Only in periods of particularly high prices or during supply shocks has popular will existed to do something about our common nemesis, imported oil.

Technology of the Future Available Today

There is really not much dispute over the feasibility of manufacturing liquid fuels from non-petroleum sources. In the US, substantial quantities of ethanol are already manufactured by fermenting sugar from corn. Brazil has achieved energy independence, in large part by producing ethanol from sugarcane. During years of isolation from international markets and the world oil trade because of apartheid, South Africa developed an extensive synthetic fuel industry, which processes coal and natural gas into liquid fuels. Although apartheid is long-dead, the industry is still going strong and produces almost half of the fuel consumed in South Africa.[5]

With all of the negative consequences of foreign oil dependence, a greater emphasis on alternatives is imperative. Unfortunately, the corn fermentation process prevalent in the US will never bring about energy independence. It is simply too inefficient on a variety of fronts, the most important of which is land use. Growing corn takes a lot of land for relatively small crop yields. As for a sugarcane program similar to Brazil's, the climate in the US just isn't suitable for production of sugar cane in quantities sufficient for achieving energy independence.

The US does have abundant coal and biomass resources to efficiently produce hydrocarbon fuels. Both can play a major role in the future of transportation fuel manufacturing, but biomass has the key advantage of carbon neutrality. Plants consume carbon dioxide during photosynthesis, thereby removing it from the atmosphere. A plant can contain no more carbon than it has absorbed, so when biomass fuels are produced and burned, the maximum amount of carbon emitted is equal to the total carbon intake of the plant. From an atmospheric perspective, nothing has changed; it is as if the plant never existed. Assuming no fossil fuel was consumed in the cultivation and collection of the biomass, the result is net-zero carbon emission.

Some claim production of fuel from biomass may even be carbon negative, actually resulting in a net removal from the atmosphere by permanently storing some carbon in the soil. Estimations for soil carbon build-up are highly site-specific and vary widely depending on the type of biomass produced; they range from net carbon emission of two tons per acre to net sequestration of about 18 tons per acre over the crop rotation cycle.[6] In practice, biomass cultivation will probably have the effect of removing slightly more carbon from the atmosphere than it emits.

There are a variety of technologies capable of producing fuels from biomass. For a large scale effort of sufficient scope and scale to impact foreign oil dependence, thermochemical processes have several important advantages and are generally superior due to implicit efficiency and flexibility.

Thermochemical fuel production can use virtually any organic matter as a raw material (including natural gas; residual oil; petroleum coke; coal; and biomass from the wood in construction debris, residue from logging, agricultural and yard waste, and dedicated energy crops).[7] A wide range of fuel products including ethanol, methanol, low-sulfur diesel, gasoline, kerosene, and jet fuel can be produced. The technology is actually closer to petroleum refining than it is to the fermentation process used to produce ethanol from corn in the US. Accordingly, in addition to fuels, there is the possibility of manufacturing many ancillary products associated with petroleum such as plastics and chemicals. Capital costs of building a thermochemical synthetic fuel plant are substantial, but operation is efficient and economical.

Thermochemical conversion of biomass to liquid fuels can take several paths, but the easiest to explain and the most established technology is referred to as indirect liquefaction. It combines the processes of gasification and fuel synthesis.

Gasification

Gasification has come a long way since it was pioneered by Scottish engineer William Murdock in 1792. Gasification has been used commercially worldwide for more than 50 years in the refining, fertilizer, and chemical industries, and for more than 35 years in the electric power industry. There are more than 140 gasification plants operating worldwide, 19 of which are in the US. Most of the US plants are used in chemical manufacturing.[8] Gasification technology benefits from several decades of significant operating experience. Today's market boasts multiple vendors for both gasification technology and equipment, all of which have been operated successfully on a commercial scale.

As the name implies, gasification is the process of taking a solid material (such as coal or biomass) and converting it to a gas, a mixture comprised mostly of hydrogen (H_2) and carbon monoxide (CO) — commonly referred to as synthesis gas or "syngas." For purposes of producing transportation fuel, syngas is an intermediate product, but it can also be used directly for energy production. In an integrated gasification combined-cycle (IGCC) power plant, for example, it is piped directly into a gas-turbine to be combusted without any further processing. "Combined-cycle" refers to the use of excess heat from the gas-turbine to produce steam for a secondary turbine, thereby making the plant much more efficient that if that heat were wasted.

There are dozens, perhaps even hundreds, of variations of gasification technologies. Explaining differences between the technologies goes far beyond the scope of a general audience book like this one, falling more in the realm of graduate study in chemical engineering. Because it has a material impact on the economics, it is worth mentioning that there are generally two classes of gasifiers: partial oxidation gasifiers and indirectly heated gasifiers. Partial oxidations (POX) gasifiers use the exothermic reaction between oxygen and organics to provide the heat necessary to drive the gasification process. Reactors that use the POX usually require pure oxygen, which necessitates construction of an oxygen production plant to accompany the gasifier. Oxygen plants are expensive, which means that this technology typically is only used in very large plants where significant economies of scale can be gained.

Indirectly-heated gasifiers, on the other hand, derive the heat required for the gasification process from a source external to the reaction. The heat is commonly produced by diverting and combusting some of the syngas, but can also be generated using natural gas or electricity purchased from the grid. The heat is then transferred to the gasifier, often using a hot solid (like sand) or a heat transfer surface. Indirectly-heated gasifiers tend not to be quite as efficient as POX gasifiers, but can be competitive at a much smaller size because an oxygen plant is not required.[9]

Fuel Synthesis

Once syngas has been produced, it is fairly simple to produce a liquid fuel. The process has been well understood for nearly a century. Like gasification, synthesis chemistry comes in many varieties with hundreds of variations on plant designs and product spectrums. By far the most well-established process is known as Fischer-Tropsch (FT) synthesis, developed in 1923 by German chemists Franz Fischer and Hans Tropsch. The process involves reaction of syngas in the presence of a catalyst to produce various liquid hydrocarbons, energy, water (H_2O), and carbon dioxide (CO_2). Temperature of the reaction, pressure, ratio of the syngas components, and formulation of the catalyst determines the range of products produced. The products of FT synthesis reactions can be further refined (similar to the process of refining petroleum) to produce precisely the desired finished product.[10] Because fuels are synthesized from a purified gas, the finished product has none of the impurities associated with crude oil distillates such as sulfur and heavy metals.[11]

Germans were the first to begin using FT fuels on a commercial scale, which provided a large portion of their fuel during World War II, but South Africa is the most successful modern case study. In 1955, the South African refiner Sasol (then owned by the government of South Africa) built its first FT production plant. Because of availability of relatively cheap oil on the world market, the FT process has generally been applied in situations where access to global free market has been constrained for political reasons (such as in Germany during World War II and in South Africa during apartheid).[12]

Over the years, Sasol has been able to improve its technology to increase output and gain economies of scale. Today, both coal and natural gas are used to produce liquid fuels in South Africa. Sasol's plant in Secunda, south-east of Johannesburg, is the largest coal-based synthetic fuel plant in the world. It produces 160,000 barrels of fuel per day (or about 2.5 billion gallons per year) from coal using gasification and FT synthesis,[13] a quantity of fuel equivalent to nearly half the output of the entire US ethanol industry.

With the elimination of apartheid and South Africa's re-integration in the world community, Sasol has been aggressively pursuing opportunities to increase its footprint internationally. The company commissioned its first international joint-venture plant in Qatar in 2006, and has another under construction in Nigeria. Both plants are designed to produce FT liquids from natural gas.[14] The company has also signed agreements to develop new plants in China, India, and Uzbekistan.[15]

There are also quite a few other companies, among them Syntroleum Corporation and Range Fuels in the US, actively pursuing thermochemical fuel production technologies. Several large oil multinationals have also been developing FT technology, although they tend to focus, not surprisingly, on using natural gas feedstocks. The most active oil company is Royal Dutch Shell, which has an FT plant in Bintulu, Malaysia. A significant portion of the middle distillates (like diesel) produced at the Bintulu plant has actually ended up in the US market where they are used to meet California's stringent emissions regulations.[16] In 2005, Shell began expanding its Bintulu plant's capacity, and, in 2007, began construction of another large FT plant in Qatar.[17]

The most aggressive moves, however, are being made in China. China has at least two large coal-to-liquids facilities currently under construction. The first of the facilities, developed by mostly state-owned Shenhua Group, China's largest coal company, will be capable of producing 24,000 barrels per day of liquid fuels (primarily diesel) and is estimated to cost $1.5 billion.[18]

The Fischer-Tropsch synthesis reaction is actually quite simple. The constituent molecules of syngas, carbon monoxide (CO) and hydrogen gas (H_2) react to form water (H_2O) and a hydrocarbon. The nature of the hydrocarbons produced vary, but the most important reactions form compounds known as alkanes, also known as paraffins. The reaction is depicted as:

$$(x)CO + (2x+1)H_2 = (x)H_2O + C_{(x)}H_{(2x+2)}$$

The $C_{(x)}H_{(2x+2)}$ molecule is an alkane representative of a hydrocarbon chain, which could be of varying length (CH_4, C_2H_6, C_3H_8, etc.).[19] The "x" can be any whole number; the higher the value, the more complex the chain. Length of the molecular chain is a function of catalyst selectivity and reaction conditions (temperature, pressure, etc.).[20] The most well known alkane is methane (natural gas), but longer chains, such as gasoline components hexane and octane, take liquid form.

Catalysts like those needed in FT reactions are also used in petroleum refining. Demand for better catalysts in the refining industry, which have a clear impact on profitability, has led to major technological advances. For example, suppliers now have the capability of manufacturing custom catalysts based on specific configuration of a plant, feedstock, operating environment, and finished product slate, a service referred to as "extreme customization".[21]

In recent years, major technological advances in catalysts and numerous other components of liquid synthesis systems have significantly reduced costs and increased the portion of the product yields that can be used as liquid fuels.[22] Catalyst technology is central to the FT process. In the early days of FT, the catalysts of choice were iron-based. When natural gas began to be used as a feedstock instead of coal, however, researchers discovered that cobalt-based catalysts performed better in the higher hydrogen-to-carbon ratio environment.

Recent advances in catalyst technology represent a major leap forward toward improving the economics of the FT process. One of the keys to decreasing costs is increasing catalyst lifespan. Sasol's first commercialized cobalt catalysts had an expected lifespan of, at most, one year. Now the life expectancy is five years.[23] Extending catalyst life to five years means a five-fold reduction in catalyst cost.

Longevity is not the only major advance. Nanotechnology is playing a major role as well. Reactions take place on the surface of the catalyst, so increasing surface area can greatly increase performance. Micro-channels provide much more surface on which reactions can take place.[24] Instead of a flat surface, there are many tiny tunnels, dramatically increasing surface to volume ratio.

The most important advantage of FT liquids is rather obvious: they are fuels already widely prevalent because they are the same fuels currently distilled from crude oil. FT liquids are not, however, the only potential products that can be produced from syngas. Production of mixed alcohols, for example, is another synthesis reaction that has applications for fuel production. The chemistry of alcohol synthesis is very similar to the FT alkane reaction. The basic reaction is:

$$(x)CO + (2x)H_2 = (x\text{-}1)H_2O + C_{(x)}H_{(2x+1)}OH$$

The only difference between an alkane hydrocarbon and an alcohol is that an oxygen atom is present as part of a hydroxyl group (the "OH" part of the molecule). Methanol is the most basic alcohol (CH_3OH), but the transportation fuel market is most familiar with ethanol (C_2H_5OH). Like hydrocarbons, there are many different types of alcohols. As with FT synthesis, production of alcohols can be tailored to maximize selectivity of the desired alcohol, which would be ethanol in most cases.

Commercial interest in producing mixed alcohols from thermochemical conversion is relatively new, only gaining attention in the past few decades, but catalyst technology has already progressed significantly. A variety of catalysts are capable of producing mixed alcohols, but compounds based on the element molybdenum have been shown to produce high alcohol yields and selectivity while resisting impurities such as sulfur in the reaction chamber. Most recent private and government research on mixed alcohol catalysts has focused on compounds of molybdenum.[25] Rhodium catalysts also have shown superior performance, but they are generally too expensive to be useful for commercial operations.[26] Molybdenum is used to manufacture stainless steel, so it is widely available. At the pinnacle of the building boom, the cost of molybdenum topped out at nearly $40 per pound, but it has since dropped to below $10 per pound.[27] At either price, the cost does not significantly impact fuel production economics.

The Refinery of the Future

The word "refinery" has come to mean a manufacturing plant that takes crude oil and converts it into usable liquid fuel such as gasoline, kerosene, or diesel. That concept need not be exclusive. In the alternative energy world, people often discuss the concept of the bio-refinery. In a nutshell, a bio-refinery, just like a traditional refinery, takes a raw material (in this case biomass) and changes it into usable products. Of course, like a traditional refinery, there can also be ancillary products for the chemical, fertilizer, and pharmaceutical industries. Not all crude oil becomes gasoline. In fact, chemicals make up 17% of the volume of products manufactured from petroleum.[28]

The bio-refinery of the future may be configured to take advantages of any number of technologies. As was discussed earlier, there are many potential configurations. An indirect liquefaction bio-refinery, which will be the technology addressed throughout the remainder of this book, would have five separate phases: feedstock handling and preparation (where biomass is dried and sized to meet the plant's specifications); gasification; gas "cleanup" (where particulates, impurities, and carbon dioxide are removed); synthesis (which converts the syngas to liquid fuel); and, finally, product separation.[29] Separation is necessary because synthesis reactions yield multiple compounds. In fact, much of the research into synthesis catalysts has centered on catalyst selectivity;[30] that is the ability of a catalyst to yield higher percentages of a specifically desired product. Catalyst formulations tend to be proprietary, heavily guarded trade secrets.

The most important analysis when considering any alternative means of manufacturing fuels is cost. Therefore, it is vital to gain a complete understanding of the economics of production.

Operating Efficiency

The most important aspect of a biorefinery is its conversion efficiency, or, plainly, the amount of fuel that can be produced from a given ton of raw materials. Not all raw materials are the same. Different organic materials have different relative quantities of carbon, hydrogen, oxygen, and other elements.[31] Maximum yield depends on the molecular composition.

As a baseline for comparison purposes, fuel and chemical products produced in petroleum refining contain 70.6% of the energy of the crude oil and auxiliary energy inputs.[32] Fuel production from biomass or coal is not as efficient as petroleum refining, but there are plenty of other good reasons to use alternative fuels.

The actual efficiency of thermochemical conversion depends on the specific engineering and configuration of a biorefinery. Energy is always going to be lost in any conversion process. In the case of a biorefinery, energy is lost through production of heat as well as in production of non-fuel by-products. A portion of the syngas must be diverted to meet the power requirements of running the plant itself, making it unavailable to produce fuels, and not all syngas produces usable products.

There are a variety of estimates available for the volume of fuel that can be produced in a modern operating plant. Various studies indicate that anywhere between 35% and 55% of the energy contained in raw biomass feedstock can be converted to fuel regardless of whether the end products are mixed alcohols or Fischer-Tropsch gasoline and diesel.[33] A 2007 report prepared by the National Renewable Energy Laboratory, a government laboratory under the direction of the US Department of Energy, specifically estimated the conversion efficiency of a small scale POX reactor combined with mixed alcohol synthesis to be 47%.[34] The author's analysis indicates an energy conversion yield of 49%, which will be used for calculating potential yields for the remainder of this book.[35] Saleable fuel products would constitute 75% to 85% of its yield.[36] The remaining products would also have economic value and would likely be sold for use in manufacturing plastics, textiles, cosmetics, cleaners, pharmaceuticals, and numerous other products. This book will assume that 85% of a plant's production can be sold as fuels.

Capital Costs

The most common criticism of thermochemical fuel production technology is the high capital costs of constructing refineries. Even proponents sometimes classify the technology as uneconomic. A close examination of a wide variety of government research and publicly available information shows that, contrary to conventional wisdom, thermochemical production of fuels from biomass can be profitable, highly profitable.

A biomass-to-liquids plant designed to compete with petroleum is a significant undertaking. For years the biofuel industry, which has been almost exclusively comprised of corn-based ethanol production, has been characterized by relatively small plants that are often owned locally by farmer co-ops. Even the largest corn-based ethanol plants built with Wall Street backing are quite modest compared with even the smallest petroleum refineries. For thermochemical biomass processing to maximize efficiency and economies of scale, plants will be large and look much more like a petroleum refinery than a corn-ethanol plant (both visually and in terms of investment capital).

Economies of scale are very important for bio-refineries. A study by the Energy Research Centre of the Netherlands (ECN) suggests that capital cost as a percentage of capacity falls dramatically until a plant reaches the equivalent of around 20,000 barrels per day, after which it continues to improve modestly. Scaling also improves efficiency, landing it toward the high end of the range of theoretical conversion rates.[37]

Probably the single most important component determining the cost of constructing a biorefinery is the price of steel.[38] Between 2003 and 2008, steel prices shot up dramatically, but onset of the global recession at the end of 2008 caused prices to drop significantly. All cost figures in this book's analyses have been adjusted to 2007 dollars based on the *Chemical Engineering* Plant Cost Index.[39] That year marked a point when steel prices were at near record levels.

As a baseline, consider that the projected cost of an installed new crude oil refinery is about $20,000 per barrel per day of capacity in 2007 dollars.[40] For simplicity, all estimates in this section are listed in barrel per day of oil equivalent. Estimates for capital costs of thermochemical fuel plants vary significantly, but assumptions underlying those estimates (plant configuration, scale, product slate) also diverge. The often-sited National Renewable Energy Laboratory study places capital costs at roughly $65,000 per barrel per day equivalent, but the study also assumes a very small plant with about 2,500 barrels per day of capacity.[41] The ECN study, which assumes a much larger plant with a 20,000 barrel per day capacity, estimates capital costs of about $60,000 per barrel per day. But it also indicates that if capacity reaches 80,000 barrels per day, the capital costs may fall below $40,000 per barrel.[42] This author also completed an independent costing study. The results indicated a total capital cost of approximately $65,000 per barrel per day, which equates to about $3.85

per gallon of gasoline equivalent production capacity per year.[43] For purposes of this book, this author will continue to use the conservative estimate of $3.85 per gallon of gasoline equivalent.

The cost of constructing a biorefinery is indeed significantly higher than constructing an oil refinery, but, again, the smallest investment does not necessarily make the most long-term financial sense. Capital cost is spread over a long useful life of a plant, and savings show up in other places. It is an investment that will indeed pay dividends, both figuratively and literally.

Operating Costs

Operating costs are very important because they determine the minimum price at which biofuels can be competitive with petroleum. The most important operating cost of a manufacturing facility is the price of raw materials. The entire following chapter is devoted to a discussion of biomass feedstock including costs and the quantities that can be available for fuel production. Although energy is a key factor in production as well, this analysis assumes that energy requirements are met using an on-site generator fueled using a portion of the syngas produced in the gasification process. Such a configuration eliminates the costs of an external energy source but also reduces the amount of net product available for sale.

Operating costs generally fall into the categories of fixed (don't change based on the level of production) and variable. Expenses such as biomass and chemical inputs would be the primary variable costs, while expenses such as labor, maintenance, and overhead are generally fixed. Although labor is a cost, the job creation aspect of plant development has a public policy benefit. Government forecasts indicate that a biorefinery with capacity of processing around 2,000 tons per day of biomass would employ approximately 54 people.[44] By analyzing the nature of the jobs and comparing them to similar positions in other industries, it can be determined that the average salary would be around $45,000 per year, not including benefits, taxes, etc (which typically are assumed to add 25% based on national averages). Since this figure is an average, some employees would make more, other less; salaries would also go up or down in accordance with the local labor market. To the extent that plant capacity is greater than 2,000 tons per day, scale efficiencies would result in additional employees, but not on a one-to-one basis with capacity expansion. For example, doubling capacity might only result in the addition of only 50% more employees.

Besides biomass, the main raw material needed for thermochemical processing is water. Corn ethanol plants, such as those already operating all over the US, use about four gallons of water for every gallon of fuel ethanol they produce. Thermochemical fuel production is significantly more water-efficient, using less than two gallons of water for every gallon of fuel produced.[45] Furthermore, when feedstock is delivered to the plant, it contains significant quantities of moisture that can be counted toward the water requirement further reducing the need for an external water source. The cost of water, at least at present rates, would not have a major material impact on profitability of a plant.

Another important expense of plant operation is the cost of catalysts and chemicals essential to a plant's chemical processes. Based on current prices and assuming a five year useful life for catalysts, catalysts and chemicals should add roughly 2.5¢ to the cost of each gallon of fuel produced. There are also other miscellaneous costs that should be included as well: permits, taxes, insurance, overhead, and hundreds of other small charges. All of these things fall under the operating expense category.

As with capital costs, an extensive literature review as well as the author's own cost study was considered when evaluating potential operating costs. As expected, operating costs on a per-unit-of-output basis decline substantially as the size of the plant increases. Cost estimates range from 15¢ to 38¢ per gallon of gasoline equivalent fuel production. The author's study indicates (and this book will use for purposes of all calculations) 35¢ per gallon of gasoline equivalent products produced.[46]

Throughout this chapter conservative estimates have been used. While these choices will very likely underestimate performance of the technology and overestimate cost, the goal is to demonstrate that thermochemically produced fuels can be economical. Exploring the technical and financial aspects of a biorefinery is not the end, but rather a beginning. In the following chapters, this analysis will show how thermochemical fuel production technology, combined with an ample supply of biomass in the US (along with still more that can be produced), can finally achieve the elusive goal of energy independence.

12
My Stalk is Longer than Yours

At the dawn of the automobile age, approximately 25% of agricultural land in the US was devoted to growing food for horses.[1] Horses were the primary means of transportation. The US was, quite simply, a biomass-based society. Nobody is suggesting going back to riding around on horses, but a return to a biomass-based society with a modern twist is an idea worth exploring.

In the early twentieth century, there was a movement focused on promoting a more concrete link between agriculture and industry whereby farmers would produce the raw material from which industry would manufacture a wide range of products. Henry Ford was a prominent member of this movement, which came to be known as chemurgy. Leaders recognized that it was technically possible to produce anything from agricultural products (biomass) that could be produced from petroleum. With an abundance of cheap petroleum during that time, however, the movement lost its steam.[2]

Having established that it is possible to produce fuel from biomass, the next challenge is to quantify the potential supply of biomass and determine how much oil it can displace. To avoid the same dilemma faced with petroleum, dwindling supply, biofuel production can be thought of as having an upper limit where use of biomass outstrips the amount created in a given year by new growth. Strict adherence to such a limit ensures that the supply is "sustainable," a heavily overused word but an important concept. The supply potential is further constrained by the biomass that is economically accessible.

Fortunately, the federal government has done significant research into determining available biomass resources. An April 2005 joint report of the US Department of Agriculture (USDA) and the Department of Energy ascertained that annual national biomass potential "exceeds 1.3 billion dry tons – the equivalent of more than one-third of the current demand for transportation fuels."[3] As great as that sounds, it is prudent to examine the subject in significantly greater detail, particularly since quite a few assumptions were involved in extrapolating that conclusion.

Usable energy in biomass ranges from about 6500 to 8500 British thermal units (Btu) per pound of dry material. This figure is important to note because biomass contains significant quantities of water (typically by 40-50%) that substantially increase its weight.[4] Therefore, the energy value *per pound* of wet material is reduced, which becomes very important when shipping material (since the more something weighs, the more it costs to ship).

Biomass resources come from two major categories: crops grown specifically for energy production and everything else. The "everything else" is actually somewhat easier to quantify because these resources are already being produced in known quantities. The biomass potentially available from dedicated agricultural endeavors, however, is dependent upon various assumptions, including crop yields per acre, number of acres planted, and types of crops cultivated.

Existing Biomass Resources

Non-cultivated biomass resources are comprised of: residues generated by traditional logging operations and clearing of timberlands; forest thinning for purposes of fire suppression; processing wastes (including primary mills, secondary mills, and paper mills); and urban wood residues.[5] Urban residues may include construction and demolition debris; yard wastes; and municipal wood wastes such furniture, cabinets, pallets and containers, and other scrap wood.[6]

About 33 percent of US land area (749 million acres) is forest, down from roughly half at the time our country was settled.[7] Forests contain the largest standing inventory of biomass resources. Simply cutting down all the trees is not an option because prudence dictates that no more biomass should be taken from forests than is produced in new growth each year. Fortunately, there are already harvesting operations that supply the timber industry. It is possible to "piggy-back" on those operations to access a substantial biomass supply.

Current harvesting operations on the nation's forest lands, as well as historical operations for all years that the US Forest Service has kept records, have taken less biomass material than has been replenished by new growth; the result has been perennial net biomass increases (33% more growth than removal).[8] Logging operations produce saw-timber, but leave tree tops and branches as waste. In 2001, the total volume of these logging residues and other removals was 4,532 million cubic feet.[9] After adjusting for limitations inherent in the recovery of the material and converting volume to dry weight, that volume equates to 41 million dry tons of biomass material available each year for fuel production without cutting down a single additional tree.[10] Available material must be collected and processed into a form suitable for biofuel production, the cost of which is estimated to be $21 per ton.[11]

In recent years, the US has been plagued by major forest fires, which, in some cases, have threatened high value residential communities. Even homes of celebrities in southern California have been at risk. A primary means of preventing forest fires is to limit the amount of fuel available through the removal of excess dead and dying timber. This removal provides another excellent source of renewable biomass. While 8.4 billion tons of total material has been targeted for removal, the USDA calculates the potentially available biomass for fuel production on an annual basis is 60 million dry tons after adjusting for accessibility, recoverability, and resource quality.[12]

The cost of processing, collecting, and removing fuel treatments is significantly greater than for logging residues. The reason for this is quite obvious: logging residues are collected in conjunction with logging activities that are already ongoing, but fuel treatment activities require separate crews and equipment to extract the materials. The US Forest Service estimates that processing fuel treatments to chips and extracting them to a major roadway would cost $34-$48 per dry ton.[13]

Waste materials, when available, tend to be excellent sources of biomass. They are naturally geographically concentrated. There is typically some explicit disposal cost (such as a landfill tipping fee) that provides a tangible cash incentive for their productive use. It is also clearly advantageous from an environmental perspective to reuse waste biomass rather than have it buried in landfills.

Processing wastes, by virtue of the fact that they are already concentrated at processing facilities where they originate, provide the most easily captured biomass resources. There is no need to go out into forests to retrieve them. Furthermore, they are highly desirable for energy production because they tend to be clean, uniform, and low in moisture content.[14]

At primary wood processing facilities (sawmills), the processing wastes are small pieces of scrap, sawdust, and tree bark. Secondary processing mills (manufacturing plants that use processed wood to make such products as furniture, flooring, and paper) also produce scrap and sawdust, but in smaller quantities. Total residue volume from both primary and secondary processing mills is 159 million tons per year. Because most of this waste is already recycled (often for energy production on site), the USDA estimates that only 7.7 million tons are available for biofuel production.[15] At higher values, however, plants may have an economic incentive to make more available for fuel production. There is also considerable research and development ongoing with respect to co-locating fuel plants with processing mills, allowing them to take advantage of waste heat and syngas to power the plant while profitably producing significant quantities of fuel.[16]

Although it varies by region, a representative price for this type of waste in high value markets is $31 per dry ton.[17] To the extent that a biofuel manufacturer pays more than $31 per ton for feedstock, there will be a greater potential for penetration into these markets and more material available. To determine total cost, however, a biomass facility would have to calculate not only the actual cost of feedstock, but also the cost of processing it (estimated to be $5.5 per ton).[18]

The final type of non-agricultural biomass resource is urban wood residues. Construction and demolition debris account for the preponderance of material that could be available in this category. In 2002, 77.8 million tons of wood was used in construction. The USDA estimates that 15% of this wood ends up as waste material; 75% of the waste material is recoverable. Therefore, construction waste has the potential to contribute 8.6 tons of material to biofuel production each year.[19]

Demolition wastes, as the name implies, is the product removed from demolished homes and other buildings that are torn down. It is very hard to recycle demolition wastes because there are often many types of building materials mixed together. Such waste often includes concrete, insulation, wood, metal, sheet rock, glass, and sometimes hazardous materials. To make the wood component of this waste useable, it must be separated from the other materials. Although this process would be time consuming and expensive, the USDA estimates that another 10.6 million tons of biomass could be available for fuel production annually, assuming a 30% recovery rate.[20] The recovery rate, however, is difficult to estimate.

Obviously, greater processing would be required for this type of material. Estimates for collection and processing are roughly $15 per ton.[21] Construction and demolition debris, however, has an added economic advantage to the biofuel producer; it costs an average of $24.50 per ton to dispose of it in the form of landfill or incinerator tipping fees.

The final potential source of non-agricultural biomass is municipal solid waste, which includes yard trimmings and wood product wastes. Most yard trimmings are already recycled, generally as mulch. More than half of all wood product wastes are also already recycled. The combination of these two sources could, according to the USDA, provide 7.7 million tons of feedstock for biofuel production.[22] The same collection and processing costs ($15 per ton) are assumed for biomass derived from municipal solid waste (MSW).[23]

The combination of all of these non-agricultural biomass resources could provide 135.6 million dry tons per year on a sustainable basis.

Agricultural Wastes

With most agricultural crops, only a part of the plant is actually used. Anyone who has grown a garden is quite familiar with the concept. Suffice it to say, there is a lot more stalk than there is bean. In recent decades, the US has seen serious challenges from other countries in almost every industry – but not agriculture. When it comes to growing things efficiently, the US is the undisputed king. With such a massive agricultural industry, naturally there is a tremendous amount of biomass material that is currently unused or underused.

The USDA estimates that total agricultural residue that can be used on a sustainable basis for production of bioenergy is 113.2 million dry tons.[24] The preponderance of this material (74.8 million dry tons)[25] is corn stover (part of the corn plant other than the ear of corn). The remaining plant volume is spread among many other types of agricultural crops grown in the US.

Crop residues are particularly attractive for biofuel production because growth is controlled and is incidental to other crop production. The resources can be easily harvested and moved through existing supply chains. The cost of accessing crop wastes is relatively modest, and production does not require the recovery of land costs because it is a byproduct of existing crops.

The USDA has done an extensive study of the cost of using biomass feedstocks for fuel production. With some basic mathematics, we can extrapolate from their data that 90% of total biomass crop residue in the US not currently being used for animal feed (estimated to be 102 million tons) could be available at a maximum cost of approximately $33.25 per dry ton.[26]

In addition to the material available from crop residues, there is also a significant amount of animal product waste. This material includes manure as well as the unused portions of agriculturally produced animals (beef, pork, chicken, etc.). About 59.7 million dry tons of animal related waste is projected to be available.[27]

All major sources of biomass discussed so far are waste products or are gleaned by removing material from existing forest growth. While each of these supplies is relatively modest by itself, the combination is a formidable supply of biomass that could be refined to supplant a portion of the petroleum the US currently imports.

As the following table shows, total biomass available from existing resources is roughly 308 million tons, available at roughly $33 per dry ton, not including transportation costs to a bio-refinery.

Type of Biomass	Available Biomass (million dry tons)	Estimated Cost ($/dry ton)
Logging Residues	41	$21
Fire Prevention Removals	60	$48
Wood Processing Residues	7.7	$37
Construction Debris	8.6	$15
Demolition Debris	10.6	$15
MSW*	7.7	$15
Crop Residues	113.2	$33
Manure & Animal Residues	59.7	$34[†]
Total	**308.5**	**$33[‡]**

* Includes yard trimmings and municipal wood product wastes.
† Based upon $50 per dry ton costs for the manure component (35.1 million tons) and $12 per dry ton costs for animal residue (derived from analysis for other MSW feedstocks that incur disposal costs such as landfill tipping fees).
‡ Weighted average cost.

Energy Crops

If the US is to go beyond the fuel production capabilities from the country's existing supply of biomass, dedicated agriculture will be necessary. The US already produces ethanol from corn, making it the first crop grown in the US specifically for the production of energy. Corn-derived ethanol has become widely accepted in the United States, with 173 ethanol plants now operating (and a reported 9 additional plants under construction), almost all of which produce ethanol from the starch in corn. The combined current operating capacity of 11.9 billion gallons will grow to 13.4 billion gallons per year with completion of plants already under construction,[28] a volume representing a modest 5.3% (6.0% with scheduled completions) of the total 222.7 billion gallons of transportation fuel consumption in the US in 2008.[29]

Unfortunately, the use of corn for ethanol has several distinct disadvantages, the most important of which is its relative land efficiency. Corn tends to yield about 3.3 dry tons per acre per year.[30] In 2008, there were approximately 86 million acres of planted corn in the US that yielded an estimated 153.9 bushels per acre.[31] Much of that corn is used as feed, with around 15% going to the production of ethanol.[32] With current crop yields and the technology used in most of today's plants, corn is capable of producing only about 400 gallons of ethanol for each acre of corn that is planted and dedicated to energy production.[33] If all of the corn planted in the US in 2008 was used exclusively for ethanol production, the result would be 34.4 billion gallons of ethanol, which is still only 15.4% of the total 222.7 billion gallons of transportation fuels consumed in 2008.[34] In other words, even if every ear of corn in the US were devoted ethanol production (which is not feasible since corn also has other critical uses), the resulting fuel would have only a small impact on foreign oil imports.

With estimates for conversion efficiency and crop yields, it is relatively simple to calculate the amount of land that would be needed to produce enough ethanol to offset the nation's supply of foreign oil. If average corn yields could be held steady over the entire land mass of the United States (which is also not feasible since land and climate most suitable for corn production is already devoted to its growth), a total of 561 million acres would need to be planted to produce enough ethanol to fully supplant all of the transportation fuel consumed in the US that comes from imported oil.[35] That amount of land represents 29.7%

of the 1,894 million acre total land area of the contiguous 48 states.[36] Of the 360.2 million acres of cropland that are not already planted in corn, about 220 million acres are planted in some other crop (such as wheat, soybeans, hay, and cotton), which leaves only 102 million acres of additional cropland available to be planted in corn without changing land use.[37]

Although corn yields have been steadily increasing over time,[38] the pace of improvement would need a hyper-drive before it could come close to producing enough corn to make a dent in imported oil given the land available for planting. Most experts believe (and the trend lines indicate) that there will be more corn yield increases in the future but on a modest scale. To double the yield or even triple the yield on a per acre basis (which is not realistic in the foreseeable future) would not be nearly enough.

Since clearing a vast expanse of forestland to make way for energy crops is both unrealistic and undesirable, there is really only one option for the US to realistically replace foreign oil with agriculturally derived biofuels. Alternative crops must be used that have much higher yields. By using thermochemical fuel production technology, crops that contain large quantities of sugar or starches are no longer required. There are certainly crops that are easier to produce (much less labor intensive) and yield significantly greater volumes of material per acre than corn. With the availability of thermochemical fuel technology and the reality that crops offering much higher yields are available, high yielding energy crops clearly make more sense than relying on expensive and land intensive crop production process.

High Yielding Perennials

Growing crops for energy is just like anything else in the world: cheaper, easier, and more efficient tends to win the day. When producing crops for food, most people tend to think of a very traditional agricultural cycle – planting crops in the spring, harvesting in the fall, and repeating the process all over again the next year. The traditional agricultural cycle is labor intensive and, therefore, expensive. Not all crops have to be planted each spring; some varieties of plants just keep growing year after year. The two that are most common, and probably most often overlooked, are grass and trees. Imagine if we could find varieties of grass and trees that grow rapidly, producing more biomass than seed crops like corn.

In fact, there are quite a few varieties of grasses and a few types of trees that produce enough biomass material to make their growth substantially more land-efficient than corn. Brazil has actually achieved energy independence by basing a biofuel industry on a common variety of perennial grass – a favorite for those with a sweet tooth – sugar cane. The USDA does classify sugar cane as perennial, but it is really more of a semi-perennial due to the fact that it must be replanted every four to five years.[39]

As it turns out, sugar cane is indeed much more land efficient than corn. Where it is grown in the US, it does produce very high comparative yields – a 2005 average of 28.8 tons per acre.[40] While corn yields about 100 gallons of ethanol for each ton of corn (about 2.7 gallons per bushel), sugarcane yields only 19.5 gallons per ton.[41] Factoring all of that together, sugarcane yields about 560 gallons per acre, which is a sure improvement over corn's yield at 400 gallons per acre.

Unfortunately, sugarcane doesn't grow very well outside of tropical areas. In the US, it is grown only in south Florida, Louisiana, parts of Texas, and, to a limited extent, in Hawaii.[42] There is limited land available for expansion in areas that are climatically suitable.

Although ethanol produced from sugarcane in Brazil is much more economical than corn-based ethanol produced in the US, producing ethanol from sugarcane in the US is quite expensive by comparison. Projected costs for producing feedstock and ethanol were $2.45 per gallon for sugarcane and $2.34 for sugar beets in 2005 dollars.[43] The cost to consumers, however, would be significantly higher due to transportation costs, overhead, and profit for the manufacturer and others in the supply chain.

The cost of production in Brazil averaged $0.80 per gallon[44] (including feedstock cost of about $0.30 per gallon[45]), which is quite a dramatic savings compared to sugar-based production in the US, a product of the availability of much more cultivatable acreage that can be devoted to sugarcane production without displacing crops devoted to food production. Public policy also has played a major role. Brazil ended sugar price supports, drastically lowering the price of sugarcane, while establishing relatively high blending requirements for ethanol with gasoline, supporting the price of ethanol.[46] In the US, there are multiple schemes to support sugar prices that keep them well above world market prices. Finally, sugarcane can be harvested throughout much of the year in Brazil (typically nine months), but can only be harvested three to six months of the year in the US. This would limit ethanol plants to operation at only 25-50% of their annual capacity.[47]

Switchgrass

Since sugarcane, or sugar beets for that matter, are not really well suited for ethanol production in the US, most of the discussion and research has been focused on a crop called switchgrass. Switchgrass has gotten much attention since it was mentioned by name in the State of the Union Address by President Bush in 2006. Despite that attention, a survey discovered that only 21% of farmers had ever heard of the possibility of growing switchgrass for profit.[48] Presumably, that percentage is even less among the population at large.

First of all, to be clear, policy makers and advocates often use "switchgrass" as a catch-all term intended to encompass all energy crops that are not also consumable as food. When they speak of switchgrass, they may mean a variety of perennial grasses that have potential as energy crops. Most often, however, switchgrass indeed does mean switchgrass, a variety of perennial grass native to the Eastern two-thirds of the US.

Like any crop, switchgrass has its advantages and disadvantages, but it has been chosen as a "model crop" by government researchers for several reasons. It is native to the US and has the capacity for relatively high yields, even on poor soils with limited water availability. Relatively low inputs of energy and agrochemicals are required per unit of energy produced by switchgrass. It can be produced by conventional farming operations using standard equipment for seeding, crop management, and harvesting. As a result, management intensity and capital spending requirements for its production are low, and equipment to plant and harvest is already widely available.[49]

The yield of switchgrass varies depending on geographic area and the conditions of soil and climate at that location. Extensive studies on crop yields indicate that poor soil would yield an average of 7.1 tons per acre and good soils would yield an average of 9.8 tons per acre on an annual basis.[50]

Switchgrass has deep roots, often with as much mass below-ground as there is above-ground. It can be grown on depleted and eroded croplands where years of agricultural production have reduced the soil's organic matter, helping to restore soil fertility and capacity to hold nutrients and water. For this reason, it is one of the preferred crops planted in lands within the Conservation Reserve Program, which encompasses around 30 million acres.[51]

The economics of switchgrass are clearly important to understand when evaluating its value as a bioenergy feedstock. Its establishment cost is about $500 per acre.[52] A normal switchgrass crop has a useful life of 10 years,[53] which results in an amortized establishment cost of $50 per year. Ongoing production and harvest costs for switchgrass are estimated to be $250 per acre,[54] for a total cost of $300 including the establishment costs. Assuming an average production yields equivalent to those described above, the resulting cost of production would be $42 per ton on poor quality soils and $31 per ton on good quality soils.

Arundo

Perhaps the best energy crop is a crop almost nobody in the US is talking about, the perennial grass *Arundo donax* – more commonly known as the giant reed. Arundo is one of the most resilient and fastest growing crops in the world. Like switchgrass, it is a perennial grass, but its yield potential is significantly higher.

Governmental research on arundo has been quite limited in the US, where researchers have tended to favor switchgrass because it is native to the US, it requires less maintenance and irrigation, and it works well with existing agricultural equipment. Switchgrass also lends itself well to producing cellulosic ethanol using the bio-processing method where polysaccharides are broken down and then ethanol is produced by fermentation. Arundo does not work as well as a feedstock for bio-processing; rather it is more ideally suited to thermochemical fuel production. Substantially more arundo research has been conducted in Europe where it is a native plant species.

In the process of estimating yield potential for arundo, a very wide range of data was considered. It indicates that natural stands of arundo in warm temperate and tropical regions would yield up to 23 dry tons per acre annually.[55] Even under severe drought conditions, it remains remarkably resilient and can still produce high yields.[56]

Commercially-produced arundo, however, could have still higher yields. Warm climates, with the use of fertilizer and underground irrigation, can produce a continuous stream of biomass equal to 45 dry tons per acre per year.[57] Studies for colder climates in the northern US are limited, but European research has indicated that arundo will grow well in the cooler climates of northern Europe, albeit with yield reduced by about 50%.[58]

Arundo is native to areas stretching from the Mediterranean to the lower Himalayas, but it has been introduced to many subtropical and warm temperate regions of the world. It grows in clumps up to 6 meters tall (about 20 feet). It can tolerate annual rainfall of 12 to 155 inches and average temperatures of 48 to 83 degrees Fahrenheit.[59] It does best, however, with ample sunlight and water, and can often be found growing on riverbanks or on sand dunes near seashores. Due to its extended root system and full-year canopy, arundo is an excellent crop for preventing soil erosion.[60]

Because of its extraordinary growth properties, arundo has garnered a bit of a bad reputation. It has found its way on to lists of invasive species in several states. The problem seems to be that arundo thrives in riparian habitats, often growing with such vigor that it crowds out other plant varieties.[61] Arundo is sterile outside its native habitat. It only spreads in the US by movement of plant fragments – either on equipment, carried by animals, and through deliberate introduction by humans. Some environmental groups have objected to the use of arundo as a crop for biofuels, believing that it could spread and grow outside intended farm areas, but that risk is relatively low.[62] Furthermore, the benefits of arundo for biofuel production far outweigh the risk of it spreading to unintended habitats.

In addition to being highly attractive as a potential energy crop, arundo may also be quite useful in other industries as well. It makes an excellent substitute for wood in manufacturing pulp for the paper industry.[63] It may also have a variety of uses in pharmaceutical manufacturing.[64]

Without question, arundo's greatest potential is as a biofuel feedstock. At the top end of its yield range (45 tons per acre) arundo is capable of yielding about 3,200 gallons of gasoline equivalent (roughly equal to 4,725 gallons of ethanol) per acre per year.[65] That is nearly twelve times the land use efficiency of corn (which can produce about 400 gallons of ethanol per acre). The other important consideration, however, is cost.

The exact economics of growing arundo on a large scale have yet to be demonstrated, but they can be estimated based on a variety of assumptions. Since arundo is a perennial crop, the annual costs of seeding it are eliminated. The tradeoff, however, is that arundo is particularly expensive to initially establish. Estimates for the cost of establishing arundo range from about $1,250 (using high tech means) to more than $8,000 per acre (using decidedly low-tech stem cuttings).[66] All indications are, however, that modern technologies will allow costs to be toward the bottom of that range, perhaps decreasing further in the future. For this analysis, a conservative estimate of $2,500 per acre is reasonable. If amortized over an expected 20-year planting cycle for arundo,[67] the result is a cost of $125 per acre per year.

Ongoing costs of producing arundo are likely to be relatively high on a per acre basis when compared with a crop like corn or even switchgrass, but very low on a per-ton basis. Reasonable estimates are $250 per acre per year for crop management (including irrigation) and $500 per acre for harvesting and processing.[68] When all are combined, the result is a total annual production cost for arundo of $875 per acre, or about $20 per ton based on a 45 ton per acre yield. Advances in technology could greatly reduce harvest costs, further reducing per ton cost.

In addition to the crops discussed above, there are a variety of other crops that could be useful for production of biofuels. Among those crops are hybrid poplar,[69] miscanthus, and reed canary grass.[70] Each of these plants is relatively high yield, but they are probably not capable of achieving the yields or costs on par with arundo. Advancements in technology may improve the prospects of these plants (and potentially others) in the future.

There are also efforts underway to develop algae as a biomass feedstock. Technology for algae production and processing are in early stages of development, and algae may ultimately prove to be an important factor in biomass production. Heavyweights such as Bill Gates' Cascade Investments and the Rockefeller Foundation's venture capital arm are making bets on algae. Some believe it could eventually produce as much as 3,000 gallons per acre per year,[71] an amount roughly equivalent to the high end of arundo yields. At this point, however, it is too early to estimate when it could be deployed commercially and at what cost, but commercial fuel production from algae is probably at least a decade away. For that reason (and due to the urgent national need for alternatives to foreign oil that can be deployed quickly), the evaluation and possible inclusion of algae is beyond the scope of this book.

Calculating Potential Energy Crop Yields

The powerhouse US agricultural sector produces its bounty from just 340 million acres of active cropland, about 15% of total US land area.[72] The reason for discussing land use is that energy crops cannot be planted just anywhere. Climates vary significantly, and it would be pointless to plant crops where they simply won't grow (like the arctic tundra or the desert). So, a realistic method of determining where energy crops could be planted is needed. After yields are calculated, it is a simple additional step to estimate the amount of actual fuel that can be produced to displace imported petroleum.

The place to start when estimating potential land available for production of energy crops is with idle cropland. There are almost 39.7 million acres of cropland sitting idle in the US. As discussed earlier, arundo is among the highest yielding crops for energy production. Arundo tends to favor warmer climates, and generally, the warmer the climate the better yields will be. Because of arundo's climate requirements, much of the northern plains states and upper Midwestern states are not suitable for its growth. When land is available for energy crop cultivation but not suitable for arundo, it can still be planted with switchgrass.

For purposes of allocating land between arundo and switchgrass as well as for projecting arundo yields, the primary tool is climatic data from the US Department of Agriculture (USDA).[73] The highest arundo yields will be in the warmest climates in the US. The coldest areas where arundo can be expected to succeed have climates comparable to those in northern Europe.[74] Arundo will grow at some level in at least 38 of the lower 48 states,[75] but yields in cooler climates, as previous research has indicated, will b6 reduced to half the level of yields in warmer climates.[79]

About 63% of idle cropland in the lower 48 states is suitable for growing arundo, but the remaining lands can be expected to support switchgrass. Although switchgrass has lower potential yields, it can still produce around 104 million tons of biomass on the 14.6 million acres of idle cropland not suitable for arundo (assuming average yields of 7.1 tons per acre, the low end of its yield potential).[77]

Arundo yields are a little more complex to calculate. To get an accurate estimate, it can be assumed that yields are at their maximum in the warmest climates and gradually decrease (by about 20% for each climate zone) until reaching half the maximum yield in the cooler northern climates.[78] Assuming the warmest climates (such as Florida and Louisiana) produce maximum yields of 45 tons per acre, the average projected yield over the whole idle cropland area planted in arundo would be just over 32 tons per acre.[79] For the 25 million available acres, over 805 million tons of biomass could be produced.

Coincidentally, based on the amount of available idle cropland and climate, the top biomass-producing state would also be the top petroleum producer, Texas.[80] Texans need not fear a biofuel revolution; on the contrary, Texas is the state that will likely benefit most as domestic oil production continues while the new biofuel industry emerges. Texas alone could gain as many as one million new jobs.

So far, only idle cropland has been considered, but there is also the potential to convert croplands used for grazing without sacrificing land currently used to produce other crops or converting non-agricultural land (such as prairie) to agricultural use. Cropland used as pasture is not the same as the 587 million acres of grasslands and permanent pasture in the US; only the 61.8 million acres of cropland that has been converted to or used as pasture will be considered in this analysis. Using all of the methods described earlier, an estimated 49.1 million acres are suitable for arundo with the remaining 12.6 million acres planted in switchgrass. Switchgrass production could be 90 million tons (still assuming 7.1 tons per acre), while the climate-adjusted yield of arundo would be 1,671 million tons, an average of 34 tons per acre on the cropland used as pasture area (slightly higher than for idle cropland). If cropland used as pasture and idle cropland are combined, the total biomass yield potential is 2.67 billion tons. The energy crop yield combines with existing biomass resources (forest resources, agricultural residues, etc.) for a grand total of 2.98 billion tons.

Impact on the Food Supply

There was a serious spike in world food prices leading up to the onset of the recession in 2008. The oil industry, as evidenced by an editorial in *Oil and Gas Journal*, places the blame for increased food costs squarely and solely on biofuels. They claim, "the verdict is clear: The biofuel craze, while raising costs for everyone, is devastating the chronically hungry."[81] Such an assertion is, of course, preposterous. The editors are not alone in their opinions; they have strong allies in Fidel Castro and Hugo Chavez, both of whom have criticized the US biofuel industry for its alleged impact on the food market.[82]

Because of all of the criticism leveled at the use of crops for energy production, a serious analysis of the situation is needed. Although it is popular to blame increased food prices on the use of corn to produce ethanol in the United States, evidence of such a causal relationship is noticeably missing. For starters, corn used in biofuel production is not lost from the agricultural sector. In fact, most of the nutrients in corn used to produce ethanol are returned to the feed market as distillers' grains. Very little corn goes directly into food; livestock feed is the primary market.[83]

Most of the recent world food crisis relates to the high cost of wheat and rice. Rice is a minor crop in the US, but wheat is among the major agricultural exports. Some have claimed that potential profits from the biofuel industry have caused farmers to plant corn on land previously devoted to wheat, reducing its production and driving up the price.[84] But there has been very little variation in wheat plantings over the last 5 years – an average deviation of only 2.9%.[85] Wheat plantings actually increased annually from 2006 to 2008, the same period as significant world food price increases, with actual production increasing by a whopping 38% over the same period.[86]

The data seems to tell a very different story from conventional wisdom. To the extent that there were trade-offs, the data clearly shows that they were not between corn and wheat, but rather between corn and soybeans. Soybeans prices, although important in processed foods and for manufacturing soybean oil (neither of which are staples among poorer consumers), had very little impact on the overall cost of food on the world stage.

Among the many factors that did contribute to world food price increases were large grain crop failures in Ukraine and rice crop failures in Australia resulting from unfavorable weather. Oil prices actually had a much greater effect on food prices than did the biofuel industry. Farming costs spiked because of increased expenses for diesel fuel and fertilizer, both of which are petroleum derived.[87] Transportation, the cost of which is also strongly correlated with petroleum, also contributed to the cost of grocery items.[88] The depreciation of the US dollar, which contributed to the petroleum price spike, was yet another significant factor.[89]

The reality is that all food commodities have been increasing in price despite record harvests. Even with the many challenges to the agricultural sector, grain harvests in 2007 were the largest in world

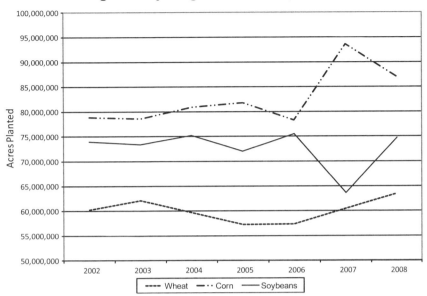

Plantings of Major Agricultural Crops in the US

Data from the US Department of Agriculture, National Agricultural Statistics Service.

history.[90] If prices can increase in the face of record harvests, forces other than biofuels must be at work.[91]

At the core of the problem is a structural increase in demand. As development continues throughout the world, especially in China and India, those populations begin to enjoy an improved diet. Particularly in China, meat and dairy consumption is way up. Animals, of course, also have to eat, which greatly increases grain demand. Grain is the largest cost associated with raising livestock.[92] As wealth increases in China and other developing countries, those populations' overall diet will continue to improve resulting in the consumption of more meat and greater food demand. Use of biofuels is, at most, a trivial factor in food price increases.

Whether or not corn-based biofuels continue to be a factor in the US energy landscape, grain prices will continue to increase unless crop yields can be improved not just in the US but internationally. In theory, the addition of arundo and switchgrass to the agricultural scheme should have very little effect if energy crops are grown on land that is currently not used for other agricultural production. In practice, however, to the extent that energy crops are more profitable than food crops, there may be some trade-offs until the market is able to reach a new equilibrium. Short term price spikes in food commodities are possible, but is that really too great a price for energy independence?

13
I Love It When a Plan Comes Together

The US is a large country with the world's largest economy, and it consumes more energy and more fuel than any other country by a wide margin.[1] Despite the massive consumption, if history has any lessons to teach that are useful in today's world, it has shown that it is possible to shift away from undesirable methods of producing energy. After the 1973 oil crisis, it became obvious that using petroleum to generate electricity was unwise. Within five years, the US was able to begin a major shift away from petroleum-generated electricity toward coal and natural gas. By 2007, the US had completed a more than 80% reduction in use of petroleum for electricity generation compared to the highest levels in 1978.[2] If the US can cut the amount of power generated from oil so dramatically, there is absolutely no reason why it can't do the same in the transportation sector.

Most potential solutions to the foreign energy dependence quagmire that the US faces encompass some mixture of conservation, improvement in efficiency, and alternative fuels. In that respect, the ideas offered in this book are no different. Voluntary conservation and avoiding wasteful transportation habits can make a significant contribution. Increased fuel efficiency requirements, and implementation of new technologies that promote greater fuel economy, such as hybrid vehicles, will also be a part of a comprehensive solution, but conservation and fuel efficiency can only take the US so far. With around two-thirds of the transportation fuel consumed in the US coming from abroad, it would be foolish to think energy independence can be achieved on the demand side alone absent major changes in the way society and the US economy functions – changes that most Americans are not prepared to make. Taking freedom and mobility away from people is not the American way. Public transportation is great if you live in New York City, but what about the suburbs and rural America? The bottom line is that any solution to America's energy problems must include fuel sources that can replace foreign oil.

Is Energy Independence Possible?

Is energy independence just a fantasy? Unfortunately, there are far too many people convinced that it is and still more who have an ax to grind by making it seem impossible. The previous two chapters began the process of explaining how biomass can be converted to clean renewable fuels using thermochemical processing technology, but there is an entrenched establishment that would love nothing more than to discredit the facts. In the words of investor Vinod Khosla,

> The oil interests and the American Petroleum Institute keep propagating myths like insufficient land, poor energy balance, and high production costs to curb enthusiasm for [alternative fuel]. For me this is reminiscent of the tobacco companies funding studies to prove that smoking does not cause cancer...In my opinion, these are either bogus or ill-informed claims...[3]

In 2008, the US consumed 232.5 billion gallons of petroleum fuel products.[4] Because the US imported 4.7 billion barrels of petroleum compared to only 2.5 billion barrels produced domestically, the import share of the petroleum fuel products market is 65.7%, which amounts to 152.8 billion gallons (or 159.6 billion gallons of gasoline equivalent fuel). It is the import share of the fuel market that must be displaced with primary products from refined biomass.

In the previous chapter, an analysis of potential resources indicated that the quantity of existing biomass that can be sustainably used for fuel production is 308.5 million tons per year. Using a 49% conversion efficiency assumption and assuming that 85% of a plant's output (on an energy content basis) is fuel, that quantity of biomass is capable of producing 21.8 billion gallons of gasoline equivalent fuel. Likewise, if, as described in the previous chapter, energy crops were produced on idle cropland yielding 909 million tons of biomass, 64.1 billion gallons could be produced. Cropland used as pasture converted to produce biomass could generate another 1,761 million tons, yielding 124.3 billion gallons of gasoline equivalent fuel:

Potential Fuel Market

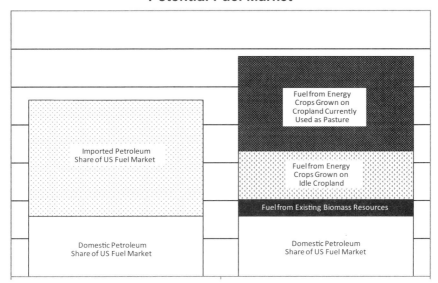

Data from US Department of Energy, Energy Information Administration and author's calculations of fuel that could be produced from domestic biomass resources.

Production estimates are, as stated earlier, based on conservative assumptions. They are not a static boundary but rather can be improved given modest technological advances. Given these assumptions, biomass resources could produce a total of 210.2 billion gallons of gasoline equivalent fuel, a figure more than 31% higher than the 159.6 billion gallons of gasoline equivalent fuel derived from imported oil. Using optimal crop selection, further analysis of the data indicates that devoting just 70.5 million acres to biomass production (when taken with the existing supply) would be sufficient to produce enough fuel to displace all foreign imports. For perspective, consider that the amount of land that would need to be devoted to energy crops is less than the amount of land devoted to either corn or soybean production and only slightly more than was devoted to wheat production as of 2008.

My conclusion is simple: energy independence is possible. It can be accomplished using carbon neutral technology – clean biomass. The biomass can be grown without deforestation and without taking land away from food production. Millions of jobs can be created, and economic growth can be spurred.

A Closer Look at Costs

The Natural Resources Defense Council, a proponent of biomass-derived fuels, projects that ethanol can be manufactured for $1.26 per gallon from biomass using currently available cellulosic technology. They also believe that those costs can be cut in half to about $0.63 per gallon by improving process efficiency with the investment of around $1.1 billion in research.[5] These forecasts are a good starting point, but further examination is essential.

The first step is estimating the all-important capital investment requirements. Too frequently, particularly in public policy debates, capital investment can become confused with spending. For example, if the useful life of a plant is 20 years, then the cost of building it might be spread over the output of a certain plant for a 20 year period of time. Yet, investors still have to come up with the cash to pay for all of those capital investments before the first gallon of fuel can be produced.

In an earlier chapter, an estimate of $3.85 per gallon of annual gasoline equivalent output capacity was established for the anticipated capital investment requirement of a thermochemical fuel plant. Again, the imported share of the US fuel products market is about 159.6 billion gallons of gasoline equivalent fuel, which equates to 2.66 billion tons of biomass. The capital investment needed to install that amount of biorefinery capacity in the US (assuming $3.85 per gallon) would be $723 billion.[6]

Establishing the biomass crops needed to feed the plants would also require capital investment. Based on the information calculated for crop yields and establishment costs in the previous chapter, investment of roughly $176 billion would be necessary to generate enough biomass to displace the foreign share of fuel used in 2008 after taking into account existing supply. When the capital requirements for refineries and crops are combined, the result is a total of $900 billion of investment needed to complete infrastructure capable of completely displacing foreign oil from the domestic transportation fuel market.

Investments measured in figures approaching one trillion dollars are indeed serious undertakings, but before the concept is dismissed as too expensive it should put it into context. In 2008, the US imported $453 billion of petroleum.[7] When the capital cost is viewed in context of cash spent on foreign oil, it doesn't seem like so much. If the US can invest, just one time, so that our country never again has to pay overseas suppliers, would it be worth it? Put another way: if you could buy a home and pay off the mortgage in just a few years, wouldn't that be better than paying rent forever?

If the investment amount still seems like a stretch, perhaps the $700 billion Troubled Asset Relief Program (TARP), better known as the bank bailout, and the $787 billion American Recovery and Reinvestment Act of 2009 (the stimulus package) can provide some additional context. Those two programs spent nearly $1.5 trillion in the span of just a few months. Suddenly, investment of $900 billion to make the US truly strong again seems like an incredible bargain by comparison.

Is the capital investment really worth it? Can biofuel be produced economically? Or, more precisely, can alternatives compete with foreign oil in an open market? Earlier, an estimate for operating cost equal to 35¢ per gallon of gasoline equivalent fuel produced was established. Based on the ongoing maintenance and harvest costs for both arundo and switchgrass, assuming the average crop yields described in the previous chapter, the weighted average cost of producing biomass feedstock is estimated to be $22.46 per ton, or 32¢ per gallon of gasoline equivalent produced. The existing biomass resources would cost $33 per ton (see previous chapter).

Lastly, cost of transporting biomass to the plant must be considered. Transporting biomass is estimated to cost $0.26 per ton-mile.[8] Generally, plants will be constructed near biomass feedstock to minimize transportation costs. If a plant draws from a 100 mile radius, an average haul distance to the plant of 70.7 miles can be assumed,[9] which results in an average transportation cost of $18.38 per ton, or about 26¢ per gallon of gasoline equivalent fuel produced. The total ongoing cost of fuel production is the sum of plant operating cost, biomass cost, and transportation cost, which amounts to 93¢ per gallon of gasoline equivalent produced using energy crop feedstocks. Using existing biomass resources, the cost would be $1.08 per gallon, for a weighted average production cost of 95¢ per gallon.

It is typical to assume a useful life of 20 years for capital equipment in a plant such as a biorefinery. Arundo has an anticipated replanting cycle of 20 years, and switchgrass has a replanting cycle of 10 years. The lifespan of these assets matters because a true per-gallon cost estimate requires the up-front investment to be apportioned over the useful life. If all capital costs are included and depreciated on a straight-line basis, the total per gallon cost can be estimated to be $1.23. Improvements in efficiency or more advanced proprietary technology can provide greater yields at lower costs.

The appropriate number to which our final cost estimate should be compared is the wholesale price of unleaded gasoline. The Energy Information Administration, which has been an invaluable source of data throughout this book, provides historical information on spot prices at various locations in the US. The difference between prices at the various locations is generally quite small. Because the cost of crude oil is highly volatile, the price of gasoline experiences wide price swings as well. Over the last five years, the wholesale price of unleaded gasoline has fluctuated widely. The following graph shows the price of crude oil, the wholesale price of gasoline, and the cost of biomass-derived gasoline equivalent fuel.

The wholesale price of a gallon of gasoline over the five years ending in August 2008 was, on average, 116% of the price of a gallon of crude oil.[10] This is a way of expressing the "crack spread," a means of calculating refinery margins. Using that ratio, you can extrapolate that the $1.23 cost estimate is equivalent to oil at just under $45 per barrel.

Until the onset of the global recession in 2008, oil had been trading well in excess of $45 per barrel, topping out at nearly three times that price. When fears of a worldwide economic collapse were at their peak, the price of oil plummeted to lows around $30 a barrel, a point at which biofuels would not be competitive. The trough was short-lived, and the price has rebounded to well above the break-even level, which only demonstrates the reality that oil prices are highly volatile. Shocks and counter-shocks aside, most economists agree that a long term stable oil price based on structural supply and demand would be in excess of the $60 threshold. Furthermore, increasing demand in China, India, and other emerging markets, coupled with the questionable longevity of world reserves even at current consumption rates, creates an economic climate where long term upward pressure on oil prices is a certainty. All things considered, an investment in biorefineries is not only good for the US from a national policy perspective; it is good business that carries with it the promise of long term profits.

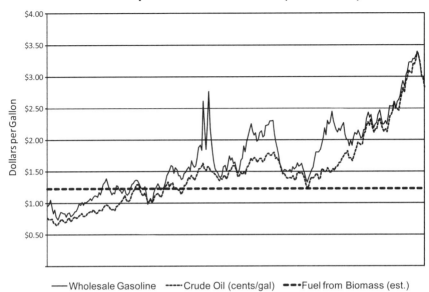

Price Comparison for US Fuels (2003-2008)

—— Wholesale Gasoline   ----- Crude Oil (cents/gal)   ●━●Fuel from Biomass (est.)

Data from US Department of Energy, Energy Information Administration for August 2003 to August 2008, FOB US Gulf Coast. Break-even cost of producing biomass fuel as calculated by the author.

Financing Independence

If $900 billion is to be invested in new energy infrastructure, the obvious question is: who is going to pay for it? It is tempting to turn to the deepest pockets around, the US government. Although the capital needs are substantial, the US government has not historically engaged in commercial enterprise. On the occasions when it has, it has tended to fail miserably. Certain political forces have, once again, as happens from time to time, encouraged deeper government involvement in the private sector. The most glaring example of this trend is US government ownership of General Motors.

For a whole host of reasons, private capital should be strongly preferred to finance industrial assets such as biorefineries. The private sector is much more efficient at deploying capital. Government, sadly, is beholden to far too many special interests to engage in efficient investment. Furthermore, as few seem to remember in our modern world, government actually can't pay for anything; it is merely a means of involuntarily spreading costs over the people. As the Soviet Union has proven, the prospect of individual financial success is essential for an economy to survive and prosper. That said, the government is not without a role, and, while it can do much to hinder development of alternative energy, it can also do much to help.

One of the most important things a government can do is conduct and fund basic research. The US government is and should continue to be the largest provider of funding for basic energy research and development. Much of the technology that will be needed to achieve energy independence has been developed with funding from the US Department of Energy or another government agency. Government should continue to fill that role and drive efforts for more new breakthroughs in energy technologies, particularly research on fuel cells and solar energy.

Energy independence is not a new goal, and the US government is certainly not an inexperienced participant in the quest for it. A new push would by no means be the first attempt at achieving energy independence, nor would it be the first attempt at developing transportation fuels based on energy sources other than oil. As early as the 1940s, the United States Bureau of Mines oversaw a program to develop a coal-to-liquids technology to produce coal-based synthetic fuel. The Synthetic Liquid Fuels Act of 1944 authorized use of $30 million over a five year period for:

> ...the construction and operation of demonstration plants to produce synthetic liquid fuels from coal, oil shale, agricultural and forestry products, and other substances, in order to aid the prosecution of the war, to conserve and increase the oil resources of the Nation, and for other purposes.[11]

The US program got a significant boost in technical prowess from Operation Paperclip (the program to extract German scientists and move them to the US), which allowed the US to capitalize on expertise developed in Germany where liquid fuels were manufactured from coal during World War II. In the three years after the end of the War several new laboratories were constructed. By 1951, several small scale demonstration plants had been built. Just two years later, however, interest in synthetic fuels had diminished and Congress ended funding for the program.[12] Government continued to limp along, supporting alternative fuel sources with varying vigor over the next two decades until the oil shocks of the 1970s.

What Not to Do!

After the Iranian Revolution precipitated a second oil shock in 1979 (the first shock was the spike after the Arab oil embargo), President Carter emerged from a week-long retreat at Camp David to propose the most ambitious effort aimed at achieving energy independence in US history.[13] His proposal culminated in the Energy Security Act of 1980, a part of which was the United States Synthetic Fuels Corporation Act. The legislation established a unique quasi-government agency called the US Synthetic Fuels Corporation (SFC). The SFC was supposed to, "improve the nation's balance of payments, reduce the threat of economic disruption from oil supply interruptions, and increase the nation's security by reducing its dependence on foreign oil."[14]

In practice, the SFC was designed to function like a bank, providing financial assistance in the form of loans, loan guarantees, price guarantees, purchase agreements, or joint ventures to projects that would produce synthetic fuel from coal and other alternatives to petroleum.[15] The Energy Security Act authorized up to $88 billion for alternative fuels development; $20 billion would be available immediately, and $68 billion would become available upon Congressional approval of the required "comprehensive strategy document" that the SFC was required to submit by June 30, 1984. Of the $20 billion authorized, $19 billion was actually appropriated. The appropriation was broken down as follows: $12.2 billion directly for the SFC, $5.5 billion to the Department of Energy (DOE) for an interim program until the SFC was up and running and another $1.3 billion to the DOE and the US Department of Agriculture (USDA) for an alternative fuels program based on biomass feedstocks.[16]

From the start, the SFC was plagued by problems. Among the strongest advocates of synthetic fuels in the US Senate was Idaho Republican James McClure, who became Chairman of the Senate Committee on Energy and Natural Resources in 1981.[17] Just three months after passage of the Energy Security Act, he warned of "inherent problems in the Synthetic Fuels Corporation concept, as enacted."[18]

The most glaring problem, in the view of McClure, was that the production targets set out – 500,000 barrels of crude equivalent per day by 1987 and 2 million barrels of crude equivalent per day by 1992 – were unachievable given the financial incentives that the SFC was allowed to provide under the law. He warned that,

> If the SFC is unable to meet its objectives as stipulated by the legislation, it is possible that much harm could be done to the overall synfuels program. The Congress as well as the American public might become disillusioned with the industry and the people who administer the SFC – the end result being that a great deal of support would be lost for synfuels in general.[19]

McClure also warned that, although the SFC was intended to be a "banking organization, not staffed with bureaucrats but with hard-nosed businessmen trained in high finance and possessed with the expertise to make the synthetic fuels program a reality," the diverse and complex responsibilities delegated to the SFC might hinder those efforts.[20]

In practice, the SFC was laden with all kinds of cumbersome regulatory requirements. In researching the SFC, much discussion is made of reporting requirements and bureaucracy. If the goal of Congress was to avoid a tangling bureaucratic mess of red tape, they failed miserably. As J. F. Trautschold, Jr., who was general manager of Mobil's synfuels division, explained, "If we had solicited money from the [SFC], we would have had to hire probably ten more auditors just to meet the [government's] demand for information."[21]

Although the intent was to hire "hard-nosed businessmen" to run the SFC, such individuals don't always fit neatly in a government bureaucracy. Government investment and private investment are two entirely different worlds. A good CEO of a private company does not necessarily make a good public servant. The SFC was supposed to help create a new industry, but the managers, partly because of an emphasis placed on the SFC being a "banking institution", saw themselves as bankers. They had a tendency to sit back and screen projects, approving or disapproving based on their perception of the credit-worthiness of a given deal.[22] A more proactive approach was needed.

McClure's third issue with the SFC related to intellectual property. Production of liquid fuels usually involves technologies that, although perhaps rooted in public basic research, are developed with private sector financing and are proprietary in nature. As such, investors want to see a return on their technology investment. Under the SFC rules, however, details of the technologies would have to be publicly disclosed, which created a disincentive to do business with the SFC. The result could be a scenario, as McClure warned, that resulted in only projects of lesser quality, using inferior technology, being funded by the SFC.[23]

McClure's final concern also resonates in issues felt by the industry today. The SFC, under the law, had no authority to authorize or expedite the permitting or licensing of proposed projects.[24] The process of permitting a major liquid fuels plant can be extremely cumbersome. As testament to this fact, one needs to look no further than the refinery industry. No new refineries have been built since 1986,[25] largely because of the difficulty in obtaining permits, a process that requires working with numerous state and federal agencies, few of which coordinate with each other and many of which have divergent agendas. Gaining regulatory approval for a liquid fuels plant is further complicated by the fact that few such facilities already exist, which means that regulators tend to have limited understanding of the technology and no templates for how to proceed through the permitting process. Responsibility falls on project sponsors to educate regulators. The result of all of these factors is that it often takes years to procure a permit, if one can be obtained at all.

One serious problem that McClure didn't foresee was the impact of the politicalization of selecting the SFC's managers on its ability to do business. The Energy Security Act was passed less than four months before the 1980 Presidential Election. Carter was facing a losing battle for reelection against Ronald Reagan. Reagan, a strong believer that government should not mettle in free markets, made elimination of the SFC part of his platform. Immediately, Carter faced opposition to his appointees for the board of directors who could not assume their positions until confirmed by the Senate. The Senate inevitably chose to delay the matter until after the election,[26] forcing Carter to appoint a chairman on an interim basis. Once Reagan took office, he immediately fired Carter's nominee for chairman, John Sawhill. As president, Reagan did see the merit of synfuels and decided keep the SFC framework, at least for a while. He picked Edward Noble, an Oklahoma oilman, as his choice for chairman.[27]

It didn't take long for the SFC's first president, Victor Schroeder, to resign amid a flurry of accusations that included allegations he improperly charged personal expenses (including interest on his home mortgage) to the SFC. He was replaced by Victor Thompson, who survived in the post only two months before he was also forced to resign after being accused of trying to sell stock in a bank he had formerly headed to Belton Johnson, a rich Texan who was seeking subsidies from the SFC.[28] After Thompson's departure, the Board of Directors went seven months without a quorum, rendering the SFC unable to conduct business for a majority of 1984.[29] By then, the SFC had almost as many former employees as current ones.

Although the SFC framework was fraught with problems, the real nail in the coffin was not related to its structure, but to changes in international petroleum markets. Although consensus opinion and historical context indicated that oil prices would continue to rise, after passage of the Energy Security Act, a worldwide recession and oil conservation programs reduced petroleum use while US domestic production increased.[30] Changes in the market rendered uneconomic many of the projects being contemplated by the SFC. By 1984, there were eight to ten billion barrels per day of worldwide excess capacity, prices had been declining for three straight years, energy conservation measures and recession had succeeded in reducing demand, and new taxes had reduced the incentive to invest in synthetic fuels projects.[31]

In his transmittal of the proposed "Energy Security Reserved Amendments of 1984", President Reagan summed up, as only the Great Communicator could, the core of the SFC's most serious problem,

> Synthetic fuels held promise as an economically competitive alternative to traditional fuel sources...In the intervening years, the energy outlook has improved dramatically. The price of imported crude oil has declined more than 25 percent since I took office, and our oil imports are down 33 percent compared to 1980 levels...As a consequence of these major changes, the presumptions that underlie the current synthetic fuels program have proven at variance with the realities of the market place. It is now apparent that developing a commercial synthetic fuels industry at the pace

envisioned by the Energy Security Act of 1980 would require enormous direct budget outlays that would not be offset by any economic benefits.[32]

Congress terminated the SFC experiment under the Consolidated Omnibus Budget Reconciliation Act of 1985,[33] and the SFC was finally closed in 1986.[34] At the end of the day, only six synthetic fuels projects received financial assistance awards.[35] As an executive of SFC explained, "Because neither the technical nor market realities of project development were as positive as had been forecast, the corporation's award process has been much slower than proponents of the program had wished."[36]

The SFC was truly an abysmal failure, but the failure of the SFC does not mean that synfuels are a bad idea. Government has had many failed programs and initiatives, but the goals of those efforts were often nonetheless desirable and achievable if pursued using a different strategy. To denounce synfuels as a failure because of the US Synthetic Fuels Corporation fiasco is either a gross oversimplification or outright propaganda in favor of the petroleum industry. A variety of complex inherent problems and market forces spelled the end for the SFC, not a fundamental inferiority of non-petroleum-derived fuels. Some have suggested that pursuing alternative fuels now is to repeat a grave mistake of history. Would those people also argue that we should do away with doctors and medicine because the federal government mismanages its healthcare programs or that the US Army should be disbanded because a defense contractor was caught fleecing the defense procurement system?

We can draw some valuable lessons from the SFC experience. The legislation forming the SFC was the product of hard-fought battles and compromise. Our founders intended government to operate with a system of checks and balances. Because legislation can affect the lives of so many people, enacting it is supposed to be difficult. Such a structure does not lend itself well to the operation of a business. Commercial ventures operated by consensus almost invariably under-perform or fail outright. Bureaucracy is one of the dirtiest words in the business world. In a corporation, solid and often uncompromising leadership gets results.

Furthermore, accountability for financial management takes on entirely different context in the private sector. You often hear people advocate the idea that government should be run more like a business.

Never do you hear anyone suggest that a business should be run more like the government.

The synthetic fuels program was established without sufficient flexibility to meet changes in market conditions, such as a decrease in the price of fuel. In a private corporation, leadership would have the flexibility to change its strategy to adapt to market conditions. A legislated quasi-governmental organization, however, has to operate under the parameters of the legislation that created it based on political, not economic, considerations. For example, certain projects under the SFC were to be allocated to each of the 50 states regardless of economic viability.[37] Successful corporations do not spread around their operations to make sure that each politician's constituency gets its share of government pork.

A Market Driven Approach with Government Support

Any government attempt to directly invest $900 billion is, for the reasons afore described, not likely to yield ideal results. There is, however, much that can be done to encourage action in the private sector. To convince investors to pour billions of dollars into the cause of energy independence and the technologies necessary to achieve it, there will have to be some legislative action. There are many steps that government can take to grow and protect an alternative fuels industry. The following are a few of the most important ways that government can help achieve energy independence.

Keeping the Wolves at Bay

The greatest risk to a nascent alternative fuel industry is attack from powerful predators – oil exporters and multi-national oil companies. It was a precipitous drop in oil prices in the mid-1980s that doomed the SFC. The same thing could happen again for a new generation of aspiring alternative fuel entrepreneurs. It is essential to the long term survival of the industry that it be protected from a reactionary drop in prices.

Vinod Khosla, one of the largest investors in cutting-edge alternative fuel production, came to prominence and became quite wealthy as a co-founder of Sun Microsystems. He is now bringing his considerable personal resources to bear in the world of alternative fuels. Mr. Khosla rightly recognizes that one of the greatest risks to an alternative fuels industry is a rapid decline in petroleum prices. In testimony before the Senate Foreign Relations Committee, Khosla described an encounter with a senior executive from a major oil company at which he was informed, "You know, we can drop the price of gasoline to drive [alternative fuel] producers out of business."[38]

The extent to which oil companies can control prices in the modern market is suspect, but there is little question that the government of Saudi Arabia has substantial influence. Their crude production costs are much lower than those in the US and most of the world. A frighteningly large percentage of the price of crude is pure profit to the Saudis; their actual production costs are reportedly somewhere around $1 per barrel.[39] They could see a huge fall in oil prices and still continue to profit handsomely. Of course, the Saudis need massive oil profits; their economy depends on them as does the reign of their monarchy.

In addition to the Saudis, there is the larger construct of OPEC, which has proven itself remarkably unpredictable. It has not embraced a consistent strategy since it first began to successfully exercise market power. How OPEC would respond to a major decline in US petroleum demand (resulting from alternative fuels or some other domestic change) isn't clear. A decrease in US demand would force OPEC to choose among reducing production to hold prices steady, holding production steady while allowing prices to fall, or an intermediate course.[40] A concern, however, is that OPEC decisions might be more strategic, focusing less on their short-term profit in favor of maintaining long-term market share. There is a risk that predatory actions could be employed if oil dominance was threatened by a domestic alternative fuels industry. In other words, oil exporters might flood the market with petroleum, forcing a drop in prices with the goal of putting alternatives out of business. Once that goal is accomplished, they could simply raise prices back to their previously high levels.

OPEC has previously shown awareness of the potential for competition from alternative fuels. In April 1978, OPEC appointed a committee of representative oil ministers with the objective of establishing long term price policy. The report of the committee, leaked in late 1979, stated their specific pricing goal: to raise the price to a level just below the cost of producing synthetic liquid fuels.[41] They were conspiring to set prices at exactly the level to ensure that non-petroleum-derived fuels were uneconomic to produce, thereby perpetuating their monopoly.

The concept wasn't new considering the Shah of Iran had made a similar proposal several years earlier. This evidence confirms the possibility that oil-rich nations could engage in predatory pricing schemes in an attempt to drive alternative producers to bankruptcy. Alternatives are competitive with the oil market, but they are not necessarily competitive with the actual cost of oil extraction, particularly among low cost producers, a very important distinction.

Absent monopolistic behavior by participants with market power, the production of biofuels may itself result in falling petroleum prices. In most situations, competition does decrease prices. The same principles could be expected to apply to the alternative fuel and petroleum industry. Unfortunately, the very act of forcing down petroleum prices would have the effect of making biofuels appear less attractive.[42] This could have a particularly unfortunate impact with policy makers who must please their constituents – a populace that too often fails to understand the long term implications of policy decisions made based on short term market conditions.

The solution to this unfortunate problem, although on the surface it may seem to be at odds with the premise of this book, is for the US government to stabilize and defend the price of oil. From the country's birth, generations of leaders have embraced policies designed to protect America's industry from foreign predators. From Alexander Hamilton to Ronald Reagan, many great statesmen in America's history have recognized the need for (and embraced the use of) policies to selectively protect industries determined to be of vital national importance. Few would suggest that the US should rely on foreign producers for advanced weapon systems vital to national security. The same concept applies to energy.

One potential mechanism for protecting the energy industry is the establishment of a price floor for crude oil. The floor price could be set to ensure that alternatives, including fuel produced from biomass, could sustainably compete with oil even in a falling market. If the floor were ever triggered, proceeds could be used for a "price stabilization fund"[43] or could be used to make purchases for the Strategic Petroleum Reserve (SPR).

Just such legislation was proposed in 1986 by none other than George Keller, then Chairman of Chevron Corp. and head of the American Petroleum Institute.[44] His position was that the US should impose an import fee to establish a minimum price for oil in the US. The fee would be designed to take effect if the price fell below a certain level.[45]

Another surprising proponent of such a price floor has been conservative columnist Charles Krauthammer, who has written several editorials embracing a price floor for gasoline. He advocates a federal gas tax that would effectively fix a minimum price at $3 to $4 per gallon. If prices fell below that level, a tax would kick in and the difference would go into the US treasury. If prices were above that level, the tax would be abandoned until the market price fell back below the tax threshold.[46]

Mr. Krauthammer's rational is that a price floor "obviates the waste and folly of an army of bureaucrats telling auto companies what cars in which fleets need to meet what arbitrary standard of fuel efficiency. Abolish all the regulations and let the market decide."[47] In effect, he contends that higher prices will allow the market to choose between conservation, better vehicle technologies, and alternative fuels. His approach makes sense, but has the added advantage of washing out any predatory action by the oilocracy.

An adequate domestic fuel supply is a matter of national and economic security. It is clear that such a goal will only be achievable if the domestic alternative fuel industry is protected against rapid declines in world petroleum prices. If world petroleum markets were indeed free markets, such a suggestion might grate against the prevailing free-trade dogma, but the reality is that petroleum markets are not free markets. Governments already have the power to heavily influence – if not directly determine – prices. Instead of that power resting with the US government, however, it is held by regimes in places like Saudi Arabia, Venezuela, Russia, and Iran.

Rational choices to defend domestic industry might include a tax like the one proposed by Mr. Krauthammer, an oil import duty, government guaranteed minimum prices for alternative fuel, an aggressive purchasing program for an increased Strategic Petroleum Reserve, a combination of these, or some other program. Although advocating a particular set of legal machinery to protect the price of oil in the US domestic market is beyond the scope of this book, this author tends to favor an import duty. Regardless of the structure, some mechanism will be essential to ensure the survival of an alternative fuel industry and the long term safety of investment in it.

Cutting Through the Red Tape

An essential step toward construction of numerous domestic bio-refineries is to make the permitting of such plants much easier and faster. Obtaining a permit to construct and operate a major chemical processing plant (such as a bio-refinery) can be a very expensive and cumbersome process. The prospect of spending years attempting to obtain permits with no assurance of ever receiving approval is a huge impediment to a major expansion effort. It can cost sponsors of a bio-refinery project up to $10 million for engineering and environmental studies just to apply for a permit. More than a few projects have died because investors were unwilling to provide the large sums needed to initiate a project without assurance that a permit would eventually be issued.

Permitting for alternative fuel facilities should be accomplished solely at the federal level to make sure that policies are uniform throughout the nation and that experienced regulators are available to evaluate each application. Furthermore, the process should be streamlined to minimize costs. Provisional permits should be issued without demanding the massive reams of engineering data that is usually required before a project is approved. This policy would have the effect of assuring investors that a final permit would eventually be issued to construct and operate a given facility as long as a set of pre-established conditions are met.

Using the Tax System to Your Advantage

Through the use of tax policy, government can play a major role in expanding the pool of investment capital in the private sector available to invest in alternative fuel. Policies that allow investments in capital assets to be treated as expenses for tax purposes (instead of being depreciated), tax credits, and other commonly used incentive mechanisms can play a central role in efforts to direct capital toward investments in alternative fuels. Such tax advantages have had a major impact in the power generation sector, prompting rapid growth of wind energy.

A prominent national law firm that specializes in, among other things, financing for alternative energy assets estimates that, with some creative financial structuring, various tax incentives already exist that could be used to pay for as much as 55% of the capital cost of a thermochemical fuel plant.[48]

Existing tax incentives are a start, but there remains much that the government can do to spur investment. Complexity of the rules should be reduced, and, most importantly, rules should be changed to make it easier for plant developers to sell tax credits or other tax advantages in the market to raise capital. Tax advantages are only beneficial to tax payers. Since taxes are only due when there is income, a plant in the development stage has no direct use for tax advantages. Such a plant does not yet produce fuel and, therefore, has no revenue or income. If plant developers sell their tax advantages to corporations that owe significant tax bills (like utilities and banks, for example), they can use the cash to finance the plant. In some circumstances, this process is already legal, but it needs reform and simplification to create a more open and transparent market.

Getting Them Built

Besides the obvious challenge of gathering massive sums of investment capital, another key to the widespread production of alternative fuel is the ability to physically construct the plants. The universe of engineering and construction contractors who have the capability to build these types of facilities is limited. Most of the firms that do have such capabilities perform the preponderance of their work (not surprisingly) for the petroleum industry. In at least one instance, a major contractor pulled out of a deal to construct an alternative energy project because of a relationship with an oil company. Undoubtedly, there have been similar occurrences on other occasions. With such substantial building requirements, a whole new stable of contractors with the willingness and capability to construct these facilities is necessary. Although this is a challenge for the alternative fuel industry, it is an opportunity for ambitious contractors interested in diversification into a new and profitable business line.

The limited universe of contractors and technology risk has another side-effect. It makes procurement of loans or issuance of bonds to finance plants quite challenging. Not surprisingly, investors and lenders want to know that after all of those millions of dollars are spent, not only will the plant be complete but also that it will actually work when someone flips the switch for the first time. That assurance typically comes from guarantees or bonds from the contractor, but because of inexperience with the technology, contractors have proven reluctant to provide such formal commitments.

To exacerbate the problem, for a guarantee to be meaningful, the contractor must be sufficiently creditworthy to back it. With projects costing hundreds of millions of dollars, only very large, financially solid contractors would fit the bill. Once the technologies in question are commonplace in the US, these issues should no longer be a concern.[49] In the mean time, it is a significant challenge.

The best solution is for the US government to institute a program to certify and guarantee technological performance if a plant is build according to approved specifications. In many cases, the Department of Energy developed significant portions of the process technologies and already has the expertise to evaluate them. By relieving concerns about technology risk, the government can play a major role in enhancing investor comfort and directing private investment toward alternative energy technologies.

A Salute from Our Men and Women in Uniform

The largest fuel buyer in the US, the Department of Defense (DOD), is already doing its part to promote alternative fuel. The military has long recognized the strategic vulnerabilities associated with such overwhelming dependence on foreign oil and has been a leader in encouraging the development of domestic alternatives. In September 2007, the Department of Defense issued a request for information (RFI) to determine what contract terms would be necessary to develop long term domestic sources of synfuel for military use. The results revealed that potential suppliers would only invest in synfuel production plants if the DOD were able to offer incentives such as long-term (10 to 30 years) contracts, accelerated cost recovery, loan guarantees, tax credits, and a floor price mechanism. Industry responses to the RFI indicate that longer term contracts are particularly important for creating conditions that bring more companies into the market. Federal procurement law, as it is currently written, does not allow long term contracts. The maximum length currently allowable is five years, with an option (by the government, not the supplier) to extend for five additional years,[50] which is generally not sufficient for investors to recoup the capital investment required to build a plant.

Plants need long term contracts for price and demand stability, which will assure investors that there will be a revenue steam adequate to provide a return on their investment. To qualify for project financing from banks, a plant must generally have sales contracts that are at least as long in duration as would be needed to fully pay-off the debt. Lenders have been historically unwilling to take a risk on "merchant" plants (plants built to sell product into the short term or "spot" market). As you will remember from earlier chapters, one of the great benefits of fuel synthesis technology is the flexibility of producing a wide range of fuel products. Aviation fuel is of particular interest because it is the primary fuel purchased by the US Department of Defense for use in military aircraft and many ground vehicles (including tanks). The Defense Energy Support Center, the fuel logistics agency of the Department of Defense, is the largest single purchaser of fuel in the United States. In 2007, it purchased over 5.7 billion gallons of petroleum fuel of various types, more than half of which was JP-8 aviation fuel.[51]

In April 2006, the Air Force began efforts to procure synthetic aviation fuel to test, evaluate, and certify aircraft using a 50/50 blend of synthetic fuel and traditional petroleum-derived fuel. The Defense Energy Support Center subsequently purchased 315,000 gallons of Fischer-Tropsch ISO-Paraffinic Kerosene (FT-IPK) from Shell Oil Products in June 2007 for $3.41 per gallon.[52] The fuel was tested successfully in a B-52 bomber jet that used the mixture in all eight of its turbine engines.[53] The Air Force has set a goal of receiving 50% of its fuel supply used in the contiguous 48 states from synthetic production by 2016.[54]

Thomas Friedman, a columnist for the *New York Times*, has predicted that the next great technological revolution will be energy technology.[55] This new sector will create fortunes in much the same way as information technology created fortunes over the last three decades. Already, stock prices of alternative energy companies are much more heavily correlated with the price of technology stocks than on the price of oil. This phenomenon suggests that investors view alternative energy companies as similar to other high technology companies. Unfortunately, studies have shown that most investors perceive widespread alternative fuels as being far-off and uncertain.[56]

Alternative energy is anything but uncertain; it is inevitable. The question is not if, but when? A dwindling world supply of oil and rising demand in the developing world prescribe that a transition will occur, and it will be sooner than many people think. Few saw the information revolution coming, but it came just the same. Only a few years ago, mobile telephones did not exist. Today, almost everyone has one. Technological revolutions happen quickly, generally not over the course of generations. A transition to alternatives could bear some resemblance to the technological revolution, but there is a major distinction. Unlike information processing, energy production is massively capital intensive.

Fortunately, the estimated $900 billion is not needed all at one time. Frankly, the magnitude of the challenge in planting millions of acres of new energy crops and constructing an entirely new web of bio-refineries will take some time. An optimal transition would be spread over a ten year period, but the pace will ultimately depend on availability of capital. There is already a community of entrepreneurs and startups that can make a huge difference. Still more are needed, but the greatest need is for more investors willing to take the lead.

For a shift to alternative fuels to succeed, what is most needed is a commitment from the American people. We need to invest not only in America's future but in our own. The greatest rewards will inure to those who invest early, just as it has for the early investors in the information technology revolution.

With all investments there are short term value fluctuations, which are to be expected. Asset values, including energy investment values, will rise and fall in the short run based on perception much more than fundamentals. In the long run, however, fundamentals always carry the day. A global supply of oil that has become harder to find and extract, growing global petroleum demand (especially in emerging economies), and attractive economics of biofuel production are those fundamentals. They spell rewards for ambitious investors and entrepreneurs willing to take a risk on the future.

Oil has caused conflict throughout the world. It has taken the US into wars. American fighting men and women have shed their blood because of it. Modern terrorism against the West can be traced to oil-led decisions going back decades. Oil holds the promise of future struggles, certainly with radical Islamists in the Middle East and with Russia in the Caucasus, but also perhaps with China as competition for resources increases.

Foreign oil is like a dead weight on the economy. Each driven mile transfers wealth from Americans to despots, dictators, and terrorists around the world. Its continued purchase threatens to drive up the national debt and drive down the value of the dollar. If the US continues on this path, eventually the standard of living will degrade, and while the US military may still be powerful, the economy will look more than that of a third-world country with extreme levels of debt and run-away inflation.

Domestically-produced alternative fuels would solve these problems. No longer must the economy suffer. No longer must the US find itself entangled in geopolitical struggles over resources in the Middle East and in other corners of the globe where it has little strategic interest other than maintaining its oil addiction. No longer must the wealth created by the hard work of the American people inevitably become the property of enemies and adversaries.

In the future, it will become increasingly clear that small business is America's salvation while multinational conglomerates are all-too-often the curse. Nowhere is that more evident than in the oil industry, where the economies of scale and government control of resources act to centralize power and control. The logistics of the biomass raw material supply more aptly lends itself to smaller regional biorefineries rather than large centralized refineries.[57] The agricultural production of energy crops also provides opportunities for many land owners and farmers.

As much as oil takes the world toward war, poverty, hopelessness, and despair, biofuel offers the promise of peace and economic strength; jobs and growth; and more power for individuals with less for despotic regimes. A transition is not going to happen tomorrow, but action must be swift. Foreign oil dependence is a cancer, slowly but surely growing and spreading its evils.

Economic Fallout

Going from foreign dependence to energy self-sufficiency would have many far-reaching implications for the economy, and all of them would be good. A plan like the one outlined in this book would have a very dramatic effect, spurring economic growth and creating millions of jobs.

Using economic impact models developed by the Department of Energy and information from the US Department of Commerce's Bureau of Economic Analysis (BEA) it is possible to estimate the impact that a shift to domestically-produced alternative fuel would have on various aspects of the economy, including job creation, earnings, and GDP. The concept is simple: for each dollar invested in domestic alternative fuel (plant construction and crop establishment), there is a ripple-effect through the economy that creates more jobs and new businesses.

Investing in biorefineries would benefit many dependent industries. Equipment manufacturers, technology providers, railroads, trucking companies, and local economies where plants would be located (along with many, many others) would all see growth from the effort. The greatest impact, however, would likely be felt in the struggling US steel industry. With hundreds of billions worth of new steel orders, the US steel industry would be primed for a major resurgence.

The greatest job creation and growth would come from building plants. Constructing enough plants to displace all foreign oil would contribute about $2 trillion to US GDP and create annual earnings of $730 billion. Assuming a ten year transitional period, the contribution would be on the order of $200 billion per year (assuming for simplicity that each year's investment is equal), an amount that could increase US annual GDP by over 1.3%. As for employment, the construction effort alone could generate over 12 million new jobs.[58]

Once all of the facilities are up and operating, a tremendous positive impact on the economy would continue. The new industry would provide almost two million jobs in biomass production, transportation, and fuel production.[59] These would be good, permanent jobs across a broad spectrum of disciples, including agricultural and manufacturing labor; scientific and research jobs; management; and independent business owners. It would offer to millions of Americans the opportunity to join the middle class, an upgrade that, in many cases, would not otherwise be available.

As for the impact on national output, a permanent addition of at least $340 billion to US GDP would provide a substantial boost in economic growth.[60] Economic growth benefits everyone. Even the government's perennial fiscal disorder could be alleviated by the substantial new tax revenue that could be used to balance the budget, decrease taxes on individuals, and strengthen the Social Security and Medicare systems as the US population ages.

Many struggling industries could be strengthened. As mentioned, the steel industry stands to benefit substantially from the construction effort, but there are also long term structural benefits available for many other industries. Perhaps no industry is better poised to reinvent itself than the seemingly perennially-bankrupt airline industry.

The commercial aviation fuel market is a natural leaping-off point for synthetic fuels. Transportation carriers are among the hardest hit in times of increasing fuel prices. Long term fixed-price contracts offer the potential for absolute cost stability for carriers while eliminating market risk for fuel manufacturers. It is a natural partnership that could guaranty not only the profitability of the biorefineries but also of the airlines. There are also clear logistical advantages since a high percentage of the consumption of aviation fuel is concentrated among only a few major buyers (airlines and cargo shipping companies), which allows fuel to be delivered to or plants co-located at a central location (major airports). Continental Airlines has already taken a strong interest. In January 2009, Continental became the first airline to test biofuel in a commercial airliner (a Boeing 737-800) in the US.[61]

Arguably the most important consequences of energy self-sufficiency involve the US place in the global economy. A major component of the trade deficit would be erased, and, consequently, the need for foreign capital to support the economy would be eased. No longer would net foreign ownership of US assets continue to climb out of control. The US could remain forever the property of the American people.

A New Face of Global Geopolitics

During the 2008 Presidential campaign, both Barack Obama and John McCain called openly for the US to pursue energy independence. Of course, this is not a surprise considering that every president since Richard Nixon has called for energy independence. Rhetoric has flowed in abundance, but commitment has failed to keep pace.

Part of the problem is confusion over what energy independence really means. When some speak of energy independence, what they really seek is something referred to as "energy security". In practice, energy security means oil can be imported from abroad but only from "friendly" countries. The idea is, of course, that America's friends would not endanger its access to oil. As the National Defense Council Foundation points out, however, "the only truly secure sources of supply are those that exist within our borders."[62]

Because supply lines that exist outside controlled borders always have at least some inherent vulnerability and because regimes can and do change, converting today's ally into tomorrow's adversary, there is no such thing as long term energy security when supplies are sourced from outside the US. More importantly, whether oil comes from nations with friendly regimes or hostile ones, the economic disadvantages associated with imported oil are no different.

To retain access to and secure the world's largest oil supplies, the US has been forced to climb into bed with some of the world's most corrupt and despotic leaders. In exchange for their cooperation and petroleum supply, we have provided arms, military training, technical assistance, diplomatic support, and White House access. Meanwhile, we have ignored their decidedly non-American values, egregious human rights violations, and contempt for democracy.[63]

Gone could be the days of supporting regimes that embody everything against which our founders fought. America should not and would no longer have to support despotic regimes that repress their people in ways far more grievous than even those experienced by the colonists at the dawn of the American Revolution. How could supporting such regimes possibly be in harmony with American values?

In fact, supporting unpopular regimes in the Middle East is one of the primary reasons the US finds itself the target of terrorists. Although many experts ascribe terrorists' hatred of the West to support for Israel, or, as George W. Bush once claimed, they hate us for our freedom, the reality is that (while those may be factors) it is the presence of troops in the region and US support for certain unpopular Arab regimes that are the most immediate causes of most terrorist actions.

The US did not become the "great Satan" overnight. As recently as the 1956 Suez crisis, the US was viewed favorably in the Arab world. The current path began when the US started choosing sides in the battles between monarchial forces and Arab nationalists to protect oil interests.

In Iran, the timing was similar. In 1953, the US staged a *coup d'état* that removed the democratically-elected government and in its place vested authoritarian rule in the Shah. His reign of terror poisoned the Iranian people against America and set the stage for the rise of the anti-American theocratic government that today seeks nuclear weapons and supports terrorist groups, a truly unsavory combination.

Meanwhile, all of the enemies who hate America stand by as American consumers unwittingly shovel cash in their direction. Funding for Islamic extremism and terrorism has come predominately from two countries, Saudi Arabia and Iran. It is no coincidence that these countries are the top two petroleum exporting nations. These countries are so awash in cash that no matter what controls are in place from their governments, some of the money is going to end up with radical groups.[64] It is, in fact, the US consumer who is the ultimate source for financing to support terrorism. It need not be so.

Because of America's overwhelming dependence on foreign oil, access to it is obviously a matter of national security. The US military, having responsibility for that security, has long been a voice of reason promoting energy independence. Their attitude is perhaps best summarized in the Defense Energy Support Center's 2006 Fact Book,

> [Biofuels] not only protect the environment on which all life depends; they also reduce the obvious dependency the United States has on foreign countries for its energy needs. This factor alone substantiates the need for widespread use of these alternative energy sources.[65]

Eliminating the need for imported petroleum would have so many positive effects for America and its place in the world that the repercussions are too far-reaching to fathom. According to journalist and foreign policy expert Fareed Zakaria, "Reducing [US] dependence on oil would be the single greatest multiplier of American power in the world."[66]

American power, when used wisely, is a positive force doing much good for the world. When used shortsightedly and selfishly, it becomes a trap for its own masters. Imagine a world where the US acts in accordance with its values because, finally, our values and our interests lead to the same policy choices. The US has been a beacon of freedom, a leader for the world; it is time to regain that status.

Energy independence is much more than a fantasy, a worthy goal that can never actually be achieved in our lifetimes such as, for example, world peace. Energy independence is systematically attainable through a concerted national effort of entrepreneurs, political leaders, and investors. This book has shown how it could happen, but the ideas within these pages are not to the exclusion of other great ideas and innovations.

Whether the motivation is patriotism or self interest is not particularly relevant, as long as action is taken. Such a large and important undertaking requires the commitment of millions of Americans all working toward the same goal. This book is a small step, but on these last pages the baton must pass to the reader. In the words of Gandhi, "You must be the change you want to see in the world." The opportunity, the challenge starts now.

Notes

Telling All My Secrets

1   Bureau of Economic Analysis, US Department of Commerce;
http://www.bea.gov (accessed October 1, 2008).

2   National Defense Council Foundation, "The Hidden Cost of Oil: An Update," p. 1.

3   The method of calculation for potential job creation is discussed in the final chapter.

Chapter 1
Going Up in Smoke

1   Copulos, *America's Achilles Heel*, p. 1.

2   Deficit includes all goods and services. US Department of Commerce, Bureau of
Economic Analysis, http://www.bea.gov (accessed November 9, 2009).

3   Japan Ministry of Finance, http://www.mof.go.jp/english/ (access November 9, 2009).

4   US Department of Commerce, Bureau of Economic Analysis,
http://www.bea.gov (accessed November 9, 2009); Department of Energy, Energy
Information Administration, http://www.eia.doe.gov (accessed November 9, 2009).

5   Some economists define wealth transfer as economic profit gained by oil producers by
virtue of the monopoly power of OPEC and the fact that the price of oil is set above its
natural level in a truly competitive market. For purposes of this book, however, wealth
transfer shall be the entire cost of imported petroleum because each dollar spent on
imported petroleum must be financed either with exports or external capital resulting in a
direct one to one relationship between the importation of petroleum and the acquisition
of US assets by foreigners.

6   US Department of Commerce, Bureau of Economic Analysis, http://www.bea.gov
(accessed November 9, 2009).

7   Salvatore, "US Trade Deficits, Structural Imbalances, and Global Monetary Stability," p. 698.

8   US Department of Commerce, Bureau of Economic Analysis, http://www.bea.gov
(accessed November 9, 2009).

9   Mussa, "The Dollar and the Current Account Deficit," p. 693.

10   Mussa, "The Dollar and the Current Account Deficit," p. 693; and Bollino, "Oil Prices and
the U.S. Trade Deficit."

11   Salvatore, "US Trade Deficits, Structural Imbalances, and Global Monetary Stability," p. 699.

12   Ibid.

13   Ibid.

14   Clark, *Petrodollar Warfare*, pp. 17-18.

15   Ibid., pp. 18-19, 37.

16   Ibid., p. 30.

17   Ibid., p. 30.

18   Spiro, *The Hidden Hand of American Hegemony*, p. 121.

19   Clark, *Petrodollar Warfare*, p. 28.

20   Spiro, *The Hidden Hand of American Hegemony*, p. 130.

21   Alnasrawi, *Arab Nationalism, Oil, and the Political Economy of Dependency*, pp. 104-7.

22   Spiro, *The Hidden Hand of American Hegemony*, p. 128.

23   Clark, *Petrodollar Warfare*, pp. 20-22.

24   Organization of Petroleum Exporting Countries. *OPEC Annual Statistical Bulletin, 2008*, p. 15.

25   Saudi Arabian Monetary Agency, *Annual Report*, p. 270.
26   US Department of Commerce, Bureau of Economic Analysis,
      http://www.bea.gov (accessed November 9, 2009).
27   US Department of the Treasury, Treasury International Capital Reporting System,
      http://www.treas.gov/tic/ (accessed November 16, 2009).
28   Ibid.
29   Clark, *Petrodollar Warfare*, p. 22.
30   Bernanke, "Deflation: Making Sure 'It' Doesn't Happen Here."
31   US Department of the Treasury, Treasury International Capital Reporting System,
      http://www.treas.gov/tic/ (accessed November 16, 2009).
32   Calculated from Outstanding Mortgage Balances of One-to-Four Family Residences. Board
      of Governors of the Federal Reserve System, Statistical Supplement to the Federal Reserve
      Bulletin, December 2006, http://www.federalreserve.gov/pubs/supplement/2006/12
      /200612StatSup.pdf (accessed June 8, 2010); and Board of Governors of the Federal Reserve
      System, Statistical Releases and Historical Data, March 2010, http://www.federalreserve.gov
      /econresdata/releases/mortoutstand/current.htm (accessed June 8, 2010).
33   Cavallo, "Oil Prices and the US Trade Deficit."
34   Bernanke, "Deflation: Making Sure 'It' Doesn't Happen Here."
35   Zhang et al., "Spillover Effect of US Dollar Exchange Rate on Oil Prices."
36   International Monetary Fund, IMF Statistical Databases, International Financial Statistics.
37   Bollino, "Oil Prices and the U.S. Trade Deficit."
38   Clark, *Petrodollar Warfare*, p. 141.
39   Leone and Wasow, "George Bush's Fiscal Finger of Fate Inflates Gas Prices."
40   Ibid.
41   *Economist*, "The Disappearing Dollar."
42   Zhang et al., "Spillover Effect of US Dollar Exchange Rate on Oil Prices."
43   Lizardo and Mollick, "Oil Price Fluctuations and US Dollar Exchange Rates."
44   Barsky and Kilian, "Oil and the Macroeconomy Since the 1970s," p. 126
45   Bénassy-Quéré et al., "China and the Relationship between the Oil Price and the Dollar."
46   Leone and Wasow, "George Bush's Fiscal Finger of Fate Inflates Gas Prices."
47   Faisal, "When Will We Buy Oil in Euros?"
48   Clark, *Petrodollar Warfare*, p. 117.
49   Faisal, "When Will We Buy Oil in Euros?"
50   Clark, *Petrodollar Warfare*, p. 121.
51   Spiro, *The Hidden Hand of American Hegemony*, p. 122.
52   Alnasrawi, *Arab Nationalism, Oil, and the Political Economy of Dependency*, p. 136.
53   Koplow and Martin, "Fueling Global Warming."
54   Greene and Leiby, *The Oil Security Metrics Model*, p. 23.
55   Copulos, *America's Achilles Heel*, p. 31.
56   Budget of the United States Government, Fiscal Year 2009 – Appendix,
      http://www.whitehouse.gov/omb/budget/fy2009/pdf/appendix/mil.pdf (accessed June
      18, 2008)
57   Copulos, *America's Achilles Heel*, p. 35.
58   Congressional Research Service, *The Cost of Iraq, Afghanistan, and Other Global War on
      Terror Operations Since 9/11*, p. 9.
59   Congressional Budget Office, *Withdrawal of U.S. Forces from Iraq: Possible Timelines and
      Estimated Costs*, p. 18.
60   Copulos, *America's Achilles Heel*, p. 36.
61   US Department of Energy, Energy Information Administration, http://www.eia.doe.gov
      (accessed October 20, 2009).

62 Barsky and Kilian, "Oil and the Macroeconomy Since the 1970s," p. 117.
63 Greene and Ahmad, *Costs of Oil Dependence: A 2005 Update*, p. 9.
64 Ibid., p. 13.
65 Balke, Brown and Yucel, "Oil Price Shocks and the US Economy."
66 Data has been adjusted to 2005 dollars. Greene and Ahmad, *Costs of Oil Dependence: A 2005 Update*, p. 31.

Chapter 2
It's Getting Hot in Here

1   National Oceanic and Atmospheric Administration, http://www.ozonelayer.noaa.gov (accessed February 20, 2008).
2   Chicago Climate Exchange, http://www.chicagoclimatex.com/content.jsf?id=221 (accessed February 7, 2008).
3   Exxon Valdez Oil Spill Trustee Council, 2009 Status Report, p. 4-6. http://www.evostc.state.ak.us/ (accessed June 17, 2010).
4   US Department of Energy, Energy Information Administration, http://www.eia.doe.gov (accessed November 18, 2009).
5   Alyeska Pipeline Service Company, http://www.alyeska-pipe.com/about.html (accessed June 18, 2010).
6   International Monetary Fund, http://www.imf.org (accessed June 18, 2010).
7   National Research Council, *Surface Temperature Reconstructions for the Last 2,000 Years*, p. 5.
8   Ibid., pp. 2-3.
9   National Oceanic and Atmospheric Administration, http://lwf.ncdc.noaa.gov/oa/climate/globalwarming.html (accessed February 6, 2008).
10 Petit et al., "Climate and Atmospheric History of the Past 420,000 Years from the Vostok Ice Core, Antarctica," p. 429.
11 Ibid., p. 435.
12 Ibid., p. 429.
13 Etheridge et al., "Historical CO_2 Records from the Law Dome DE08, DE08-2, and DSS Ice Cores."
14 Dr. Pieter Tans, US Department of Commerce, National Oceanic and Atmospheric Administration, Earth System Research Laboratory, http://www.esrl.noaa.gov/gmd/ccgg/trends (accessed February 6, 2008).
15 Canadell et al., "Contributions to Accelerating Atmospheric CO_2 Growth from Economic Activity, Carbon Intensity, and Efficiency of Natural Sinks," p. 18866.
16 US Department of Commerce, National Oceanic and Atmospheric Administration, National Environmental Satellite, Data, and Information Service, National Climatic Data Center, http://lwf.ncdc.noaa.gov/oa/climate/globalwarming.html (accessed February 6, 2008).
17 *Crude*, television documentary directed and written by Richard Smith.
18 Raupach et al., "Global and Regional Drivers of Accelerating CO_2 Emissions," p. 10288.
19 Ibid., p. 10289.
20 Petit et al., "Climate and Atmospheric History of the Past 420,000 Years from the Vostok Ice Core, Antarctica," p. 429.
21 Tett et al., "Estimation of Natural and Anthropogenic Contributions to Twentieth Century Temperature Change."
22 Brewer, "Direct Injection of Carbon Dioxide in the Oceans," p. 44.
23 Brewer, "Feasibility of Large-Scale Ocean CO_2 Sequestration."
24 Raupach et al., "Global and Regional Drivers of Accelerating CO_2 Emissions," p. 10292.
25 Canadell et al., "Contributions to Accelerating Atmospheric CO_2 Growth from Economic Activity, Carbon Intensity, and Efficiency of Natural Sinks," p. 18868.

26 Haugen and Eide, "CO_2 Capture and Disposal: The Realism of Large Scale Scenarios."
27 Brewer, "Feasibility of Large-Scale Ocean CO_2 Sequestration."
28 Brewer, "Direct Injection of Carbon Dioxide in the Oceans," p. 44.
29 International Maritime Organization, http://www.imo.org (accessed February 8, 2008).
30 Caldeira, "The Effectiveness and Unintended Consequences of Ocean Fertilization," p. 54.
31 Ibid., p. 55.
32 Orr, "Sequestration via Injection of Carbon Dioxide in the Deep Earth," p. 18.
33 Ibid., p. 19.
34 Ibid., p. 20.
35 Hill, "Using Carbon Dioxide to Recover Natural Gas and Oil," p. 23.
36 Jacobs, "Using Terrestrial Ecosystems for Carbon Sequestration," p. 62.
37 Raupach et al., "Global and Regional Drivers of Accelerating CO_2 Emissions," p. 10288.
38 Walsh, "Can Emissions Trading of Carbon Dioxide Bootstrap the Transition?" p. 108.
39 Ibid., p. 112.
40 Chicago Climate Exchange, Carbon Financial Instrument, http://www.chicagoclimateexchange.com/market/data/summary.jsf (accessed October 20, 2008).
41 Kyoto Protocol to the United Nations Framework Convention on Climate Change, http://unfccc.int/resource/docs/convkp/kpeng.html (accessed January 15, 2008).
42 Marland, Boden, and Andres, "Global, Regional, and National Fossil Fuel CO_2 Emissions."
43 US Department of Energy, Energy Information Administration, *Impacts of the Kyoto Protocol on U.S. Energy Markets and Economic Activity.*
44 US Department of Energy, Energy Information Administration, http://www.eia.doe.gov (accessed November 17, 2009).
45 US Department of Energy, Energy Information Administration, *Impacts of the Kyoto Protocol on U.S. Energy Markets and Economic Activity.*
46 Ibid.
47 Ibid.
48 Ibid.
49 Internal Revenue Service, http://www.irs.gov (accessed February 20, 2008)

Chapter 3
And on the 8th Day, Oil

1   BP plc, *Statistical Review of World Energy June 2009.*
2   Tarbell, *The History of the Standard Oil Company*, pp. 4-5.
3   Ibid., p. 31.
4   Ibid., p. 21.
5   US Department of Energy, Energy Information Administration, http://www.eia.doe.gov (accessed November 5, 2009).
6   Tarbell, *The History of the Standard Oil Company*, p. 42.
7   Ibid., p. 43.
8   Ibid., p. 44.
9   Maugeri, *The Age of Oil*, p. 18.
10 Klepper and Gunther, *The Wealthy 100: From Benjamin Franklin to Bill Gates-A Ranking of the Richest Americans, Past and Present.*
11 Forbes, "The World's Billionaires."
12 Bureau of Economic Analysis, http://www.bea.gov/national/index.htm#gdp (accessed November 5, 2009).
13 Maugeri, *The Age of Oil*, p. 15.

14   Ibid., p. 11.
15   Ibid., p. 12.
16   Ibid., p. 13.
17   Ibid., p. 14.
18   Ibid., p. 22.
19   Catherwood, *Churchill's Folly,* p. 23.
20   Ibid., pp. 24-25.
21   Ibid., p. 25.
22   Ibid., p. 26.
23   Maugeri, *The Age of Oil*, p. 22.
24   BP plc, http://www.bp.com (accessed March 15, 2008).
25   Maugeri, *The Age of Oil*, pp. 23-24.
26   Catherwood, *Churchill's Folly*, p. 63.
27   Ibid., p. 65.
28   Ibid., p. 45.
29   Ibid., p. 46.
30   Ibid., p. 45.
31   Ibid., p. 46.
32   Ibid., p. 49.
33   Ibid., p. 53.
34   Ibid., p. 44.
35   Maugeri, *The Age of Oil*, p. 26.
36   Ibid., p. 28.
37   Catherwood, *Churchill's Folly*, p. 60.

Chapter 4
The Foundations of Oil Geopolitics

1   Yergin, *The Prize*, pp. 212-17.
2   Ibid., pp. 262-68.
3   Maugeri, *The Age of Oil*, p. 53.
4   Yergin, *The Prize*, p. 334.
5   Ibid., p. 335.
6   Ibid., p. 334.
7   Ibid., p. 337.
8   Ibid., p. 343.
9   Harold L. Ickes's son, Harold M. Ickes, served as President Clinton's Chief of Staff and is a
     prominent member of the Democratic National Committee.
10   Yergin, *The Prize*, p. 274.
11   Maugeri, *The Age of Oil*, p. 53.
12   Yergin, *The Prize*, p. 382.
13   Ibid., p. 330.
14   Ibid., p. 333.
15   Ibid., pp. 344-45.
16   Maugeri, *The Age of Oil*, p. 51.
17   Yergin, *The Prize*, pp. 309-10.
18   Ibid., p. 307.
19   Ibid., p. 318.
20   Ibid., p. 318.
21   Ibid., p. 322.
22   Ibid., p. 356.

23   Ibid., p. 357.
24   Ibid., p. 358.
25   Maugeri, *The Age of Oil*, p. 55.
26   Ibid., p. 53.
27   Yergin, *The Prize*, p. 393.
28   Ibid., p. 394.
29   Maugeri, *The Age of Oil*, p. 54.
30   Klare, *Blood and Oil*, p. 12.
31   Yergin, *The Prize*, pp. 403-5.
32   North Atlantic Treaty Organization, http://www.nato.int (accessed March 15, 2008).
33   US Department of State, Bureau of Public Affairs, Office of the Historian, http://www.state.gov/r/pa/ho/time/lw/98683.htm (accessed March 15, 2008).
34   US Central Intelligence Agency, *The Break-Up of the Colonial Empires and Its Implications for US Security*, p. 1.
35   Maugeri, *The Age of Oil*, p. 93.
36   Ibid., p. 93.
37   Ibid., p. 95.
38   Ibid., p. 96.
39   Ibid., p. 87.
40   US Department of State, Bureau of Public Affairs, Office of the Historian, http://www.state.gov/r/pa/ho/time/lw/98683.htm (accessed March 15, 2008).
41   Aden Refining Company, http://www.arc-ye.com/ (accessed October 16, 2008).
42   Pelletière, *Yemen and Stability in the Persian Gulf*.
43   Ibid.
44   US Department of State, *Near East, 1962-1963,* Vol. XVIII of *1961-1963, John F. Kennedy,* In *Foreign Relations of the United States*, Document 215.
45   Ibid., Document 293.
46   US Central Intelligence Agency, *Main Trends in the Arab World*, p. 7.
47   US Department of State, *Near East, 1962-1963,* Vol. XVIII of *1961-1963, John F. Kennedy,* In *Foreign Relations of the United States*, Document 361.
48   Ibid., Document 363.
49   Pelletière, *Yemen and Stability in the Persian Gulf*.
50   Metz, *Iran: A Country Study*.
51   Yergin, *The Prize*, pp. 269-71.
52   Maugeri, *The Age of Oil*, p. 63.
53   BP plc, http://www.bp.com (accessed March 15, 2008).
54   Maugeri, *The Age of Oil*, p. 65.
55   Ibid., p. 65.
56   Ibid., p. 66.
57   Ibid., p. 67.
58   Ibid., p. 68.
59   Ibid., p. 69.
60   Ibid., p. 70.
61   BP plc, http://www.bp.com (accessed March 15, 2008).

Chapter 5
Losing Control

1   Maugeri, *The Age of Oil*, p. 48.
2   Ibid., p. 84.
3   Yergin, *The Prize*, p. 512.

4   Ibid., pp. 513-14.
5   Ibid., p. 518.
6   Ibid., p. 522.
7   Ibid., p. 522.
8   Maugeri, *The Age of Oil*, p. 85.
9   Yergin, *The Prize*, p. 523.
10   Maugeri, *The Age of Oil*, p. 86.
11   Yergin, *The Prize*, p. 525.
12   Israeli Ministry of Foreign Affairs, Historical Documents, 1947-1974.
     http://www.mfa.gov.il/MFA/Foreign+Relations/Israels+Foreign+Relations+since+1947
     /1947-1974/THE+SIX-DAY+WAR+-+INTRODUCTION.htm (accessed April 2, 2008).
13   Maugeri, *The Age of Oil*, p. 101.
14   US Department of State, *Arab-Israeli Crisis and War, 1967*, Vol. XIX of *1964-1968,
     Lyndon B. Johnson*, In *Foreign Relations of the United States*, Document 12.
15   Yergin, *The Prize*, p. 554.
16   US Central Intelligence Agency, *The Situation and Prospects in Egypt*.
17   Israeli Ministry of Foreign Affairs, Historical Documents, 1947-1974,
     http://www.mfa.gov.il/MFA/Foreign+Relations/Israels+Foreign+Relations+since+1947
     /1947-1974/THE+SIX-DAY+WAR+-+INTRODUCTION.htm (accessed April 2, 2008).
18   US Department of State, *Arab-Israeli Crisis and War, 1967*, Vol. XIX of *1964-1968,
     Lyndon B. Johnson*, In *Foreign Relations of the United States*, Document 25.
19   Israeli Ministry of Foreign Affairs, Historical Documents, 1947-1974, Statement by
     President Nasser to Arab Trade Unionists, May 26, 1967.
20   Salameh, "Oil Crises, Historical Perspective."
21   Ibid.
22   Maugeri, *The Age of Oil*, p. 100.
23   Yergin, *The Prize*, pp. 557-58.
24   US Central Intelligence Agency, *Current Status of UAR President Nasser's Health*.
25   Yergin, *The Prize*, p. 557.
26   The name of the Libyan leader has many different English spellings. This is the version
     used by the US Central Intelligence Agency.
27   Akins, "The Oil Crisis: This Time the Wolf Is Here," p. 470.
28   Maugeri, *The Age of Oil*, p. 102.
29   Ibid., p. 105.
30   Yergin, *The Prize*, p. 582.
31   Salameh, "Oil Crises, Historical Perspective."
32   Ibid.
33   Maugeri, *The Age of Oil*, p. 104.
34   Quandt, "U.S. Energy Policy and the Arab-Israeli Conflict," pp. 282-83.
35   Akins, "The Oil Crisis: This Time the Wolf Is Here," p. 487.
36   Adelman, *The Genie Out of the Bottle*, p. 102; and Quandt, "U.S. Energy Policy and the
     Arab-Israeli Conflict," pp. 282-83.
37   Yergin, *The Prize*, p. 590.
38   Ibid., p. 593.
39   Ibid., pp. 595-96.
40   Akins, "The Oil Crisis: This Time the Wolf Is Here," p. 483.
41   Ibid., pp. 467-68.
42   Yergin, *The Prize*, pp. 602-3.
43   Maugeri, *The Age of Oil*, p. 112.
44   Yergin, *The Prize*, p. 605.

45 Maugeri, *The Age of Oil*, p. 112.
46 Sankari, "The Character and Impact of Arab Oil Embargoes," p. 271.
47 Maugeri, *The Age of Oil*, p. 112.
48 Sankari, "The Character and Impact of Arab Oil Embargoes," p. 272.
49 Yergin, *The Prize*, p. 608.
50 Alnasrawi, *Arab Nationalism, Oil, and the Political Economy of Dependency*, p. 185.
51 Morgan and Faisal, "Saudi Dove in the Oil Slick."
52 Barsky and Kilian, "Oil and the Macroeconomy Since the 1970s," p. 130.
53 Adelman, *The Genie Out of the Bottle*, p. 113.
54 Yergin, *The Prize*, p. 617.
55 Ibid., p. 614.
56 Maugeri, *The Age of Oil*, p. 114.
57 Yergin, *The Prize*, p. 615.
58 Ibid., p. 617.
59 Maugeri, *The Age of Oil*, p. 114.
60 Yergin, *The Prize*, p. 625.
61 Ibid., p. 632.
62 Maugeri, *The Age of Oil*, p. 114.
63 Adelman, *The Genie Out of the Bottle*, p. 112.
64 Yergin, *The Prize*, p. 637.
65 Pelletière, *America's Oil Wars*, p. 71.
66 Ibid., p. 72.
67 Based on the change in the Consumer Price Index from November 1973 to November 1974, US Department of Labor, Bureau of Labor Statistics, http://www.bls.gov (accessed March 15, 2008).
68 US Department of Labor, Bureau of Labor Statistics, http://www.bls.gov (accessed March 15, 2008).
69 Yergin, *The Prize*, p. 637.
70 Ibid., p. 638.
71 Maugeri, *The Age of Oil*, p. 106.
72 Pelletière, *America's Oil Wars*, pp. 72-73.
73 Ibid., p. 73.
74 Ibid., p. 73.
75 Ibid., p. 74.
76 Bowden, "Among the Hostage-Takers."
77 Ibid.
78 Adelman, *The Genie Out of the Bottle*, p. 168.
79 Klare, *Blood and Oil*, p. 46.

Chapter 6
Everything Changed in 1979

1 Copulos, *America's Achilles Heel*, p. 50.
2 Schofield, "Position, Function, and Symbol: The Shatt al-Arab Dispute in Perspective."
3 Pelletière, *America's Oil Wars*, pp. 88-89.
4 Ibid., p. 89.
5 Ibid., pp. 89-90.
6 Ibid., p. 90.
7 US Central Intelligence Agency, *Iran-Iraq War: Increased Threat to Persian Gulf Oil Exports*.
8 Pelletière, *Iraq and the International Oil System*, p. 197.

9   Pelletière, *America's Oil Wars*, p. 91.
10   Hollis, "The US Role: Helpful or Harmful?"
11   Nonneman, "The Gulf States and the Iran-Iraq War: Pattern Shifts and Continuities."
12   Pelletière, *Iraq and the International Oil System*.
13   Pelletière, *America's Oil Wars*, p. 94.
14   Hollis, "The US Role: Helpful or Harmful?"
15   Pelletière, *Iraq and the International Oil System*, p. 186.
16   Maugeri, *The Age of Oil*, p. 146.
17   Pelletière, *America's Oil Wars*, p. 97.
18   Adelman, *The Genie Out of the Bottle*, p. 255.
19   Pelletière, *America's Oil Wars*, p. 98.
20   Maugeri, *The Age of Oil*, p. 146.
21   Ibid., p. 146.
22   Pelletière, *America's Oil Wars*, p. 99.
23   Pelletière, *Iraq and the International Oil System*, pp. 218-19.
24   Nyang and Hendricks, *A Line in the Sand*, p. 63.
25   Pelletière, *Iraq and the International Oil System*, pp. 218-19.
26   Nyang and Hendricks, *A Line in the Sand*, pp. 63-66.
27   Blair, *At War in the Gulf: A Chronology*.
28   Nyang and Hendricks, *A Line in the Sand*.
29   Chollet and Goldgeier, *America Between the Wars: From 11/9 to 9/11*, p. 9.
30   Dannreuther, *The Gulf Conflict*, pp. 20-21.
31   Blair, *At War in the Gulf: A Chronology*.
32   Maugeri, *The Age of Oil*, p. 149.
33   Ibid., p. 150.
34   Blair, *At War in the Gulf: A Chronology*.
35   House Committee on Foreign Affairs, *Foreign Policy and National Security Implications of Oil Dependence*, Rep. Tom Lantos.
36   BP plc, *Statistical Review of World Energy June 2009*.
37   Pelletière, *America's Oil Wars*, p. 24.
38   Ibid., p. 32.
39   Chollet and Goldgeier, *America Between the Wars: From 11/9 to 9/11*, p. 263.
40   Ibid., pp. 185-86.
41   Ibid., pp. 13-15.
42   Ibid., pp. 187-89.
43   Alfonsi, *Circle in the Sand*.
44   BP plc, *Statistical Review of World Energy June 2009*.
45   Jaffe, "Geopolitics of Energy," p. 852; and Palast, "OPEC on the March."
46   Palast, "OPEC on the March."
47   Ibid.
48   Ibid.
49   Ibid.
50   Mufson, "A Crude Case for War?"
51   Ibid.
52   BP plc, *Statistical Review of World Energy June 2009*.
53   Klare, *Blood and Oil*, pp. 115-16.
54   BP plc, *Statistical Review of World Energy June 2009*.
55   CITGO Petroleum Corporation, http://www.citgo.com (accessed October 18, 2008).
56   Ingham, "Chavez Calls for Anti-US Alliance."
57   Jaffe, "Geopolitics of Energy," p. 849.

58 International Monetary Fund et al., *A Study of the Soviet Economy*.
59 Ticktin, *Origins of the Crisis in the USSR*, pp. 130-31.
60 International Monetary Fund et al., *A Study of the Soviet Economy*.
61 Shelton, *The Coming Soviet Crash*, p. 86.
62 Ibid., pp. 81-84.
63 Ibid., p. 88.
64 Ibid., p. 86.
65 International Monetary Fund et al., *A Study of the Soviet Economy*.
66 Shelton, *The Coming Soviet Crash*, pp. 84-85.
67 International Energy Agency, *World Energy Investment Outlook 2007*.
68 Chollet and Goldgeier, *America Between the Wars: From 11/9 to 9/11*, pp. 122-24.
69 Ibid., pp. 231-32.
70 Official Site of the Bush Putin Slovenia Summit 2001,
    http://www.ljubljana-summit.gov.si/en/index.html (accessed October 20, 2008).
71 Kaufman, "The Ethnic Conflicts in Georgia."
72 US Central Intelligence Agency, *Caspian Region Oil Pipelines*; and BP plc,
    http://www.bp.com (accessed October 19, 2008).
73 US Central Intelligence Agency, *Caspian Region Oil Pipelines*.

Chapter 7
The Oil Bidniz

1   US Department of Energy, Energy Information Administration,
    http://www.eia.doe.gov (accessed November 17, 2009).
2   BP plc, *Statistical Review of World Energy June 2009*.
3   Lake, "Nuclear Energy: Large Scale, Zero-Emissions Technology," p. 95.
4   US Department of Energy, Energy Information Administration,
    http://www.eia.doe.gov (accessed November 18, 2009).
5   US Nuclear Regulatory Commission,
    http://www.nrc.gov/info-finder/reactor/ (accessed November 19, 2009).
6   International Atomic Energy Agency, http://www.iaea.org (accessed July 7, 2008).
7   *Crude*, television documentary directed and written by Richard Smith.
8   Hyne, *Nontechnical Guide to Petroleum Geology, Exploration, Drilling and Production*, p. 149.
9   Ibid., p. xxxiv.
10 Downey, "Oil and Natural Gas Exploration."
11 Hyne, *Nontechnical Guide to Petroleum Geology, Exploration, Drilling and Production*, p. 24.
12 Ibid., p. 26.
13 Maugeri, *The Age of Oil*, p. 205.
14 Hyne, *Nontechnical Guide to Petroleum Geology, Exploration, Drilling and Production*, p. 4.
15 Peterson and Mahnovski, *New Forces at Work in Refining*, p. 103.
16 Hyne, *Nontechnical Guide to Petroleum Geology, Exploration, Drilling and Production*, pp. 4-5.
17 Peterson and Mahnovski, *New Forces at Work in Refining*, p. 104.
18 Hyne, *Nontechnical Guide to Petroleum Geology, Exploration, Drilling and Production*, p. 164.
19 Deffeyes, *Beyond Oil*, p. 122.
20 Hyne, *Nontechnical Guide to Petroleum Geology, Exploration, Drilling and Production*, p. 165.
21 Petroleum Communication Foundation, *Canada's Oil Sands and Heavy Oil*.
22 Canadian Association of Petroleum Producers, http://www.capp.ca (accessed November 18, 2009).
23 US Department of Energy, Energy Information Administration, http://www.eia.doe.gov (accessed July 7, 2008).

24 Hyne, *Nontechnical Guide to Petroleum Geology, Exploration, Drilling and Production*, p. 423.
25 Ibid., p. 425.
26 Ibid., p. 422.
27 Ibid., p. 439.
28 Ibid., p. 441.
29 Deffeyes, *Beyond Oil*, p. 27.
30 Ibid., p. 28.
31 Ibid., p. 28.
32 Peterson and Mahnovski, *New Forces at Work in Refining*, p. 103.
33 Ibid., p. 105.
34 Ibid., p. 104.
35 Hyne, *Nontechnical Guide to Petroleum Geology, Exploration, Drilling and Production*, p. 7.
36 Peterson and Mahnovski, *New Forces at Work in Refining*, pp. 105-6.
37 Ibid., p. 107.
38 Speight, *The Chemistry and Technology of Petroleum*, pp. 684-86.
39 *The Columbia Encyclopedia*, s.v. "Internal Combustion Engine,"
    http://www.bartleby.com/65/in/intern-co.html (accessed January 17, 2008).
40 Watts, *The People's Tycoon: Henry Ford and the American Century*, p. 36.
41 Ibid., pp. x-xi.
42 Ibid., p. 37.
43 Ibid., p. 54.
44 Ibid., p. 57.
45 Ibid., p. 111.
46 Maugeri, *The Age of Oil*, p. 21.
47 Ibid., p. 22.
48 Schafer, "Passenger Demand for Travel and Energy Use."

Chapter 8
A Few 800-Pound Gorillas

1   Greene, *Modeling the Oil Transition*, p. 21.
2   Ibid., p. 18.
3   Storchmann, "Long-Run Gasoline Demand for Passenger Cars: The Role of Income
    Distribution," p. 28.
4   Ibid., p. 55.
5   Greene, *Modeling the Oil Transition*, p. 29.
6   Ibid., p. 31.
7   BP plc, *Statistical Review of World Energy June 2009*.
8   Ibid.
9   Levine and Sinton, "National Energy Policy: China."
10 Klare, *Blood and Oil*, p. 175.
11 Levine and Sinton, "National Energy Policy: China."
12 US-China Economic and Security Review Commission, *2007 Report to Congress*, p. 161.
13 National Bureau of Statistics of China, "Energy," in *China Statistical Yearbook - 2006*.
14 BP plc, *Statistical Review of World Energy June 2009*.
15 International Energy Agency, *World Energy Investment Outlook 2007*.
16 Greene, *Modeling the Oil Transition*, p. 28.
17 Wang, et al., *Projection of Chinese Motor Vehicle Growth, Oil Demand, and CO_2 Emissions
    through 2050*.
18 Klare, *Blood and Oil*, p. 22.

19 Jaffe, "Geopolitics of Energy," p. 847.
20 House Committee on Science, *Improving the Nation's Energy Security*, Testimony by Gal Luft.
21 US-China Economic and Security Review Commission, *2007 Report to Congress*, p. 177.
22 Ibid., p. 157.
23 Ibid., p. 178.
24 Ibid., p. 179.
25 International Energy Agency, *World Energy Investment Outlook 2007*; and BP plc, *Statistical Review of World Energy June 2009*.
26 Philip, *The Political Economy of International Oil*, p. 180.
27 Baer, "The Fall of the House of Saud," p. 55.
28 Ross and Rackmill, "Secrets of the Saudi Royal Family."
29 Baer, "The Fall of the House of Saud," p. 62.
30 Ibid., p. 58.
31 Ibid., p. 56.
32 Ibid., p. 58.
33 Ibid., p. 60.
34 Askari and Krichene, "Oil Price Dynamics (2002–2006)."
35 Greene, *Modeling the Oil Transition*, p. 2.
36 House Committee on Foreign Affairs, *Foreign Policy and National Security Implications of Oil Dependence*, Testimony of John M. Deutch.
37 Kaufmann et al., "Determinants of OPEC Production," p. 334.
38 Morgan and Faisal, "Saudi Dove in the Oil Slick."
39 Barsky and Kilian, "Oil and the Macroeconomy Since the 1970s," p. 125.
40 Kaufmann et al., "Determinants of OPEC Production," p. 334.
41 Ibid., p. 343.
42 Ibid., p. 347.
43 Ibid., p. 334.
44 Ibid., p. 346.
45 Spot market price is the price at this "spot" in time. When you buy gasoline for your car, you pay the spot price – the price posted for gasoline at that store at that time.
46 Congressional Research Service, *Oil Shale: History, Incentives and Policy*, p. 11.
47 Kohl, "National Security and Energy," p. 197.
48 Adelman, *The Genie Out of the Bottle*, p. 194.
49 Palast, "OPEC on the March."
50 Jaffe, "Geopolitics of Energy," p. 846.
51 Kaufmann et al., "Determinants of OPEC Production," p. 346.
52 Yousefi and Wirjanto, "The Empirical Role of the Exchange Rate on the Crude-Oil Price Formation."
53 Kohl, "National Security and Energy," pp. 199-200.
54 Jaffe, "Geopolitics of Energy," p. 853.
55 US Department of Energy, http://www.spr.doe.gov/dir/dir.html (accessed November 18, 2009).
56 BP plc, *Statistical Review of World Energy June 2009*.
57 US Department of Energy, http://www.fe.doe.gov/programs/reserves/ (accessed June 25, 2008).
58 Author's calculations based on data from US Department of Energy, Energy Information Administration, http://www.eia.doe.gov (accessed November 18, 2009).
59 Gary and Karl, *Bottom of the Barrel*, p. 18.
60 Ibid., p. 21.
61 Ibid., p. 12.

62   Ibid., p. 20.
63   Ibid., p. 10.
64   Klare, *Blood and Oil*, p. 22.
65   Gary and Karl, *Bottom of the Barrel*, p. 19.
66   Klare, *Blood and Oil*, p. 22.
67   Gary and Karl, *Bottom of the Barrel*, p. 23.
68   International Institute for Strategic Studies, *The Military Balance*.
69   Gary and Karl, *Bottom of the Barrel*, p. 18.
70   Ross, "Does Oil Hinder Democracy?" p. 356.
71   Gary and Karl, *Bottom of the Barrel*, p. 20.
72   Karl, "The Impact of Oil Booms on Oil-Exporting Countries," p. 43.
73   Deffeyes, *Beyond Oil*, p. 179.
74   Gary and Karl, *Bottom of the Barrel*, p. 21.
75   Central Intelligence Agency, CIA World Factbook,
     https://www.cia.gov/library/publications/the-world-factbook/ (accessed May 13, 2008).
76   Gary and Karl. *Bottom of the Barrel*, p. 21.
77   Olien and Olien, *Oil and Ideology*, p 251.
78   Cooper, *Time to Change the Record on Oil Policy*, p. 6.
79   Ibid., p. 3.
80   Ollinger, *Organizational Forms and Business Strategy in the US Petroleum Industry*, pp. 102-103.
81   ExxonMobil Corporation, Form 10-K filed with the US Securities and Exchange
     Commission for the year ended December 31, 2007.
82   BP plc, http://www.bp.com (accessed October 23, 2008).
83   BP plc, Form 20-F filed with the US Securities and Exchange Commission for the year
     ended December 31, 2007; BP Alternative Energy,
     http://www.bp.com/genericarticle.do?categoryId=11&contentId=7045549 (accessed
     October 23, 2008).

Chapter 9
I Think I Lost My Appetite

1   DeCicco, Griffin, and Ertel, "Putting the Brakes on U.S. Oil Demand."
2   House Committee on Science, *Improving the Nation's Energy Security*, Testimony by David
     L. Greene.
3   DeCicco, Griffin, and Ertel, "Putting the Brakes on U.S. Oil Demand."
4   House Committee on Science, *Improving the Nation's Energy Security*, Testimony by K. G.
     Duleep.
5   Report of the Committee on the Effectiveness and Impact of Corporate Average Fuel
     Economy (CAFE) Standards, p. 3.
6   House Committee on Science, *Improving the Nation's Energy Security*, Testimony by K. G.
     Duleep.
7   Report of the Committee on the Effectiveness and Impact of Corporate Average Fuel
     Economy (CAFE) Standards, p. 5.
8   World Business Council for Sustainable Development, *Mobility 2030*, p. 81.
9   Ibid.
10   World Business Council for Sustainable Development, *Mobility 2030*, p. 81; and US
     Environmental Protection Agency, *Light Duty Automotive Technology and Fuel Economy
     Trends*.
11   Lovins et al., *Winning the Oil Endgame*, pp. 56-58.
12   National Highway Traffic Safety Administration,
     http://www.nhtsa.dot.gov/cars/rules/cafe/overview.htm (accessed January 24, 2008).

13 Ibid.
14 House Committee on Science, *Improving the Nation's Energy Security.*
15 House Committee on Science, *Improving the Nation's Energy Security*, Testimony by David L. Greene.
16 Ibid.
17 BP plc, *Statistical Review of World Energy June 2009.*
18 House Committee on Science, *Improving the Nation's Energy Security*, Testimony by David L. Greene.
19 Ibid.
20 Report of the Committee on the Effectiveness and Impact of Corporate Average Fuel Economy (CAFE) Standards, p. 3.
21 House Committee on Science, *Improving the Nation's Energy Security*, Testimony by Michael J. Stanton.
22 DeCicco, Griffin, and Ertel, "Putting the Brakes on U.S. Oil Demand."
23 Ibid.
24 House Committee on Science, *Improving the Nation's Energy Security*, Testimony by K. G. Duleep.
25 Ibid., Testimony by David L. Greene.
26 US Department of Transportation, National Highway Traffic Safety Administration, http://www.nhtsa.dot.gov (accessed November 18, 2009).
27 House Committee on Science, *Improving the Nation's Energy Security*, Testimony by David L. Greene.
28 Ibid.
29 Plotkin, "Fuel Economy Initiatives: International Comparisons."
30 House Committee on Science, *Improving the Nation's Energy Security*, Testimony by K. G. Duleep.
31 Plotkin, "Fuel Economy Initiatives: International Comparisons."
32 Plotkin, "Fuel Economy Initiatives: International Comparisons;" and Brons et al., "A Meta-Analysis of the Price Elasticity of Gasoline Demand: A SUR Approach."
33 Clerides and Zachariadis, "The Effect of Standards and Fuel Prices on Automobile Fuel Economy."
34 Brons et al., "A Meta-Analysis of the Price Elasticity of Gasoline Demand. A SUR Approach."
35 House Committee on Science, *Improving the Nation's Energy Security*, Testimony by K. G. Duleep.
36 US Department of Energy, Energy Information Administration, http://www.eia.doe.gov (accessed September 10, 2008).
37 Ibid.
38 House Committee on Science, *Improving the Nation's Energy Security*, Testimony by David L. Greene.
39 Ibid.
40 BP plc, *Statistical Review of World Energy June 2009.*
41 House Committee on Science, *Improving the Nation's Energy Security*, Testimony by Michael J. Stanton.
42 German, "Hybrid Electric Vehicles."
43 Greene, *Modeling the Oil Transition*, p. 55.
44 Heywood, "Fueling our Transportation Future."
45 House Select Committee on Energy Independence and Global Warming, *Geopolitical Implications of Rising Oil Dependence and Global Warming*, Testimony by James Woolsey.
46 German, "Hybrid Electric Vehicles."
47 US Environmental Protection Agency, *Light Duty Automotive Technology and Fuel Economy Trends*, p. 38.

48 World Business Council for Sustainable Development, *Mobility 2030*, p. 71.
49 House Committee on Science, *Improving the Nation's Energy Security*, Testimony by K. G. Duleep.
50 General Motors Corporation, http://www.chevrolet.com/pages/open/default/future/volt.do (accessed April 8, 2010).
51 House Committee on Science, *Improving the Nation's Energy Security*, Testimony by Gal Luft.
52 Dunn, "History of Hydrogen."
53 Dunn, "History of Hydrogen."
54 Lovins, *Twenty Hydrogen Myths*, p. 10.
55 Dunn, "History of Hydrogen."
56 Lovins, *Twenty Hydrogen Myths*, p. 5.
57 Energy Future Coalition, *Challenge and Opportunity: Charting a New Energy Future*, p. 52.
58 Ibid.
59 DeCicco, "Fuel Cell Vehicles."
60 Rifkin, "Hydrogen: Empowering the People."
61 DeCicco, "Fuel Cell Vehicles."
62 US Department of Energy, *Basic Research Needs for the Hydrogen Economy*, p. ix.
63 Ibid., p. 55.
64 Ahluwalia and Wang, "Fuel Cell Systems for Transportation: Status and Trends," p. 169.
65 US Department of Energy, *Basic Research Needs for the Hydrogen Economy*, p. 56.
66 Ibid., p. 4.
67 American Physical Society, *The Hydrogen Initiative*, p. 3.
68 Lovins, *Twenty Hydrogen Myths*, p. 4.
69 American Physical Society, *The Hydrogen Initiative*, p. 10.
70 Petersen, Erickson, and Kahn, *A Strategy: Moving America Away from Oil*, p. 61.
71 US Department of Energy, *Basic Research Needs for the Hydrogen Economy*, p. 32.
72 Lovins, *Twenty Hydrogen Myths*, p. 5.
73 US Department of Energy, *Basic Research Needs for the Hydrogen Economy*, p. 33.
74 American Physical Society, *The Hydrogen Initiative*, p. 8.
75 US Department of Energy, *Basic Research Needs for the Hydrogen Economy*, p. 49.
76 Petersen, Erickson, and Kahn, *A Strategy: Moving America Away from Oil*, p. 33.
77 World Business Council for Sustainable Development, *Mobility 2030*, p. 76.
78 Lovins, *Twenty Hydrogen Myths*, pp. 10-11.
79 US Department of Energy, *Basic Research Needs for the Hydrogen Economy*, p. 11.
80 American Physical Society, *The Hydrogen Initiative*, p. 6.
81 Ibid.
82 Deffeyes, *Beyond Oil*, pp. 157-58.
83 Lovins, *Twenty Hydrogen Myths*, p. 8.
84 Energy Future Coalition, *Challenge and Opportunity: Charting a New Energy Future*, p. 52.
85 Petersen, Erickson, and Kahn, *A Strategy: Moving America Away from Oil*, p. 33.
86 Lovins, *Twenty Hydrogen Myths*, p. 12.

Chapter 10
Drill, Baby, Drill!

1 Hyne, *Nontechnical Guide to Petroleum Geology, Exploration, Drilling and Production*, p. 26.
2 Deffeyes, *Beyond Oil*, p. 27.
3 BP plc, *Statistical Review of World Energy June 2009*.
4 US Department of Energy, Energy Information Administration, http://www.eia.doe.gov/emeu/international/reserves.html (accessed November 19, 2009).

5   Campbell, *Regular Conventional Oil Production to 2100 and Resource Based Production Forecast.*
6   Clark, *Petrodollar Warfare*, p. 81.
7   Ibid., p. 82.
8   Greene, *Modeling the Oil Transition*, p. 4.
9   Figures from US Geological Survey, *World Petroleum Assessment 2000* adjusted reference date of Jan. 1, 1996 to year end 2008 using production figures from BP plc, *Statistical Review of World Energy June 2009* and BP plc, *Statistical Review of World Energy June 2007.* Estimate of existing reserves includes projected conventional reserve growth (occurs as the full extent of a newly discovered field is learned in the process of producing oil).
10 US Geological Survey, *World Petroleum Assessment 2000.*
11 Among those claiming the USGS figure are too optimistic are Klare, *Blood and Oil*, p. 116; and Deffeyes, *Beyond Oil.*
12 Campbell, *Regular Conventional Oil Production to 2100 and Resource Based Production Forecast.*
13 Deffeyes, *Beyond Oil*, p. 18.
14 BP plc, *Statistical Review of World Energy June 2009.*
15 Ibid.
16 Klare, *Blood and Oil*, p. 185.
17 Clark, *Petrodollar Warfare*, p. 83.
18 BP plc, *Statistical Review of World Energy June 2009.*
19 US Department of Energy, Energy Information Administration, http://www.eia.doe.gov (accessed November 19, 2009).
20 National Defense Council Foundation, "The ANWR Imperative," p. 3.
21 US Department of Interior, Minerals Management Service, *Comprehensive Inventory of US OCS Oil and Natural Gas Resources*, p. 20.
22 Based on estimates of reserves and projected new discoveries as of the end of 2005 from Campbell, *Regular Conventional Oil Production to 2100 and Resource Based Production Forecast*, adjusted to year end 2008 using production figures from BP plc, *Statistical Review of World Energy June 2009.*
23 Combines estimate of proved reserves from BP plc, *Statistical Review of World Energy June 2009* and estimates of future discoveries from US Geological Survey, *World Petroleum Assessment 2000.*
24 BP plc, *Statistical Review of World Energy June 2009.*
25 Adelman, *The Genie Out of the Bottle*, p. 11.
26 Yergin, "Imagining a $7-a-Gallon Future."
27 Kohl, "National Security and Energy," p. 197.
28 Deffeyes, *Beyond Oil*, p. 31.
29 Kohl, "National Security and Energy," p. 197.
30 World Business Council for Sustainable Development, *Mobility 2030*, p. 68.
31 Yergin, "Imagining a $7-a-Gallon Future."
32 Deffeyes, *Beyond Oil.*
33 BP plc, *Statistical Review of World Energy June 2009.*
34 Davis, Diegel, and Boundy, *Transportation Energy Data Book.*
35 Greene, Hopson, and Li, "Have We Run Out of Oil Yet?"
36 US Department of Energy, Energy Information Administration, http://www.eia.doe.gov (accessed June 17, 2008).
37 Deffeyes, *Beyond Oil*, p. xiii.
38 Based on data from the US Department of Energy, Energy Information Administration, http://www.eia.doe.gov, and US Department of Transportation, Federal Highway Administration, http://www.fhwa.dot.gov (accessed June 27, 2008).

39 Cooper, *Time to Change the Record on Oil Policy*, p. 9.
40 Peterson and Mahnovski, *New Forces at Work in Refining*, p. 38.
41 Gasohol is a term coined during the 1970s for fuel that is a mixture of gasoline and ethanol. Although ethanol is still blended with gasoline, the terminology fell out of favor in the mid-1980s when gas prices dropped, dooming the Carter-era programs.
42 US Department of Energy, Energy Information Administration, http://www.eia.doe.gov (accessed October 28, 2009); and Renewable Fuels Association, http://www.ethanolrfa.org (accessed October 28, 2009).
43 US Department of Energy, Energy Information Administration, http://www.eia.doe.gov (accessed April 3, 2008).
44 Internal Revenue Service, Publication 510 and Form 720, 2008.
45 Calculated from data in Wright et al., *Biomass Energy Data Book*, p. 22.
46 Shockey et al., *Optimal Ethanol Blend-Level Investigation*.
47 International Energy Agency, 2007 Energy Balance for Brazil. http://www.iea.org/stats/balancetable.asp?COUNTRY_CODE=BR (accessed June 8, 2010).
48 Coelho and Goldemberg, "Alternative Transportation Fuels: Contemporary Case Studies."
49 Ibid.
50 US Department of Agriculture, Foreign Agricultural Service, *Brazilian Sugar*, p. 2.
51 Sandalow, "Ethanol: Lessons from Brazil," p. 3.
52 Coelho and Goldemberg, "Alternative Transportation Fuels: Contemporary Case Studies." (figures in 2001 dollars).
53 Ibid.
54 Ibid.
55 Coelho, "Agriculture & Biomass: Competition or a Synergy? Brazilian Experience on Biofuels."
56 Yergin, *The Prize*, p. 333.

Chapter 11
How to Squeeze Oil from a Twig

1 BP plc, *Statistical Review of World Energy June 2009*.
2 Navigant Consulting Inc., "North American Natural Gas Supply Assessment."
3 BP plc, *Statistical Review of World Energy June 2009*.
4 Petersen, Erickson, and Kahn, *A Strategy: Moving America Away from Oil*, p. 21.
5 US Department of Energy, Energy Information Administration, "Country Analysis Briefs: South Africa," October, 2008, http://www.eia.doe.gov/emeu/cabs/South_Africa/pdf.pdf (accessed November 23, 2009).
6 Mann and Spath, *Life Cycle Assessment of a Biomass Gasification Combined-Cycle System*, p. 47.
7 Spath and Dayton, *Technical and Economic Assessment of Synthesis Gas to Fuels and Chemicals*, p. i.
8 Gasification Technologies Council, *Gasification: Redefining Clean Energy*.
9 Phillips et al., *Thermochemical Ethanol via Indirect Gasification and Mixed Alcohol Synthesis of Lignocellulosic Biomass*, pp. 3-4.
10 Greene, *An Assessment of Energy and Environmental Issues Related to the Use of Gas-to-Liquid Fuels in Transportation*, p. 7.
11 Bergin, "Annual Report for the Ultra-Clean Fischer-Tropsch Fuels Production and Demonstration Project."
12 Greene, *An Assessment of Energy and Environmental Issues Related to the Use of Gas-to-Liquid Fuels in Transportation*, p. 7.
13 Sasol Limited, *Reaching New Energy Frontiers through Competitive GTL Technology*.
14 Ibid.
15 Ramon, *Update from the Chief Financial Officer*.

16 Knott, "Gas-to-Liquids Projects Gaining Momentum as Process List Grows."

17 Royal Dutch Shell plc, http://www.shell.com/home/content/qatar/ (accessed October 28, 2008).

18 Sun, "CTL Development in China;" and Shenhua Group, http://www.shenhuagroup.com.cn/english/index.htm (accessed September 30, 2008).

19 Ciferno and Marano, *Benchmarking Biomass Gasification Technologies for Fuels, Chemicals and Hydrogen Production*, p. 15.

20 Bergin, "Annual Report for the Ultra-Clean Fischer-Tropsch Fuels Production and Demonstration Project."

21 Peterson and Mahnovski, *New Forces at Work in Refining*, p. 44.

22 Greene, *An Assessment of Energy and Environmental Issues Related to the Use of Gas-to-Liquid Fuels in Transportation*, p. 1.

23 Bergin, "Annual Report for the Ultra-Clean Fischer-Tropsch Fuels Production and Demonstration Project."

24 Ibid.

25 West Virginia University and Union Carbide Technical Center, *The Economical Production of Alcohol Fuels from Coal-Derived Synthesis Gas.*

26 Nexant Inc., *Mixed Alcohols from Syngas - State of Technology.*

27 Phillips et al., *Thermochemical Ethanol via Indirect Gasification and Mixed Alcohol Synthesis of Lignocellulosic Biomass*, p. 22; International Molybdenum Association, http://www.imoa.info/ (accessed November 22, 2009).

28 Elliott, "Chemicals from Biomass."

29 Phillips et al., *Thermochemical Ethanol via Indirect Gasification and Mixed Alcohol Synthesis of Lignocellulosic Biomass*, pp. 10-11.

30 Foley and Mills, "Design of a High Activity and Selectivity Alcohol Catalyst."

31 Monti, Di Virgilio, and Venturi, "Mineral Composition and Ash Content of Six Major Energy Crops."

32 Lynd et al., "The Role of Biomass in America's Energy Future," p. 119.

33 Boerrigter, *Economy of Biomass-to-Liquids (BTL) Plants*, p. 19; Kreutz et al., "Fischer-Tropsch Fuels from Coal and Biomass," p. 24; Laser et al., "Comparative Analysis of Efficiency, Environmental Impact, and Process Economics for Mature Biomass Refining Scenarios," p. 252; and Phillips et al., *Thermochemical Ethanol via Indirect Gasification and Mixed Alcohol Synthesis of Lignocellulosic Biomass*, p. 84.

34 Phillips et al., *Thermochemical Ethanol via Indirect Gasification and Mixed Alcohol Synthesis of Lignocellulosic Biomass*, p. 33.

35 Author's calculations based on data from Bridgwater, "Renewable Fuels and Chemicals by Thermal Processing of Biomass;" Greene, *An Assessment of Energy and Environmental Issues Related to the Use of Gas-to-Liquid Fuels in Transportation*; Foley and Mills, "Design of a High Activity and Selectivity Alcohol Catalyst;" Hamelinck et al., *Production of FT Transportation Fuels from Biomass*; Nexant Inc., *Mixed Alcohols From Syngas - State of Technology*; and Phillips et al., *Thermochemical Ethanol via Indirect Gasification and Mixed Alcohol Synthesis of Lignocellulosic Biomass.*

36 Phillips et al., *Thermochemical Ethanol via Indirect Gasification and Mixed Alcohol Synthesis of Lignocellulosic Biomass*, p. 84.

37 Boerrigter, *Economy of Biomass-to-Liquids (BTL) Plants.*

38 Phillips et al., *Thermochemical Ethanol via Indirect Gasification and Mixed Alcohol Synthesis of Lignocellulosic Biomass*, p. 8; and Lozowski, "Economic Indicators: Business News," *Chemical Engineering.*

39 Lozowski, "Economic Indicators: Business News," *Chemical Engineering.*

40 Bergin, "Annual Report for the Ultra-Clean Fischer-Tropsch Fuels Production and Demonstration Project.", adjusted to 2007 dollars based on information from Lozowski, "Economic Indicators: Business News," *Chemical Engineering*.

41 Calculated from Phillips et al., *Thermochemical Ethanol via Indirect Gasification and Mixed Alcohol Synthesis of Lignocellulosic Biomass*, p. 84.

42 Boerrigter, *Economy of Biomass-to-Liquids (BTL) Plants*.

43 Bergin, "Annual Report for the Ultra-Clean Fischer-Tropsch Fuels Production and Demonstration Project."; Ciferno and Marano, *Benchmarking Biomass Gasification Technologies for Fuels, Chemicals and Hydrogen Production*, p. 22; Greene, *An Assessment of Energy and Environmental Issues Related to the Use of Gas-to-Liquid Fuels in Transportation*, p. 15; and Spath and Dayton, *Technical and Economic Assessment of Synthesis Gas to Fuels and Chemicals*.

44 Phillips et al., *Thermochemical Ethanol via Indirect Gasification and Mixed Alcohol Synthesis of Lignocellulosic Biomass*, p. 39.

45 Ibid., p. 34.

46 Range estimates and author's calculations based on data from Boerrigter, *Economy of Biomass-to-Liquids (BTL) Plants*, p. 23; Kreutz et al., "Fischer-Tropsch Fuels from Coal and Biomass," p. 50; Laser et al., "Comparative Analysis of Efficiency, Environmental Impact, and Process Economics for Mature Biomass Refining Scenarios," p. 264; Phillips et al., *Thermochemical Ethanol via Indirect Gasification and Mixed Alcohol Synthesis of Lignocellulosic Biomass*, pp. 38-41, 84; and Zhu et al., *Analysis of the Effects of Compositional and Configurational Assumptions on Product Costs for the Thermochemical Conversion of Lignocellulosic Biomass to Mixed Alcohols*, p. 3.3.

Chapter 12
My Stalk is Longer than Yours

1 Greene, *Modeling the Oil Transition*, p. 55.

2 Elliott, "Chemicals from Biomass."

3 Perlack et al., *Biomass as Feedstock for a Bioenergy and Bioproducts Industry*, p. 34.

4 Gunderson et al., *Barrier Issues to the Utilization of Biomass*, p. 7.

5 Perlack et al., *Biomass as Feedstock for a Bioenergy and Bioproducts Industry*, p. 4.

6 McKeever, "Inventories of Woody Residues and Solid Wood Waste in the United States, 2002."

7 Smith et al., *Forest Resources of the United States, 2002*, p. 3.

8 Ibid., p. 6.

9 Ibid., p. 135.

10 Perlack et al., *Biomass as Feedstock for a Bioenergy and Bioproducts Industry*, p. 7.

11 Fehrs, "Secondary Mill Residues and Urban Wood Waste Quantities in the United States," p. 27. Source states material prices in green ton, which have been converted based on moisture content average for wood and woody biomass from Vassilev et al., "An Overview of the Chemical Composition of Biomass."

12 Perlack et al., *Biomass as Feedstock for a Bioenergy and Bioproducts Industry*, p. 7.

13 US Department of Agriculture, US Forest Service, *A Strategic Assessment of Forest Biomass and Fuel Reduction Treatments in Western States*, p. 11.

14 Perlack et al., *Biomass as Feedstock for a Bioenergy and Bioproducts Industry*, p. 14.

15 Ibid., p. 51.

16 Consonni, Katofsky, and Larson, "A Gasification-Based Biorefinery for the Pulp and Paper Industry."

17 Fehrs, "Secondary Mill Residues and Urban Wood Waste Quantities in the United States," p. 40. Source states material prices in green ton, which have been converted based on moisture content assumptions for wood residue from Vassilev et al., "An Overview of the Chemical Composition of Biomass."

18 Fehrs, "Secondary Mill Residues and Urban Wood Waste Quantities in the United States,"
    p. 27. Source states material prices in green ton, which have been converted based on
    moisture content assumptions for wood residue from Vassilev et al., "An Overview of the
    Chemical Composition of Biomass."

19 McKeever, "Inventories of Woody Residues and Solid Wood Waste in the United States,
    2002."

20 Ibid.

21 Fehrs, "Secondary Mill Residues and Urban Wood Waste Quantities in the United States,"
    p. 27. Source states material prices in green ton, which have been converted based on
    moisture content average for wood and woody biomass from Vassilev et al., "An Overview
    of the Chemical Composition of Biomass."

22 Perlack et al., *Biomass as Feedstock for a Bioenergy and Bioproducts Industry*, p. 52.

23 Fehrs, "Secondary Mill Residues and Urban Wood Waste Quantities in the United States,"
    p. 27. Source states material prices in green ton, which have been converted based on
    moisture content average for wood and woody biomass from Vassilev et al., "An Overview
    of the Chemical Composition of Biomass."

24 Perlack et al., *Biomass as Feedstock for a Bioenergy and Bioproducts Industry*, p. 55.

25 Ibid.

26 Based upon data from Gallagher et al., "Biomass from Crop Residues: Cost and Supply
    Estimates." Calculated based upon cost estimates for each geographic region, combined as
    a weighted average based upon biomass volume in each region. Data is further adjusted to
    cost for dry ton based upon 22.0% implied average moisture content.

27 Perlack et al., *Biomass as Feedstock for a Bioenergy and Bioproducts Industry*, p. 55.

28 Renewable Fuels Association,
    http://www.ethanolrfa.org/industry/locations/ (accessed October 29, 2009).

29 Calculation based on the total finished petroleum products supplied (an accepted means
    of estimating consumption) in the US in 2008. US Department of Energy, Energy
    Information Administration, http://www.eia.doe.gov (accessed October 29, 2009).

30 Perlack et al., *Biomass as Feedstock for a Bioenergy and Bioproducts Industry*, p. 55.

31 US Department of Agriculture, Economic Research Service,
    http://www.ers.usda.gov (accessed October 29, 2009).

32 Wright et al., *Biomass Energy Data Book*, p. 98.

33 Based on average production rate of 2.7 gallons per bushel of corn.

34 US Department of Agriculture, Economic Research Service,
    http://www.ers.usda.gov (accessed October 29, 2009); US Department of Energy, Energy
    Information Administration, http://www.eia.doe.gov (accessed October 29, 2009).
    Transportation fuel is defined as gasoline, aviation gasoline, jet fuel, and distillate fuel oil
    (diesel).

35 Calculation on an energy content equivalent basis (adjusting for lower energy content of
    ethanol) using data from US Department of Energy, Energy Information Administration,
    Monthly Energy Review, October 2009, p. 157. Assumes the percentage of transportation fuel
    from imports is equivalent to the percentage of crude oil imported from outside the US.

36 US Department of Agriculture, Economic Research Service, *Major Uses of Land in the
    United States, 2002*, p. 4.

37 Ibid., pp. 4-31.

38 Wright et al., *Biomass Energy Data Book*, p. 99.

39 US Department of Agriculture, *The Economic Feasibility of Ethanol Production from Sugar
    in the United States*, p. 7.

40 Ibid., p. 7.

41 Ibid., p. 17

42 Ibid., p. 7.
43 Ibid., p. 25.
44 Sandalow, "Ethanol: Lessons from Brazil," p. 3.
45 US Department of Agriculture, *The Economic Feasibility of Ethanol Production from Sugar in the United States*, p. 20.
46 Ibid., p. 29.
47 Ibid., p. 31.
48 Jensen et al., "Farmer Willingness to Grow Switchgrass for Energy Production."
49 Lewandowski et al., "The Development and Current Status of Perennial Rhizomatous Grasses as Energy Crops in the US and Europe."
50 McLaughlin and Kszos, "Development of Switchgrass (*Panicum virgatum*) as a Bioenergy Feedstock in the United States."
51 Senate Committee on Agriculture, Nutrition and Forestry, *Biomass Use in Future Energy Production*, Testimony by Samuel B. McLaughlin.
52 US Department of Agriculture, Natural Resources Conservation Service, *Estimated Production Cost Budgets for Biomass*.
53 Duffy and Nanhou, *Costs of Producing Switchgrass for Biomass in Southern Iowa*.
54 US Department of Agriculture, Natural Resources Conservation Service, *Estimated Production Cost Budgets for Biomass*.
55 Angelini et al., "Comparison of *Arundo donax* L. and *Miscanthus x giganteus* in a Long-Term Field Experiment in Central Italy," p. 640; Mantineo et al., "Biomass Yield and Energy Balance of Three Perennial Crops for Energy Use in the Semi-arid Mediterranean Environment," p. 211; Christou et al., "Environmental Studies on *Arundo donax*," p. 103; and Westlake, "Comparisons of Plant Productivity."
56 Christou et al., "Environmental Studies on *Arundo donax*," p. 104.
57 Southern Sun Biosystems, "Biomass Energy Plants;" supported by data in Spencer et al., "Estimating *Arundo donax* Shoot Biomass."
58 Lewandowski, Christian, and Elbersen, "Perennial Rhizomatous Grasses Overview."
59 Duke, *Handbook of Energy Crops*.
60 Christou et al., "Environmental Studies on *Arundo donax*," p. 103.
61 Rieger and Kreager, "Giant Reed (*Arundo donax*): A Climax Community of the Riparian Zone."
62 Florida Native Plant Society, *Policy Statement on Arundo donax*.
63 Shatalov and Pereira, "Papermaking Fibers from Giant Reed (*Arundo donax*);" and Lewis and Jackson, "Nalgrass: A Nonwood Fiber Source Suitable for Existing US Pulp Mills."
64 Plants for a Future Database, http://www.pfaf.org/index.html (object name *Arundo donax*; accessed November 1, 2007).
65 Based on 8,000 Btu/pound energy content and previously discussed assumptions for operating efficiency; includes energy content of ancillary products.
66 Lewandowski, Christian, and Elbersen, "Perennial Rhizomatous Grasses Overview," p. 21.
67 Ibid., p. 19.
68 Estimated from information contained in Lewandowski, Christian, and Elbersen, "Perennial Rhizomatous Grasses Overview;" US Department of Agriculture, *The Economic Feasibility of Ethanol Production from Sugar in the United States*; Southern Sun Biosystems, "Biomass Energy Plants;" US Department of Agriculture, *The Economic Impacts of Bioenergy Crop Production on U.S. Agriculture*; http://www.ers.usda.gov/Data; and US Department of Agriculture, http://www.ers.usda.gov/Briefing/WaterUse.
69 US Department of Agriculture, *The Economic Impacts of Bioenergy Crop Production on U.S. Agriculture*.
70 Lewandowski, Christian, and Elbersen, "Perennial Rhizomatous Grasses Overview."
71 Reed, "Chicken Parts as Jet Fuel? Pond Scum? It's Possible."

72 US Department of Agriculture, Economic Research Service, *Major Uses of Land in the United States, 2002.*

73 US Department of Agriculture, Agricultural Research Service, US National Arboretum, http://www.usna.usda.gov/Hardzone/index.html (accessed August 6, 2008).

74 Lewandowski, Christian, and Elbersen, "Perennial Rhizomatous Grasses Overview."

75 Arundo could also be grown in Hawaii, but for purposes of simplifying calculations, Hawaii's production potential has not been included.

76 Lewandowski, Christian, and Elbersen, "Perennial Rhizomatous Grasses Overview."

77 McLaughlin and Kszos, "Development of Switchgrass (*Panicum virgatum*) as a Bioenergy Feedstock in the United States."

78 Only full zones (5, 6, 7, and 8) were used, sub-zones were disregarded.

79 To calculate yields, states were assigned a climate factor based on the hardiness zones in that state weighted by approximate land area for each zone.

80 US Department of Energy, Energy Information Administration, http://www.eia.doe.gov (accessed August 7, 2008).

81 *Oil & Gas Journal*, "The New Imperative."

82 Sheridan, "Blame It on Biofuels."

83 Hemphill, "Don't Blame the Biofuels."

84 *Economist*, "Cheap No More - Food Prices."

85 Average deviation from the arithmetic mean acres planted over the period 2002-2008. Data from US Department of Agriculture, National Agricultural Statistics Service, http://www.nass.usda.gov (accessed August 18, 2008).

86 Data from US Department of Agriculture, National Agricultural Statistics Service, http://www.nass.usda.gov (accessed August 18, 2008 and March 11, 2010).

87 Nordland and Gross, "Now It's the $6 Loaf of Bread."

88 Hemphill, "Don't Blame the Biofuels."

89 World Bank, *Addressing the Food Crisis: The Need for Rapid and Coordinated Action*; and Sheridan, "Blame It on Biofuels."

90 Nordland and Gross, "Now It's the $6 Loaf of Bread."

91 *Economist*, "Cheap No More - Food Prices."

92 Nordland and Gross, "Now It's the $6 Loaf of Bread;" and *Economist*, "Cheap No More - Food Prices."

Chapter 13
I Love It When a Plan Comes Together

1 International Energy Agency, *World Energy Investment Outlook 2007.*

2 US Department of Energy, Energy Information Administration, http://www.eia.doe.gov (accessed August 8, 2008).

3 Senate Committee on Foreign Relations, *Energy Security and Oil Dependence*, Testimony by Vinod Khosla.

4 US Department of Energy, Energy Information Administration, http://www.eia.doe.gov (accessed November 9, 2009).

5 Greene and Mugica, *Bringing Biofuels to the Pump*, pp. 5-6.

6 Figures include adjustment to account for 85% of plant production going to fuel products.

7 US Department of Commerce, Bureau of Economic Analysis, http://www.bea.gov (accessed November 9, 2009); Department of Energy, Energy Information Administration. http://www.eia.doe.gov (accessed November 9, 2009).

8   Cost estimate from Fehrs, "Secondary Mill Residues and Urban Wood Waste Quantities in the United States," p. C-3, adjusted to May 2008 cost levels based on the US Department of Transportation, Research and Innovative Technology Administration, Bureau of Transportation Statistics, "Transportation Services Index – Freight," http://www.bts.gov/xml/tsi/src/index.xml (accessed July 31, 2008); and supported by Brechbill and Tyner, "The Economics of Biomass Collection, Transportation, and Supply," pp. 54-56.

9   Mean haul distance is estimated by first calculating the area of a circle with a radius of 100 miles; the radius is then calculated for a circle with half that area. It is that radius that will be used for the mean haul distance. In other words, half of the area lies on each side of the midpoint.

10   FOB US Gulf Coast. US Department of Energy, Energy Information Administration, http://www.eia.doe.gov (accessed August 12, 2008).

11   *Encyclopedia of Chemistry, Analytics and Pharmaceutics*, s.v. "Synthetic Liquid Fuels Program," http://www.chemie.de/lexikon/e/Synthetic_Liquid_Fuels_Program (accessed May 28, 2008).

12   Ibid.

13   Grieves, "Portrait of a Federal Fiasco."

14   Congressional Research Service, *Oil Shale: History, Incentives and Policy*, pp. 27-28.

15   Ibid., p. 28.

16   US General Accounting Office, "The Synthetic Fuels Corporation's Progress in Aiding Synthetic Fuels Development," pp. 2-3.

17   Scharff, "Some Setbacks for Synfuels."

18   McClure, "The Background of the United States Synthetic Fuel Corporation."

19   Ibid.

20   Ibid.

21   Scharff, "Some Setbacks for Synfuels."

22   Landsberg, "The Death of Synfuels."

23   McClure, "The Background of the United States Synthetic Fuel Corporation."

24   Ibid.

25   Deffeyes, *Beyond Oil.*

26   McClure, "The Background of the United States Synthetic Fuel Corporation."

27   Scharff, "Some Setbacks for Synfuels."

28   Grieves, "Portrait of a Federal Fiasco."

29   Axelrod, "The Role of the Synthetic Fuels Corporation."

30   US General Accounting Office, "The Synthetic Fuels Corporation's Progress in Aiding Synthetic Fuels Development," p. 4.

31   Ibid., p. 6.

32   Reagan, "Message to the Congress Transmitting Proposed Legislation to Implement the National Synthetic Fuels Program."

33   Congressional Research Service, *Oil Shale: History, Incentives and Policy*, p. 11.

34   Report of the Panel on the Government Role in Civilian Technology.

35   US General Accounting Office, "The Synthetic Fuels Corporation's Progress In Aiding Synthetic Fuels Development," p. 3.

36   Axelrod, "The Role of the Synthetic Fuels Corporation."

37   Report of the Panel on the Government Role in Civilian Technology.

38   Senate Committee on Foreign Relations, *Energy Security and Oil Dependence*, Testimony by Vinod Khosla.

39   Copulos, *America's Achilles Heel*, p. 44.

40   Greene and Leiby, *The Oil Security Metrics Model*, p. 44.

41   Adelman, *The Genie Out of the Bottle*, p. 160.

42   Greene, *Growing Energy*, p. 7.

43   Senate Committee on Foreign Relations, *Energy Security and Oil Dependence*, Testimony
     by Vinod Khosla.

44   Taylor, "US Oil Policy, Under Review, Isn't Seen Embracing Import Fee or Price Supports."

45   Adelman, *The Genie Out of the Bottle*, p. 233.

46   Krauthammer, "Energy Independence? A Serious Plan Requires Taxes, ANWR and
     Nukes;" Krauthammer, "Pump Some Seriousness into Energy Policy;" and Krauthammer,
     "Tax and Drill."

47   Krauthammer, "Pump Some Seriousness into Energy Policy."

48   Alexander, Susalka, and Kogan, "Coal-to-Liquids Projects in the United States."

49   Ibid.

50   US Department of Defense, Defense Logistics Agency, Defense Energy Support Center,
     Fact Book 2007.

51   Ibid.

52   Ibid.

53   US Department of Energy, National Energy Technology Laboratory, *Fischer-Tropsch Fuels*.

54   Gray et al., *Increasing Security and Reducing Carbon Emissions of the U.S. Transportation
     Sector*, p. viii.

55   Friedman, *Hot, Flat, and Crowded*.

56   Henriques and Sadorsky, "Oil Prices and the Stock Prices of Alternative Energy Companies."

57   World Business Council for Sustainable Development, *Mobility 2030*, p. 74.

58   Data derived from Urbanchuk, *Contribution of the Ethanol Industry to the Economy of the
     United States*; US Department of Commerce, Bureau of Economic Analysis,
     http://www.bea.gov/ (accessed November 9, 2009), and US Department of Energy,
     National Renewable Energy Laboratory, Job and Economic Development Impact (JEDI)
     Model, Cellulosic Biofuels Model rel. C1.09.01.

59   Ibid.

60   Ibid.

61   Continental Airlines, "Continental Airlines Flight Demonstrates Use of Sustainable
     Biofuels as Energy Source for Jet Travel," News Release, January 7, 2009,
     http://www.continental.com/web/en-US/apps/vendors/default.aspx?i=PRNEWS
     (accessed March 11, 2010).

62   National Defense Council Foundation, "The ANWR Imperative," p. 3.

63   Klare, *Blood and Oil*, p. 185; and Gary and Karl, *Bottom of the Barrel*, p. 20.

64   Zakaria, "How to Escape the Oil Trap."

65   US Department of Defense, Defense Logistics Agency, Defense Energy Support Center,
     Fact Book 2006, p. 83.

66   Zakaria, "How to Escape the Oil Trap."

Bibliography

Adelman, Morris A. *The Genie Out of the Bottle: World Oil Since 1970*. Cambridge, MA: MIT Press, 1995.

Adelman, Morris A. "The Real Oil Problem." *Regulation* 27, No. 1 (2004): 16-21.

Ahluwalia, Rajesh K. and Xiaohua Wang. "Fuel Cell Systems for Transportation: Status and Trends." *Journal of Power Sources* 117 (2008): 167-76.

Air Products and Chemicals, Inc. *Development of Alternative Fuels and Chemicals from Synthesis Gas*. Final Technical Report to the U.S. Department of Energy. Allentown, PA: Air Products and Chemicals, Inc., 2003.

Akins, James. "The Oil Crisis: This Time the Wolf Is Here." *Foreign Affairs* 51, No. 3 (1973): 462-90.

Alexander, Todd, Richard Susalka, and Jeff Kogan. "Coal-to-Liquids Projects in the United States." *Project Finance NewsWire*, June 2008. http://www.chadbourne.com/files/Publication/fcf2cf74-27d7-4f7a-882e-b384f42a177f/Presentation/PublicationAttachment/5ea1f6c2-b0d3-45f3-b809-b6911cd72426/pfn0608.pdf (accessed June 16, 2008).

Alfonsi, Christian. *Circle in the Sand: Why We Went Back to Iraq*. New York: Doubleday, 2006.

Alnasrawi, Abbas. *Arab Nationalism, Oil, and the Political Economy of Dependency*. New York: Greenwood Press, 1991.

Amano, Robert A. and Simon van Norden. "Oil Prices and the Rise and Fall of the US Real Exchange Rate." *Journal of International Money and Finance* 17, No. 2 (1998): 299-316.

American Physical Society. *The Hydrogen Initiative*. College Park, MD: American Physical Society, March 2004. http://www.aps.org/policy/reports/popa-reports/upload/hydrogen.pdf (accessed October 12, 2007).

Andrews, Anthony. *See* Congressional Research Service.

Angelini, Luciana G., Lucia Ceccarini, Nicoletta Nassi o Di Nasso and Enrico Bonari. "Comparison of *Arundo donax* L. and *Miscanthus x giganteus* in a Long-Term Field Experiment in Central Italy: Analysis of Productive Characteristics and Energy Balance." *Biomass and Bioenergy* 33, No. 4 (2009): 635-43.

Askari, Hossein and Noureddine Krichene. "Oil Price Dynamics (2002–2006)." *Energy Economics* 30, No. 5 (2008): 2134-53.

Axelrod, L. "The Role of the Synthetic Fuels Corporation." In *Synthetic Fuels - Status and Directions*. Proceedings of the Conference on Coal Gasification Systems and Synthetic Fuels for Power Generation, San Francisco, CA, April 14-18, 1985. Palo Alto, CA: Electric Power Research Institute, 1985.

Baer, Robert. "The Fall of the House of Saud." *Atlantic Monthly* 291, No. 4 (2003): 53-62.

Baez, Alba. *See* US Department of Agriculture.

Balke, Nathan S., Stephen P.A. Brown and Mine K. Yucel. "Oil Price Shocks and the US Economy: Where Does the Asymmetry Originate?" *Energy Journal* 23, No. 3 (2002): 27–52.

Barnett, Jon, Suraje Dessai, and Michael Webber. "Will OPEC Lose from the Kyoto Protocol?" *Energy Policy* 32, no. 18 (2004): 2077–88.

Barsky, Robert B. and Lutz Kilian. "Oil and the Macroeconomy Since the 1970s." *The Journal of Economic Perspectives* 18, No. 4 (2004): 115-34.

Bechtel Corporation. *Baseline Design/Economics for Advanced Fischer-Tropsch Technology.* Final Report to the Federal Energy Technology Center. Washington, DC: U.S. Department of Energy, 1998.

Belasco, Amy. *See* Congressional Research Service.

Bénassy-Quéré, Agnès, Sophie Béreau and Valérie Mignon. "The Dollar in the Turmoil." *Journal of the Japanese and International Economies* 23, No. 4 (2009): 427-36.

Bénassy-Quéré, Agnès, Valérie Mignon and Alexis Penot. "China and the Relationship Between the Oil Price and the Dollar." *Energy Policy* 35, No. 11 (2007): 5795-805.

Berg, Christoph. *World Fuel Ethanol Analysis and Outlook.* Tunbridge Wells, United Kingdom: F.O. Licht, 2004.

Bergendahl, Goran. *The Management of OPEC's Financial Surpluses.* Oxford: Oxford Institute for Energy Studies, 1984.

Bergin, Steve, ed. *Annual Report for the Ultra-Clean Fischer-Tropsch Fuels Production and Demonstration Project.* Report prepared for the U.S. Department of Energy. Sterling Heights, MI: Integrated Concepts and Research Corporation, October 14, 2005.

Bernanke, Ben S. "Deflation: Making Sure 'It' Doesn't Happen Here." Remarks before the National Economists Club, Washington, DC, November 21, 2002. http://www.federalreserve.gov/boardDocs/speeches/2002/20021121/default.htm (accessed November 12, 2009).

Blair, Arthur H. *At War in the Gulf: A Chronology.* College Station, TX: Texas A&M University Press, 1992.

Boehmel, Constanze, Iris Lewandowski and Wilhelm Claupein. "Comparing Annual and Perennial Energy Cropping Systems with Different Management Intensities." *Agricultural Systems* 96, No. 1-3 (2008): 224-36.

Boerrigter, Harold. *Economy of Biomass-to-Liquids (BTL) Plants.* Petten, The Netherlands: Energy Research Centre of the Netherlands (ECN), 2006. http://www.ecn.nl/docs/library/report/2006/c06019.pdf (accessed November 20, 2009)

Bollino, Carlo Andrea. "Oil Prices and the U.S. Trade Deficit." *Journal of Policy Modeling* 29, No. 5 (2007): 729-38.

Bowden, Mark. "Among the Hostage-Takers." *The Atlantic,* December 2004. http://www.theatlantic.com/doc/200412/bowden (accessed September 1, 2009).

BP plc. *Statistical Review of World Energy June 2009.* London: BP plc, 2009.

Brechbill, Sarah C. and Wallace E. Tyner. "The Economics of Biomass Collection, Transportation, and Supply to Indian Cellulosic and Electricity Utility Facilities." Working Paper, Department of Agricultural Economics, Purdue University, April 2008. http://www.agecon.purdue.edu/papers/biofuels/Working_Paper_Fina.pdf (accessed July 31, 2008).

Brewer, Peter G. "Direct Injection of Carbon Dioxide in the Oceans." In *The Carbon Dioxide Dilemma: Promising Technologies and Policies.* Proceedings of a Symposium, April 23-24, 2002. Washington, DC: National Academies Press, 2003.

Brewer, Peter G. *Feasibility of Large-Scale Ocean CO2 Sequestration.* Annual Report Prepared for the US Department of Energy. Moss Landing, CA: Monterey Bay Aquarium Research Institute, 2006.

Bridgwater, A.V. "Renewable Fuels and Chemicals by Thermal Processing of Biomass." *Chemical Engineering Journal* 91, No. 2 (2003): 87-102.

Brons, Martijn, Peter Nijkamp, Eric Pels and Piet Rietveld. "A Meta-Analysis of the Price Elasticity of Gasoline Demand. A SUR Approach." *Energy Economics* 30, No. 5 (2008): 2105-22.

Brown, Marilyn A., Mark D. Levine, Walter Short, and Jonathan G. Koomey. "Scenarios for a Clean Energy Future." *Energy Policy* 29, No. 14 (2001): 1179–96.

Bucholtz, Shawn. *See* US Department of Agriculture.

Caldeira, Ken. "The Effectiveness and Unintended Consequences of Ocean Fertilization." In *The Carbon Dioxide Dilemma: Promising Technologies and Policies.* Proceedings of a Symposium, April 23-24, 2002. Washington, DC: National Academies Press, 2003.

Campbell, Colin J. *Regular Conventional Oil Production to 2100 and Resource Based Production Forecast.* August 2006. http://www.hubbertpeak.com/campbell/ (accessed November 19, 2009).

Canadell, Josep G., Corinne Le Quéré, Michael R. Raupach, Christopher B. Field, Erik T. Buitenhuis, Philippe Ciais, Thomas J. Conway, Nathan P. Gillett, R. A. Houghton, and Gregg Marland. "Contributions to Accelerating Atmospheric CO2 Growth from Economic Activity, Carbon Intensity, and Efficiency of Natural Sinks." *Proceedings of the National Academy of Sciences* 104, No. 47 (2007): 18866-70.

Catherwood, Christopher. *Churchill's Folly: How Winston Churchill Created Modern Iraq.* New York: Barnes & Noble, 2007.

Cavallo, M. "Oil Prices and the US Trade Deficit." *FRBSF Economic Letter*, No. 24 (2006).

Central Intelligence Agency. *The Break-Up of the Colonial Empires and Its Implications for US Security.* ORE 25-48, Langley, VA, September 3, 1948.

Central Intelligence Agency. *Caspian Region Oil Pipelines.* PCL Map Collection, Langley, VA, April 2002. http://www.lib.utexas.edu/maps/map_sites/oil_and_gas_sites.html (accessed October 19, 2008).

Central Intelligence Agency. *Current Status of UAR President Nasser's Health.* Intelligence Information Cable, Langley, VA, July 31, 1967.

Central Intelligence Agency. *Iran-Iraq War: Increased Threat to Persian Gulf Oil Exports.* Special National Intelligence Estimate No. 34/36.2-83, Langley, VA, October 13, 1983.

Central Intelligence Agency. *Main Trends in the Arab World.* National Intelligence Estimate No. 36-64, Langley, VA, April 8, 1964.

Central Intelligence Agency. *Nasser's Prospects and Problems in Yemen.* Special Memorandum 9-65, Langley, VA, February 18, 1965

Central Intelligence Agency. *The Outlook for the United Arab Republic.* National Intelligence Estimate No. 36.1-66, Langley, VA, May 19, 1966.

Central Intelligence Agency. *The Situation and Prospects in Egypt.* National Intelligence Estimate No. 36.1-67, Langley, VA, August 17, 1967.

Chaudhry, Kiren Aziz. *The Price of Wealth: Economies and Institutions in the Middle East.* Ithaca, NY: Cornell University Press, 1997.

Chollet, Derek and James Goldgeier. *America Between the Wars: From 11/9 to 9/11, The Misunderstood Years Between the Fall of the Berlin Wall and the Start of the War on Terror.* New York: BBS PublicAffairs, 2008.

Christou, M., M. Mardikis and E. Alexopoulou. "Biomass Production from Perennial Crops in Greece." Paper presented to the 14th European Conference and Technology Exhibition on Biomass for Energy, Industry and Climate Protection, Paris, France, October 17-21, 2005.

Christou, M., M. Mardikis, E. Alexopoulou, S. L. Cosentino, V. Copani and E. Sanzone. "Environmental Studies on *Arundo donax*." In Vol. B, *Proceeding of the 8th Conference on Environmental Science and Technology*, Lemnos Island, Greece, September 8-10, 2003, edited by T. D. Tekkas. Lesvos, Greece: University of the Aegean, 2004. http://www.cres.gr/bioenergy_chains/files/pdf/Articles/3-Lemnos.pdf (accessed February 2, 2008).

Ciferno, Jared P. and John J. Marano. *Benchmarking Biomass Gasification Technologies for Fuels, Chemicals and Hydrogen Production*. Pittsburg, PA: National Energy Technology Laboratory, 2002.

Clark, William R. *Petrodollar Warfare: Oil, Iraq and the Future of the Dollar*. Gabriola Island, Canada: New Society Publishers, 2005.

Clarke, Duncan. *The Battle for Barrels: Peak Oil Myths & World Oil Futures*. London: Profile Books, 2007.

Clerides, Sofronis and Theodoros Zachariadis. "The Effect of Standards and Fuel Prices on Automobile Fuel Economy: An International Analysis." *Energy Economics* 30, No. 5 (2008): 2657-72.

Coelho, S. T. and José Goldemberg. "Alternative Transportation Fuels: Contemporary Case Studies." Vol. 1, *Encyclopedia of Energy*, edited by Cutler J. Cleveland, 67-80. San Diego: Elsevier, 2004.

Coelho, Suani. "Agriculture & Biomass: Competition or a Synergy? Brazilian Experience on Biofuels." Presentation to the Latin American Carbon Forum, Lima, Peru, September 7, 2007.

Committee on the Effectiveness and Impact of Corporate Average Fuel Economy (CAFE) Standards. *Effectiveness and Impact of Corporate Average Fuel Economy (CAFE) Standards*. Washington, DC: National Academies Press, 2002.

Congressional Budget Office. *Estimated Cost of U.S. Operations in Iraq and Afghanistan and Other Activities Related to the War on Terrorism*. Prepared Testimony of Peter Orszag to the U.S. Congress, House of Representatives, Committee on the Budget. 110th Congress, 1st Session, October 24, 2007. http://www.cbo.gov/ftpdocs/86xx/doc8690/10-24-CostOfWar_Testimony.pdf (accessed June 19, 2008).

Congressional Budget Office. *Withdrawal of U.S. Forces from Iraq: Possible Timelines and Estimated Costs*. Letter to the Honorable John F. Tierney, U.S. Congress, House of Representatives, Committee on Oversight and Government Reform, Subcommittee on National Security and Foreign Affairs. 111th Congress, 1st Session, October 7, 2009. http://www.cbo.gov/ftpdocs/105xx/doc10523/10-07-TierneyTroopWithdrawal.pdf (accessed October 20, 2009).

Congressional Research Service. *Oil Shale: History, Incentives and Policy*. By Anthony Andrews. Washington, DC: Library of Congress, April 13, 2006. http://www.fas.org/sgp/crs/misc/RL33359.pdf (accessed May 28, 2008).

Congressional Research Service. *The Cost of Iraq, Afghanistan, and Other Global War on Terror Operations Since 9/11*. By Amy Belasco. Washington, DC: Library of Congress, April 11, 2008.

Consonni, Stefano, Ryan E. Katofsky and Eric D. Larson. "A Gasification-Based Biorefinery for the Pulp and Paper Industry." *Chemical Engineering Research and Design* 87, No. 9 (2009): 1293-317.

Cooper, Mark. *Time to Change the Record on Oil Policy: Record Gasoline Prices and Oil Company Profits Require Aggressive Policies to Reduce Demand and Protect Consumers from Abusive Business Practices.* Yonkers, NY: Consumers Union, August 2006.

Cooper, Richard N. "Living with Global Imbalances: A Contrarian View." *Journal of Policy Modeling* 28, No. 6 (2006): 615-27.

Copulos, Milton R. *America's Achilles Heel: The Hidden Cost of Imported Oil, A Strategy for Energy Independence.* Washington, DC: National Defense Council Foundation, 2003. http://ndcf.homeip.net/ndcf/energy/NDCF_Hidden_Costs_of_Imported_Oil.pdf (accessed May 24, 2008).

Crompton, Paul and Yanrui Wu. "Energy Consumption in China: Past Trends and Future Directions." *Energy Economics* 27, No. 1 (2005): 195-208.

Crude. Television Documentary First Broadcast May 24, 2007 by Austrailian Broadcasting Corporation. Directed and written by Richard Smith.

Dannreuther, Roland. *The Gulf Conflict: A Political and Strategic Analysis.* London: International Institute for Strategic Studies, 1992

David Gardiner & Associates, LLC. *Addicted to Oil: Ranking States' Oil Vulnerability and Solutions for Change.* New York: Natural Resources Defense Council, 2007.

Davis, Stacy C., Susan W. Diegel, and Robert G. Boundy. *Transportation Energy Data Book.* 28th ed. Oak Ridge, TN: Oak Ridge National Laboratory, 2009.

De La Torre Ugarte, Daniel G. *See* US Department of Agriculture

DeCicco, John M. "Fuel Cell Vehicles." Vol. 2, *Encyclopedia of Energy*, edited by Cutler J. Cleveland, 759-70. San Diego: Elsevier, 2004.

DeCicco, John, Rod Griffin, and Steve Ertel. *Putting the Brakes on U.S. Oil Demand.* Washington, DC: Environmental Defense, 2003. http://www.environmentaldefense. org/documents/3115_OilDemand.pdf (accessed October 10, 2007).

Deffeyes, Kenneth S. *Beyond Oil: The View from Hubbert's Peak.* New York: Hill and Wang, 2005.

Delucchi, Mark A. and James J. Murphy. *U. S. Military Expenditures to Protect the Use of Persian Gulf Oil for Motor Vehicles.* 2nd rev. Report No. 15, *The Annualized Social Cost of Motor-Vehicle Use in the United States, based on 1990-1991 Data.* Davis, CA: Institute of Transportation Studies, University of California, Davis, 2004.

Downey, Marlan W. "Oil and Natural Gas Exploration." Vol. 4, *Encyclopedia of Energy*, edited by Cutler J. Cleveland, 549-58. San Diego: Elsevier, 2004.

Dry, Mark E. "High Quality Diesel via the Fischer–Tropsch Process – A Review." *Journal of Chemical Technology and Biotechnology* 77, No. 1 (2002): 43-50.

Duffy, Mike and Virginie Y. Nanhou. *Costs of Producing Switchgrass for Biomass in Southern Iowa.* Ames, IA: University Extension, Iowa State University, 2001.

Duke, James A. *Handbook of Energy Crops.* 1983. http://www.hort.purdue.edu/newcrop/duke_energy/Arundo_donax.html (accessed January 15, 2008).

Dunn, Seth. "History of Hydrogen." Vol. 3, *Encyclopedia of Energy*, edited by Cutler J. Cleveland, 241-52. San Diego: Elsevier, 2004.

Economist. "Cheap No More - Food Prices." December 8, 2007.

Economist. "The Disappearing Dollar." December 4, 2004.

Elliott, Douglas C. "Chemicals from Biomass." Vol. 1, *Encyclopedia of Energy*, edited by Cutler J. Cleveland, 163-74. San Diego: Elsevier, 2004.

Elobeid, Amani, Simla Tokgoz, Dermot J. Hayes, Bruce A. Babcock, and Chad E. Hart. *The Long-Run Impact of Corn-Based Ethanol on the Grain, Oilseed, and Livestock Sectors: A Preliminary Assessment.* Ames, IA: Center for Agricultural and Rural Development, Iowa State University, 2006.

Energy Future Coalition. *Challenge and Opportunity: Charting a New Energy Future.* Washington, DC: Energy Future Coalition, 2003. http://www.energyfuturecoalition.org/pubs/EFCReport.pdf (accessed October 11, 2007).

Etheridge, D.M., L. P. Steele, R. L. Langenfelds, R. J. Francey, J. M. Barnola, and V. I. Morgan. "Historical CO_2 Records from the Law Dome DE08, DE08-2, and DSS Ice Cores." In *Trends: A Compendium of Data on Global Change.* Oak Ridge, TN: Carbon Dioxide Information Analysis Center, Oak Ridge National Laboratory, 1998. http://cdiac.ornl.gov/trends/co2/lawdome.html (accessed February 6, 2008).

Fairbanks, J. Nelson. *See* US Department of Agriculture.

Faisal, Islam. "Iraq Nets Handsome Profit by Dumping Dollar for Euro." *The Observer*, February 16, 2003. http://www.guardian.co.uk/business/2003/feb/16/iraq.theeuro (accessed June 16, 2008).

Faisal, Islam. "When Will We Buy Oil in Euros?" *The Observer*, February 23, 2003. http://www.guardian.co.uk/business/2003/feb/23/oilandpetrol.theeuro (accessed June 16, 2008).

Fehrs, Jeffrey. *Secondary Mill Residues and Urban Wood Waste Quantities in the United States.* Washington, DC: Northeast Regional Biomass Program, 1999. http://www.nrbp.org/pdfs/pub21.pdf (accessed October 17, 2007).

Fisk, Robert. "The Demise of the Dollar." *The Independent*, October 6, 2009. http://www.independent.co.uk/news/business/news/the-demise-of-the-dollar-1798175.html (accessed October 21, 2009).

Florida Native Plant Society. *Policy Statement on Arundo donax.* Melbourne, FL: Florida Native Plant Society, 2006.

Foley, Henry C. and G. Alex Mills. "Design of a High Activity and Selectivity Alcohol Catalyst." Research Report for the U.S. Department of Energy, Center for Catalytic Science and Technology, University of Delaware, 1994.

Forbes. "The Forbes 400," edited by Matthew Miller, September 20, 2007. http://www.forbes.com/2007/09/19/richest-americans-forbes-lists-richlist07-cx_mm_0920rich_land.html (accessed July 17, 2008).

Forbes. "The World's Billionaires," edited by Luisa Kroll, Matthew Miller and Tatiana Serafin. March 11, 2009. http://www.forbes.com/2009/03/11/worlds-richest-people-billionaires-2009-billionaires_land.html (accessed November 5, 2009).

Frankel, Jeffrey. "Could the Twin Deficits Jeopardize US Hegemony?" *Journal of Policy Modeling* 28, No. 6 (2006): 653-63.

Friedman, Thomas. *Hot, Flat, and Crowded.* New York: Farrar, Straus and Giroux, 2008.

Gallagher, Paul, Mark Dikeman, John Fritz, Eric Wailes, Wayne Gauther, and Hosein Shapouri. "Biomass from Crop Residues: Cost and Supply Estimates." Agricultural Economic Report No. 819, U.S. Department of Agriculture, Office of the Chief Economist, February 2003.

Gary, Ian and Terry Lynn Karl. *Bottom of the Barrel: Africa's Oil Boom and the Poor.* Baltimore, MD: Catholic Relief Services, June 2003.

Gasification Technologies Council. *Gasification: Redefining Clean Energy.* Arlington, VA: Gasification Technologies Council, 2008. http://www.gasification.org/pdfs/Final_whitepaper.pdf (accessed September 11, 2008).

Gelbspan, Ross. *The Heat is On: The High Stakes Battle over Earth's Threatened Climate.* Reading, MA: Addison-Wesley, 1997.

German, John M. "Hybrid Electric Vehicles." Vol. 3, *Encyclopedia of Energy*, edited by Cutler J. Cleveland, 197-213. San Diego: Elsevier, 2004.

Graham, Robin L., Erik Lichtenberg, Vernon O. Roningen, Hossein Shapouri, and Marie E. Walsh. "The Economics of Biomass Production in the United States." Paper presented at the Second Biomass Conference of the Americas: Energy, Environment, Agriculture, and Industry, Portland, OR, August 21-24, 1995.

Gray, David, Charles White, Glen Tomlinson, Mark Ackiewicz, Ed Schmetz, and John Winslow. *Increasing Security and Reducing Carbon Emissions of the U.S. Transportation Sector: A Transformational Role for Coal with Biomass.* Report prepared for the US Department of Energy, National Energy Technology Laboratory, and the US Department of Defense, Air Force. Pittsburg: National Energy Technology Laboratory, 2007.

Greene, David L. *An Assessment of Energy and Environmental Issues Related to the Use of Gas-to-Liquid Fuels in Transportation.* Oak Ridge, TN: Oak Ridge National Laboratory, 1999.

Greene, David L., ed. *Modeling the Oil Transition: A Summary of the Proceedings of the DOE/EPA Workshop on the Economic and Environmental Implications of Global Energy Transitions.* Oak Ridge, TN: Oak Ridge National Laboratory, 2007.

Greene, David L. and Sanjana Ahmad. *Costs of Oil Dependence: A 2005 Update.* Oak Ridge, TN: Oak Ridge National Laboratory, 2005.

Greene, David L., Janet L. Hopson, and Jia Li. "Have We Run Out of Oil Yet? Oil Peaking Analysis from an Optimist's Perspective." *Energy Policy* 34 (2006): 515-31.

Greene, David L. and Paul N. Leiby. *The Oil Security Metrics Model: A Tool for Evaluating the Prospective Oil Security Benefits of DOE's Energy Efficiency and Renewable Energy R&D Programs.* Oak Ridge, TN: Oak Ridge National Laboratory, 2006.

Greene, David L., Paul N. Leiby, Brian James, Julie Perez, Margo Melendez, Anelia Milbrandt, Stefan Unnasch, Daniel Rutherford, and Matthew Hooks. *Analysis of the Transition to Hydrogen Fuel Cell Vehicles and the Potential Hydrogen Energy Infrastructure Requirements.* Oak Ridge, TN: Oak Ridge National Laboratory, 2008. http://cta.ornl.gov/cta/Publications/Reports/ORNL_TM_2008_30.pdf (accessed June 19, 2008).

Greene, Nathanael. *Growing Energy: How Biofuels Can Help End America's Oil Dependence.* New York: Natural Resources Defense Council, 2004.

Greene, Nathanael and Yerina Mugica. *Bringing Biofuels to the Pump; An Aggressive Plan for Ending America's Oil Dependence.* New York: Natural Resources Defense Council, 2005.

Grieves, Robert T. "Portrait of a Federal Fiasco." *Time*, May. 14, 1984.

Gross, Daniel. "The Prius and the Olive Tree: Why Are Conservatives Supporting Higher Gas Taxes?" *Slate*, May 27, 2004. http://www.slate.com/id/2101349/ (accessed October 5, 2007).

Grunwald, Michael. "The Clean Energy Scam." *Time*, April 7, 2008.

Gunderson, Jay R., Bruce C. Folkedahl, Darren D. Schmidt, Greg F. Weber, and Christopher J. Zygarlicke. *Barrier Issues to the Utilization of Biomass*. Report Prepared for the National Energy Technology Laboratory. Grand Forks, ND: Energy & Environmental Research Center, University of North Dakota, 2002.

Hamelinck, Carlo N., Andre P.C. Faaij, Herman den Uil, and Harold Beorrigter. *Production of FT Transportation Fuels from Biomass; Technical Options, Process Analysis and Optimization, and Development Potential*. Utrecht, Netherlands: Copernicus Institute, Universiteit Utrecht, 2003.

Hansen, James, Makiko Sato, Reto Ruedy, Ken Lo, David W. Lea, and Martin Medina-Elizade. "Global Temperature Changes." *Proceedings of the National Academy of Sciences* 103, No. 39 (2006): 14288-93.

Haugen, Hans Aksel and Lars Ingolf Eide. "CO2 Capture and Disposal: The Realism of Large Scale Scenarios." *Energy Conversion and Management* 37, No. 6-8 (1996): 1061-66.

Hellman, Christopher. *U.S. Security Spending: How Much Do We Really Spend?* Washington, DC: Center for Arms Control and Non-Proliferation, October 1, 2007. http://www.armscontrolcenter.org/policy/securityspending/articles/how_much_do_we_spend/# (accessed October 5, 2007).

Hemphill, Peter. "Don't Blame the Biofuels." *The Weekly Times (Australia)*, May 14, 2008.

Henriques, Irene and Perry Sadorsky. "Oil Prices and the Stock Prices of Alternative Energy Companies." *Energy Economics* 30, No. 3 (2008): 998-1010.

Hershey, Jr., Robert D. "Synfuels Corp. is Running on Empty." *New York Times*, August 25, 1985.

Hess, J. Richard, Thomas D. Foust, Reed Hoskinson and David Thompson. *Roadmap for Agricultural Biomass Feedstock Supply in the United States*. Idaho Falls, ID: Idaho National Laboratory, November 2003.

Heywood, J. B. "Fueling our Transportation Future." *Scientific American* 295, No. 3 (2006): 60-63.

Higman, Christopher and Maarten van der Burgt. *Gasification*. New York: Gulf Professional Publishing, 2003.

Hill, Gardiner. "Using Carbon Dioxide to Recover Natural Gas and Oil." In *The Carbon Dioxide Dilemma: Promising Technologies and Policies*. Proceedings of a Symposium, April 23-24, 2002. Washington, DC: National Academies Press, 2003.

Hollis, Rosemary. "The US Role: Helpful or Harmful?" In *Iran, Iraq, and the Legacies of War*, edited by Lawrence G. Potter and Gary G. Sick, 193-211. New York: Palgrave Macmillan, 2004.

Hoogwijk, Monique, André Faaij, Richard van den Broek, Göran Berndes, Dolf Gielen and Wim Turkenburg. "Exploration of the Ranges of the Global Potential of Biomass for Energy." *Biomass and Bioenergy* 25, No. 2 (2003): 119-33.

Hudson, Randy, ed. *Giant Reed (Arundo donax) and its Potential as a New Georgia Crop*. Athens, GA: Center for Emerging Crops and Technologies, University of Georgia, n.d. http://www.cropsoil.uga.edu/Special/Hudson%27s%20Documents/Hudson-GiantReed.pdf (accessed November 5, 2007).

Hyde, Roderick A., Edward Teller, and Lowell L. Wood. "Active Climate Stabilization: Practical Physics-Based Approaches to Preventing Climate Change." In *The Carbon Dioxide Dilemma: Promising Technologies and Policies*. Proceedings of a Symposium, April 23-24, 2002. Washington, DC: National Academies Press, 2003.

Hyne, Norman J. *Nontechnical Guide to Petroleum Geology, Exploration, Drilling and Production.* 2nd ed. Tulsa, OK: Pennwell Books, 2001.

Ikenberry, G. John. *Reasons of State: Oil Politics and the Capacities of American Government.* Ithaca, NY: Cornell University Press, 1988.

Ingham, James. "Chavez Calls for Anti-US Alliance." *BBC News*, January 28, 2008. http://news.bbc.co.uk/2/hi/americas/7212457.stm (accessed December 7, 2008).

Intergovernmental Panel on Climate Change. *Special Report on Emissions Scenarios*, edited by Nebojsa Nakicenovic and Rob Swart. Cambridge: Cambridge University Press, 2000. http://www.grida.no/climate/ipcc/emission/ (accessed February 7, 2008).

International Energy Agency. *World Energy Investment Outlook 2007.* Paris: International Energy Agency, 2007.

International Energy Agency. *Analysis of the Impact of High Oil Prices on the Global Economy.* Paris: International Energy Agency, May 2004. www.iea.org/Textbase/Papers/2004/High_Oil_Prices.pdf (accessed October 10, 2007).

International Institute for Strategic Studies. *The Military Balance.* London: International Institute for Strategic Studies, 2008

International Monetary Fund, World Bank, Organization for Economic Cooperation and Development, and European Bank for Reconstruction and Development. *A Study of the Soviet Economy.* Paris: International Monetary Fund, World Bank, Organization for Economic Cooperation and Development, and European Bank for Reconstruction and Development, 1991.

Jacobs, Gary K. "Using Terrestrial Ecosystems for Carbon Sequestration." In *The Carbon Dioxide Dilemma: Promising Technologies and Policies*. Proceedings of a Symposium, April 23-24, 2002. Washington, DC: National Academies Press, 2003.

Jaffe, Amy Myers. "Geopolitics of Energy." Vol. 2, *Encyclopedia of Energy*, edited by Cutler J. Cleveland, 843-57. San Diego: Elsevier, 2004.

Jechura, John. *Maximum Yield of Liquid Fuels from Biomass Based on Stoichiometry.* Technical Memorandum. Golden, CO: National Renewable Energy Laboratory, 2006.

Jensen, Kimberly, Christopher D. Clark, Pamela Ellis, Burton English, Jamey Menard, Marie Walsh, and Daniel de la Torre Ugarte. "Farmer Willingness to Grow Switchgrass for Energy Production." *Biomass & Bioenergy* 31 (2007): 773-81.

Jensen, Marc W. and Marc Ross. "The Ultimate Challenge: Building an Infrastructure for Fuel Cell Vehicles." *Environment* 42, No. 7 (2000): 10-22.

Jones, Susanne B. and Yunhua Zhu. *Techno-economic Analysis for the Conversion of Lignocellulosic Biomass to Gasoline via the Methanol-to-Gasoline (MTG) Process.* Report prepared for the US Department of Energy. Richland, WA: Pacific Northwest National Laboratory, 2009. http://www.pnl.gov/main/publications/external/technical_reports/PNNL-18481.pdf (accessed November 22, 2009).

Karl, Terry Lynn. "The Impact of Oil Booms on Oil-Exporting Countries: Reflections on *The Paradox of Plenty*." *Journal of International Affairs* 53, No. 1 (1999): 31-48.

Karl, Terry Lynn. *The Paradox of Plenty: Oil Booms and Petro-States.* Berkeley, CA: University of California Press, 1997.

Kaufman, Stuart J. "The Ethnic Conflicts in Georgia." *Encyclopedia of Modern Ethnic Conflicts,* edited by Joseph R. Rudolph, Jr., 199-206. Westport, CT: Greenwood Press, 2003.

Kaufmann, Robert K., Andrew Bradford, Laura H. Belanger, John P. McLaughlin and Yosuke Miki. "Determinants of OPEC Production: Implications for OPEC Behavior." *Energy Economics* 30, No. 2 (2008): 333-51.

Khadduri, Majid. *The Gulf War: The Origins and Implications of the Iraq-Iran Conflict.* New York: Oxford University Press, 1988.

Khadduri, Majid and Edmund Ghareeb. *War in the Gulf, 1990-91: The Iraq-Kuwait Conflict and its Implications.* New York: Oxford University Press, 1997.

Kilian, Lutz, Alessandro Rebucci and Nikola Spatafora. "Oil Shocks and External Balances." *Journal of International Economics* 77, No. 2 (2009): 181-94.

Klare, Michael. *Blood and Oil: The Dangers and Consequences of America's Growing Oil Dependency.* New York: Metropolitan, 2004.

Klein, Lawrence R. "Issues Posed by Chronic US Deficits." *Journal of Policy Modeling* 28, No. 6 (2006): 673–77.

Klepper, Michael and Robert Gunther. *The Wealthy 100: From Benjamin Franklin to Bill Gates – A Ranking of the Richest Americans, Past and Present.* Secaucus, NJ: Carol Publishing Group, 1996.

Knott, David. "Gas-to-Liquids Projects Gaining Momentum as Process List Grows." *Oil & Gas Journal,* June 23, 1997.

Kohl, Wilfrid L. "National Security and Energy." Vol. 4, *Encyclopedia of Energy,* edited by Cutler J. Cleveland, 193-206. San Diego: Elsevier, 2004.

Koplow, Douglas and Aaron Martin. "Fueling Global Warming: Federal Subsidies to Oil in the United States." Report prepared for Greenpeace, June 1998.

Krauthammer, Charles. "Energy Independence? A Serious Plan Requires Taxes, ANWR and Nukes." *Washington Post,* January 26, 2007.

Krauthammer, Charles. "Pump Some Seriousness Into Energy Policy." *Washington Post,* November 11, 2005.

Krauthammer, Charles. "Tax and Drill." *Washington Post,* May 21, 2004.

Kreutz, Thomas G., Eric D. Larson, Guangjian Liu and Robert H. Williams. "Fischer-Tropsch Fuels from Coal and Biomass." Paper presented at the Twenty Fifth Annual International Pittsburgh Coal Conference, Pittsburgh, PA, September 29-October 2, 2008.

Kszos, L. A., M. E. Downing, L. L. Wright, J. H. Cushman, S. B. McLaughlin, V. R. Tolbert, G. A. Tuskan, and M. E. Walsh. *Bioenergy Feedstock Development Program Status Report.* Oak Ridge, TN: Oak Ridge National Laboratory, 2000.

Lake, James A. "Nuclear Energy: Large Scale, Zero-Emissions Technology." In *The Carbon Dioxide Dilemma: Promising Technologies and Policies.* Proceedings of a Symposium, April 23-24, 2002. Washington, DC: National Academies Press, 2003.

Landsberg, Hans H. "The Death of Synfuels." *Resources* 82 (1986): 7-8.

Laser, Mark, Eric Larson, Bruce Dale, Michael Wang, Nathanael Greene, and Lee R. Lynd. "Comparative Analysis of Efficiency, Environmental Impact, and Process Economics for Mature Biomass Refining Scenarios." *Biofuels, Bioproducts and Biorefining* 3, No. 2 (2009): 247 - 70.

LeBlond, Doris. "IEA: $16 Trillion in Energy Investment Needed by 2030," *Oil & Gas Journal*, November 10, 2003.

Leduc, Sylvain and Keith Sill. "A Quantitative Analysis of Oil-Price Shocks, Systematic Monetary Policy, and Economic Downturns." *Journal of Monetary Economics* 51, No. 4 (2004): 781-808.

Leone, R.C. and B. Wasow. "George Bush's Fiscal Finger of Fate Inflates Gas Prices." *Los Angeles Times*, April 1, 2004.

Levine, Mark D. and Jonathan E. Sinton. "National Energy Policy: China." Vol. 4, *Encyclopedia of Energy*, edited by Cutler J. Cleveland, 127-39. San Diego: Elsevier, 2004.

Lewandowski, Iris, Dudley Christian, and Wolter Elbersen. "Perennial Rhizomatous Grasses Overview." In *Renewable Energy and Sustainable Agriculture: The Impact of Perennial Grass Research*. Bioenergy Workshop Report of the Fifth Framework Programme, Research Directorate-General, European Commission, October 20, 2000.

Lewandowski, Iris, Jonathan M. O. Scurlock, Eva Lindvall, and Myrsini Christou. "The Development and Current Status of Perennial Rhizomatous Grasses as Energy Crops in the US and Europe." *Biomass & Bioenergy* 25 (2003): 335-61.

Lewis, Mark and Michael Jackson. "Nalgrass: A Non-wood Fiber Source Suitable for Existing US Pulp Mills." In *Trends in New Crops and New Uses*, edited by J. Janick and A. Whipkey. Alexandria, VA: ASHS Press, 2002.

Lizardo, Radhamés A. and André V. Mollick. "Oil Price Fluctuations and US Dollar Exchange Rates." *Energy Economics* 32, No. 2 (2010): 399-408.

Lovins, Amory B. "Comment on APS Hydrogen Report." *Forum on Physics and Society,* July 2004. http://units.aps.org/units/fps/newsletters/2004/july/commentary.cfm (accessed October 10, 2007).

Lovins, Amory B. *Twenty Hydrogen Myths*. Snowmass, CO: Rocky Mountain Institute, June 20, 2003. Corrected and updated February 17, 2005. http://www.rmi.org/images/other/Energy/E03-05_20HydrogenMyths.pdf (accessed October 10, 2007).

Lovins, Amory B., E. Kyle Datta, Odd-Even Bustnes, Jonathan G. Koomey, and Nathan J. Gasgow. *Winning the Oil Endgame: Innovation for Profits, Jobs and Security*. Snowmass, CO: Rocky Mountain Institute, 2005.

Lozowski, Dorothy. "Economic Indicators: Business News." *Chemical Engineering,* July 15, 2008, p. 64. http://www.che.com/download/ei/pdf/2008/ei_200807.pdf?dl (accessed July 21, 2008).

Lubowski, Ruben N. *See* US Department of Agriculture.

Lugar, Richard E. and R. James Woolsey. "The New Petroleum." *Foreign Affairs* 78, No. 1 (1999): 88-102.

Lynd, Lee R., Eric Larson, Nathanael Greene, Mark Laser, John Sheehan, Bruce E. Dale, Samuel McLaughlin and Michael Wang. "The Role of Biomass in America's Energy Future: Framing the Analysis." *Biofuels, Bioproducts and Biorefining* 3, No. 2 (2009): 113-23.

Mankiw, N. Gregory. "Reflections on the Trade Deficit and Fiscal Policy." *Journal of Policy Modeling* 28, No. 6 (2006): 679-82.

Mann, Margaret K. and Pamela L. Spath. *Life Cycle Assessment of a Biomass Gasification Combined-Cycle System*. Golden, CO: National Renewable Energy Laboratory, 1997.

Mantineo, M., G. M. D'Agosta, V. Copani, C. Patanè and S. L. Cosentino. "Biomass Yield and Energy Balance of Three Perennial Crops for Energy Use in the Semi-arid Mediterranean Environment." *Field Crops Research* 114, No. 2 (2009): 204-13.

Marland, G., T.A. Boden, and R. J. Andres. "Global, Regional, and National Fossil Fuel CO2 Emissions." In *Trends: A Compendium of Data on Global Change.* Oak Ridge, TN: Oak Ridge National Laboratory, 2007.

Mattione, Richard P. *OPEC's Investments and the International Financial System.* Washington, DC: Brookings Institution, 1985.

Maugeri, Leonardo. *The Age of Oil: The Mythology, History, and Future of the World's Most Controversial Resource.* Westport, CT: Praeger Publishers, 2006.

McClure, James A. "The Background of the United States Synthetic Fuel Corporation." In Vol. 1, *Conference Proceedings of the Conference on Synthetic Fuels – Status and Directions*, San Francisco, CA, October 13-16, 1980, edited by S. B. Alpert. Palo Alto, CA: Electric Power Research Institute, 1981.

McKeever, David B. "Inventories of Woody Residues and Solid Wood Waste in the United States, 2002." Paper presented to the Ninth International Inorganic-Bonded Fiber Composites Conference, Vancouver, BC, October 10-13, 2004.

McKinnon, Ronald and Gunther Schnabl. "Devaluing the Dollar: A Critical Analysis of William Cline's Case for a New Plaza Agreement." *Journal of Policy Modeling* 28, No. 6 (2006): 683-94.

McLaughlin, Samuel B., and Lynn Adams Kszos. "Development of Switchgrass (*Panicum virgatum*) as a Bioenergy Feedstock in the United States." *Biomass and Bioenergy* 28 (2005): 515-35.

McLaughlin, Samuel B., Daniel G. De La Torre-Ugarte, C. T. Garten, Jr., L. R. Lynd, M. A. Sanderson, V. R. Tolbert, and D. D. Wolf. "High-Value Renewable Energy from Prairie Grasses." *Environmental Science & Technology* 36, No. 10 (2002): 2122-99.

Metz, Helen Chapin, ed. *Iran: A Country Study.* 4th edition. Federal Research Division, Library of Congress. Washington, DC: USGPO, 1989. http://lcweb2.loc.gov/frd/cs/irtoc.html (accessed October 29, 2008).

Monti, Andrea, Nicola Di Virgilio and Gianpietro Venturi. "Mineral Composition and Ash Content of Six Major Energy Crops." *Biomass and Bioenergy* 32, No. 3 (2008): 216-23.

Morgan, Oliver and Islam Faisal. "Saudi Dove in the Oil Slick." *The Observer*, January 14, 2001. http://www.guardian.co.uk/business/2001/jan/14/globalrecession.oilandpetrol (accessed June 9, 2008).

Mufson, Steven. "A Crude Case for War?" *Washington Post*, March 16, 2008.

Mussa, Michael. "The Dollar and the Current Account Deficit: How Much Should We Worry?" *Journal of Policy Modeling* 29, No. 5 (2007): 691-96.

Myers, N. and J. Kent. *Perverse Subsidies: How Tax Dollars Can Undercut the Environment and the Economy.* London: Island Press, 2001.

National Bureau of Statistics of China. "Energy." Chapter 7 in *China Statistical Yearbook - 2006.* Beijing, China: China Statistics Press, 2006. http://www.stats.gov.cn/tjsj/ndsj/2006/indexeh.htm (accessed February 1, 2008).

National Defense Council Foundation. "The ANWR Imperative." *Issue Alert*, August 2, 2005. http://ndcf.homeip.net/ndcf/energy/TheANWRImperative.pdf (accessed May 24, 2008).

National Defense Council Foundation. "The Hidden Cost of Oil: An Update." *Issue Alert*, January 8, 2007. http://ndcf.homeip.net/ndcf/energy/NDCF_Hidden_Cost_2006_summary_paper.pdf (accessed May 24, 2008).

National Hydrogen Association. *Hydrogen Commercialization Plan.* n.d. http://www.hydrogenassociation.org/general/commercializationPlan.pdf (accessed May 11, 2008).

National Petroleum Council. *Balancing Natural Gas Policy: Fueling the Demands of a Growing Economy Volume II: Integrated Report.* Washington, DC: National Petroleum Council, 2003.

National Renewable Energy Laboratory. *Advanced Biomass Gasification Projects.* Golden, CO, August 1997.

National Research Council. *Surface Temperature Reconstructions for the Last 2,000 Years.* Washington, DC: National Academies Press, 2006.

Navigant Consulting Inc. *North American Natural Gas Supply Assessment.* Report prepared for the American Clean Skies Foundation. Chicago: Navigant Consulting Inc., July 2008. http://www.cleanskies.org/pdf/navigant-natural-gas-supply-0708.pdf (accessed February 10, 2010).

Nexant Inc. *Mixed Alcohols from Syngas – State of Technology.* Task 9 of *Equipment Design and Cost Estimation for Small Modular Biomass Systems, Synthesis Gas Cleanup and Oxygen Separation Equipment.* Golden, CO: National Renewable Energy Laboratory, 2006. http://www.nrel.gov/docs/fy06osti/39947.pdf (accessed January 15, 2008).

Nonneman, Gerd. "The Gulf States and the Iran-Iraq War: Pattern Shifts and Continuities." In *Iran, Iraq, and the Legacies of War,* edited by Lawrence G. Potter and Gary G. Sick. New York: Palgrave Macmillan, 2004.

Nordland, Rod and Daniel Gross. "Now It's The $6 Loaf of Bread; As Prices Soar, Food Has Replaced Oil as the Big Threat to the Long-Running Global Economic Expansion." *Newsweek,* May 5, 2008.

Nyang, Sulayman and Evan Hendricks. *A Line in the Sand: Saudi Arabia's Role in the Gulf War.* Washington, DC: PT Books, 1995.

Oil & Gas Journal. "The New Imperative." April 28, 2008.

Olien, Roger M. and Diana Davids Olien. *Oil and Ideology: The Cultural Creation of the American Petroleum Industry.* Chapel Hill, NC: University of North Carolina Press, 2000.

Ollinger, Michael. *Organizational Forms and Business Strategy in the US Petroleum Industry.* Lanham, MD: University Press of America, 1993.

Organization of Petroleum Exporting Countries. *OPEC Long Term Strategy.* Vienna, March 2006.

Organization of Petroleum Exporting Countries. *OPEC Annual Statistical Bulletin, 2008.* Vienna, 2009.

Orr, Franklin M. "Sequestration via Injection of Carbon Dioxide in the Deep Earth." In *The Carbon Dioxide Dilemma: Promising Technologies and Policies.* Proceedings of a Symposium, April 23-24, 2002. Washington, DC: National Academies Press, 2003.

Orszag, Peter. *See* Congressional Budget Office.

Paisley, M.A. and R.P. Overend. "Verification of the Performance of Future Energy Resources' SilvaGas Biomass Gasifier – Operating Experience in the Vermont Gasifier." Paper presented at the Nineteenth Annual International Pittsburgh Coal Conference, Pittsburgh, PA, September 23-27, 2002.

Palast, Greg. "OPEC on the March." *Harper's Magazine,* April 2005.

Panel on the Government Role in Civilian Technology. *The Government Role in Civilian Technology: Building a New Alliance.* Washington, DC: National Academics Press, 1992.

Pelletière, Stephen C. *America's Oil Wars*. Westport, CT: Praeger, 2004.

Pelletière, Stephen C. *Iraq and the International Oil System: Why America Went to War in the Gulf*. Westport, CT: Praeger, 2001.

Pelletière, Stephen C. *Yemen and Stability in the Persian Gulf: Confronting the Threat from Within*. Carlisle Barracks, PA: Strategic Studies Institute, U.S. Army War College, 1996.

Perdue, Jr., Robert E. "*Arundo donax*: Source of Musical Reeds and Industrial Cellulose." *Economic Botany* 12 (1958): 368-404.

Perlack, Robert D. and Anthony F. Turhollow. "Feedstock Cost Analysis of Corn Stover Residues for Further Processing." *Energy* 28, No. 14 (2003): 1395-1403.

Perlack, Robert D., Lynn L. Wright, Anthony F. Turhollow, Robin L. Graham, Bryce J. Stokes and Donald C. Erbach. *Biomass as Feedstock for a Bioenergy and Bioproducts Industry: The Technical Feasibility of a Billion-Ton Annual Supply*. Oak Ridge, TN: Oak Ridge National Labs, 2005.

Peterson, D. J. and Sergej Mahnovski. *New Forces at Work in Refining: Industry Views of Critical Business and Operations Trends*. Santa Monica, CA: RAND Corporation, 2003.

Petersen, John L., Dane Erickson, and Humera Kahn. *A Strategy: Moving America Away from Oil*. Arlington, VA: Arlington Institute, August 2003.

Petit, J.R., J. Jouzel, D. Raynaud, N.I. Barkov, J.-M. Barnola, I. Basile, M. Benders, et al. "Climate and Atmospheric History of the Past 420,000 Years from the Vostok Ice Core, Antarctica." *Nature* 399, No. 6735 (1999): 429-36.

Petroleum Communication Foundation. *Canada's Oil Sands and Heavy Oil: Developing the World's Largest Petroleum Resource*. Calgary: Petroleum Communication Foundation, 2000.

Philip, George. *The Political Economy of International Oil*. Edinburgh: Edinburgh University Press, 1994.

Phillips, S., A. Aden, J. Jechura, D. Dayton, and T. Eggeman. *Thermo-chemical Ethanol via Indirect Gasification and Mixed Alcohol Synthesis of Lignocellulosic Biomass*. Golden, CO: National Renewable Energy Laboratory, 2007.

Pickering, Andrew. "Oil Reserves Production Relationship." *Energy Economics* 30, No. 2 (2008): 352-70.

Plotkin, Steven. "Fuel Economy Initiatives: International Comparisons." Vol. 2, *Encyclopedia of Energy*, edited by Cutler J. Cleveland, 791-806. San Diego: Elsevier, 2004.

Quandt, William B. "U.S. Energy Policy and the Arab-Israeli Conflict." In *Arab Oil: Impact on the Arab Countries and Global Implications*, edited by Naiem A. Sherbiny and Mark A. Tessler. New York: Praeger, 1976.

Raghu, S., R. C. Anderson, C. C. Daehler, A. S. Davis, R. N. Wiedenmann, D. Simberloff, and R. N. Mack. "Adding Biofuels to the Invasive Species Fire?" *Science* 313 (September 22, 2006): 1742.

Ramon, Christine. *Update from the Chief Financial Officer*. Johannesburg: Sasol Limited, June 2009. http://www.sasol.com/sasol_internet/downloads/CFO_newsletter_to_investors_30June2009_final_1246367964853.pdf (accessed October 8, 2009).

Raneses, Anton, Kenneth Hanson, and Hosein Shapouri. "Economic Impacts from Shifting Cropland Use from Food to Fuel." *Biomass and Bioenergy* 15, No. 6 (1998): 417-22.

Raupach, Michael R., Gregg Marland, Philippe Ciais, Corinne Le Quéré, Josep G. Canadell, Gernot Klepper, and Christopher B. Field. "Global and Regional Drivers of Accelerating CO_2 Emissions." *Proceedings of the National Academy of Sciences* 104, No. 24 (2007): 10288-93.

Reagan, Ronald. "Message to the Congress Transmitting Proposed Legislation to Implement the National Synthetic Fuels Program." May 25, 1984. In *Public Papers of the President: Ronald Reagan, 1981-1989.* Ronald Reagan Presidential Library. http://www.reagan.utexas.edu/archives/speeches/1984/52584a.htm (accessed May 28, 2008).

Rieger, John P. and Ann D. Kreager. "Giant Reed (*Arundo donax*): A Climax Community of the Riparian Zone." Paper Presented to the California Riparian Systems Conference, Davis, CA, September 22-24, 1988.

Rifkin, Jeremy. "Hydrogen: Empowering the People." *The Nation*, December 23, 2002. http://www.thenation.com/doc/20021223/rifkin (accessed October 4, 2007).

Rifkin, Jeremy. *The Hydrogen Economy: The Creation of the Worldwide Energy Web and the Redistribution of Power on Earth.* New York: Penguin, 2003.

Ringlund, Guro Børnes, Knut Einar Rosendahl and Terje Skjerpen. "Does Oilrig Activity React to Oil Price Changes: An Empirical Investigation?" *Energy Economics* 30, No. 2 (2008): 371-96.

Roberts, Michael J. *See* US Department of Agriculture.

Roberts, Paul. "The Undeclared Oil War." *Washington Post*, June 28, 2004.

Ross, Brian and Jill Rackmill. "Secrets of the Saudi Royal Family." *ABC News.com*, October 15, 2004. http://abcnews.go.com/2020/News/Story?id=169246&page=1 (accessed October 24, 2008).

Ross, Michael. "Does Oil Hinder Democracy?" *World Politics* 53, No. 3 (2001): 325-61.

Salameh, Mamdouh G. "Oil Crises, Historical Perspective." Vol. 4, *Encyclopedia of Energy*, edited by Cutler J. Cleveland, 633-48. San Diego: Elsevier, 2004.

Salassi, Michael. *See* US Department of Agriculture.

Salvatore, Dominick. "US Trade Deficits, Structural Imbalances, and Global Monetary Stability." *Journal of Policy Modeling* 29, No. 5 (2007): 697-704.

Sandalow, David. "Ethanol: Lessons from Brazil." In *A High Growth Strategy for Ethanol.* Aspen, CO: Aspen Institute, 2006.

Sankari, Farouk A. "The Character and Impact of Arab Oil Embargoes." In *Arab Oil: Impact on the Arab Countries and Global Implications*, edited by Naiem A. Sherbiny and Mark A. Tessler. New York: Praeger, 1976.

Sasol Limited. *Reaching New Energy Frontiers through Competitive GTL Technology.* Johannesburg: Sasol Limited, 2006. http://www.sasol.com/sasol_internet/downloads/GTL_brochure12_6_1150180264478.pdf (accessed September 11, 2008).

Saudi Arabian Monetary Agency. *Annual Report.* 45th ed. Riyadh: Saudi Arabian Monetary Agency, 2009.

Schafer, Andreas. "Passenger Demand for Travel and Energy Use." Vol. 4, *Encyclopedia of Energy*, edited by Cutler J. Cleveland, 793-804. San Diego: Elsevier, 2004.

Scharff, Edward E. "Some Setbacks for Synfuels." *Time*, September 14, 1981.

Schofield, Richard. "Position, Function, and Symbol: The Shatt al-Arab Dispute in Perspective." In *Iran, Iraq, and the Legacies of War*, edited by Lawrence G. Potter and Gary G. Sick. New York: Palgrave Macmillan, 2004.

Shapouri, Hosein. *See* US Department of Agriculture.

Shatalov, Anatoly A. and Helena Pereira. "Papermaking Fibers from Giant Reed (*Arundo donax*) by Advanced Ecologically Friendly Pulping and Bleaching Technologies." *BioResources* 1, No. 1 (2006): 45-61.

Shelton, Judy. *The Coming Soviet Crash: Gorbechev's Desperate Pursuit of Credit in Western Financial Markets.* New York: The Free Press, 1989.

Shen, Laihong, Yang Gao and Jun Xiao. "Simulation of Hydrogen Production from Biomass Gasification in Interconnected Fluidized Beds." *Biomass and Bioenergy* 32, No. 2 (2008): 120-27.

Sheridan, Barrett. "Blame It on Biofuels; Cornflake Makers and Socialists Alike are Pointing to Green Fuel for High Food Prices. Are They Right?" *Newsweek*, August 20, 2007.

Shockey, Richard E., Ted R. Aulich, Bruce Jones, Gary Mead, and Paul Stevens. *Optimal Ethanol Blend-Level Investigation.* Sioux Falls, SD: American Coalition for Ethanol, 2007. http://www.ethanol.org/pdf/contentmgmt/ACE_Optimal_Ethanol_Blend_Level_Study_final_12507.pdf (accessed July 23, 2008).

Shultz, George P. *See* US Department of State.

Slinsky, Stephen P. *See* US Department of Agriculture.

Smeets, Edward M. W., Andre P. C. Faaij, Iris M. Lewandowski, and Wim C. Turkenburg. "A Bottom-Up Assessment and Review of Global Bio-Energy Potentials to 2050." *Progress in Energy and Combustion Science* 33, No. 1 (2007): 56-106.

Smith, W. Brad, Patrick D. Miles, John S. Vissage, and Scott A. Pugh. *Forest Resources of the United States, 2002.* St. Paul, MN: U.S. Department of Agriculture, Forest Service, North Central Research Station, April 2004. http://ncrs.fs.fed.us/pubs/gtr/gtr_nc241.pdf (accessed October 16, 2007).

Southern Sun Biosystems. "Biomass Energy Plants." http://www.sosun.com/affiliates.html (accessed November 6, 2007).

Spath, P., A. Aden, T. Eggeman, M. Ringer, B. Wallace, and J. Jechura. *Biomass to Hydrogen Production Detailed Design and Economics Utilizing the Battelle Columbus Laboratory Indirectly-Heated Gasifier.* Golden, CO: National Renewable Energy Laboratory, 2005.

Spath, P. and D.C. Dayton. *Preliminary Screening - Technical and Economic Assessment of Synthesis Gas to Fuels and Chemicals with Emphasis on the Potential for Biomass-Derived Syngas.* Golden, CO: National Renewable Energy Laboratory, 2003.

Speight, James G. *The Chemistry and Technology of Petroleum.* 3rd ed. New York: Marcel Dekker, 1999.

Spencer, David F., Pui-Sze Liow, Wai Ki Chan, Gregory G. Ksander, and Kurt D. Getsinger. "Estimating *Arundo donax* Shoot Biomass." *Aquatic Botany* 84 (2006): 272-76.

Spiro, David E. *The Hidden Hand of American Hegemony: Petrodollar Recycling and International Markets.* Ithaca, NY: Cornell University Press, 1999.

Staudt, Amanda, Nancy Huddleston, and Sandi Rudenstein. *Understanding and Responding to Climate Change.* Washington, DC: National Research Council, 2005. http://dels.nas.edu/basc (accessed February 13, 2008).

Stern, Jonathan P. *Soviet Oil and Gas Exports to the West: Commercial Transaction or Security Threat.* Brookfield, VT: Gower Publishing Company, 1987.

Storchmann, Karl. "Long-Run Gasoline Demand for Passenger Cars: The Role of Income Distribution." *Energy Economics* 27, No. 1 (2005): 25-58.

Sun, Qingyun. "CTL Development in China." Presentation to the Congressional Noontime Briefing, Rayburn House Office Building, Washington, DC, April 24, 2008. http://www.researchcaucus.org/docs/CTL%20Development%20in%20China.pdf (accessed September 30, 2008).

Tarbell, Ida M. *The History of the Standard Oil Company*. New York: McClure, Phillips and Co., 1904. http://www.history.rochester.edu/fuels/tarbell/main.htm (accessed January 15, 2008).

Taylor, Robert E. "US Oil Policy, Under Review, Isn't Seen Embracing Import Fee or Price Supports." *Wall Street Journal*, November 17, 1986.

Tett, Simon F. B., Gareth S. Jones, Peter A. Stott, David C. Hill, John F. B. Mitchell, Myles R. Allen, William J. Ingram, et al. "Estimation of Natural and Anthropogenic Contributions to Twentieth Century Temperature Change." *Journal of Geophysical Research* 107, No. D16 (2002): 4306.

Ticktin, Hillel. *Origins of the Crisis in the USSR: Essays on the Political Economy of a Disintegrating System*. Armonk, NY: M. E. Sharpe, Inc., 1992.

Trottman, Melanie. "Increased Oil Prices Jeopardize Recovery in U.S. Airline Industry." *Wall Street Journal*, May 20, 2004.

Urbanchuk, John M. *Contribution of the Ethanol Industry to the Economy of the United States*. Washington, DC: Renewable Fuels Association, 2008.

Urbanchuk, John M. *The Relative Impact of Corn and Energy Prices in the Grocery Aisle*. Washington, DC: Renewable Fuels Association, 2007.

US Congress. House of Representatives. Committee on Foreign Affairs. *Foreign Policy and National Security Implications of Oil Dependence: Hearing before the Committee on Foreign Affairs; House of Representatives*. 110th Congress, 1st Session, March 22, 2007.

US Congress. House of Representatives. Committee on Science. *Improving the Nation's Energy Security: Can Cars and Trucks Be Made More Fuel Efficient? Hearing before the Committee on Science, House of Representatives*. 109th Congress, 1st Session, February 9, 2005.

US Congress. House of Representatives. Select Committee on Energy Independence and Global Warming. *Geopolitical Implications of Rising Oil Dependence and Global Warming*. 110th Congress, 1st Session, April 18, 2007.

US Congress. Senate. Committee on Agriculture, Nutrition and Forestry. *Biomass Use in Future Energy Production: Demonstration and Commercial Application for Agricultural Bioproducts and Cellulosic Biomass Use: Hearing before the Committee of Agriculture, Nutrition and Forestry, US Senate*. 108th Congress, 2nd Session, May 6, 2004.

US Congress. Senate. Committee on Foreign Relations. *Energy Security and Oil Dependence: Hearing before the Committee on Foreign Relations, US Senate*. 109th Congress, 2nd Session, May 16, 2006.

US Department of Agriculture. Economic Research Service. *Major Uses of Land in the United States, 2002*. By Ruben N. Lubowski, Marlow Vesterby, Shawn Bucholtz, Alba Baez and Michael J. Roberts. Economic Information Bulletin Number 14, Washington, DC, May 2006.

US Department of Agriculture. Foreign Agricultural Service. *Brazilian Sugar*. Production, Market and Trade Feature Reports, Washington, DC, October 2003. http://www.fas.usda.gov/htp/sugar/2003/Brazilsugar03.pdf (accessed January 15, 2008).

US Department of Agriculture. Natural Resources Conservation Service. Plant Materials Program. *Estimated Production Cost Budgets for Biomass: Switchgrass, 'Highlander' Eastern Gamagrass, Indiangrass, and Big Bluestem*. By Jamie L. Whitten. Plant Materials Technical Note No. 102, Washington, DC, May 2007.

US Department of Agriculture. Office of the Chief Economist. *The Economic Feasibility of Ethanol Production from Sugar in the United States*. By Hosein Shapouri, Michael Salassi and J. Nelson Fairbanks. Washington, DC, July 2006.

US Department of Agriculture. Office of the Chief Economist. *U.S. Biobased Products Market Potential and Projections through 2025*. By Marvin Duncan, Irene M. Xiarchos, John Whims, Tom Scott, Mark Stowers, Bernie Steele, and Don Senechal. Washington, DC, 2008. http://www.usda.gov/oce/reports/energy/BiobasedReport2008.pdf (accessed August 18, 2008).

US Department of Agriculture. Office of the Chief Economist. *The Economic Impacts of Bioenergy Crop Production on U.S. Agriculture*. By Daniel G. De La Torre Ugarte, Marie E. Walsh, Hosein Shapouri, and Stephen P. Slinsky. Agricultural Economic Report No. 816, Washington, DC, 2003.

US Department of Agriculture. US Forest Service. *A Strategic Assessment of Forest Biomass and Fuel Reduction Treatments in Western States*. Washington, DC, March 2005. http://www.fs.fed.us/rm/pubs/rmrs_gtr149.pdf (accessed October 17, 2007).

US Department of Defense. Defense Logistics Agency. Defense Energy Support Center. *Fact Book 2006*. 29th ed., 2007. http://www.desc.dla.mil/DCM/Files/FactBook_FY06.pdf (accessed September 28, 2007).

US Department of Defense. Defense Logistics Agency. Defense Energy Support Center. *Fact Book 2007*. 30th ed., 2008. http://www.desc.dla.mil/DCM/Files/Factbook_2007_Final.pdf (accessed May 12, 2008).

US Department of Energy. Energy Information Administration. *Emissions of Greenhouse Gases in the United States 2006*, edited by John Conti and Glen E. Sweetnam. Washington, DC: Energy Information Administration, 2007.

US Department of Energy. Energy Information Administration. *Impacts of the Kyoto Protocol on U.S. Energy Markets and Economic Activity*. Washington, DC: Energy Information Administration, 1998.

US Department of Energy. Energy Information Administration. *Monthly Energy Review, October 2009*. Washington, DC: Energy Information Administration, 2009.

US Department of Energy. National Energy Technology Laboratory. *Fischer-Tropsch Fuels*. R&D Facts. Pittsburg, PA, April 2007.

US Department of Energy. Office of Energy Efficiency and Renewable Energy and US Environmental Protection Agency. *Fuel Economy Guide*. Washington, DC, 2007.

US Department of Energy. Office of Science. *Basic Research Needs for the Hydrogen Economy: Report of the Basic Energy Sciences Workshop on Hydrogen Production, Storage, and Use*. 2nd Printing. Argonne, IL: Argonne National Laboratory, February 2004. http://www.sc.doe.gov/bes/hydrogen.pdf (accessed October 12, 2007).

US Department of Interior. Minerals Management Service. *Comprehensive Inventory of US OCS Oil and Natural Gas Resources.* Report to Congress, February 2006.

US Department of State. Bureau of Public Affairs. Office of the Historian. *Arab-Israeli Crisis and War, 1967.* Vol. XIX of *1964-1968, Lyndon B. Johnson.* In *Foreign Relations of the United States,* edited by Harriet Dashiell Schwar. Washington, DC: USGPO, 2004. http://www.state.gov/r/pa/ho/frus/johnsonlb/xix/ (accessed April 1, 2008).

US Department of State. Bureau of Public Affairs. Office of the Historian. *Near East, 1962-1963.* Vol. XVIII of *1961-1963, John F. Kennedy.* In *Foreign Relations of the United States,* edited by Nina J. Noring. Washington, DC: USGPO, 1995. http://www.state.gov/r/pa/ho/frus/kennedyjf/xviii/ (accessed March 15, 2008).

US Department of State. *U.S. Interests in the Persian Gulf.* By George P. Shultz. Washington, DC, 1987.

US Environmental Protection Agency. *Light Duty Automotive Technology and Fuel Economy Trends: 1975 through 2008.* Washington, DC, 2008.

US General Accounting Office. "The Synthetic Fuels Corporation's Progress in Aiding Synthetic Fuels Development." Report to the US Congress, House of Representatives, Committee on Energy and Commerce, Subcommittee on Fossil and Synthetic Fuels. 98th Congress, 2nd Session, July 11, 1984.

US Geological Survey. *US Geological Survey World Petroleum Assessment 2000.* Washington, DC, 2000. http://pubs.usgs.gov/dds/dds-060/ (accessed September 11, 2008).

US-China Economic and Security Review Commission. *2007 Report to Congress of the US-China Economic and Security Review Commission.* Washington, DC: US Government Printing Office, 2007. http://www.uscc.gov/annual_report/2007/report_to_congress.pdf (accessed August 27, 2008).

Varvel, G.E., K.P. Vogel, R.B. Mitchell, R.F. Follett and J.M. Kimble. "Comparison of Corn and Switchgrass on Marginal Soils for Bioenergy." *Biomass and Bioenergy* 32, No. 1 (2008): 18-21.

Vassilev, Stanislav V., David Baxter, Lars K. Andersen and Christina G. Vassileva. "An Overview of the Chemical Composition of Biomass." *Fuel* 89, No. 5 (2010): 913-933.

Vesterby, Marlow. *See* US Department of Agriculture.

Walsh, Marie E. "Biomass Resource Assessment." Vol. 1, *Encyclopedia of Energy,* edited by Cutler J. Cleveland, 237-49. San Diego: Elsevier, 2004.

Walsh, Marie E. *See also* US Department of Agriculture.

Walsh, Michael J. "Can Emissions Trading of Carbon Dioxide Bootstrap the Transition?" In *The Carbon Dioxide Dilemma: Promising Technologies and Policies.* Proceedings of a Symposium, April 23-24, 2002. Washington, DC: National Academies Press, 2003.

Wang, Lijun, Curtis L. Weller, David D. Jones, and Milford A. Hanna. "Contemporary Issues in Thermal Gasification of Biomass and Its Application to Electricity and Fuel Production." *Biomass and Bioenergy* 32, No. 7 (2008): 573-81.

Wang, M., H. Huo, L. Johnson, and D. He. *Projection of Chinese Motor Vehicle Growth, Oil Demand, and CO2 Emissions through 2050.* Argonne, IL: Argonne National Laboratory, December 2006. http://www.transportation.anl.gov/pdfs/TA/398.pdf (accessed October 12, 2007).

Watts, Steven. *The People's Tycoon: Henry Ford and the American Century.* New York: Alfred A. Knopf, 2005.

Wender, Irving. "Reactions of Synthesis Gas." *Fuel Processing Technology* 48, No. 3 (1996): 189-297.

West Virginia University and Union Carbide Technical Center. *The Economical Production of Alcohol Fuels from Coal-Derived Synthesis Gas*. Report for the US Department of Energy. Morgantown, WV: West Virginia University, 1999.

Westlake, D.F. "Comparisons of Plant Productivity." *Biological Reviews* 38 (1963): 385-425.

Whitten, Jamie L. *See* US Department of Agriculture.

Wiltsee, G. *Urban Wood Waste Resource Assessment*. Golden, CO: National Renewable Energy Laboratory, 1998.

World Bank. *Addressing the Food Crisis: The Need for Rapid and Coordinated Action*. Presentation to the Group of Eight Meeting of Finance Ministers, Osaka, Japan, June 13-14, 2008.

World Business Council for Sustainable Development. *Mobility 2030: Meeting the Challenges to Sustainability*. Geneva: World Business Council for Sustainable Development, 2004.

Wright, Lynn, Bob Boundy, Bob Perlack, Stacy Davis, and Bo Saulsbury. *Biomass Energy Data Book*. 1st ed. Oak Ridge, TN: Oak Ridge National Laboratory, 2006.

Yanarella, Ernest J. and William C. Green, eds. *The Unfulfilled Promise of Synthetic Fuels: Technological Failure, Policy Immobilism, or Commercial Illusion*. New York: Greenwood Press, 1987.

Yergin, Daniel. "Imagining a $7-a-Gallon Future." *New York Times*, April 4, 2004.

Yergin, Daniel. *The Prize: The Epic Quest for Oil, Money, and Power*. New York: Simon & Schuster, 1991.

Yousefi, Ayoub and Tony S. Wirjanto. "The Empirical Role of the Exchange Rate on the Crude-Oil Price Formation." *Energy Economics* 26, No. 5 (2004): 783-99.

Zakaria, Fareed. "How to Escape the Oil Trap." *Newsweek*, August 29, 2005.

Zhang, Wennan. "Automotive Fuels from Biomass via Gasification." *Fuel Processing Technology*, In Press.

Zhang, Yue-Jun, Ying Fan, Hsien-Tang Tsai and Yi-Ming Wei. "Spillover Effect of US Dollar Exchange Rate on Oil Prices." *Journal of Policy Modeling* 30, No. 6, (2008): 973-991.

Zhu, Yunhua, Mark A. Gerber, Susanne B. Jones and Don J. Stevens. *Analysis of the Effects of Compositional and Configurational Assumptions on Product Costs for the Thermo-chemical Conversion of Lignocellulosic Biomass to Mixed Alcohols – FY 2007 Progress Report*. Report prepared for the US Department of Energy. Richland, WA: Pacific Northwest National Laboratory, 2009. +http://www.pnl.gov/main/publications/external/technical_reports/PNNL-17949rev1.pdf (accessed November 22, 2009).

Index

Y